A CONCISE COMPANION TO HISTORY

EDITED BY **ULINKA RUBLACK**

OXFORD
UNIVERSITY PRESS

OXFORD
UNIVERSITY PRESS

Great Clarendon Street, Oxford OX2 6DP
United Kingdom

Oxford University Press is a department of the University of Oxford.
It furthers the University's objective of excellence in research, scholarship,
and education by publishing worldwide. Oxford is a registered trade mark of
Oxford University Press in the UK and in certain other countries

© Oxford University Press 2012

The moral rights of the author have been asserted

First Edition published in 2012
First published in paperback 2012

Impression: 2 4 6 8 10 9 7 5 3 1

Reprinted with corrections 2012

British Library Cataloguing in Publication Data

Data available

Library of Congress Cataloging in Publication Data

Data available

ISBN 978–0–19–929121–2(Hbk.)
ISBN 978–0–19–966030–8(Pbk.)

Printed in Great Britain
on acid-free paper by
Clays Ltd, St Ives plc

1006899449

A CONCISE COMPANION TO HISTORY

Ulinka Rublack teaches in the History Faculty at Cambridge University, and is a Fellow of St John's College. Her books include *Reformation Europe; The Crimes of Women in Early Modern Germany;* and *Dressing Up: Cultural Identity in Renaissance Europe,* which received the Roland H. Bainton Prize and was a finalist for the Cundill Prize. The last two titles are also published by Oxford University Press.

Praise for *A Concise Companion to History*:

'How has the writing of history changed over the past half century? What are the topics and issues that interest historians today? These questions, and many more, are addressed in the Concise Companion, a pioneering and exceptionally stimulating volume of essays which indicate some of the ways in which the challenges of globalization are forcing historians to rethink their approaches to the past.'
Sir John Elliott, Regius Professor Emeritus of Modern History, University of Oxford

'Ulinka Rublack has created a true companion volume for readers of recent and current historical writing. In an astonishing feat of editorship, she brings together some of the best living historians and some insuperable essays on the state and drift of the subject.'
Felipe Fernández-Armesto, William P. Reynolds Professor of History, Notre Dame University

'Ulinka Rublack's editing shows the right blend of sympathetic autocracy...It resembles David Cannadine's symposium *What is History Now* more closely than any of the larger surveys of global historiography or guides to historical theory that are now filling the bookshelves.'
Michael Bentley, *English Historical Review*

'The stellar cast of authors...[introduce] the reader to some of the most exciting developments in the field of history....the book achieves a great deal.'
Stefan Berger, *Times Literary Supplement*

'Ambitious...rich and challenging...'
Alix Green, *Reviews in History*

For João and Sophie, beloved children
of the twenty-first century

Acknowledgements

I wish to thank Christopher Wheeler at Oxford University Press, who entrusted me with the task of thinking about a Companion, for being such an exceptional editor. I have been deeply grateful for his real companionship whenever I needed it. Matthew Cotton from Oxford University Press once more provided outstandingly reliable and effective help. It is a pleasure to acknowledge a discussion with Chris Bayly when I first drafted proposals for this book, alongside helpful suggestions from several anonymous reviewers, whom I now have the opportunity to thank. All contributors have more than rewarded my expectations with their writing, and I applaud them for making this book such an exciting departure. Francisco Bethencourt shared the Companion coming to life with enthusiasm and invaluable critique. Sophie was not even twelve months old when I started envisaging the Companion. I dedicate it to her and her brother João, as they grow up with history and historians.

U.R.

Contents

Preface

During the twentieth century, traditional concepts of objectivity and narratives of Western exceptionalism have been forcefully challenged. Does that mean that our relationship with the past and the content and purpose of history are now less self-evident than before? Is history writing really no more than 'us, just back there', as historians project their own concerns into the past? Historians have, it seems, often given up earlier 'certainties', with their deceptive impression of solid moorings for our understanding of the past. The unsettling question remains: what might be put in their place? Few today will endorse John Seeley's famous nineteenth-century dictum: 'History is past politics, and past politics is present history'. But who feels at ease with the postmodernist Michel Foucault's crisp reply to an interviewer in 1979: 'I practice a sort of historical fiction'? Foucault happily conceded that historians might well write that his history of madness was untrue. It was a partial and exaggerated account, which quite possibly had ignored elements contradicting his argument. The truth of his books lay in their political effects in his own and future societies: 'I hope', he concluded, 'that the truth of my books is in the coming.'[1] This lent Foucault a messianic spirit as he radically rewrote history as past and present politics.

What are we to make of that unnerving relationship between history, reality, and truth at the beginning of the twentieth-first century? History appears not merely as a comforting companion, illuminating informant, or resource to critically reread, but also an uncanny shadow we often struggle with and try to shake off while it follows us around to trap us into further tragedy and human catastrophe. Where do we move with this companion and what new questions do we ask of pasts that can seem overwhelming, yet elusive, disturbingly strange as well as all too familiar? How can history today respond to interests of increasingly interconnected and mobile people, so deeply beset by problems of inequality, conflict, and environmental collapse? How does it address broad questions about global themes in a serious and nuanced way, without once more fashioning facile meta-narratives of unilinear change and fixed identities, or by simply replacing these with ready-made relativisms?

This Companion is only a book; but it offers itself as a guide to be inspired by and rethink history. Through description, explication, and analysis, it maps some of the most significant directions and themes in contemporary ways of writing history designed to take us forward. It assesses how leading scholars currently regard their own practice and approach issues that are powerful determinants of the ways in which twenty-first-century people locate themselves historically. Many of these have developed as exciting new sub-fields in history only during the last forty years: communication, gender, emotions, ethnicity, science, and the environment, for instance. Alongside them lies a range of core themes which remains essential to understand societies: commerce, power, religion, ideas, populations. These topics make up the second part of the Companion, which resonates with four opening chapters in its first part: history and historians, the status of historical knowledge, and the role of causation in historical explanation. I invited contributors to connect in an ambitiously informative, reliable, and critical way with large themes, across time and space, as well as theoretical elements which help us to interrogate present categories of conceiving history. Rather than necessarily presenting tight historiographical overviews, contributors were asked to feel free to write incisive, stimulating essays on their theme while engaging with the historiographies they judged particularly relevant. This, in contrast to statements such as Foucault's in 1979, was done in full acknowledgement of nuances, lacunae, and question marks over evidence and interpretations as crucial elements of historians' craft, while retaining the aim to counter nostalgic or Whiggish visions of the past. The result, I hope, is an intellectual adventure both fruitful and alive.

This volume cannot be a 'complete' companion, nor can it be an assemblage of authors who speak with one voice and do the same thing. It has, nonetheless, one unified aim. This is to mark a significant departure in a genre still shaped by stories about history which are predominantly Western. Such a relationship with the past badly fits our world, and also fails to reflect the proliferation of perspectives and skills achieved within the profession. The Companion therefore most distinctively advocates a practice of history that seeks global connections and pioneers a sustained dialogue between historians specializing in the history of particular continents. It does not, to use Niall Ferguson's sharply ridiculing phrase, compare the Ashanti Empire to the British Empire.[2] But we need to build on the much greater awareness that 'Western' achievements and 'modernities' were often not as unique as once portrayed, and that the history of interconnections and multi-centric developments of different civilizations is crucial for a proper critical understanding of the past. No *Companion to History* should any more read like a *Companion to Western History*, in which the West is taken as a universal model and overall provides the central experience of the past. Yet startlingly, nothing like this book with its comparative discussions around themes and concepts which concern all of us in this world so far exists. In this sense, the Companion is best approached as an enquiry which I invite readers to explore alongside contributors, who all are outstandingly original historians of diverse specializations—from Africa to the Caribbean, China and Japan to India, and Europe to Latin America.

This exploration, I hope, is further facilitated visually through artefacts and contemporary art I have chosen to accompany texts. With the exception of the Nigerian and London artist Yinka Shonibare's work, introduced by Megan Vaughan, and an image from the Brazilian artist Rivane Neuenschwander's evocative installation 'Continent Cloud', these objects come from the magnificent collection of the British Museum. They stimulate questions about what historians, publics, collectors, and particular institutions have taken and take to be a society's cultural artefacts, what politics inform choices, and what will constitute the future archive of artefacts from our contemporary world. So when I pair Chris Bayly's opening article with a badge from anti-globalization activists the point is not to endorse the slogan, but to reference the prominence of these concerns which begin to be registered as future evidence of ways in which the global is increasingly part of how we represent the world to ourselves. A contemporary object of this kind moreover quickly prompts questions we likewise need to ask of any piece of historical evidence: who turned this badge into an object worth preserving, where did it come from, and why? How has this kind of evidence been categorized, contextualized, or displayed? Looking at other museum objects, as well as Shonibare's work, we can then go on to ask to whom it matters in what way art or artefactual evidence of societies should be 'authentic', 'representative', and ascribed historicity? What questions suggest themselves about each of these frames of reference in connection with the image we see? What order do we place on objects which are produced, exchanged, adapted, and displayed in more than one society?[3]

In January 1550, Sebastian Münster sent his pioneering cosmography to King Gustav of Sweden with an elegant Latin apology: 'I did what I could, not what I wanted. This is why I do not want it to be seen as my fault that I disseminate some subjects in an incomplete and faulty manner, much perhaps in an unordered way and some, as I fear, contradictory; for historians do not always agree.'[4] We might say that little has changed: historians still don't agree, and every work attempting to be more comprehensive as well as authoritative still usually begins with an apology for all it is not in order to accommodate its readers' disappointments. Münster did in fact omit any discussion of the Americas. Yet, as I hope we have already seen, this volume does not simply present a universalistic history to counter the predominantly nationalistic one. It experiments with new forms of collaboration among historians of different societies to stimulate its readers to approach history from multiple and comparative perspectives, to provide an appropriate critical reading of the discipline and its categories, the past and the present. There are urgent concerns that prompt us to do so.

Chris Bayly thus opens the volume with a powerful evaluation of the increasing centrality of world history for our understanding of the many trans-national problems confronting us today, such as migration. John McNeill later in the book provides an encompassing overview of the discipline of environmental history, barely forty years old and now one of the fastest growing sub-fields, as ecological concerns press on current generations. The impact of colonialism and capitalism shape these historians' agenda. McNeill and Bayly agree in their prognoses that 'struggles over resources of water, oil and food as well as the impact of global epidemics' significantly impact 'on the way history is written'—now and in the future, which will of necessity look across national boundaries to a trans-national arena.

Commerce has been the greatest connector of societies. Ken Pomeranz thus charts how cultures across the globe have lived with commerce and been shaped by their increasing market integration. He identifies agents of change as well as enquiring about the interrelationship between economic developments and culture. Pomeranz cautions that Europe before *c*.1800 does not qualify as a case study of proto-globalization in contemporary terms. Nor was market integration 'necessarily further advanced' in Europe than in China before the building of railroads, even though Europe is still 'often imagined as the homeland of open, competitive markets'. Chris Bayly, in commenting on this important debate about the final and rather late divergence between Asia and Europe around 1800, emphasizes that the key European breakthrough economically 'took place, ultimately, in relations between the state, military technology and the elite citizens who operated various forms of surveillance on state and society', primarily in north-western Europe. Bayly suggests that particularly developed forms of taxation, state formation, and military organization lay at the heart of Western economic advances and empire building in the periods after 1800, but were seeded and cultivated in the two preceding centuries. Both Pomeranz and Bayly endorse the need to argue comparatively and to further research the multi-causal nature of economic success.

This can only be highlighted further once we consider Chris Clark's account of power in relation to Bayly's contention about the advances of European state formation. Clark, a historian of Europe, sets out that 'Power' is a concept historians hardly every investigate, let alone across cultures. It is best analysed as something that 'is in flux, it disperses, becomes localised and in doing so changes its character'. In his view it has a tendency to resist concentration and does not reach a steady state: 'all relationships are subject in the longer term to re-negotiation and social upheavals and wars can always intervene to recalibrate the balance'. Clark therefore points out that state power in Europe was still relatively limited even by the end of the eighteenth century, and comparisons of forms of distributed power with Asia and Latin America once more present themselves as extremely fruitful.

R. Bin Wong's chapter on Causation proves particularly valuable here. Wong argues that it is beneficial to return to questions of historical causation for complex phenomena in a comparative mode. With reference to developments of states, warfare, and taxation in eighteenth-century Europe and China, for instance, he explains that both continents saw popular protests against taxation, but these were 'embedded in distinct political ideologies and institutions that defined the larger meanings of protest to participants and the impact of their actions'. While Europeans and Americans could link taxation with political representation, 'Chinese expectations of what was fair and equitable depended on beliefs shared with their officials that were not translated into formal institutional mechanisms for political voice.' This was in part because paternalist ideologies informed a consistent Chinese policy of grain supplies for its population and sustained established hierarchies more effectively than in the West. The difference between the vast domestic empire of the Chinese and belligerent European states fighting for supremacy created the fatal European need to spend on war at the expense of domestic civilian projects, but inadvertently also helped to strengthen European voices for political resistance and rights. Wong concludes: 'The existence of comparable episodes in different paths of change means that similar causal chains or mechanisms are embedded in larger patterns of difference.' This means that we 'can replace the single and simple path of historical change and development', as in traditional modernization theories, 'with multiple paths'. Our explanations for cultural changes need to be flexible enough to allow both for interrelations and distinctiveness.

These approaches seamlessly connect with Peter Burke's analysis of why we likewise need to conceive of changes in communication in a multi-centric way, rather than by focusing on Europe as the only centre of change. The 'printing revolution', for instance, needs to be thought of as a series of separate revolutions in China, Korea, and the West, and it is possible that Gutenberg knew about Korean techniques. However, the commercialization of print advanced rapidly in the West, and then spread in other parts of the world. Many other forms of communication coexisted and had different effects on parts of society, so that it would be unwise ever to assume that new media have predictable consequences and cyber-democracies are accessible to all. Nor are cyber-democracies tools of quintessential modern Western liberation. Thus, Chris Bayly in his contribution maintains that political 'ideas' had many locales and the West should be careful about any claims to be the only cradle of democratic forms of thinking. He asks: 'How would the "Cambridge School" analysis of the birth of civic republicanism fare if one sought analogies in the Islamic world, India or China?', stating that 'India's Locke was Rammohan Roy.'

When planning this Companion, I asked myself what would happen if a particular historian of Africa should write on 'Culture' and a specific historian of China wrote on 'Gender'. The results are incisive overviews by Megan Vaughan and Dorothy Ko, which critically interrogate themes which have categories that underlie many accounts written by scholars of Western history. Ko shows how there can be a vision of sex as something beyond perceived differences between the binary categories of male and female—a 'more fluid system' and different ways of ordering the body and sex. Her chapter discusses case studies outside Europe and America, such as Iran, Latin America, and Japan. It contextualizes the frameworks which have often problematically informed historians' writing, for instance normative models of the male breadwinner heading a family. Ko highlights work that has drawn attention to the tremendous cultural labour involved in achieving particular ideas of masculinity and femininity, neither of which is 'made within a day'. Ko further makes links to interests in the gendering of world history, colonialism, and ethnicity. Gendered reproduction was at the heart of the Spanish conquest of the New World, for example, as mestiza daughters could 'figure as a kind of "cultural capital" for their fathers'. Sex, like science and ethnicity, in Ko's account is treated as product of culture, and nature itself can only be apprehended through that culture.

Vaughan, in turn, examines critically what we then take to be 'culture'. Vaughan recalls the unease of anthropologists with this category as early as the 1960s, when 'it began to look dangerously like all and nothing. Culture was society, human consciousness, economic structure, religion, politics.' So was it different from 'nature'? She puts considerable methodological pressure on this category by looking at the legacies of its enlightenment connotations as romanticized diversity or progressive civilization, at colonial politics, and by examining its intricate role in the identity politics of the postcolonial world, with its re-inventions of cultural difference to claim rights. Vaughan's approach stresses the necessity of a politically informed discursive reading of definitions of culture in particular fields of power: 'No histories of cultural production in Africa', she argues, 'can avoid the politics of the definition of the cultural sphere.' In a postcolonial context, notions of culture and cultural history become problematic with their implication that 'culture' is a distinctive field; how can we determine what is or is not culture? Cultural history, she concludes, does not operate well as a separate sphere of analysis; it needs to be history as such in asking how different institutions and actors in societies make and remake meaning. This history, then, traces processes rather than origins or distinct, fixed identities, and not least their emotional effects on people. These encompass trauma, loss, and conflict, and give the lie to a happy notion of easy, joyful hybridity which some portray as coming dancing along with everything more global. In this, the chapters of both Vaughan and Ko meet in stressing the need to keep notions of nature and culture unstable and yet to draw attention, for instance, to the struggle involved in subverting fixed conventional sexual identifications or even to conceive of and find adequate languages for them.

Analogous to Vaughan's critique of the notion of culture as distinct from nature or other spheres of society is Elizabeth Buettner's argument against the politics of difference that often informs the use of 'ethnicity' as a category. We need, she posits, to consistently address 'ethnicity' as a historical category 'with reference to the "self" and the "other" alike—to the ethnic majority "mainstream" as much as minorities'. She demonstrates the power of colonialism in inventing deeply gendered notions of tribalism and race, which obscured the lived heterogeneity of peoples. Ethnicity, then, is not an objective category for historians designating a 'natural' origin, but needs to be analysed in its historical construction as an identity enforced, assumed, or adapted by people in different contexts in different times. Buettner reminds us that this is an ongoing process in our own societies, as many new ethnicities are to come. Here, once more, her work is best read alongside Vaughan's similarly compelling analysis of the dynamics of postcolonial identity politics. Pat Thane meanwhile provides an account of how and why historians have studied population and how they have dealt with the vastly increased levels of accurate data compiled in the last fifty years. She carefully assesses the use of different sources throughout her chapter, and brings us up to date with wide-ranging research on key contemporary concerns, such as changes in mortality and fertility, in interrelationship with gender, class, population policies, or slave trading. The relevance of comparative data is evident: as Chris Clark writes, for instance, only in 1975 did Africa reach population densities comparable with those of Europe around 1500; in 1900 Africa accounted for 18 per cent of the world's surface but only 5 to 7 per cent of its population. Both Thane and Clark provide models of how to ask questions about and analyse the effects of such constitutive divergences to deeply understand the development of world societies.

Pamela Smith next introduces us to the important perspectives developed by historians of science in the past thirty years. Scientific knowledge is firmly seen as a product not so much of isolated geniuses as of human society. Such knowledge is 'constructed within particular communities and their place in social and intellectual structures, as people make use of ideas, information, and techniques available in that society'. Many discoveries across human history result from collective and collaborative processes, and were not necessarily dependent on writing. Smith likewise draws attention to the impact of colonialism and the way in which the 'possession' of science facilitated social demarcations. Science was embedded in ideologies of European superiority through modernity. Historians of science therefore attempt to destabilize straightforward associations of Western science with objectivity and reason through pointing to the global origins of knowledge about nature and the contingency of its formation in social processes.

Historians of science have in effect transformed how we conceive of knowing the world, and their impact on accounts of historical forms of knowing is evident in work summarized in Chapter 3 of this volume. Scientists since Heisenberg and historians of science have dispelled an idealized notion of 'objectivity' that is untainted by the observer. They have replaced the category of objectivity with the notion that we use 'trained judgement' in order to make nature or the world intelligible. This applies to historians' understanding of the past, which depends on their tools, forms, and contexts of work. Idealistic notions of truth can thus be replaced with concepts of fidelity and reliability, rather than arbitrary relativism or fictional history. We need, moreover, a complex analysis of what it is that historians involve themselves in doing when they create knowledge about the past and what values and concepts they resort to in defending their ideals. Historians, in other words, can be subjected to the same kinds of analysis in the making of the past as scientists have been in their making of knowledge about nature. This broadens the intellectual history from a concern with ideas to a concern with practices of knowledge making embedded in particular contexts and conventions of particular communities across the world.

This theme is magisterially developed in Bonnie Smith and Donald Kelley's account of who counted as a 'historian' doing 'proper' history where, for whom, and in what period. They set out how different definitions of history operated for the way Chinese history was typically written as dynastic history and European history came increasingly to be written as nation-based. 'Historians' moreover charts the effects of the professionalization of history in universities, while drawing attention to the considerable vigour and alternative visions of 'amateur' historians and other practitioners of history, many of them female, in different parts of the globe. Smith and Kelley interestingly stress the twentieth-century European notion that the historian had to become an *Übermensch*, 'stretching to cover a wider swath of past experience and to learn methods outside of history, becoming geographer, sociologist, critique of the arts and literature and many other things', especially with the *Annales* notion that history writing should be 'total history', encompassing all aspects of societies. This development led to concomitant anxieties about the scope of history and professional roles, giving rise to fears of over-specialization as much as over-generalization. At the same time, it introduced a new scale of professional variation in terms of what kinds of history are now written and how.

These changes are given excellent expression in Miri Rubin's contribution. She sets out how fundamentally the writing on religious history has diversified since the late twentieth century. It is no longer written predominantly by practitioners of particular confessions about their religion or about ideas as allegedly set doctrines. Religious history, like other fields, is also far less the preserve of male scholars than it used to be. Through a dialogue with anthropological approaches scholars now pay greater attention 'to the experience of the multitude of believers, to the ways in which a religious cosmology—an understanding of the world—structures people's lives'. The relation of gender, the body, and space to religious identities has been central to these endeavours. Rubin brings out the richness of questions to be asked about spiritual cultures as constitutive of identities and their transmission across world religions. Conversations with the supernatural are an important element of how cultures have channelled emotions such as grief or hope. Eiko Ikegami investigates how societies more widely have developed methods of governing and expressing emotions, and thus introduces us to the most recent among a contemporary Clio's sub-disciplines: the history of emotions. She challenges any notion of a natural dualism of mind and body and draws on evidence from Japan to question Norbert Elias's narrative of a progressive and distinctly Western development towards more civilized forms of behaviour. This prompts new questions: why would it not even occur to medieval Japanese courtiers to blow their noses on sleeves, and why did the humanist Erasmus still have to write against such customs in sixteenth-century Europe? Do different body techniques tell us most about the way in which people maintained boundaries between each other or had internalized a sense of shame? How are we to think about neuroscientific claims which often seem to treat us as human species without distinct histories and societies?

For historians, rather, ideas and ways of understanding and categorizing humans are transmitted and adapted over long periods of time. One of the largest challenges is to account for final 'paradigm shifts', in which former ideas suddenly seem worn out and ready to be discarded, as Anthony Grafton sets out in the final contribution to this Companion. He draws attention to the vigorous debates among historians of ideas about how best to explain the contexts out of which ideas arise and take shape, and why any determinism about precise causal factors is typically defied by complexities. Grafton also shows why central master narratives, such as Max Weber's idea that Western capitalism was exceptional and causally connected to a Protestant attitude towards work and consumption, no longer command support. Like Chris Bayly, Grafton powerfully underlines that the history of ideas can yield 'new understandings of many stories in world history' if it crosses cultural boundaries and works together with other historical sub-disciplines.

I have introduced the chapters of this book not in strict chronological order but in terms of their interconnections. All contributors exhibit the extraordinary dynamic historical research has shown in recent decades. I have pointed to threads which for me make up the warp and weft of this book from which a new weave of history might eventually be seen to emerge. It is for different readers to judge how much of a patchwork with disfiguring holes this still seems, or whether the density, texture, colour, and sense of rich possibility already on display compensate for incompleteness.

U.R.

St John's College, Cambridge, May 2010

Notes on Contributors

C. A. Bayly is Vere Harmsworth Professor of Imperial and Naval History at the University of Cambridge and fellow of St Catherine's College. He has worked on the history of modern India and world history, publishing *Imperial Meridian: The British Empire and the World, 1780–1830* (1989) and *The Birth of the Modern World 1780–1914: Global Connections and Comparisons* (2004). He is at present studying the history of Indian liberalism in world context.

Elizabeth Buettner is Senior Lecturer in History at the University of York. Her book *Empire Families: Britons and Late Imperial India* (2004) was joint winner of the Women's History Network Book Prize for 2004. Her articles have appeared in the *Journal of Modern History*, *Ab Imperio*, *History & Memory*, the *Scottish Historical Review*, and *Food and History*. She has contributed to a number of edited collections, including Robert Bickers (ed.), *Settlers and Expatriates: Britons over the Seas*, Oxford History of the British Empire Companion Series (2010). She is completing a comparative study entitled *Europe after Empire: Decolonization, Society, and Culture*.

Peter Burke was Professor of Cultural History, University of Cambridge, until his retirement in 2004 and remains fellow of Emmanuel College. He has written more than twenty books, most of them on the cultural and social history of early modern Europe, including *Culture and Society in Renaissance Italy* (1972), *Popular Culture in Early Modern Europe* (1978), *The Fabrication of Louis XIV* (1992), and *Languages and Communities in Early Modern Europe* (2004). Together with Asa Briggs he is the author of *A Social History of the Media* (3rd edn. 2009).

Christopher Clark is Professor of Modern European History at St Catharine's College, Cambridge University. He is the author of *The Politics of Conversion: Missionary Protestantism and the Jews in Prussia, 1728–1941* (1995), *Kaiser Wilhelm II* (2000), and *Iron Kingdom: The Rise and Downfall of Prussia, 1600–1947* (2006), as well as of articles on themes drawn from the history of religion and culture in modern Europe. He is currently working on a study of the July Crisis of 1914.

Anthony Grafton teaches the history of early modern Europe at Princeton. His books include *What was History? The Art of History in Early Modern Europe* (2007), *Codex in Crisis* (2008), and *Worlds made by Words* (2009).

Eiko Ikegami is Professor of Sociology at the New School of Social Research in New York. She is best known for her books *The Taming of the Samurai: Honorific*

Individualism and the Making of Modern Japan (1995) and *Bonds of Civility: Aesthetic Networks and the Political Origins of Japanese Culture* (2005).

Donald R. Kelley is James Westfall Thompson Professor Emeritus of History at Rutgers University and former editor of the *Journal of the History of Ideas*. He has published widely in intellectual history and is currently writing a history of encyclopedias.

Dorothy Ko is Professor of History at Barnard College, Columbia University. She is the author of, among other books, *Teachers of the Inner Chambers: Women and Culture in Seventeenth-Century China* (1994) and *Cinderella's Sisters: A Revisionist History of Footbinding* (2005).

John R. McNeill is Professor of History at Georgetown University, and in 2011–12 President of the American Society for Environmental History. He studied at Swarthmore College and Duke University and is the author or editor of ten books, including *The Mountains of the Mediterranean World: An Environmental History* (1992); *Something New under the Sun: An Environmental History of the Twentieth-Century World* (2000); *The Human Web* (2003); *Mosquito Empires: Ecology and War in the Greater Caribbean, 1640–1914* (2010).

Kenneth Pomeranz is Chancellor's Professor of History at the University of California, Irvine. His publications include *The Making of a Hinterland: State, Society, and Economy in Inland North China, 1853–1937* (1993); *The Great Divergence: China, Europe, and the Making of the Modern World* (2000); and (with Stephen Topik) *The World That Trade Created: Society, Culture, and the World Economy, 1400 to the Present* (2nd edn. 2006).

Miri Rubin is Professor of Medieval and Early Modern History at Queen Mary, University of London. She was educated in Jerusalem and Cambridge and has researched various aspects of medieval religious and social life, in studies on charity, ritual, and the cult of the Virgin Mary. She is also very much interested in Jewish–Christian relations. Her most recent book is *Mother of God: A History of the Virgin Mary* (2009).

Ulinka Rublack teaches at Cambridge University and is a fellow of St John's College. She has published *The Crimes of Women in Early Modern Germany* (1999); *Reformation Europe* (2005); and *Dressing Up: Cultural Identity in Renaissance Europe* (2010), as well as edited a volume on *Gender in Early Modern German History* (2002). She serves on the editorial boards of the *Historical Journal* and *German History*.

Bonnie G. Smith is Board of Governors' Professor of History at Rutgers University. She has published in women's and gender, European, and world history. Her most recent publication is the *Oxford Encyclopedia of Women in World History* (2008), of which she was general editor.

Pamela H. Smith is a Professor of History at Columbia University and the author of *The Business of Alchemy: Science and Culture in the Holy Roman Empire* (1994) and *The Body of the Artisan: Art and Experience in the Scientific Revolution* (2004). She co-edited *Merchants and Marvels: Commerce, Science, and Art in Early Modern Europe* (with Paula Findlen, 2002) and *Making Knowledge in Early Modern Europe: Practices, Objects, and Texts, 1400–1800* (with Benjamin Schmidt, 2008). In her present research, she attempts to reconstruct the vernacular knowledge of early modern European metalworkers from a variety of disciplinary perspectives, including hands-on reconstruction of historical metalworking techniques.

Pat Thane is Professor of Contemporary British History at King's College, London. She has published, among other books, *The Foundations of the Welfare State* (2nd edn. 1996), *Old Age in English History: Past Experiences, Present Issues* (2000), and is editor of *The Long History of Old Age* (2005).

Megan Vaughan is Smuts Professor of Commonwealth History at the University of Cambridge and Director of the Centre of African Studies there. Her most recent book is *Creating the Creole Islands: Slavery in Eighteenth Century Mauritius* (Duke University Press, 2005). She is working on a history of death in East and Central Africa.

R. Bin Wong is Director of the UCLA Asia Institute and Professor of History. Among his books are *China Transformed: Historical Change and the Limits of European Experience* (Cornell University Press, 1997) and with Jean-Laurent Rosenthal, *Before and Beyond Divergence: The Politics of Economic Change in China and Europe* (Harvard University Press, 2011).

List of Illustrations

Part I
Writing History

1. Anti-globalization badge, 'This world is not for Sale'. © By permission of the Trustees of the British Museum

I History and World History

CHRISTOPHER BAYLY

This chapter considers some major themes which have recently emerged in the writing of the world history of the last three centuries. It examines and critiques recent discussions about the timing and origins of the 'rise of the West' to global dominance and the decline of its hegemony in the twentieth century. Turning to historical method, it examines the way in which long-held notions of national and racial historical evolution ('historicism') have continued to grip the public, and even academic imagination across the globe, despite advances in professional history and the challenge of a multi-polar world. It argues that world history writing is still dwarfed by the persistence of nationalist historical narratives, though it can be brought into useful dialogue with them. The chapter then takes a case study. It considers the possibilities for writing a global intellectual history or a world history of ideas, turning outward a sophisticated form of historical writing, which has remained resolutely European- and American-based until quite recently. Finally, the chapter considers some emerging themes which will preoccupy world historians in the future: demography, environmentalism, and disease. This chapter, therefore, reflects broadly on the way in which the experience of contemporary 'globalization' has modified our perspective on the emergence of the modern world. It argues that world history can no longer be regarded as an 'add-on-extra' to national or regional histories, but can fundamentally change the way we understand historical narratives. A radical change of perspective, however, still lies some way off.

The scope of World History: European and American dominance and their demise

Until twenty years ago origins of Euro-American world dominance from the eighteenth to the twentieth century were still largely debated in terms of European achievement: commercial, military, moral, and scientific. The Asian, Middle Eastern, and African story was one of 'what went wrong?' Even on the Left, bar a few dissenters such as Andre Gunder Frank,[1] it was argued that the West's superior technology and taste for aggression allowed it to capture the wealth of the non-West and recycle it into the machine of the industrial revolution. The sole exception to this story was the interest in Japan's rise after 1870, but here the explanatory model also remained the characteristics of 'modernization' which had been isolated for Western Europe.

The recent economic rise of India and China, alongside the proliferation of migrations across the globe, has significantly changed this perspective. The 'great divergence' of the West from the non-West, particularly China, is now more likely to be dated to about 1800, rather than to the Renaissance or even the later Middle Ages, as was the case until recently.[2] The existence in Asia of strong states, commercialized agriculture, even the existence of incipient indigenous 'public spheres', has been emphasized. If the continuing superior wealth of the East until at least 1750 was long recognized, now the technological, intellectual, and scientific prowess of the West has been downplayed, or at least made highly relative.

This historiographical trend has been a healthy one and has broadened the political significance of the study of history in the global age. But, pushed to extremes, it does run the risk of obscuring the origins of what has clearly been a fundamental feature of early modern and modern history and cannot really be explained away entirely as a 'late divergence'. One aspect of the upward trajectory of Europe which needs to be re-emphasized is the importance of the early modern Iberian empires and also the Dutch in the Atlantic and New World, a point that did not escape the notice of Adam Smith. Most of the relativist, revisionist histories of recent decades take the perspective of the later north-west European empires: France and Britain. They were written by historians of China, Japan, and India. True, some of them, notably Kenneth Pomeranz, pointed to the New World as a great and exploitable resource for Britain and France, but this was seen as a matter of the mobilization of resources rather than imperial culture.

Yet the Spanish Empire in Mexico and Peru was a remarkable model for later empire, while it was the Portuguese who created the first truly global polity, stretching from Brazil to Malacca and beyond.

These empires pioneered long-distance expatriate migration and cre-ated remarkably resilient structures of imperial control long before modern communications developed. In combination with the colo-nial viceroyalties, the Church, particularly the Jesuits, developed new types of colonial statistical knowledge that only had limited analogies in the great indigenous empires of Asia and North Africa. The impera-tive to 'save souls' demanded a more pervasive proto-anthropology of the colonized. Equally, the Spanish and Portuguese pioneered the super-exploitation of peasant and slave labour, which was characteris-tic of the era of European dominance until the twentieth century. This involved the creation of new systems of bio-political control, trans-port, risk management, and warfare which changed the face of Europe and later Asia and Africa.

Equally significant, the further monetization of the world economy through the export and diffusion of New World silver created the first intimations of the dependency which was to tie China, the Ottoman Empire, and Africa to Europe. This was as early as 1600. For instance, as Sevket Pamuk has shown, the Ottoman Empire was severely weak-ened economically by its dependence on silver transmitted through European sources which raised the level of inflation without creating new resources for the empire.[3] Silver from the New World and Euro-pean arms were among the few commodities that the Mughals and Qing initially desired from Europe and here again, new dependencies were created quite early.

Two other measures of the significance of the New World to what was once called 'the rise of Europe' were, first, the diffusion of new spe-cies of plants, animals, and diseases to the rest of the world and, sec-ondly, the development of forms of creole independence movements which were to have major effects in Europe and Asia after 1750, effects which were as striking as the 'contagion of sovereignty' which spread from the United States after 1783. It has sometimes been assumed that, because it was the British, French, and other north European pow-ers which completed European dominance in the nineteenth century, rather than Spain, Portugal, Genoa, or Venice, this meant that there was little connection between the Atlantic and the Asian–African phases of European colonial expansion. But not only has the pre-capitalist nature of these earlier empires been exaggerated, but also nineteenth-century empire builders often relied on the models, connections, and even personnel of their predecessors. Portuguese remained the most widely spoken European language in British India and Dutch South-East Asia as late as 1820, while much of the British Indian Empire's lower bureaucracy, for instance, was staffed by Indo-Portuguese. So-called 'Dutch burgers' in Ceylon and most of Batavia's creoles were also of Portuguese origin, while some of the earliest creole separatist movements took place in the Spanish Philippines.

Many of the arguments for the very late dating of the 'great divergence' have resulted from careful consideration of the Chinese and Japanese economic data along the lines developed for European economic history a generation earlier. Yet we should recognize that the conclusions have been ambiguous and contested. If Chinese coastal provinces were indeed as productive as north European farmlands in the eighteenth century and if Japan saw its own 'industrious revolution', European historians have responded that productivity, as opposed to total production, was much higher in north-western Europe. If historians of Asia have continued to note the wealth and complexity of the Chinese porcelain industry and Chinese, Ottoman, and Indian textile production, European historians respond that, even before 1700, industries in northern Europe showed rather greater capacity for innovation and technological development than was evident in Asia or the Middle East. The industrial revolution was itself preceded by a gathering momentum of medium-level technical changes, driven by new scientific knowledge, particularly in the areas of astronomy, armaments, agriculture, and transport. In addition, much of the innovation which was later seen in the Indian, Chinese, or Ottoman artisan industries itself became dependent on distant European demand.

This is a critical point: it was European commercial agencies which were able to expand and project their demand overseas on a large scale and protect their resources with advanced forms of armed shipping. Asian and Islamic societies certainly had sophisticated commercial cultures and had developed forms of double-entry bookkeeping and promissory notes; they even continued to have a majority of the world's richest merchants. There were, however, no equivalents to the great European joint stock companies such as the Dutch or the English East India companies. Much has been made of the voyages of Admiral Cheng Ho and early Chinese expansion into the Indian Ocean and the African coast. But during the Qing dynasty, Chinese commercial activity continued only in the form of trade diasporas of individual merchants in small and generally unarmed shipping. Chinese expansion was land-based expansion into inner Asia, while Western European expansion was predominantly seaborne, if we exclude Russian entrepreneurs' expansion into Siberia in search of furs.

The key European breakthrough took place, ultimately, in relations between the state, military technology, and the elite citizens who operated various forms of surveillance on state and society—broadly Jürgen Habermas's public sphere.[4] This occurred above all in northwestern Europe. This is not to deny that the Mughals, Ottomans, and Qing displayed increasingly sophisticated forms of 'governmentality' or that their management of ethnic diversity did not compare favourably in human terms with some of the so-called 'persecuting states' of the early modern West. But the difference was early and stark. The Dutch East India Company and its imitators harnessed capital and risk on an unparalleled scale. The English (later British) state taxed heavily and highly effectively, as John Brewer pointed out,[5] but elite surveillance of the state by Parliament ensured that money was spent relatively productively.

This was especially so in the case of the British Royal Navy, a force which by the early eighteenth century could deploy up to 30,000 men permanently stationed on ships hundreds of miles from the British coast and constantly replace and feed them. Even supposedly less efficient continental absolute monarchies maintained powerful and intrusive taxation systems which mobilized resources highly effectively and were only undermined by the excessive ambition of European overseas conflicts. China, by contrast, as historians such as Pamela Crossley have shown, imposed a light taxation regime to pacify its provinces and gained resources by external conquest on its land frontiers.[6] Its army was highly effective, but logistically unsophisticated and politically weak by contemporary European standards.

Even here, China was something of an exception. As a state form and empire, it soldiered on through the later eighteenth-century revolts until ideological dissidence and local state formation came together in the Taiping rebellion of the 1850s, finally bringing the Qing Empire to its knees. Other extra-European states and societies, notably the Ottomans, Safavids, Mughals, and Javanese kingdoms, faced internal disintegration much earlier—at the beginning of the eighteenth century—and European trades in silver and arms served only to undermine them further. It may well be that the 'great divergence' did not become fully apparent until about 1800, or become totally irreversible before 1750, but Europe's competitive advantages had firmly revealed themselves up to two centuries earlier. World historians have rightly concentrated on the polycentric nature of change in world societies and economies in the early modern period and the way in which this has determined the nature of 'the modern'. Yet this does not mean that the early and dynamic growth of a particular style of European political economy can be downplayed.

The nation state and 'the subaltern' as global actors

Conceptually linked to the debate about the rise of the West has been the study of the origins and nature of the modern nation state. This stretches back to the mid-nineteenth century and the work of Leopold von Ranke and Ernst Renan, for instance. But the tradition was reinvigorated during the 1970s and 1980s by a group of historians and sociologists which included Eric Hobsbawm and Ernest Gellner.[7] These scholars argued for the very late emergence of nationalism in the nineteenth century as a result of international conflict, urbanization, and the growth of print capitalism. Just as the expansion of Europe was post-dated, so then was the modern state and modern nationalism.

This new scepticism in the 1970s and 1980s about the longevity and dominance of the nation state seems to have reflected the assumption that the state was actually on the point of demise as trans-national flows of capital and people speeded up during those decades following the 'fall of Communism'. The view that nationalism emerged no earlier than the 1870s critiqued much of the earlier historiography of the nation state. Earlier European historians had traced nationalities back to the Middle Ages, or even late antiquity. This was also true of nations outside Europe. For instance, George Antonius, writing in the 1930s, identified a sense of Arab nationality in the days of the Prophet Muhammad when the Arabic language emerged.

The evident recovery of the nation state following the small wars of the 1990s and, more recently, the 2008 financial crisis now seems to be re-empowering a more traditional style of historiography of nations and nationalism. The main difference from the history writing of the 1970s is that the nation state is often now studied from the perspective of those who are apparently excluded from its workings: migrants, minorities, and, above all, women, who were still poorly represented in high office and business across much of the world. But the state is now firmly back in the historical saddle. Several scholars have also recently revisited the theme of the medieval origins of nationalities, while the conservative turn in politics has tended to revive benign views of the antiquity of nations both within and outside Europe. The superficiality of much of the 'world history' taught in schools and universities has aided the 'return of nation and empire' in curricula in several countries, including Britain, France, and Turkey. What surely has to be stressed in future history lessons at all levels is that the transnational, the 'cosmopolitan', the migration of people, goods, and ideas across borders, expanded as powerfully and at the same time as the reach of the nation state itself.

Alongside the 1970s interest in, and expected demise of, the state was a parallel phenomenon, a new version of 'history from below': often called Subaltern Studies. On the face of it, this was an important historical moment because it represented the first major incursion into global historiography of a group of historians drawn from formerly colonized people. The writing of the history of 'people without history' in India soon sparked analogies in South-East Asia, Latin America, and Africa. This was not a wholly new development, of course. Even nineteenth-century literary figures, such as the Bengali novelist Bankim Chandra Chatterjee, had taken an interest in the lives of the poor. Marxist scholars, especially in China, had discarded the nice distinctions amongst the peasantry described by Westerners and hailed a unified global proletariat. In British history Christopher Hill and E. P. Thompson,[8] among others, had analysed popular mentalities. But the Subaltern Studies Collective,[9] developing among Indian and Indianist scholars in Europe and the United States, certainly acted as a powerful shock to the international historical establishment and made main-line political and economic historians more circumspect in their claims. The Subaltern Studies writers abandoned much of the teleology and social structuralism of earlier Marxist and liberal historians. They emphasized instead the distinct consciousness and political forms of the 'people without power' who came in time to include colonized elites.

Many in the Western academy, however, are unaware of the fact that Subaltern Studies has not been readily accepted in India itself or other postcolonial societies, either in its counter-Marxist or in its postmodernist guise. One reason for this is that Marxist social analysis, as opposed to the epistemological and psychic traumas of elites, which Subaltern historians came increasingly to study, held significant advantages for historians and sociologists studying contested and internally fragmented popular movements in many locales across the world. The recent resurgence of self-styled Maoist movements in Nepal, Bihar, and in various Latin American countries may well help to revive Marxist historiography, though it is unlikely that it will regain the clout it wielded between about 1930 and 1970. Even the most abstract of French Marxists now doubt the imminence of revolution. The popular objects of study in liberal democracies—migrants, gender, women, freed slaves, déclassé urban proletarians—were never central to the teleologies of orthodox Marxism. Nevertheless, history writing across the world is likely to see a revival of late Marxist history and the history of political economy, in reaction to Subaltern and cultural history.

American hegemony and international Communism: absent presences

Considerations of the rise of the West, the modern state, and the 'people without power' bring this opening discussion, finally, to absences in modern world history writing. The rise of the USA, European decolonization, and the relative decline of Europe itself have inevitably dominated this story. The world wars, the Cold War, and, very recently, the rise of Islamism have provided the causal motors for much of this work. In some respects, the first of these—US history itself—remains a paradox in regard to its relationship with world history. The history of this dominant world power and consumer, home of modern capitalism and democracy, site of the largest and most diverse historical profession in the world, remains quite incomplete across much of its span. As with British history until the Second World War, it may be that this very dominance has created a degree of introversion. Certainly, relatively few outstanding works have been devoted to analysing the worldwide influence of the USA and reactions to it, compared with the huge corpus of American domestic histories.

For the nineteenth century, the notion of national independence, what David Armitage called the 'contagion of sovereignty', is receiving attention, for instance.[10] But the significance of the expansion of US trade on the global economy of free trade is little examined. There are, again, relatively few studies of the wider impact of the US Civil War, not simply on Mexico, but on Western Europe, and, through cotton prices and new methods of warfare, on societies as distant as Egypt and India. The 'Wilsonian moment' of 1917–20 has recently come to the fore.[11] But the international diplomatic history of the USA has rarely been brought into dialogue with regional social histories to create a convincing picture of the significance of US power and reactions to it. Recent studies of the American war in Vietnam, for instance, have generally retreated to a resolutely American perspective, leaving the domestic history of resistance to anthropologists. Compared with the myriad of studies of European decolonization, the concomitant, and connected, rise of American power, culture, and influence is represented in a myriad of smaller studies, but has not been effectively synthesized, except in somewhat triumphal narratives of the spread of 'American freedoms'.

So, studies of American hegemony have been relatively small in number and limited in scope. Similarly, its mirror image, the worldwide Communist *ecumene*, which survived from 1917 to at least 1989, and much longer thereafter in an occluded form in China, North Korea, and Vietnam, has also been neglected. One problem here was the proliferation of specialists on Communism during the Cold War. Their work was devoted to explaining the power and menace emanating from the Soviet Bloc. When that Bloc suddenly collapsed in the late 1980s, this genre of political science and history withered almost as quickly. Yet the Communist world was much more than a fragile despotism. Doctors, teachers, engineers, and other specialists moved from one Communist country to another in large numbers; economic systems became interdependent in an unbalanced way.[12] The cultural progress of Communist nations was lauded in many varieties of media, preparing people for the re-emergence of those tropes of national historicism discussed in the next section. Indeed, the very vastness of the record of the last century and the plethora of voices reporting on it has made it difficult to research, write, and teach 'the day before yesterday'.

World historical methodologies: the fall and rise of historicism

This section moves from considerations of the scope and limitations of world history and writing over the last generation to the question of style and narrative. The classic nineteenth-century historicist mode of thought posited the evolution of races, nations, or institutions through time as their essential characteristics were gradually revealed. World history, insofar as it was written at all, consisted of a description of competition between these evolving entities. In very different ways, both Hegel and Comte promoted this kind of thinking and it was foundational, too, in early Marxism, though here it was the evolution of social classes that was emphasized. Later in the nineteenth century, this idea became complicated by a more scientific view of evolution, which drew to one degree or another on the thought of Charles Darwin and Herbert Spencer.

Some typical examples concern the evolution of Anglo-Saxon freedom, as portrayed by E. A. Freeman and of India's unity and 'ancient constitution' as portrayed by contemporary Indian liberals. Freeman's generation built on Macaulay's histories to portray English institutions groaning under the 'Norman Yoke' but eventually flourishing, as Norman administrative genius fused with Teutonic proto-democracy to produce an imperial nation. In the latter case, Indians argued that India had also once been a great nation governed by popular will acting through a local deliberative body, the *panchayat*, which was proposed as the equivalent of the Anglo-Saxon *witenagemot*. To these writers, the genius of the race was also embodied in its heroes. The revered Indian historians and novelists turned the god Krishna into a historic figure and founder of Indian unity, not unlike King Alfred or the German chieftains who repelled the Emperor Augustus's legions and created the free German polity. World history became the history of heroes, a development consummated by Nietzsche.

This sort of evolutionary historicism was treated with some suspicion by competing schools of history. Pupils of Ranke and the followers of Lord Acton subjected it to deep empirical scepticism and often dismissed it for romanticism. Later Marxists stressed rupture and class conflict rather than evolution. Social and political historians qualified the notion of liberty, showing it meant something very different in the later Middle Ages from the nineteenth century. Late twentieth-century postmodernist scholars rejected the whole idea of the historical evolution of forms, stressing instead the fragment, the unique experience, and arguing that, far from an objective, evolving process, history was constituted by the discourses of the present. World history therefore became, following Foucault, the history of discourses of global power.

It is striking, therefore, that evolutionary nationalist historicism remains, at the beginning of the twentieth-first century, the dominant form of historical understanding across much of the world. This is true not simply in basic education and the popular media, but in many parts of the academy itself. Indeed, far from being two opposing traditions, popular history and academic history of this sort have tended to reinforce and validate each other through publishing and the book trade. Despite the work of the specialist historians on the Indian Schoolbook Commission, for instance, the notion of ancient Indian freedoms, challenged by Alexander, then Muslim invaders, and finally the British, has persisted in popular understanding and school textbooks, sometimes reinforced by Bollywood films and Indian television. Even the historicist understanding of the role of divine figures in history has remained powerful, as witness the recent conflict over Adam's Bridge in South India, which is still seen as the crossing point of the hero-god Ram to Sri Lanka. World history teaching remains dominated by narratives of nation states evolving since antiquity.

The situation in Communist and former Communist societies is even more striking. In China, Confucius, whom nineteenth-century historians turned into a kind of divine prophet figure, has now re-emerged as something akin to Plato and Aristotle for modern Greeks, the originary philosophers of the race. Indeed, Confucius is once again the subject of direct worship, which would presumably have appalled him. Mao Zedong, by comparison, has been downgraded or turned into a 'mere' nationalist, both in schoolbooks and academic writing. After the Communist revolution and reunification of Vietnam, Ho Chih Minh (*Bac Ho* or 'Uncle Ho') retained a special, almost divine role, but the veneration of other heroes and spirits of Vietnam's past was discouraged. Now, here too, socialist history has been reconnected with the national. Historical figures, especially those who are credited with repelling the Chinese, French, and American invaders, have been reinstated as the true repositories of the history of Vietnam.

Similarly, in a recent Russian poll, Tsar Nicholas II trumped Stalin as the greatest Russian in history. But this runner-up Stalin was generally no longer the Stalin of the Marxist 'nationality question'. Rather he was Stalin, the defender of Russia, a hero in the great tradition of Alexander Nevsky and Ivan the Terrible.

It might be thought that this has not happened in Western Europe or the USA. Here, surely, critical social and political history, followed by postmodernism, has flowed out from the academy to 'correct' the public understanding of the past. World history has surely emerged as a dispassionate master narrative. Broadly speaking, this has not been the case. National histories exuding a faintly triumphal tone still rule the roost. More significantly, the histories of European national empires continue to command great public admiration and are often directly claimed as the precursors of today's 'humanitarian interventionism', the imposition of a simulacrum of Western culture or democracy by armed force. This is not confined to the understanding of the northern European empires of the nineteenth century. A 2009 British Museum exhibition on the Aztecs, for instance, was castigated by several commentators for 'moral neutralism'. The Aztec rulers, it was said, were akin to the Nazis and therefore, by implication, the Spanish invasion was a benign imposition of civilization. These commentators disregarded the fact that the exploits of Cortes and Pizarro ultimately led to the death of perhaps 80 per cent of the Amerindian population from disease and oppression.

Politics intervened more directly in French educational textbooks to save the idea of the *mission civilisatrice* of France in Africa from its detractors. In the English-speaking world again, liberal and conservative historians, many of them first-class exponents of their trade, have stepped in to update themes that would have been comfortable to Macaulay, E. A. Freeman, and G. M. Trevelyan. Niall Ferguson has re-burnished the British Empire as an empire of Free Trade.[13] Andrew Roberts has recalibrated the story of the triumph of Western freedom on both sides of the Atlantic[14] and extended this analysis to the British former empire. Conservative Party aspirants to ministerial office now aim to reinstate teaching about 'the kings and queens of England' in the national curriculum. Even Gordon Brown, the former Labour Party British Prime Minister, praised the efforts of British missionaries and educators in colonial Africa. But here he was only following a powerful academic trend which still represents God working in the African continent, albeit now against the interests of greedy imperialists. The field of African history still often exudes a historical sensibility which smacks of Christian atonement. This, though, is pitted against an understanding of African history as a story of racial oppression of black people by whites, which derives from scholarship in the United States, but is equally a product of national guilt.

The reason for the persistence, even re-invention, of nineteenth-century national and racial historicism lies partly in the policies and economics of the media. Even academic historians are constrained to write big books on wars and great statesmen, which can show us 'how we got here'. Partly, it lies in the constant revivification of the importance of the nation state, mentioned above. The perception in the 1970s and 1980s that the nation state was overwhelmed by the new world of globalized capital flows and migration has proved unfounded. Once again the nation seems the only redoubt against economic dystopia, pandemic disease, and illegal migration.

The vision of Deity working through history, which was a parallel theme to the political historicism of the nineteenth century, has also received a new impetus from the rise of evangelical Christianity and militant Islam across the world and even from events such as the election of Barack Obama as President of the United States. These movements of thought often work in complex ways. For instance, recent liberal historians of the Islamic world have attempted to downplay the themes of *jihad* and conquest in favour of the idea of Islamic brotherhood and the peaceful expansion of the faith. This is clearly a reaction to the demonization of Islam in the wake of the rise of al-Qaeda and the Taliban. Yet this 'turn' takes us back to the late nineteenth century when T. W. Arnold, fighting contemporary Islamophobia and Turcophobia, wrote of the expansion of Islam as a religion of equality, blind to race. In a sense, it takes us even further back to Gibbon and Voltaire, who praised the rationalism and equality of the Islamic *umma* against what they saw as Christian irrationalism and despotism. This chapter goes on to develop this analysis of the contest between evolutionary historicism and historical relativism in one key representative area: the realm of socially contextualized intellectual history, which has much to gain from the world history perspective.

The past and present of global intellectual history

Over the last generation, intellectual history has also witnessed a sub-tle re-emergence of teleology and historicism despite the efforts of many professional philosophers and postmodernists to banish it. The latter, determined to make us aware of the politically tainted nature of much historical scholarship, overplayed their hand by denouncing all 'grand narratives', except their own, and seemed to argue that history had no recoverable patterns at all. All the same, a more globally con-nected history of ideas seems to be coming about.

Three major traditions of the intellectual history of Euro-America emerged after the Second World War. In the English-speaking world there was a shift away from the history of the unfolding of themes (jus-tice, democracy, etc.) through genealogies of canonical thinkers, as had characterized the approach of G. H. Sabine, John Plamenatz, and the 1930s–1960s generation, to a contextual and time-aware history of ideas associated with the so-called 'Cambridge School' of Quentin Skinner, John Dunn, and John Pocock, among others.[15] The political philosopher Raymond Geuss shared an affinity with this school in his dislike of the 'moralism' of the dominant strand of liberal political phi-losophy, represented by John Rawls, and his concern for 'real politics'.[16] Some French intellectual historians, notably Pierre Rosanvallon[17] and his compeers further to the left, have also rooted the history of ideas much more closely in social and political history in comparable ways.

Secondly, and also in Western Europe, later Marxist writers emerg-ing out of the Frankfurt School, notably Jürgen Habermas, paid great attention to historical circumstances.[18] This was despite the fact that the concept of the emergence of a 'public sphere', standing between state and society and critiquing both, retained something of the earlier teleological approach. Though criticized for paying too lit-tle attention to religion, race, and gender, or those excluded from critical debate, the concept has nevertheless been highly influential among historians trying to give historical specificity to the concept of modernity. The third tendency, associated with Reinhart Kosel-leck's 'concept history', is represented as more conservative than these former approaches.[19] But it has the merit of emphasizing the impor-tance of the role of both epistemological and physical violence in the history of ideas. By contrast, English-speaking writers have seemed to make history and ideologies, at least since the English Civil War, a little too 'polite and commercial'.

Despite its aversion to teleology in intellectual history, the key argument of the first of these traditions, the 'Cambridge School', was to stress the emergence and diffusion of a set of ideas or 'speech acts' within history known as civic republicanism. The idea of the self-governing armed citizenry arose, it is argued, following the collapse of both the empire and the Papacy in Europe and the emergence of free city states, especially in northern Italy. The tradition of debate about the citizen, power, and the state, associated pre-eminently with Machiavelli, was later appropriated by northern European Protestants in their conflicts with monarchy and the Church during the 'wars of religion'. It became the basis for the Whig tradition of politics which was later appropriated again by American, Australasian, and even Indian democrats in the late eighteenth and nineteenth centuries. The history of Euro-American political thought became, to all intents and purposes, a universal history. It was not, however, a world history, since it was largely unconcerned with the appropriations and transformations of these ideas outside Europe and America.

How does the recent fate of these styles of intellectual history figure in the wider world? First, it should be emphasized that regions outside Europe and North America and the Christian world have long possessed strong traditions of intellectual history writing. These have in some ways grappled better than their Western equivalents with the role of religion in politics, not least because their historians are aware of the wide range of phenomena that the term 'religion' traditionally covers in these societies, from ritualism and cult to rationalist philosophy. Classics such as Albert Hourani's *Arabic Thought in the Liberal Age*, Joseph Levenson's *Confucian China and its Modern Fate*, or David Brading's *The First America* made this clear.

The impact of Christianity on non-Christian traditions of thought has been well documented for the age of empire in Asia and Africa. Nevertheless, it remains true that global or trans-national intellectual history remains quite underdeveloped. Intellectual historians of Europe and America do not venture much beyond their patch, while historians of Asia and Africa tend to work on national or regional issues or to relegate European ideas to the status of distant 'influences' rather than seeing them as 'speech acts', appropriated, cannibalized, hybridized, and used to effect political and economic change in particular locations. Yet an essential solvent of Western nationalist historicism must surely be a critique of the assumption of uncritical Western 'leadership' in the history of ideas, without a retreat to a banal relativism.

How would the 'Cambridge School' analysis of the birth of civic republicanism fare if one sought analogies in the Islamic world, India, or China? Here Sheldon Pollock's account of the withering of political thought in late Sanskritic India is of significance. From 1200 to 1700 great states and multi-ethnic empires continued to flourish and expand across Asia, even as warring kingdoms and city states consumed political and intellectual energies across Europe.[20] According to Pollock, the subcontinent achieved instead a cultural and intellectual equilibrium, which discouraged contestatory political thought and hastened the demise of Sanskrit as a literary language of philosophical debate.

There is obviously much truth in this. India's Machiavelli was Kautilya, a thousand years earlier; its Locke was Rammohan Roy, onehundred-and-fifty years later. Yet India and the rest of Asia did experience less profound renaissances and less rigorous enlightenments which spurred intellectual debate and provided material for later thinkers and politicians. Across the whole of Islamic and Indo-Islamic Asia, the 'mirror of princes' style of literature was taken up and embellished during the age of the Ottoman, Mughal, Safavid, and Mataram empires. Equally, localized traditions of political and social comment, such as the Indian *Panchatantra*, equivalent perhaps to Aesop's fables, continued to evolve. Most important, the nature of house-holding and good government under benign rulers continued to be discussed in all the great empires. Under the Qing in China and the Tokugawa in Japan, political debate took a Buddhist, Confucian, or Shinto form. Pamela Crossley gives a vivid analysis of the several styles of debate about the nature of Chinese celestial monarchy during the Qing period, while other writers have pointed to the continuation of themes of conciliar government both in Japan and China. In Japan, for instance, the balance between central and local powers during the Tokugawa era (*c*.1600–1870) has been seen as intellectually productive. It informed a polity which retained a centralizing ethos, yet allowed local cultural flowerings, including the appropriation of so-called 'Dutch [i.e. European] learning' in surgery, botany, and metallurgy well before the blizzard of colonialism.

In the Indo-Islamic and North African worlds discussion of the nature of government was represented by a merging of Islamic law and norms with Aristotle's *Politics* to produce a form of ethical-political literature called *akhlaq*. Cemal Kaffadar charted a veritable renaissance in the Ottoman Empire following the revitalization of studies of Aristotle there after 1453.[21] The Mughal Emperor Akbar had daily readings from some of the most important of the post-Aristotelian commentators, such as Nasiruddin Tusi. Other historians have pointed to the emergence of forms of history across Asia which became decisively separated from mythology and included comment on good government and domestic virtue. Nor were these simply abstract political debates: Asian and Middle Eastern and North African societies all possessed forms of community assembly which were supposed to play a role in local governance. How resilient or important these were depended on the nature of rule and the time and place. One example of this was the eighteenth-century *panchayat* of the pre-colonial western Indian kingdoms. Narendra Wagle has shown how these local deliberative bodies played a significant role in compromising political disputes over land and wealth.[22] They were multi-caste institutions, and agents of the rulers played a moderating, rather than a dominant, role in them. The existence of such bodies in the pre-modern and pre-colonial era proved an important mythic resource for later liberals and socialists when they sought to prove to colonial rulers that they were ready for self-government.[23]

At the very least, then, the distinction between Europe and its American colonies with vibrant political debates around real institutions and Asia and Africa mired in despotism, or the stagnant rescension of classical texts, is greatly overdone. Yet at the same time, it is true that the ending after about 1700 of the social and intellectual equilibrium of the old empires by external invasion and internal revolt did bring with it a great quickening of political debate in these societies. In the Islamic world at least, the re-emergence of political controversy pre-dated European intervention. The purist Wahhabi movement of Arabia exploded in the 1740s as the Ottoman Empire intruded more and more into the Arabian periphery. It was a political force which sought to reform the exercise of power as well as religious life and was the lineal ancestor of many of today's Islamist movements, such as the Muslim Brotherhood in Egypt or the Tablighi movement in South Asia, which have now spread to Europe and America. More orthodox patterns of Islamic scholarship and debate amongst both Sunnis and Shias responded to this challenge.

Yet there is no doubt that the conjuncture of these events with massive changes brought by the Revolutionary and Napoleonic wars and the beginnings of industrialization in Europe and America was a critical factor in the globalization of Western political thought. Liberal ideology, first in its constitutional phase and then in the form of democratic nationalism, spread from early French Algeria, through the Ottoman Empire to India, Indonesia, and the Philippines with remarkable speed after 1800. The thought of Immanuel Kant, Auguste Comte, or Guiseppe Mazzini, along with the example of George Washington, was received, reconstructed, and set to local uses in locales as far apart as Brazil, Mexico, and Japan. Later in the century, evolutionary theory, but more in the style of Herbert Spencer than Charles Darwin, had a profound impact across the world.

Christianity, moving in on the coat-tails of imperialism, merged with neo-Buddhism to prove a revolutionary force in the Chinese Taiping rebellion (1850–70). It also profoundly influenced styles of rule across sub-Saharan Africa in kingdoms such as Buganda. Even where Christian missionaries made few conversions, as for instance over much of Asia, the Middle East, and Islamic North Africa, they had a profound effect. Indigenous religious traditions were purged and modernized and re-armed with methods of publicity and organization derived from the Christian churches. These neo-Buddhist, neo-Hindu, and revived Islamic traditions sparked profound political debates wherever they arose.

Historians have shown that even in Europe later socialist and revolutionary movements built on earlier patterns of thought and often on pre-existing religious traditions. The classic work of Edward Thompson on the English working class highlighted the importance of Methodism in the emerging socialist ideology. The close relationship between democratic anti-slavery movements and evangelical religion in the USA was equally prominent. In the southern parts of united Germany, the Social Democratic Party drew on a core of Roman Catholic support. In Russia, the emergence of populist politics was closely correlated with the Old Believer sect.

There were clear analogies over much of the rest of the world. Gandhian mass politics in India blended popular Vaishnavism with ideas drawn from Christianity and the thought of Tolstoy. In China, the early nationalism of Sun Yatsen drew on the traditions of Christianity along the China coast. In several parts of East and South-East Asia, notably in French Indochina, Marxist-Leninism displayed a distinctly Buddhist tinge. Political ideologies in both East and West Africa were powerfully affected by European and American Christian missionary activities. African Christianity took a great deal from indigenous African ideas of the good life and prosperity, while downplaying the doctrines of Atonement and Sacrifice. On the one hand, its politics reconstituted ideas of the benign patriarchal provider as evidenced, for instance, in Jomo Kenyatta's *In Front of Mount Kenya*. On the other hand, African women have sometimes been at the fore of Christian movements which have challenged this patriarchy.

Recent histories have tended to treat rather sketchily the revolutionary effects of Marxist-Leninism for both political thought and political action and the once powerful socialist world system is passing out of memory, as noted earlier. Nevertheless, Marxism did represent a major rupture in intellectual history. Early socialism in Britain, the United States, and many Asian and African colonial societies tended to be influenced by the same Christian and romantic tropes as later communitarian liberalism. Yet there is no doubt that from 1917, through to Mao's Cultural Revolution and the Cuban revolution of the 1950s, public Communism and its spokesmen did attempt to reform global thought along the lines of atheist revolutionary progressivism. Even with the return of blood, race, and culture after the Communist collapse of the 1980s and the rise of Islamism, revolutionary Communism made sporadic local revivals, whether in the French academy, Nepal, Bihar, or Hugo Chavez's Venezuela.

The last generation has consequently witnessed a change of intellectual mood which has in turn affected the way intellectual history is written at world level. In the 1970s liberalism and neo-liberalism stood poised against a still powerful body of socialist and Communist ideology. On one side stood the liberal tradition of John Rawls, working in uneasy tandem with the free-market economics espoused by the World Bank and the International Monetary Fund. On the other side stood a late Marxism in which Jean-Paul Sartre had been displaced by Gramsci and Foucault. At the beginning of the twenty-first century, the situation is much more fluid, mirroring the new multi-centred form of world politics and influencing the writing of world history. Postmodernism and postcolonialism have challenged all 'foundational' views of historical change, whether market-centred or class-based. Western intellectual self-confidence has been dented by the range of works flowing from Edward Said's *Orientalism*, which charged the existing body of writings on non-European societies with complicity in imperialism.

Meanwhile, new, hybrid bodies of political theory emerged. Thus, the Ayatollah Khomeini's version of Shi'ite Islamic revivalism was laced with themes and arguments taken from earlier Marxist critiques of Western capitalism. The expansion of various forms of evangelical Christianity, particularly in Africa and Latin America, brought forth a Catholic reaction in the form of 'liberation theology'. This was, in turn, overwhelmed by the growth of Pentecostalist movements in both Latin America and Africa. These stressed the individual's relationship to God and seemed to fit well with economic neo-liberalism and the expansion of the market. At the same time, the world conflicts engendered by religion had encouraged the rise of a small group of 'militant atheists'.

Most significantly, the intellectual tempo both in the West and developing societies has been affected by the rise of new liberationist and conservationist themes, which interact in complicated ways with these more established ideologies. The women's movement, emerging in the USA in the 1970s, has profoundly affected all philosophical and human sciences, even in its mediated form as gender studies. More recently, feminism has begun to gain purchase in the Middle East, Asia, and Africa. Here small numbers of female activists and intellectuals have been embattled with various forms of neo-conservative and religious ideology. These feminists contest Islamism, Hindutva, Roman Catholicism, and various styles of late Communist disciplinarianism, which continue to stress the inviolability of the Catholic, Hindu, Muslim, or 'working-class' family. Democratic ideologies, which began to pluralize as early as the 1950s with the rise of black power or the Dalit ('untouchable') movement in India, took on new, particularistic forms, notably in the campaign for Gay Rights which began to affect the way in which churches and families regarded themselves.

Most important of all, perhaps, was the rise of environmental consciousness in the form of the Green Movement. Environmental awareness had a long lineage stretching back to the early nineteenth century, but the near doubling of world population after the 1950s and growing concerns about 'global warming' transformed this consciousness into both a philosophical position (the 'Gaia thesis'; the idea of a geological age which is fundamentally man-made) and also a form of radical political mobilization.

The importance of this widening range of political ideologies and religious sentiments was massively increased by the explosion of the worldwide web after 1990, powered forward by tools such as the blog, Facebook, and Twitter, and magnified by the spread of the cellphone. This has been particularly remarkable in Africa and China, where it may be that new, continental versions of the public sphere are emerging. If the years between 1780 and 1820s had seen a steady expansion of the public sphere brought about by the newspaper, the same short span of time two hundred years later had seen a broad democratization of knowledge and political influence through the internet. Its consequences are yet to be fully understood, but it has posed a significant challenge to governments, political parties, religious establishments, educational institutions, and even parents across the world.

These changes are cumulative. The formation of ideas reacts with changes in political economy. For instance, the global economic crisis of 2008–10 was different in reach from those of the 1840s, 1870s, 1930s, or 1970s because of the speed at which both good and bad economic news was broadcast. Once again, these socio-economic changes which arose from technical and philosophical developments fed back in turn into the way humans reflected on the history of their world. It seems likely that the idea of the market as a self-regulating entity has been driven out of economic theory as dramatically as protectionism and mercantilism were felled by the pens of Adam Smith and Condorcet. But it remains to be seen whether the revival of the power of the interventionist state in the economy will, in turn, further revivify nationalist historicism. The celebrations to mark the fiftieth anniversary of Communist China certainly seemed to point in that direction. Mao Zedong re-emerged, if somewhat diminished, as saviour of the nation from inhuman Western capitalism, pointing to a further revision of the role of European dominance in world history.

A world history for the future?

This chapter has suggested that across the world international competition, national educational systems, museums, the book trade, the media, even the recent economic crisis, have tended to reinvigorate the old themes of national historicism. It is not even clear that the expansion of migration, tourism, or what has been called 'global civil society', will immediately stimulate the study of comparative world history. Migrant communities have often been at the forefront of refashioning the national mythologies of their birthplaces.

Yet what will surely begin to change the historical perspective is the proliferation of global challenges and armed conflicts arising from demographic pressure, the degradation of environment, and the globalization of disease. A major emerging new theme in world history is the issue of the pressure of numbers on the earth itself, the growing shortages of water, the destruction of forests, and the likelihood of political conflict generated by scarcity.[24] This stands quite apart from the issue of the significance of 'global warming'.

Historians have shown that ecological awareness emerged out of proto-anthropology, romanticism, and a tutelary attitude to 'native peoples' quite early in the nineteenth century. It was, however, the trebling of world population between 1900 and 2000, the rise of Green politics in the West in the 1970s, and ecological resistance movements amongst forest-dwellers and peasants in the developing world that brought the issue to the forefront of historians' attention. Closely related to this has been a growing historiography of famine. Historians were alerted to famine by the work of Amartya Sen. Sen brought together environmental, economic, and political history with the history of ideas. He argued that lack of social entitlement, rather than absolute scarcity, produced the great famines in colonial Asia.[25] He also brought the issue into the present day by asserting that famines never occur in democracies, an argument that seemed to hold true as lethal scarcity reappeared in several 'failed states' in Africa. Some historians now argue, along with Green activists, that the world has moved into a decisively new phase when humanity itself has become the dominant influence on the natural world.

A critical dimension of the history of demography is, of course, the history of disease. For many years this was a field hived off into the history of science, which became a separate discipline from history, partly because of its technical nature. In recent decades, however, there are signs that this important sub-field has been reintegrated with main-line history. The medieval and early modern plagues were always essential features of historical analysis, the more so for Central and South America where the death of population in the sixteenth and seventeenth centuries provided the critical historical rupture. More recently, however, studies of the Eurasian cholera epidemics of the 1830s and 1890s; the connection between debates about race and the prevention of malaria in the Far East; and, most recently the ravages of HIV in Africa have brought general historians and historians of science into a new dialogue.[26] The powerful support of the Wellcome Foundation in Europe has speeded this project forward.

As the world population doubles again over the next century, it is impossible to escape the conclusion that conflicts over the consumer-driven lifestyle of the West, now exported to India, China, and Brazil, will lead to a further re-evaluation of the rise and decline of Euro-America among historians. The history of ideas, which has legitimized Western democracy and individualism, will be drawn increasingly into a worldwide, comparative framework. Struggles over resources of water, oil, and food, the impact of global epidemics, and mass migration in search of economic security will impact on the way history is written. The reactions of states to these massive problems will continue to determine their outcome in large part. But these states will inevitably be working in a trans-national arena. World history writing will reflect this fact, becoming a fundamental aspect of, and determining factor in, the writing of all national and regional histories.

2. Funerary equipment made of paper; in the form of video recorder and CDs, Singapore, 2000s. © By permission of the Trustees of the British Museum

2 Causation

R. BIN WONG

Causation of one form or another is present in most narratives. Few historical studies are without any narrative. History tells stories, whether large or small. Thus, historical studies have embedded within them assumptions about, if not evaluation of, causation. People act. Events take place. Nothing in the social or natural worlds occurs without some cause or more typically set of causes. Yet, historians today less frequently consider how causal assertions figure within their analyses and interpretations of specific topics or more general subjects than they did a generation ago. There are notable exceptions to be sure—debates over the causal importance of changes in consumption for subsequent changes in economic production, the causes of eighteenth-century witchcraft persecution, and studies of the Holocaust—but the field's broad orientations and sensibilities have been refashioned over time in ways that make attention to causality less generally salient than they once were.

Until the 1960s, historians often summarized scholarship on major historical events into presentations of the reasons for their occurrence. Political historians produced books on the causes of the American and French revolutions, while historians of religion pondered the causes of the Reformation. Economic historians reflected repeatedly on the causes of the industrial revolution. In general, the historical studies produced through the mid-1960s left out much in the way of accounts of the lives of common people, a vacuum filled by the social history new to the 1960s and 1970s. This history included causal accounts of social change for topics such as how city neighborhoods were settled, how laboring people sought to better their lives, and how families responded to daily challenges and opportunities. The subsequent turn toward cultural history in the 1980s as historical research became less closely tied to economics and political science, turning for inspiration and dialog more frequently to anthropology and literary studies, meant that causation was no longer as central a concern of historians as it once was. Consequently, causation became less relevant to the everyday practice of historians, as a younger historian captured pithily after learning that I was writing this chapter: 'Causation, isn't that something historians worried about in the 1970s?'

As the spatial sites of historical research in the late twentieth century came to include many locations outside Europe and North America, historians first found growing bodies of scholarship that could extend, qualify, and even undermine some of the themes in their work and then came to find it increasingly difficult to locate their own research without reference to a larger world, reaching in some cases a global context with influences near and far discovered to be relevant to their particular topics. Spatial grandeur of history as 'global' in the new millennium came to replace earlier temporal ambitions to chart historical changes over long periods of time. But a global framing for local subjects didn't in fact give much more guidance to locating specific cases in more general patterns than the repudiated teleologies of unilinear and developmental historical change did. How do we navigate between individual stories and larger accounts of history that avoid the pitfalls of grand narratives with teleological assumptions? Formulating coherent and persuasive responses to this question can help us consider more generally what kinds of scholarship historians can do in the twenty-first century, how they can speak to each other, and why other scholars as well as people beyond academia may want to continue to read historical studies. This chapter suggests ways in which renewed consideration of how and why causation matters to historical research can help us create more understanding of how individual and local stories connect with larger narratives of historical change.

Causal questions historians used to ask and the varied answers they proffered

In the 1960s and 1970s, historians studied significant historical events and sought to explain how and why they happened. Their research results were distilled into a rich blend of causes presented to students as a way to understand history's importance. In American schools, children learned about the causes of the American Revolution; in universities in both Europe and North America, students studied the causes of the French Revolution. This approach to history spread beyond American and European subjects. In these decades, much of twentieth-century Chinese history was oriented toward identifying the causes of the Chinese Revolution. In general, events with great consequences were deemed worthy objects of historical analysis and interpretation. Significant results meant that the reasons for their occurrence should be equally weighty.

For both the French and Chinese revolutions, scholars debated the factors they deemed most important to explaining how and why these tumultuous transformations took place. Some historians leaned heavily on economic relationships and material conditions to support their explanations of violent and dramatic political change. Others sought to avoid simple and direct connections between economic suffering and political action, arguing variously that ideas and institutions mattered crucially to enabling revolutionaries to craft strategies of political struggle and success. Precisely because revolutions were composed of complex sequences of events set in varied contexts they contained within them all manner of social, political, and economic features, the causal significance of each being difficult to disentangle.

For the Chinese Revolution a second kind of intellectual move was at least as important. As historians, among others, became more familiar with conditions in China after 1949, the revolution no longer seemed as triumphant and successful as it once had appeared to many. Growing dissatisfaction with the revolution's social, economic and political results made a search for the causes of what had previously been viewed as successful far less attractive a subject of enquiry. An increased recognition of historical continuities across the 1789 and 1949 divides further discounted the value of explaining the causes of either revolution. Finally, historians found an alternative way to honor the significance of these revolutions by considering their role in the imaginations of people in later historical eras. How the French and Chinese revolutions were remembered became important to understanding the cultural sensibilities of people living in more recent times.

Historians also used to ask about the causes of the industrial revolution. Less clearly defined in narrative terms than political revolutions, an 'industrial revolution' was nevertheless acknowledged by historians to have been a cluster of changes taking place in England after the mid-eighteenth century that culminated in a new world of economic possibilities by the early nineteenth century. Influenced by the methodology of economics, some economic historians aspired to identify the relative importance of different factors leading to the formation of cotton textile factories and the subsequent use of coal to make iron and steel that went into the building of railroads. Yet, they ultimately came up against the same sort of analytical and interpretive difficulties encountered in locating the origins and causes of political revolutions. The industrial revolution was a large and long sequence of events for which historians have stressed different factors as most crucial. Some have followed Max Weber in stressing the importance of cultural and religious beliefs; others have taken the cultural and social sensibilities encouraging science and technological change to be key. Still others have noted the crucial advantages that came from exploiting lands and resources in the New World, especially as a source of cheap cotton for England's textile mills. Yet others have focused on England's high wages which increased the relative attractiveness of investing in capital rather than labor.[1] Since the causal links among the different factors stressed by different scholars are not typically clear, they appear as separate factors, the relative importance of which is hard to assess. In fact, which are in fact necessary for the economic changes making up the industrial revolution and which simply promoted changes that were going to occur in their absence but at slower rates becomes a complex subject itself. There are even 'causes' stressed by some scholars that may well be non-causes for the industrial revolution, such as the so-called 'proto-industrialization' narratives claimed by its advocates as a stage preceding the industrial revolution. We subsequently have discovered cases within Europe as well as many more beyond Europe, including very widespread rural industry in China, that make the case for proto-industrialization as a necessary precursor to industrialization implausible.[2]

Scholars were unable to give any parsimonious account of how and why the industrial revolution occurred when and where it did, despite the dramatically visible differences in the world of material possibilities in the few decades before and after the turn from the eighteenth to the nineteenth centuries. The significance of the industrial revolution was diminished by economic historians by the 1980s. Quantitative changes were in fact quite modest in the period considered previously as crucially significant. The industrial revolution came to be seen as part of a longer-run story of economic change in Europe which first prepared for the late eighteenth-century English changes and then took full advantage of the new economic possibilities throughout the nineteenth century. In tailoring the English industrial revolution to fit a larger Western European story of economic development, economic historians highlighted what they thought made Europe special or particular in contrast to other parts of the world which did not experience the industrial revolution and by implicit extension the larger and longer context within which this revolution had been placed. Such an explicit move was less prominent for political revolutions. But both the American and French revolutions were understood to be turning points in longer-running stories of political development, the transition from kingdoms to republics. These understandings of both economic and political development framed the big picture filled in by the then 'new' social history of the 1960s and 1970s.

Causation in large-scale historical narratives and the 'new' social history of the 1960s and 1970s

For more than a century, many observers of modern life across the world have understood political and economic development to be based on some combination of the experiences of Europe and its white settler societies and relations between these Euro-American states and their economic and social elites with other populations. The basic propositions go back to Karl Marx and Max Weber. Marx stressed the negative but in his opinion necessary transformative impact of European expansion on the economies and societies of the rest of the world. Weber followed with more systematic comparative work that aimed to identify what was most crucially different about Europe that distinguished Protestant culture from other religious cultures in terms of their influence on economic behavior.

Thinking of political development as a process has meant an identification of a particular set of ideas and institutions as the ideal basis for organizing a state and its relations with its subjects who became in the nineteenth and twentieth centuries conceived to be 'citizens' who enjoyed bundles of rights and responsibilities or some shared sets of traits that distinguished them from those ruled by some other state. The historical significance of moments of crisis and change, or political processes unfolding over longer periods of time, was often determined according to their resemblances to Euro-American political developments. The English had their Glorious Revolution of 1688 with its constitutional monarchy, the Americans their independence in 1776, and the French their end to monarchy in 1789. Other parts of the world were brought into a European-defined system of states. Africa and the Americas largely entered as colonies, while Asia included European empires with formal colonies (e.g. India, Vietnam), an indigenous empire (China), states that never became colonies (Japan and Thailand), as well as areas that become colonized by an Asian power (Japan's colonies of Korea and Taiwan). The colonized world was succeeded by an era of decolonization in which political relations have been defined by a combination of international and regional organizations and networks.

Similarly, the causes for economic development looked for in Asia, Africa, and Latin America have been ones first identified in histories of the North American and West European economies. The adoption of a legal infrastructure for written contracts and Western-style firms, the formation of banking institutions, and the encouragement of entrepreneurial risk and innovation exemplify the kinds of topics chosen. Often these changes take place when economies previously unaffected by the industrial and commercial growth of developed countries become increasingly connected to an international economy. The subsequent changes are variously viewed positively (late nineteenth-century Japanese industrialization) and negatively (late nineteenth-century extraction of raw materials from parts of Africa and Asia). Paralleling political histories, stories of economic change are told as some combination of developmental narratives and stories lodged within a system of economic relations spanning much of the globe.

The formation of national states and industrial economies as two large-scale processes of historical change have provided the dynamic backdrop for looking at social change over the past several centuries. Societies shift from being rural to becoming urban as people move from largely agricultural work to industrial labor. Individuals emerge from their webs of kin and community relations to become autonomous actors defined by their relationships to the economy and the government. States create relationships of citizenship and promote national cultures which crystallize political and social identities that form modern states and societies.

Much of the social history written in the 1960s and 1970s considered what Charles Tilly once called how common people 'lived the big changes'. The social history written in the 1960s and 1970s had two salient features. First, statistical analysis of quantitative data identified the relationships that analysts chose to evaluate, including voting behavior of different kinds of people, the living conditions of slaves compared to wage workers, and social mobility among different people in American cities. Second, ordinary people, whose lives rarely enjoyed more than minor roles in historical narratives, became a major focus. Since such people had little power of their own, it was easy to see how their life possibilities were formed by forces far larger than themselves. But explaining what determined their life chances and how they navigated the possibilities presented to them hardly exhausted what scholars wished to understand about past lives. Some chose to recreate the life experiences of common people, an activity that can be very distinct from finding the causes for their life conditions.

When the actors themselves are unlikely to have had that much influence over these conditions and we are seeking to understand how they lived and what they thought and felt, then looking at the causes of their conditions becomes quite irrelevant. American slaves, European serfs, South Asian untouchables, and prisoners everywhere are among the kinds of people with very limited choices for action and equally limited opportunities for public expression, yet, as historically minded social scientist James Scott has shown in *Domination and the Arts of Resistance: Hidden Transcripts*, people have been able in their humor, folk tales, music, and theater to express their own understandings of their lives and societies at odds with those expressed by the politically powerful. When people's explanations of their conditions accommodate the political constraints imposed on them and even affirm the political logic of their leaders, encouraging them to inform on their family and friends, phenomena found in Stalinist Russia and Maoist China, rather than encourage additional resistance, their understandings can themselves contribute to the ongoing social anxiety and political insecurity that characterized those societies.

Studies of causes for a set of conditions can complement but cannot contradict the experiences of people who lived under those conditions. Among studies that speak to the causes of slavery, there can be all manner of debate over evidence and theory; witness the years of controversy that Robert Fogel and Stanley Engerman's *Time on the Cross* generated after its publication in 1974. But it makes little sense to criticize this work for arguing an economic rationality to American slavery on moral grounds or in terms of the suffering undergone by slaves, since the economic basis of slavery doesn't tell us whether we should consider the practices moral or not, nor does it say that slaves didn't suffer.

Two more features of the focus on lives of common people and the subject of historical causation are worth raising, one of which will be considered presently. Recreating the sensibilities of people can mean they have any number of preferences, desires, hopes, and fears that affect what they choose or try to do. Many of their actions will have consequences, and in a very simple and direct sense be caused by their efforts, including those outcomes they did not intend but they nevertheless helped cause to happen, such as when people rush to sell their homes before prices fall further and through their actions lower prices even further. How people feel about 'prices' may well vary across culture. But these different ideas about what 'price' means do not themselves cause different effects on supply and demand and hence on prices themselves. Instead, culturally specific ideas about 'price' act by affecting how much people are willing to spend, in other words when ideas about 'price' affect preferences which in turn affect demand for a good, the culturally specific ideas about 'prices' can affect prices. The mechanisms by which they do so, supply and demand, remain analytically the same across cases. Culturally particular ideas about price do not therefore conflict with elementary economics because price theory doesn't pretend to explain what sets people's preferences. The causes for particular preferences can well vary culturally, but their effects on prices and markets are similar—either they raise or reduce willingness to spend money on some particular good. These distinctions notwithstanding, some historians have been skeptical that neoclassical market principles apply beyond the contexts where the ideas first emerged or at least suspect that there are any number of situations in which they do not apply. We don't hold the same skepticism about theoretical propositions in physics or chemistry or biology because we assume that the relevant objects of study in the natural sciences are not affected by their spatial locations. Insofar as price theory in economics can predict certain outcomes independently of knowing why people hold particular cultural beliefs that shape their preferences, it succeeds at certain kinds of causal explanation. It does not however claim to give an account of causes for why people hold those specific beliefs. Nor does it claim to recreate the broader sensibilities of the people expressing preferences on markets. Historians concerned with interpreting cultural beliefs about prices do so without diminishing the logic of supply and demand determining prices. They can even make causal arguments about the significance of such beliefs, as Max Weber famously did when he argued that Protestant beliefs influenced attitudes toward savings and investment. Causation is present at the micro level of the individual or small group as well as at the macro levels of social, political, or economic processes writ large. Historians' efforts to recreate sensibilities can either be separate from causal explanations or they can offer causes for the sensibilities they study, thus adding to the kinds of causation historians consider, as this example of market prices suggests. What reconstructions of sensibilities cannot do, however, is claim to substitute for what causal accounts offer.

The possibilities of causal explanations complementing reconstructions of historical sensibilities have been less frequently seen as useful since historical studies typically choose one or the other, especially since the new millennium. The movement away from conscious consideration of causation to a focus on cultural topics pursued at the individual or local level simply turned away from earlier interests of the late 1960s and 1970s that continued into the 1980s and 1990s with works like David Sabean's on German villages which reconstructed the local changes in kinship relations amidst economic change to argue that kinship became more important rather than less important as new economic opportunities became available. These findings were part of a larger effort to trace the gender roles and generational conflicts that defined the life experiences of common German villagers who lived the 'big changes' commented upon by Charles Tilly for scholarship of the preceding two decades.[3]

During these same decades, the study of large-scale processes of historical change became less popular for two seemingly contradictory reasons. On the one hand, many scholars stopped believing that a unilinear model of development was able to explain historical change around the world. On the other hand, scholars, including some of those who rejected unilinear models, nevertheless subscribed to a belief that the spread and growth of capitalism caused the basic changes in people's material existences. The former view led to a rejection of a single historical path of change, whatever its causes. The latter view held that common systemic forces were remaking the conditions for people across the globe; historians accepted these changes and looked for themes and subjects that could be pursued given these basic material facts.

Acceptance did not necessarily mean approval. Criticisms of the political and economic transformations of societies are hardly new but they offer a different focus for the search for causal links and promote a rejection of the causal concerns historians previously considered. In the late twentieth-century propositions made prominent by Michel Foucault regarding the modern definitions of madness, punishment, and sexuality powered a growing skepticism regarding the enshrinement of Enlightenment reason as the positive force it was once thought to be. Historians increasingly turned to identifying features of modern society they deemed negative and for which a causal linkage between power and knowledge was posited. The interests of the powerful were affirmed by particular forms of knowledge production. It became implausible for historians influenced by Foucault to consider the kinds of causality used to account for economic and political changes since these could be explained away as the self-serving accounts of those with power and wealth.

Unable to adjudicate according to available evidence the relative importance of various factors that plausibly contributed to large-scale social changes, historians began to turn away from offering causal explanations for their occurrence. The intrinsic complexity of phenomena historians sought to explain led some to seek other kinds of subjects. A second source of skepticism about causality came from the recognition that explanations given for a particular set of events could be offered to serve the beliefs of specific actors. Historians began worrying more about the epistemology of knowledge and subsequently came to doubt how much existed independently of the subjective perspectives of individuals located in different social and political situations that encouraged them to have distinct views. People's apprehension of the world around them may well have causal elements but if people see the world differently, the causal chains they observe can also vary. Unless historians grant the existence of a world out there in which things happen that can be explained without reference to the observer's position, epistemological variety undermines belief in causal explanations. Even if a scholar doesn't give equal credence to diverse views of the same phenomenon, granting for instance the same status to arguments denying the Holocaust as to those that affirm the phenomenon, the socially constructed nature of theories, arguments, and interpretations makes them appear more fragile to scholars. Yet, theories about the natural world are also constructed. What distinguishes much of the natural sciences from the social sciences and humanities is not the socially constructed nature of their theories but the degrees to which a set of related propositions gains basic and general acceptance as the framing principles for enquiry. Because social phenomena are far more complex to explain and humanists in particular are uneasy about the kinds of conceptual simplification that scientific theories all demand to gain causal traction over their subjects, historians lack agreed upon causal explanations for many of the subjects they consider. Unlike scientists who use their theories to simplify some phenomena into more manageable sets of features, historians, like humanists more generally, often seek to celebrate the complexity and uncertainty of their topics, as well as the creativity and uniqueness of the actors they present. A devotion to recreating and affirming the multiple causes responsible for events that could well have turned out differently due to one or more contingent conditions makes the goal of identifying a few causes for big events and processes like political and economic revolutions unattractive.

This very brief sketch of some basic movements in historical studies in the past half-century, largely in English-speaking locales, suggests some important reasons for the eclipse of causation as a conscious component of historical research. Grand narratives have lost their appeal. The limitations of materialism as an approach to historical studies have diminished the faith and interest of historians in causation more generally. The complexity of historical change further renders difficult efforts at locating causes; the more we learn about the past the more complex and varied our histories become. And finally, historians have in the past quarter-century reaffirmed their engagement with topics not formulated in ways to consider causation.

Historians' practice reoriented historical scholarship away from accounts for large-scale historical change in the same period as Francis Fukuyama confidently announced the 'end of history' with the collapse of the Soviet Union and the embrace of market development and industrialization in China. Economic and political convergence based upon the practices pioneered by the West defined the only possible positive future. Those that understood this would become successful and those who did not would continue to fail. Such thinking has led to a radical simplification of ideas about the world that have been challenged most successfully by the tragic conflicts that Samuel Huntington famously labeled as a 'clash of civilizations'. The 'end of history' could not account for major conflicts promoted by Islamic radicals and their Islamic and Western foes. The collective conceptual poverty of the 'end of history' and 'clash of civilizations' theses affords historians an opportunity to contribute the riches of their research to develop more persuasive understandings of the global conditions. This will be more likely if future historians build upon the perspectives enabled by linguistic and cultural turns in historical studies and seek to replace the simple-minded 'end of history' and 'clash of civilizations' with accounts of historical change that once again consider causality consciously.

Recovering causation after the linguistic and cultural turns in historical studies

The rejection of big historical processes as a subject for historical study has been accompanied by a suspicion of European history's developmental narrative as the context for understanding others. For some this has meant redefining relations between the colonizer and the colonized. For others it has meant seeking to identify and discuss some space to be considered relatively autonomous and separate from European world views or actions. Within such spaces, historians seek to understand the experiences of people who create through their own agency meaning in their lives. Dipesh Chakrabarty's *Provincializing Europe* is an influential example of this shift in concerns. Primarily interested empirically in exploring the world of discourse for Bengali intellectuals in the 1920s and 1930s in order to give us access to their sentiments and sensibilities, he suggests how their intellectual activities create their own subjective universe quite separate from the world of power and wealth dominated by Westerners. Similar efforts can of course be made for most any group of people whose life experiences occur outside Europe or the West more generally. It helps the historian when the people being studied are literate and have a diverse set of writings for the historian to analyze. Agency matters since it is Bengali intellectuals who create their own life world but issues of causation are not a central concern. A separation between a world of discourse and the larger material world that forms the backdrop for the placement of Bengal and India more generally allows the author to concentrate on a particular scene set on a stage created by causes well beyond the actors of concern to him.

Chakrabarty, like some other historians and many scholars of literature and culture, accepts the global development of capitalism as the process defining much of the economic, political, and social system within which his subjects fashion their lives. While Marxists and others offer materialist explanations for this state of affairs, the presence of such a material world is a given. There is no point in denying these material realities and yet there is equally little need to examine them either. Issues of causation are not important because Bengali intellectuals cannot influence one way or another how the larger forces shaping their material conditions unfold. Despite an implicit critique of the global capitalist economy, the sense of inevitability that accompanies its arrival and spread is not so very different from the scenario sketched far more positively by Francis Fukuyama in his 'end of history'. These authors share with many others an assumption about the world in the recent past becoming subject to a common set of possibilities and constraints. Where Chakrabarty sees the Marxist world system as an inevitable structure within which people seek to create meaning, Fukuyama sees the triumph of capitalism over socialism to herald a common agreement on how to create human progress. The main difference lies in the decision historians make to seek out what happens beneath the relentless narrative of global capitalism's spread, be it seen as triumphal or tragic.

At its extremes, the shift from the social history of the 1960s and 1970s to the cultural history of the 1980s and 1990s meant rejecting research in which causal explanations were tied to grand narratives of historical change in order to pursue studies without causal claims and without assigned positions in a longer arc of historical time. A world made by materialist processes still existed, to be sure, but it no longer mattered directly to what historians preferred for their subjects of enquiry. Historians no longer participated frequently in the study of large-scale patterns of historical change. It is thus not surprising that historians have tended to move away from themes that link their subjects to large-scale processes of historical change that they find too complex and move toward those that place their subjects within far more limited temporal contexts. Where previous scholarship often tried to put a specific subject into a larger narrative of historical change, be it about urbanization, capitalist development, or state formation, historians began to place their subjects in larger spatial frames, rejecting national states as inappropriate spatial containers for many topics. The shift from locating historical research within the grand narratives of state formation and economic development to a focus on local sites subsequently put into a global context has taken more than two decades to complete. In the process historians have embraced many new subject areas including perhaps most importantly gender studies and evaluations of history and memory. There has been an expansion of the kinds of topics studied, new perspectives brought to older questions, and an affirmation of the historian's long-standing commitment to recovering the lived experiences of people.

At the same time, historians have rejected the old grand narratives without investing much effort in creating replacements. The older narratives move from being directly challenged to simply becoming ignored. If, however, the discourses within which people understand the world affect the ways they choose to act and these actions in turn affect what happens in the economy and polity, then it may be possible and worthwhile to seek causal connections responsible for different patterns of historical change both at the level of individual agents and in the larger structures of relations and institutions composing social life broadly. If, in other words, we don't take the relentless march of global capitalism as a master narrative of the past several centuries we could be encouraged to consider what choices people have made economically and politically and to what effect. Such efforts can build on the cultural and linguistic turn in historical studies to renew and reframe efforts to address the changing patterns of political, economic, and social experiences in different places and periods of history.

If matters of causation are to figure in these new historical studies, some attention to the difficulties presented earlier in this chapter could prove very useful. We need to move beyond the binary choice of totally rejecting or wholeheartedly accepting grand process-driven narratives. The long-standing challenge of combining ideas and material interests in explanations of causation deserves to be considered afresh. Finally, there need to be strategies developed for acknowledging the complexities of historical change and affirming the goal of constructing manageable topics for which causation can matter amidst changing tastes among historians for the types of research they wish to pursue.

Recovering causation in history after the cultural turn

The state transformations and economic growth of Europe previously taken as the basic framing for studies of social history were themselves produced by individuals great and small whose actions made these political and economic systems. Historians haven't accorded the same significance to individuals elsewhere whose actions were responsible for causal sequences that created political and economic systems different from those in Europe. But it seems highly unlikely that people's intentions could matter to explaining changes of certain polities and economies and yet not others, even if this is the implicit logic invoked for considering some sort of Western practices as the models from which political and economic changes take place in other parts of the world. More plausible is the general notion that people's ideas about their states and economies influence their beliefs and their institutions which in turn enable and constrain certain kinds of political and economic activities, except in those relatively rare situations where a very small number of individuals are able to control people in positions of extreme subordination such as prisoners, slaves, and serfs. Most other people have beliefs that influence their actions.

Consider a Chinese example about economic change. Chinese industrialization has followed a distinctive path influenced both by major policy decisions and the choices of thousands of individuals over several hundred years. For instance, the rural location of the small-scale labor-intensive industries that proved crucial to the transformation of the countryside in the 1980s and 1990s also represents a pattern of economic change different in important ways from urban-based manufacturing considered to be basic to the industrialization experiences of Western Europe and North America. The People's Republic chose in the 1950s to make a planned economy that separated industry and agriculture in a fundamental manner—urban became the virtually exclusive site for industrial, and rural which had previously included craft production became almost completely agricultural. This change represented a striking rupture with past practices and created the vacuum that the subsequent growth of township and village enterprises filled in. While the technologies and organizational formats of these township and village enterprises are certainly new, their reliance on rural laborers, many of whom stayed in their villages or moved from one rural area to another, suggests a strong link to the countryside. The strategy of bringing capital and technologies to villages and small towns in order to take advantage of the large amounts of underemployed rural labor makes economic sense, but if economic logic were the only factor that mattered we would expect other poor countries with densely settled rural areas, such as India for example, to be following the same spatial pattern of economic change. To explain the particularities of the Chinese pattern of rural development it seems reasonable to put recent practices in historical perspective and remember that many craft industries remained based in the countryside well into the twentieth century. The subsequent reform-era viability of township and rural enterprises, therefore, comes not just from the reservoir of surplus agricultural labor or the enabling policies of the government, but also from the experience of market networks, exchange, and production that people in many parts of the country knew as part of the local experiences of earlier generations. The differences from earlier practices can be explained by previously unavailable technologies, new sources of capital, and new ways of organizing a firm compared to what was possible a century or two earlier. Without these earlier practices, however, it is less clear how people would have gone about translating abstract opportunities into concrete results.

Culturally specific ideas and institutions can also help explain how particular activities based on interests that are found in widely separate settings do not themselves indicate some larger shared set of common historical changes. Again, consider a Chinese example, but this time in tandem with a European counterpart. Conflicts over food supplies in eighteenth-century China and Europe share a number of similar features—high prices, supplies threatened by exports from a locale, and hoarding or anticipated hoarding of food by the rich figure as components of the situations in which conflicts took place. People protesting high prices and supplies threatened by hoarders or export-ers, whether in China or Europe, all shared a common set of interests, namely to defend and maintain their access to food in times of scarcity. They took actions to block exports and demand lower prices because they believed they could make claims to these supplies. Similarly in both eighteenth-century China and Europe people protested taxes they felt were unfair. Protesters over food supplies and taxes in China and Europe shared common interests and professed broadly similar beliefs about government intervention to assure local food supplies and about unfair and unacceptable tax levies. The causal sequences leading to protest were alike in both China and Europe and depended on both the interests and beliefs of participants. Yet, when we step back from the events themselves and consider the larger political, social and economic contexts in which they took place, we discover that there were significant differences.[4]

An earlier generation of social historians anticipated that certain kinds of collective action were indicative of moments in large-scale sequences of historical change. Protests over food were rearguard actions against market integration and feeding growing cities. Tax resistance was also a rearguard action against centralizing states. Yet while this may have been true for European examples, it turns out that such expectations do not apply comfortably to China in the same cen-tury. Eighteenth-century popular protests in China and Europe were embedded in distinct political ideologies and institutions that defined the larger meanings of protest to participants and the impact of their actions. Where Europeans (and Americans) could link taxation with political representation (enshrined in the American revolutionary claim of 'no taxation without representation'), Chinese expectations of what was fair and equitable depended on beliefs shared with their officials that were not translated into formal institutional mechanisms for political voice.

At the same time, eighteenth-century Chinese authorities took issues of food supply management far more seriously than their Euro-pean counterparts, storing tons of grain to release onto the market or through loans in the spring when supplies from the previous year's harvests were lowest and to restock after the fall harvests came in. The French *soudure* was little different from the Chinese *qinghuang bujie* (青黄不接), but the manner in which the governments in these places responded to these conditions differed dramatically. We can think of the Chinese state's efforts to build and maintain large grain reserves for its subject population to be the product of a particular ideology, the Confucian paternalism with a long and distinguished pedigree, and thus contrast the Chinese and European efforts at food supply management in terms of the Chinese having a greater belief in paternalism. But this then poses a question about what we make of European political expressions of paternalistic concerns. Is it simply a matter of them believing less in what they say?

Perhaps the reason for the differences also involves the immediate interests of the respective states—in Europe the chronically pressing expenditure demands came more often from war making than any civilian projects, while the Chinese Empire did not face the equivalent problem as the spatial scale within which Europeans fought was all domestic territory for the Chinese—it thus makes sense that Chinese officials would be more likely to spend on domestic civilian purposes and Europeans on international military ones. If this line of reasoning is sensible, the persuasiveness of beliefs may often depend on their accord with interests; at the same time interests that lack a rhetorically compelling expression as beliefs are probably weaker than they could be.

On causation more specifically, this example suggests that the causal mechanisms producing European territorial states through competition and war making need not be a more general historical process. Chinese state efforts suggest the possibilities of alternative paths of transformation. By addressing such contrasts explicitly we can see different patterns of causation at work. Stepping back from these episodes to the larger and longer patterns of political change of which these episodes are parts, we can see that the developmental path taken by European states is hardly the only model for state transformations. By looking closely at the culturally specific political practices that emerge in late imperial China and early modern Europe we can revise earlier arguments about state transformation based on generalizations from European state formation, just as looking at the particular features of

Chinese industrialization qualifies assumptions about general patterns of economic development.

The existence of comparable episodes in different paths of change means that similar causal chains or mechanisms can be embedded in larger patterns of difference, as the food riots and tax resistance examples demonstrate. Food riots and tax resistance show how interests of people in widely separated parts of the world who have no knowledge of each other's situations can motivate similar actions and yet the consequences of their efforts can be very different, because the ideological and institutional frameworks within which they can express interests shapes the resolutions of the disputes and the linkages between these episodes and other political actions. Alternatively, different sets of causal mechanisms can produce similar outcomes, as the rural-based Chinese and urban-based European industrialization patterns suggest. Economic change need not follow a single path of development. The Chinese pattern of rural industrialization did not rely on the formal institutions of legal contract and courts made famous as key to European economic development by Nobel laureate Douglass C. North; the Chinese relied on more informal mechanisms to increase production and marketing in the 1980s that resembled their own earlier practices before 1949 more than they did Western norms for economic development.[5] More explicit attention to the limits of some causal similarities, like those of food riots or tax resistance, and to the possibilities of different kinds of causal chains producing similar results, like urban- versus rural-centered patterns of industrialization, can help us achieve a more sophisticated understanding of how longer patterns of historical change can be constructed out of shorter sequences that exhibit particular clusters of similarities and differences. We can affirm the rejection of any unilinear and teleological path of historical development without forsaking efforts to explain the causal connections within the multiple paths of historical change that have shaped the world historians study.

For earlier periods, such attention to causation alerts us against the dangers of assuming the causes of what had previously been taken to be particularly European to be so narrow when examples can be found more generally, be these long-distance trade networks, acts of religious syncretism or reform, the growth of large cities, or strong central governments. For later periods, these examples should hopefully encourage scholars, including historians, who believe in one way or another that we are at the end of history that the distinctive trajectories of political and economic change distinguishing European and Chinese history from each other may in fact help us understand some elements of variation in the contemporary world. These brief sketches of causation in the political and economic histories of China and Europe qualify the assumptions, alternatively optimistic and pessimistic, that societies more generally today are defined largely by their positions in a global system of politics and economics. To be sure, relations between domestic and foreign individual and institutional actors can be important to both politics and economics, especially in recent times and where there are great disparities of power and wealth between them. But the differences in local economic and political situations across the globe cannot be reduced to the varied roles of international actors in different places. Relations among local, regional, and global actors can all matter; the relative importance of each to a particular problem or possibility is influenced by previous practices and the ways that contexts for older issues become changed by new relations with additional actors. We can identify and evaluate these variable situations more effectively when we are better able to recognize both similar and different causal chains operating in distinct contexts.

Bringing causation back into cultural and social history

If the way we look at political and economic changes has been usefully influenced by the linguistic and cultural turns in historical studies to help refine the patterns of causation, can a symmetrical move be made? Can the approaches to political and economic change just sketched in the preceding section of this chapter suggest how more explicit attention to causation might enrich studies of cultural practice and change? Many studies of both present and past cultural social activities highlight the combination of local and global elements that create some particular phenomenon. The 'local' situates a topic in a concrete context while the 'global' alerts us to connections between people, products, and practices in one place to those elsewhere.

Going beneath and beyond the national level disrupts the spatial containers of nation within which much earlier historical research has been done. But it doesn't suggest much about the construction of social spaces between a local site and the world at large. Nor are such studies always attentive to the historical contexts in which they emerge. As a result, the causal mechanisms responsible for cultural production are rarely an explicit topic of study.

Political and economic histories of the nineteenth century forward often take the national space as a focus because there have been formal institutional practices that make national units frequently appropriate for understanding policies and practices spanning politics and economics. Cultural and social practices are more often informal, influenced as much by beliefs and passions that have little to do directly with economic motivations or political preferences. Yet clearly some of these practices do have spatial dimensions larger than the particular case examined and yet far less than the entire globe. Being mindful of what lies between the local and global may well help us explain what happens in some places rather than others. We can better offer accounts of causation behind the emergence and transformation of cultural and social practices historically.

Consider examples from the subjects of music and cuisine. For topic areas like food and music, historical studies have many purposes of enquiry other than explaining any particular musical form or kind of food. Food evokes a past remembered, while music allows people to express and even perform social and cultural identities. Forms of music and types of food as well as many other kinds of cultural production and consumption are seen at the intersection of the local and global. Such formulations allow people to look at very particular places and identify an importance to them that is general in significance. For periods within the past two centuries, scholars typically locate a local study in a national or sub-national context. For history of yet earlier periods, local studies more often exist within more flexibly defined regions since national states were not typically a meaningful spatial frame. Beyond lived experience linking people's presents and their pasts or setting human activities in a particular space located in some larger spatial frame, subjects like food and music themselves also change or are reproduced in ways that can be explained in causal terms. We can view music or food for example as lived experiences, but as I will suggest below the variable possibilities for how food and music change over time and in different locations are themselves the products of causal processes.

Music has long avoided national categories as key spatial locators. Classical music without a geographical adjective preceding it means European classical music developed before national states were a strong historical presence. Composers worked in different linguistic environments that were within a shared cultural environment. Innovation took place over time in the technical components of classical music; some compositional changes were tied to technological changes, like those from the harpsichord to the piano forte. Others were made through the creative recombination and extension of musical ideas. Influences from outside the networks of classical composers also shaped changes, such as Bartók's use of Hungarian folk themes or Dvořák's trip to the United States. We can portray the development of European classical music in the familiar terms used in history more generally to discuss developments in changing contexts that admit of new elements causing change and innovation. The primacy of the European case in music as in history more generally is suggested by the use of the geographically unmarked 'classical' from other 'classicals', such as the Japanese 'classical' or Chinese 'classical'. European classical music can be viewed as a form of cultural production that develops according to internal logics of expressive possibility at the same time as it has expanded geographically so that today it has lost much of its original tie to a European space. Both performers and consumers of European classical music are found across the globe.

Other genres of music have distinct patterns of change and different spatial locations. Some emerge out of the intersection of previously distinct musical forms and traditions to form something new. In the post-Second World War world, one of the most visible examples of this is American rock and roll, which has elements of African American blues and white hillbilly music, each of which has its own antecedents. Rock and roll became its own genre and expanded and transformed over the decades. We can also follow the emergence of American pop music more broadly and trace its transformation in other cultural settings—in East Asia there are lively and linked Chinese pop scenes spanning the Taiwan straits with Cantonese pop both distinct and connected by artists who perform in both Mandarin and Cantonese. English lyrics make their way into Japanese popular music as both individual words and phrases, while in France, English, to the dismay of many, is considered by some to be a language of French pop. If we follow heavy metal into the Middle East and Islamic areas beyond there is a surprising ability of young people to find a social space for music that speaks to them despite political and cultural opposition by government and religious leaders. Beginning in the second half of the twentieth century the migration of musical forms and increase of musical communication across previously less connected or even unconnected musical worlds makes for the juxtaposition of local and global. Yet such phenomena are not new, even if they are more common today. The American heavy metal that makes its way to areas with Muslim populations carries the musical DNA of African slaves whose Islamic prayer chants made their way into the New World to inform plantation singing which subsequently fed the blues in part informing rock and roll.

For all the complex transformations and connections among kinds of music and formation of new genres, there are evolving taxonomies of music that we can observe on the distribution or marketing side of musical production. Go into any US city with a store housing a large selection of CDs and you will find a diverse taxonomy of music selections. There will be classical music as well as jazz, and usually a section of Broadway musicals as well as Christian gospel music. By far the largest selections will be in some combination of pop and rock. Go into a store with a large collection of CDs in Paris and classical music along with jazz will take up proportionately much more floor space than they do in the USA. Pop and rock will include both anglophone and French music in separate sections. Make a similar trip into a large CD store in Taipei and the taxonomy and frequency of CDs will reflect local tastes—in addition to American pop and rock and sections for classical and jazz there will be Chinese-language CDs divided by origin as well as sections of Japanese and Korean music. Move to Hong Kong and more resemblance to Taipei than to Paris or LA will occur but there will still be differences, most dependably the scale and visibility of Canton pop, which always gets its own classification in Hong Kong. Go to Tokyo and a related but distinct taxonomy of CDs can be found with relative frequencies also different than those found in other places. Analyzing the similarities and differences in the taxonomies and frequencies and varieties of different kinds of music found in different global cities reveals varied dimensions of what is global and what is local. Those who stress global trends toward greater homogeneity and those who pinpoint the creation of new and different local practices are both correct. The challenge is to recognize both and create metrics for evaluating the significance of each.

An attention to taxonomies and frequencies of different kinds of music according to location can show what is 'global' and 'local' about particular cases. For example, the Japanese-Brazilian bossa nova singer Lisa Ono sings in Japanese, Portuguese, and occasionally English, records in Japan, but is represented by management in New York. Her CDs produced in Taiwan have lyrics in Portuguese with Japanese translations and an additional booklet of translations into Chinese. With just this description and without the context of CD consumption more generally in Taipei, it is difficult to assess the significance of this kind of music generally or her CD produced in Taiwan specifically. Unless we have some understanding of the CD market in each part of the world where her CDS are sold, it becomes difficult to put her in any context beyond the very concretely local and the abstractly global with little to connect the two.

The nature of CD consumption across the world is an example of a cultural practice that varies by location and changes over time in ways that reflect both connections among places and distinctive patterns of change. First, wherever one goes in the world there is a taxonomy of CDs that is at least partially comprehensible to anyone who buys CDs. The variety and number of CDs will vary in the categories found across multiple locations and the exact categories may not even be the same. Second, there will be categories particular to each location—Christian music, the French chanson, Japanese classical music, etc. Third, we can view the pattern of CD consumption in each location as simultaneously a product of what is of the moment more generally and what is preferred, reproduced, and transformed within specific places. The relative importance of the 'global' and the 'local' will vary regarding CD consumption. And of course CDs as a genre are themselves being subject to uneven evolutionary decline as music downloads become ever more important commercially in first the US market and increasingly other markets as well.

Related remarks can be made for cuisines. Cuisines evolve in related but separate ways. Some chefs deliberately seek to reproduce classics with as little deviation from what are deemed traditional recipes as possible, while others deliberately seek to be innovative. So important is this distinction in French cuisine that both high end cuisine and bistro food can each be classified according to whether the food is traditional or whether it is innovative. The former cleaves closely to the elements from a particular region while the latter more likely absorbs contemporary and locational influences from where it is produced, even if transplanted. Similar distinctions are also made for Chinese cuisines. For both French and Chinese cooking there is a continuum from traditional to innovative. Innovation reaches such a point that people disagree about where a kind of cooking fits within a taxonomy of cuisines, leading to the use of terms like 'fusion' to describe cooking that draws on multiple sources. But as renowned Japanese chef Nobu Matsuhisa has remarked, his food may be considered by some to be 'fusion', but he insists it is not 'confusion'. He claims his innovative cuisine to be Japanese because he has a firm foundation of training in Japanese cuisine; he has a tradition within which he is opening up new possibilities. The dynamics of change in cuisines thus include both evolution within distinct types of food and combinations among them that can either transform but keep recognizable an earlier cuisine or in fact create something deemed by many to be its own new kind of food.

The types of food produced in any particular place change over time. They evolve out of previous practices at the same time as they are subject to influences brought through connections forged by the migration of people, flows of goods, and spread of ideas. The scales of food production have also changed. Multinational restaurant chains have emerged, especially in fast-food markets, as one prominent example of multinational corporations. But unlike other product markets that become dominated by multinationals, restaurants are organized from single-unit firms to multinationals.

Even without the connections among food markets created by multinational restaurant chains, there have been increasing connections among the restaurant markets in major world cities. The emergence of some common cuisine categories means the global business traveler has a converging set of dining choices she enjoys on any given evening in many world cities. Each city will also be stronger in some cuisines than others. A city's taxonomy of choices will be finer or cruder depending on the location's relationship to the cuisine in question; even global cities have quite local cuisines as well. The production and consumption of cuisines, like those of music, are reproduced over time and space as they become more connected and change for local, regional, and global reasons.

This brief discussion of music and food as cultural phenomena that can be located in time and space in ways that show changes historically should suggest some analytical parallels to the presentations of political and economic change. Of course music and food can also be considered directly as economic and political phenomena. We can focus on their production and consumption or consider the influence of politics on cultural practices. As we discover and explore the diversity and complexities of music and cuisines in various places and many periods of history, we can also, should we wish, show the causal mechanisms responsible for the changes over time as well as the similarities and differences across space. In so doing our attention to causation for these cases turns out to be related to the ways causation for political and economic processes looks when we begin to pay attention to cultural and linguistic dimensions of historical change.

Constructing causal accounts in future historical writing

The move away from considering consciously how causation fits within historical writing is understandable given the ways in which we have come to think about history being seen from different vantage points and thus having different meanings, including meanings to people of the time and those living in subsequent times and other places. The ability to construct multiple interpretations and to recover the contingencies and non-necessity of events taking place in the ways they actually did have been constituent elements of a move away from acceptance of simple large narratives of historical change.

The shift from grand narratives to global framings of historical phenomena has allowed historians and other scholars to connect their local subjects to larger themes and thereby to suggest a broader significance to their work without making causal arguments. At the same time as we wish to avoid the kinds of large and simple teleological connections drawn between economic, political, and social changes, it would be helpful to know just how widespread some patterns are and how they are influenced by both their immediate conditions and their broader connections to other parts of the world. It could be that some patterns are found in multiple sites and represent either parallels or connected phenomena. Their subsequent differences could, like the cases of tax resistance or commercial expansion briefly suggested above, delimit similarities from differences in the contexts of the two cases.

Working within and across regions which are defined by some set of features that historians agree help organize important aspects of a situation need not be national or extremely local; such regions could easily cross political borders and yet not include all the spaces contained politically on either side of the border. Regions can be defined by connections of an economic or cultural nature that themselves can be distinguished from other links that either take place at more local levels or reach across greater stretches of space. We might better identify the causes for events, individual or group decisions, and even larger patterns of historical change through conscious attention to the spatial framing of the topics studied. If our geographical awareness remains fixed between the alternatives of national states and their rejection by moving to the polar extremes of very local or the global, we will lose important opportunities to recognize patterns of similarity and difference across our monographic studies.

The tension between the global and the local is related to the tension between wanting coherent narratives covering long periods and also searching for nuance and complexity if not indeed uncertainty and confusion in any particular historical moment. Studies that capture longer periods of time typically need to highlight selectively themes that simplify the subjects to be covered. Accounts of shorter moments or smaller groups of people frequently introduce many more elements of suspense and ambiguity that remind us that it is difficult to predict precisely what will happen tomorrow or next week, even as other elements of our lives are quite clearly shaped by larger historical dynamics working over longer periods of time. It is not easy to see how we can move from short-term uncertainties to long-run certitudes, or at least patterns that become clear when we look back at how they came to be.

One standard way of addressing the gap between temporal units of short and long duration has been to look at 'turning points' deemed to redirect subsequent historical developments and changes. We only know such moments to be turning points because of their ascribed significance to enabling subsequent events, a feature we can only know after the events. We could however include in our evaluation of any period of time the ways in which it was similar to or different from what came before and ask what its features might portend for subsequent periods. When we do so from the vantage point of the agents or actors themselves, we introduce uncertainty and recognize contingencies that owe the openness of situations to many influences, many of which are unanticipated the larger and more complex the situations are. Efforts to think consciously about when we begin and end our stories allow us to think about what kinds of causes we take as key to the events and actors we choose to study. Armed with such awareness we can better battle the difficulties of traversing the chasm between any particular moment and the long run of history.

If we consciously look for causation in the stories we reconstruct and tell and if we think about how we frame stories spatially and temporally we can begin to create a new taxonomy of historical studies that leaves behind national narratives as the organizing principle for fields and the history of European or Western sites as the metric for assessing human history elsewhere. Rather than reject Eurocentric studies, we can more comfortably aim to incorporate the European past into a larger study of history that embraces the world as it seeks to grasp more closely and clearly the many pasts that people have created.

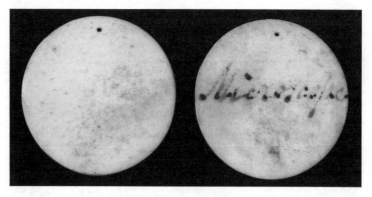

3. Circular bone token; pierced; with 'microscope' handwritten across one side in black ink. © By permission of the Trustees of the British Museum

3 The Status of Historical Knowledge

ULINKA RUBLACK

> The whole difficulty of historical reconstruction and writing lies in this fundamental truth about history: it contains a multiple situation forever on the move.
>
> (Geoffrey Elton[1])

> Anyone who has taken even the humblest part in a great battle is very well aware that it sometimes becomes impossible to be precise about a major episode after only a few hours.
>
> (Marc Bloch[2])

> L'eau à Paris a plusieurs couleurs, plusieurs facettes et functions, et elle est le support d'une activité débordante.
>
> (Arlette Farge[3])

I

On a brilliant summer morning in 1683, a man in the Dutch city of Delft set to work. His name was Antonie van Leeuwenhoek, and his passion and obsession was to perfect the making of small, powerful magnifying lenses in microscopes. For him, these were not mere instruments. He pondered the paradox: Creation in all its magnitude and inner making could only be glimpsed through smallness. Some were mad keen on telescopes. If you were a big man, was it not easy to have an astronomer show that your coat of arms was mirrored far away in the stars? Instant glorification for a bit of patronage. So Leeuwenhoek kept the fire going and shaped the glass to see the riches of life on earth as close as possible right in front of him. Here came the penis of a whale, small only in relation to the size of the beast. There were his plants from Suriname. His suppliers were fishermen, sailors of the Dutch East India Company, farmers, merchants, his maidservant, and even barbers, bringing in shaving cuts.

This morning, Leeuwenhoek looked yet again at vigorously moving sperm. Was this not the shocking essence of creation—first Adam, then Eve, created in their flesh, body, and soul, but generation after generation on earth out of the smallness of egg and spermatozoon? In a world which feared lusts, subversions, infidelities, and evil arts in women, and now sought to make visible that dark labyrinth of the womb, one of the most important questions hinged on the qualities of such sperm: might the foetus perhaps only grow from male semen? Could it be that the female only served to feed and develop it? Leeuwenhoek later that day took his pen to defend that humans certainly did not originate from an egg, but from the tiniest of animalcules in male semen.[4]

II

Antonie van Leeuwenhoek does not usually feature in essays on historical interpretation. And yet this imaginative reconstruction is of interest for two reasons: the question of how the particular is evaluated and the kind of work that is necessary to establish more general truths is central to historians. Leeuwenhoek's case shows that such evaluations relate to wider cultural attitudes towards scale. Is the small or the large, detail or broad perspective, privileged as holding access to important knowledge? What is classified as small, 'particular', or 'incidental' and what as 'general', 'essential', and patterned? Who shapes ways of looking at a subject through such terms? Do historians' change 'instruments', rather than merely pre-formed ideas, do their tools and skills make different aspects of the past visible, just as the microscope does for a biologist? For whom is what kind of knowledge important to proclaim particular narratives of origins, causation, and change, or, last but not least, to undermine the contribution of women to the shaping of human history? These are some of the key questions of historical interpretation, and they suggest that we need to examine what historians regard as their tools and skills, and how such views relate to their life-experiences, intellectual traditions, institutions, and ideals, if we wish to understand how they go about the business of interpretation. The historiography of historical interpretation is commonly approached through a body of thought variably constructed as 'Western' intellectual tradition.[5] Yet, needless to say, ideas are not exclusive to whatever is taken to be 'Western', nor are Western ideas to be treated as a model against which other developments appear as corruptions or deviations. Ideals of epistemic virtue—of how we can best approach the work of interpretation—are historically grounded and relate to practices which command trust in particular contexts at particular times. Hence I argue that we need to assess how historians in different periods and parts of the world have formed views on epistemic virtue and based their interpretations on them. My specific interest in this chapter, moreover, is to explore how scale—what people have categorized as large or small—has been related to ways in which historians have sought to create meaningful representations of the past for their own time, and how such categorizations in turn have been influenced by optical engagements with reality. For there are perhaps connections between the explanatory status ascribed to smaller or larger slices of evidence and the cultural availability and prominence of visual technologies which familiarize different ways of seeing and constituting the real. Ideas and categorizations are rooted in culture, and shared cultural experiences make plausible to others what we can know about the world, whether such knowledge matters and how it can be represented.

Leeuwenhoek's world, the Dutch Republic, is a case in point. His interest in scale and vision was not just the outcome of a series of technological inventions, but interrelated with experiences in a society which had diversified in the most extraordinary way. The Republic had defended its liberty from the Spanish monarchy and was politically multi-centric; it allowed for different religions to be practised, even though reformed religion was politically favoured; it was increasingly urbanized across its seven provinces, and since the late sixteenth century experienced a rapid and significant population increase. Commerce, professional diversification, and post-war social mobility were seen to level traditional hierarchies. Scales were experienced as shifting as cities like Haarlem and Amsterdam doubled in size through migration. Many migrants were involved in the burgeoning world trade, which since the 1590s made Amsterdam a nodal point of global exchange. Thus, by 1636, an innkeeper of that city wrote a pamphlet which commented critically on the social effects of the tulip trade, which had gripped the Republic. What disturbed him was not just that small bulbs of a perishable flower fetched such high prizes, but that 'Flora...can make the great folk so small, and the small so great, that they have much in common, and they bounce up and down together, on wagons, carts, and carriages'.[6] Such economic, social, and cultural experiences gave issues of scale their pertinence. They raised anxieties, fascinated, and already brought to the fore questions about how anything—the natural world, society, or the past—could be represented if a firm and enduring sense of scale and belonging could not be secured.

Optical experiments spurred this sense on. For, as the art historian Svetlana Alpers explains,

> an immediate and devastating result of the possibility of bringing to men's eyes the minutest of living things (the organisms viewed in the microscopic lens), or the farthest and largest (the heavenly bodies viewed through the telescopic lens), was the calling into question of any fixed sense of scale and proportion. The related problem of how we perceive distance and estimate relative size still exercises students of perception. Whatever the solution might be, there is general conclusion that the eyes cannot by themselves estimate distance and size. It is this that telescopes and microscopes made clear in the seventeenth century. To many it seemed a devastating dislocation of the previously understood measure of the world, or, in short, of man as its measure.[7]

Others enthusiastically endorsed that the microscope and telescope showed that nothing was little or large as such, but only in comparison, and that human senses were variable and open to deception.[8] The camera obscura too undercut any privileging of the central perspective onto a clearly ordered world as a window, with a clear distinction and hierarchy between foreground and background.[9] It could engender fascination with the passing of people, in its contingency as well as surprises. It provided a 'way of seeing' which could be informed by, but as a tool also could help to inform of its own, an experience of a diverse, open-ended reality which would only be captured through many stories and shifting vantage points. This undermined the social and political bias of hierarchical definitions of what people, societies, and their 'usable' past were to be about. Hierarchical and closed definitions of society and history typically legitimized elitist and imperialist concepts of governance by focusing on myths of ethnic origin, genealogy, male heroic supremacy, religious and territorial unity.

III

Optical instruments thus might be said to have influenced different responses to how actual and past reality can best be represented, though obviously not in any linear fashion. The microscope, telescope, and photographic camera, in particular, have increasingly stimulated the question of how different scales relate to accounts of the past. They are persistently invoked metaphorically to explore the notion that we only interpret by pre-selecting our evidence or field of vision. This view—remember E. H. Carr's famous request to study the historian if one wishes to understand how a particular history has been written—has heightened the awareness that a particular perspective shapes what one sees. It has brought with it contests about such selections and the arguments they furnish, as well as anxieties about foreclosure, blindness, short- or long-sightedness, and delusion in this process of seeing and knowing the past. A microscopic, grainy, or 'pixel-by-pixel' approach is typically criticized for not representing a broad enough context or not even an analytical problem as well as being too narrow in providing historical explanation. The telescopic, by contrast, is criticized as being void of sensitivity to detail, removed from any truthful complexity of historical life, and typically locked in a 'mono- or bi-causal trap of explanation'.[10] Yet another question that has gained prominence in our contemporary 'age of zoom' is how work on different scales is best combined to enrich our image of the past. Here, once more, we see a parallel between the widest ever familiarization of optical devices to capture something which people aim to represent as real and which they are enabled to repeat easily from shifting perspectives—close and far away, with less or more context, the small becoming large and the large small—and a contemporary experience of a social reality which newly emphasizes the duality of 'local' and 'global' dimensions of existence and raises questions about their connection in past and present. Technologies of vision, in other words, contribute to make self-evident that different ways of seeing and knowing are possible and raise the question what effects they produce if they are combined.

IV

The first scholar to ask how optical tools influence the ways in which we conceive of representing the world to ourselves was the German-Jewish exile Sigfried Kracauer. In 1969, Kracauer's posthumously published reflections on history, entitled 'History: The Last Things before the Last', noted that Leopold von Ranke's programme to show how 'things have essentially been' was announced only fifteen years before Daguerre's invention of photography in 1839.[11] Kracauer thus traced the story of the interrelation of visual technologies to an art of knowing back to the nineteenth century, whereas we have seen that it had a far longer history. In contrast to Ranke, Kracauer advocated an ethos and aesthetics of interpretation which built on 'empathetic absorption' in evidence and on intuition. It looked beyond traditional political narratives. To Kracauer, historians had a 'recording obligation', but merely fact-oriented, impersonal history writing was like an artless newsreel shot. Ideally, a historical account needed to be a match between pertinent data and an interpretation which 'neither overwhelms them nor leaves an undigested remainder'.[12] 'Facts' were not just names and dates, but all parts of reality, especially so if they traced not just the 'patterned' but more 'amorphous' parts of reality. These he regarded as integral to presenting life 'in its fullness', emotionality, contingency as well as 'fleetingness'.[13]

To Kracauer, the exploration of multiple meanings from a relative standpoint was the essential contribution of photography and film as an art form to how historians could open up the past from singular strands of interpretation and reclaim its complexity in other ways. Kracauer particularly attacked Christian providentialism and unilinear accounts of human 'progress'.[14] He was most interested in aspects which at first would resist interpretation, because they de-familiarized the past and opened up further contexts relevant for understanding the past. History was thus conceived as a discovery, not a process of validating preconceived hypotheses about modernization or legitimizing existing structures and hierarchies. But his work left unclear how, exactly, one was to arrive at an interpretation of all the multiple elements observed from all of human life and everywhere.

V

Just how far did twentieth-century historians manage to take claims for the importance of the particular and intuitive? The strongest defence came from one of the founding figures of an approach which labelled itself 'microhistory'. In a famous article on 'clues', first published in 1979, the Italian historian Carlo Ginzburg described the beginning of a new epistemological paradigm, a new perspective onto how we can know, in the human sciences at the end of the nineteenth century. At this time, Ginzburg set out, the Italian art historian Giovanni Morelli caused a stir with the proposal that the only method to distinguish original art work from copies would be to look at the depiction of small bodily details, such as earlobes or hands, rather than at the overall 'style' of a particular school, which was easy to copy. Morelli therefore likened an art historian's work to that of a detective, a figure newly popularized by crime novels. Sherlock Holmes precisely observed a series of small details. In *The Uncanny Parcel* (1892), he even referred to two short articles he had published on the human ear in the *Anthropological Journal*. Sigmund Freud, in turn, was fascinated by Conan Doyle and Morelli. He regarded his method as analogous. Acute observation of unguarded behaviour, of particular symptoms, everything resisting social control, in short, revealed the individual.

Ginzburg was fascinated by all three of these writers—Morelli, Conan Doyle, and Freud. In turn, he constructed the most essentialist story of human origin, arguing that such views reached back to the beginning of human history, when men (!) had been hunters for centuries. Hunters followed spurs through varying and incidental detail, through an immersion in the senses of sound, smell, and taste, which knowledge could not be abstracted from. Narrative arose from case histories. This approach to knowing had continued to be cultivated in medicine since Hippocrates, who had recognized that illness manifests itself differently in different individuals. Causes and effects could not be mathematically formalized. Intuition for the incidental, Ginzburg maintained, is innate to humans. The historian who put his nose to the ground simply cultivated this sense to a higher degree, and ascended from the unexpected incidental particular to an important general statement about a past society.[15] The process of exactly how this was meant to happen seemed to be beyond the operational.

Then, in 1998, the French historian Alain Corbin conducted probably the most extreme experiment with the indeterminate in encountering a 'completely normal' historical person.[16] Unlike Ginzburg, Corbin did not look for the extraordinary incidental detail which would open up our sense of how it was possible to think and act in the past. Unlike microhistorians with clearer structural questions indebted to Marxism, for instance, he did not think about the transformation of labour relations in capitalism, kinship structures, and local communities. Corbin looked for the ordinary detail and wished to 'stand the methods of nineteenth-century social history on their head'. Social history, not just of the elites, but of the 'people', he boldly argued, 'is based on the study of a very small sample, of people whose fates were exceptional'. The exceptional artisan who left a diary, he argued, had then been taken to represent a vast group of 'working people'. Corbin was interested in restoring someone who was destined to disappear from historical memory to our sense of the past. This was not a microhistory, he declared, just recovery, to 'repair the neglect of historians for all those things that are irrevocably relegated to oblivion'. So, he wrote engagingly, '3 pm (1995). I have chosen the archives of Orne... I close my eyes and select at random a volume from the inventory of the municipal archives... Next I open the decennial tables of vital statistics from the late eighteenth century and choose two names at random.' One of the men thus identified died young. Corbin chose the other, Louis-François Pinagot.[17] He found out where he lived and that he worked as a clog-maker. Corbin formulated a range of question, on the basis of his knowledge about nineteenth-century France—how did Louis-François experience change, with what mental equipment did he deal with impoverishment, how important was honour to him, whom did he hate?

June 1995. My sense is that a thousand pages on Pinagot, no matter how descriptive and overcautious in interpretation, would do more to satisfy the desire to understand this period than any number of minute studies of structures of proto-industrialization or hasty, pretentiously scientific comparisons of Percheron peasants with the tribesmen of New Guinea.[18]

The remainder of the book abounds with the words 'probably', 'so it is plausible to assume', 'there is no way of knowing', or, 'we need to fathom'.

Despite its considerable hermeneutic problems, such re-engagements with the particular forcefully questioned common evaluations of scale—that the particular tells us about something small and is of less significance than the general, which is brought out through a wide scope. So a village might be judged a small matter of small significance, but upon closer inspection will typically reveal itself as extraordinarily complex in its dynamic. It will force us to see that 'the village' is a generalization. 'The amorphous mass of "peasants"', Claudia Ulbrich hence notes, 'turns into individual men and women seeking their place within society.'[19] Any insignificant person's life, and this was the point of Corbin's claim, can be the subject of hundreds of questions. We might judge the history of villages in France a large subject, but then it will appear 'particular' in relation to the history of rural society all over the world. Judgement about scale, as seventeenth-century people observed, to this extent remains relative. Global change, moreover, will translate into local diversity. Both make up the story of the past, so that historians at their best are world historians and local historians at the same time.

VI

Yet as our perspectives have multiplied, one question is frequently asked: do twentieth-first-century historians still intend to come up with anything that might be called 'general truths'? How can we characterize their current relationship with the term 'objectivity' and an art of knowing? If anything, to many it seems that history has become a humble art, less certain, fatally fragmented. 'So much history is now being written that very few scholars can keep up with more than a tiny fraction of what is being published: all of us know more about less and less,' Sir David Cannadine sums up.[20] Another British historian, Jon Lawrence, starts off an essay on political history with the statement that 'it would be an exaggeration to say that there are as many conceptions of "political" history as there are political historians—but only just'.[21] Specialization, the fragmentation of knowledge, and plurality of approaches, none of which commands general trust among professionals, seem to encapsulate the dilemma of the discipline.

Richard J. Evans's highly successful 'Defence of History' against postmodernist views is particularly interesting in this context. It still deploys the notion of 'objectivity', yet it is crucial to note just how many qualifications this evocation of objectivity as epistemic ideal comes with. This is the final passage of his book:

For my own part, I remain optimistic that objective historical knowledge is both desirable and attainable. So when Patrick Joyce tells us that history is dead, and Elizabeth Deeds Ermarth declares that time is a fictional construct, and Roland Barthes announces that all the world's a text, and Hans Kellner wants historians to stop behaving as if we were researching into things that actually happened, and Diane Purkiss says that we should just tell stories without bothering whether or not they are true, and Frank Ankersmith swears that we can never know anything at all about the past so we might as well confine ourselves to studying other historians, and Keith Jenkins proclaims that all history is just naked ideology designated to get historians power and money in big university institutions run by the bourgeoisie, I will look humbly at the past and say despite them all: it really happened, and we really can, if we are very scrupulous and careful and self-critical, find out how it happened and reach some tenable though always less than final conclusions about what it all meant.[22]

How does an interpretative text of this kind work? This passage, for instance, is made rhetorically effective through a particular literary construction, which engages the readers in a brilliantly set out imaginary scene. It suggests that a humble and lone male historian of outstanding professional repute stands on one fixed point facing a whole chorus of male and female critics who deny objectivity from what is allegedly a common position, though actually they all say quite different things which seem increasingly silly. He also stands firmly on this fixed point facing the past as a defender of its truth. For 'it really happened'. This 'it' here seems to imply that we start from something 'real', and not from our questions, that there are facts we have access to. There is no emphasis at this final dramatic culmination of the book on the notion that very often we know that something happened only through the partial record of some historical person. Hence Evans here does not write 'it is said to have happened', but 'it happened'. He defends that those who do not wilfully distort this evidence and are able as much as humanly possible to detach themselves from contemporary values can then attempt a tentative historical analysis. These strong qualifications also ensure that history is presented as a highly specialized craft. For in order to be so very scrupulous and careful one needs to know what to be careful and scrupulous about and how to go about being very self-critical when faced with what really happened. These skills are not presented as anything related to common sense.

This end to *In Defence of History* provides a highly influential example of one of the ways in which epistemic virtues are currently constructed, which merges the notion that historians are highly trained experts with a residue of former, more elevated ideals of objectivity. They go hand in hand with notions of an academic self which performs a series of virtuous acts and thus becomes 'objective', though no longer in the classic sense of someone who is unbiased, but is the least biased possible. But how are biased interpretations curtailed? In his last pages, which elaborate the notion of objectivity, Evans thus quotes another historian, Thomas L. Haskell, who identifies an 'objective' pursuit of history with forms of 'ascetic self-discipline', which bear no trace of 'wishful thinking', test interpretations in terms of 'evidence and logic', and allow one to sympathetically enter the mind of people who share different values.[23] The emphasis of this discussion then is on scrupulous rational thinking combined with the ability to work out another mindset. This, most of all, is identified with virtue—ennobled by the adjective 'ascetic', because self-denial in many traditions has long been associated with greater truthfulness, as if the self and body, most of all, stand in the way of knowledge rather than their experiences being a conduit of knowledge. But how is one meant to 'detach' oneself—is this presented as learned behaviour or something one might also need a special gift for? And does the idea that the detached self should be able to merge with another involve the sense that one can then rationally work out what it is like to be that person? Such questions are difficult, but also highly productive. They certainly endorse that historians must not shy away from asking the most basic and yet fundamental questions: so how, exactly, are we meant to encounter a text and past humanity held within it? How are we meant to read, listen, see in a dialogical way that does not assume that meaning is ever transparent? What ideals are at stake in different responses to this question and which anxieties about interpretation do they typically raise?

Precision in all of these aspects of how we understand historical work matters, because they lead us to quite different conceptions of the discipline. In what contexts, we might ask, for instance, is it easier to legitimize rational modes of understanding rather than intuitive ones? We can note how Evans's struggle against the extremes of postmodern interpretations contrasts with Kracauer's and Ginzburg's strong and—in the latter case—oddly essentialized emphasis on the intuitive element in observation. It likewise contrasts with the extraordinary metaphor for historical writing which Marc Bloch found fresh from the trenches to emphasize that language as our principal descriptive tool is itself married to intuition:

Between the expression of physical and of human realities there is as much difference as between the task of a drill operator and that of a lute-maker:

both work down to the last millimetre, but the driller uses precision tools, while the lute-maker is guided primarily by his sensitivity to sound and touch. It would be unwise either for the driller to adopt the empirical methods of the lute-maker or for the lute-maker to imitate the driller. Will anyone deny that one may not feel with words as well as with fingers?[24]

In this view we do not only present a subject in terms of what logically makes sense to a controlling mind, we know it in part through the language we find to represent it. We thus, Bloch suggested, need to think of history as a sensuous and creative pursuit which incorporates but also transcends logic. And, once more, we cannot approach questions about the status of historical knowledge other than by embedding our query in a sense of practices of knowledge making, instruments, and work environments. These are crucial to how individuals establish a relationship with the past.

VII

Marc Bloch lived from 1886 to 1944, when he was shot by the Gestapo for his membership of the French Resistance. He was a medievalist and co-founder of the legendary historical journal *Annales d'histoire économique et sociale*. It set out a new vision of a richly interdisciplinary history which would encompass all aspects of human life— from its psychology and structures of symbolic meaning to modes of embodiment and economic, social, and cultural forms of exchange— and compare societies across and beyond Europe. In 1941/2 Bloch composed his final work, which has become one of the most influential books on historical interpretation. In *The Historian's Craft* Bloch replaced any notion of individual genius and 'objective' insight with an emphasis on human consciousness as a network of permanent interactions with others and the extreme limitation of personal insight. He wrote: 'A good half of what we see is seen through the eyes of others', and: 'All knowledge of mankind... will always derive a large part of its evidence from others.'[25] This in turn meant that Bloch pursued the question of what techniques were most helpful for historians to conduct a broad enquiry through 'mutual aid' and teamwork. So alongside the validation of new subject areas as significant knowledge, Bloch's real breakthrough in terms of notions of epistemic virtue lay in this cultivation of the idea of historical work as a laboratory.

Bloch was clearly in tune with contemporary shifts in scientific thinking away from traditional notions of an objectivity which could be
attained by 'will-less' scientists in search of universal, regular patterns
to the 'notion of the eternal relativity of measurement' and a much
greater flexibility of interpretation (see also Pamela Smith's chapter
below).[26] So the historian's laboratory was once again not imagined as
a place of individuals with precision drills at work on different parts
of a historical landscape. It was based on his democratic, though far
from idealistic commitment to communication and peace among
different populations after the First World War. This was grounded,
in Bloch's awareness of the importance of the medium of language,
which necessitated first the clarification and standardization of terms
generally used. Hence the *Annales* in its early years deployed the journal as a forum for such communication, to provide information about
new sources and techniques, to collect and compare results.[27] Bloch
followed Herodotus's vision in arguing that enquiry itself lay at the
core of the historical endeavour.[28] Uncertainty, the incomplete and
experimental, were no weakness. Rather they brought a freshness to
its pursuit, as long as they were subjected to critical evaluation.[29] Sensitivity for differences and differentiation needed to be trained.

This was obviously a sea change from the way history had first
been taught in France through the Napoleonic university as a
national institution in the early nineteenth century. One of its chief
duties then had been to purvey knowledge to the general public in
lectures. The audience 'consisted of rheumatic rentiers, pensioned
officers, and even the occasional lady, the latter running the risk of
being denied admittance on the grounds that she posed a threat to
moral standards'. Broad knowledge delivered in an elegant way mattered, whereas specialization and original, sparkling erudition were
not approved of in the delivery, which, French style, was annually
monitored by inspectors.[30] Such institutional frameworks, in other
words, had played their part in the cultivation of particular academic
practices and selves. Bloch, by contrast, spoke about the necessity of
'teamwork' among experts as the basis of innovative interpretation.
Academic work resided in enabling trans-national collegiate structures which would form interpretative communities. This was equally radical, because the dominant mode for the transmission of ideas
among scholars had been and often continues to be rooted in a

patriarchal and clientele-based model of discipleship, with which we are still deeply familiar. A professor mounts a thesis or approach as truth and patronizes a group of idealized brilliant 'sons' and sometimes 'daughters', who will in exchange loyally promote this truth in their works. The defence of this truth and an image of those who do not adopt it as enemies stabilizes a sense of scholarly belonging. Influence over appointments, publications, and presentations is used to minimize controversy. Scholarship is rendered relatively static and divided into fiefdoms.[31] For Bloch, the purpose of open transnational interpretative networks, by contrast, was the commitment not to personal loyalty and interpretative dominance, but again to a continuing enquiry, which was refined through the 'pooling of techniques', flows of information, a process of clarification about 'several dominant problems',[32] and then the setting up of experiments to produce and understand evidence. There existed no other truth than that of the practice of history as *craft*; 'history', his biographer Raulff sums up, 'did not legitimate itself through its eternal tomes but through its practices which are constantly to be improved'.[33] But at the beginning was not an object; at the beginning was a problem, defined by historians in historically specific sites of research.[34]

VIII

So do most historians today then unite behind general methods of historical enquiry and interpretation, instead of dominant 'general truths'? This, at least, is the argument of the British historian Ludmilla Jordanova in a further influential interpretative book, *History in Practice*. She sets out that 'what counts as successful history depends on the context in which it is being judged', while the 'most helpful way of thinking about such matters is in terms of trust, not truth'. This is because knowledge is produced within particular 'institutions, nations and particular groupings'. These obviously diverge in what they value as 'truthful'; a point all too relevant in a world in which intolerant movements often exercise considerable influence on what books are published, stocked at libraries, and used in schools and universities. In Jordanova's view, historians need to defend this 'general method' in order to be able to argue about which accounts of the past should command trust. Trust should be accorded to historians committed to the 'critical evaluation of evidence, to meticulous reasoning and to disclosing their sources, acknowledging their scholarly debts'.[35]

The American historian Natalie Davis, by contrast, equates precisely the same commitment with an epistemic ideal of truthfulness:

> we historians do not possess a monopoly of ways of telling about the past, but we have a strong responsibility to defend historical evidence, duly researched, and credible interpretation of it. I affirm this responsibility in full awareness that it is often difficult to establish the validity of evidence, that documents are never transparent (one of my books is entitled 'Fiction in the Archives!'), that historians shape disparate evidence into a narrative form, and that interpretation can be detested. But the goal of our historian's craft has been and is a quest for a truthful account of the past as full as we can make it; we try to further that goal by constantly reviewing each other's evidence, offering enlargements, and debating interpretation.[36]

Discursive claims about truthful knowledge making are thus linked to collaborative forms of work. We note that Davis's positive vision of the extent of historical collaboration, however, is far removed from David Cannadine's, or the French historian Arlette Farge's sense that historians are in danger of becoming a bunch of over-specialized, increasingly lonely people in a vastly expanded profession, who frequently express themselves in jargon, 'know more about less and less', or defend approaches particular to their sub-discipline by proprietarily speaking about 'my archives' and 'my sources'.[37]

In Jordanova's account the notion of 'truthfulness' remains in any case too closely linked to the concept of traditional objectivity and its concomitant claim that scholarly bias can be avoided. She proposes 'reliability' and 'honesty' as more helpful terms to judge the integrity of scholarship in terms of its methods. Such terms do not sit on the same pedestal as truth and are linked to commonsensical forms of judgements on consistency and plausible accuracy in everyday life. They allow for one's judgement of an account as reliable and honest, while one might not be able to regard it as truthful on the basis of one's own emotional and political attachments.[38] Jordanova's epistemic ideals rest on this openness towards different subject matters, but more crucially on a set of skills. These are described as linked to the accumulation of experience among those who practise them, to teaching, and to giftedness. These core skills are the ability to track down and thoughtfully deploy information, self-awareness of one's use of evidence, the ability to scrutinize one's emotional identification with past actors (rather than entertaining the possibility of detachment), the ability to grasp complexity, and the ability to write.[39] Questions about the past themselves are 'shaped mainly by scholarly tradition and by the concerns historians find around them'. This reiterates the position that we do not look at the past as something that self-evidently is 'there', but as something that is brought into being through our relation with it, which is mediated by pre-existing and historically situated relationships with that past and one's relationship to what is categorized as present. And yet she finally concludes that these skills do not make up a 'unifying method'. 'Taking notice and critically evaluating' are crucial, but not specific to history. What unites historians above all is historical interpretation in written form.[40] What this means is not set out other than in contrast to the notion that historians are united by archival work.

It is nonetheless clear that Jordanova, like Bloch, is guided by her interest in the twentieth-century revaluation of how scientific knowledge is produced. This leads her to emphasize that we can only conduct a debate about what history is, can be, and should be through an open-minded and honest discussion of the epistemic terms, techniques, tools, and skills which are used by different practitioners as parts of different socio-political research environments, and the questions and dilemmas they pose. The same approach is evident in a recent introduction to 'world histories', in which the Australian historian Marnie Hughes-Warrington writes:

to begin with, world history is not a thing, but an activity, and various physical forms of expressions such as lectures, books, journal papers and classroom lessons are criteria for it. "World history" should thus be defined through an examination of the various forms of expression taken as its criteria, not apart or prior to them.[41]

It exists through concrete, localized processes of making and demonstration.

IX

Historians have thus interestingly come to parallel important features of epistemic ideals in the sciences, which nowadays too focus on 'trained judgement'. For, as the American historians of science

Lorraine Daston and Peter Galison explain in their book *Objectivity*, we can distinguish between three key epistemic virtues which have been of particular relevance in particular periods of scientific endeavour. First came the ideal of 'truth-to-nature'. An eighteenth-century botanist like Linnaeus would represent a flower as one of its type, rather than with its singular characteristics with perhaps a broken leaf or more stems. The focus was on the essential and universal. Next, the mid-nineteenth century saw the ascent of 'objectivity'—the idea that the scientist should see himself above all in contrast to an individually creative artist. Scientists needed to reduce human intervention as much as possible in what they studied to be 'will-less' other than in their commitment to objectivity. They would want to reveal irregularities rather than privileging symmetry, for instance. In the twentieth century, 'trained judgement' gained prominence as epistemic ideal. Sophisticated instruments can be used to generate particular data, but experts can decide to 'smooth' the result to remove instrumental artefacts.[42] Daston and Gallison consequently argue that epistemic ideals are historically specific ways of investigating and representing nature—and we can of course paraphrase this by saying that epistemic ideals are historically and culturally specific ways of investigating and representing *the past*. It is therefore not interesting to treat objective truth, for instance, as a monolithic concept one either supports or challenges. Rather one needs to look at the way epistemic ideals function in the practices of a discipline. So the question becomes, once more, one about assumptions on which historical categories rest and about acts, how one enacts objectivity, performs acts that particular others deem to be objective, or enacts trained judgement, and how these acts are connected with beliefs which form a wider way of academic identity. 'Scientific objectivity', Daston and Gallison explain, 'resolves into gestures, techniques, habits and temperament ingrained by training and daily repetition.'[43] Acts embody and build up an ideal, and therefore implicate the knowing self physically as well as intellectually, even through the appearances particular academics cultivate and their styles of communication. In the case of Marc Bloch and the *Annales* we see that this was realized in a highly self-conscious way.

Trained judgement as epistemic ideal typically does not self-confidently believe in genius. 'The trained expert grounds his or her knowledge in guided experience, not in special access to reality.'[44] She or he is not a passive observer or someone who reveals hidden truths (from archives), but is hermeneutically aware, and implied in the making consciously and affectively, just as the recipients of knowledge thus produced are. Interestingly, judgement can thus be related to 'well schooled intuitions'. Memory and synthetic perception are given less relevance in training, and so is the production of quantitative data without training in how to analyse selection processes involved in their making. Today, the ethos of all three approaches—'truth-to-nature', 'objectivity', and 'trained judgement'—to making the past or nature intelligible is available. It can appear in particular forms—for instance when 'objectivity' or 'truthfulness' are evoked together with notions of historians as 'trained experts', as the example of Richard Evans's finishing paragraph has shown. From the commonplace that there are today more scientists at work in the world than ever before—just as there are more historians, or academics of any kind, and, as institutions of higher education expand worldwide, there are more to *come*—Daston and Galison propose an understanding of disciplinary plurality which relates to Jordanova's replacement of truth with seemingly more mundane notions of honesty and reliability. 'In this multitude', they write, 'coexist not only many individual personalities but also distinctive collective traditions of schooling and sustaining scientific selves, perpetuated by much the same mechanisms as research science is to acquire an ethos and a way of seeing.'[45] So trained judgement obviously still relates to values specific to particular communities, and how, otherwise, would one reach any agreement? But this means that we take a 'plurality of visions of knowledge' which attempt 'fidelity' to the past as a feature of history. We can then distinguish, for instance, between traditions which have informed the view that tacit knowledge is important, or fostered the view that emotional detachment must be practised and indeed that it is possible to capture a past reality.[46] Yet the purpose of such an enquiry is not to point a finger at historical ideals which fail, but to present a complex analysis of what it is that historians involve themselves in *doing* when they create knowledge about the past and what values and concepts they resort to in defending their ideals.

X

What this means is no less than that the important debate which conceived of 'art' and 'science' as opposed ways of seeing the world, which arose in the mid-nineteenth century and led to different historians declaring themselves as 'scientific' in method or not, is no longer of relevance. Epistemic ideals between the arts and sciences have considerably merged.

In addition we can conclude that there is little gain in framing 'micro-' and 'macro-historical' approaches as dichotomous, and more to be said for investigating how far away—and close up—perspectives relate and can be used to put methodological pressure on or complement each other. The question of which perspectives are best combined is highly relevant for comparative work and of increasing appeal for people who see themselves as living in a globally interconnected world. The question whether 'nation states' form the right basis for comparison in an age 'beyond the nation state' is vigorously debated (see also Chris Bayly's chapter above).[47] Jürgen Osterhammel argues that definitions of cultural identity in any case continuously shift in every nation, region, or in trans-cultural exchanges, and thus further complicate comparisons.[48]

Historians need to perceive and adapt to flows in which identifications emerge, re-emerge, proliferate, and look different from different views. A figure like Geoffrey Elton regarded this flow of life as an obstacle for historical reconstruction one needed to control with dams to reduce this complexity. But few now wish to save the authority of singular historians as seers who perform as 'sages on stages' by defining in a very limited way what matters and excluding everything else. Contemporary historians are, as we have seen, usually too critical of the costs of those dams to what knowledge of the past we create. They positively embrace ongoing debate. Some even find appropriate linguistic ways of celebrating a sense of the fluid, as Arlette Farge does, for instance, in her vivid re-creation of the Seine and water in Paris, which serves to evoke a positive sense of the many-sidedness of a historical phenomenon, in which resides its force in life: 'L'eau à Paris a plusieurs couleurs, plusieurs facettes et functions, et elle est le support d'une activité débordante.'[49] Historical creativity is hereby linked to an energetic and directed but open-ended exploration of the many-sidedness of past life, rooted—as it was for Bloch—in egalitarian ideas as well as an openness for connection and exploration.

This brings us on to the subject of historical writing as literary process. If we understand language as our principal tool not to master but creatively engage with the past, then historical writing needs to be taught. It cannot simply be regarded as something some people have more of a gift for than others, so that everyone should therefore be restricted to plain, transparent speech. It is important to analyse key narrative models which have guided history writing, in the way Hayden White influentially proposed in his book on the 'Content of Form'. Simply put, for instance, 'rise and fall narratives' will always lead one to break the story off at its most dramatic endpoint.[50] Such a model psychologically weds the historian to the spectre of tragedy, which, as the inverse of Whiggish progress narratives, has long been compelling for critical intellectuals. This nonetheless problematically closes down rather than opens up history and futurity. It is equally important to reflect on fictional configurations and rhetorical conventions which characterize different historical styles of writing and form an essential part of historians' epistemic practice. From such an awareness of different traditions and possibilities can follow an engagement with experiments in historical writing, historical novels, and films, which seek to capture different perspectives and chronologies and also to interrogate boundaries between the literary, poetical, and historical in interesting ways. We can see this in Marguerite Yourcenar's novelistic work or Natalie Davis's book *Slaves on Screen*.[51] We still represent the past to ourselves principally through the medium of language. As we explore our ability to give expression to dimensions of human existence we receptively observe, so we affect our sense of the past and how we conceive of our present.

Next we need to be aware that the key skill to transform history writing and prevent the sad sense of historians as a crowd of lonely experts is the capability to foster teamwork skills, across different periods and areas of expertise. This goes beyond listening to papers at conferences and leads back to Bloch's sense of the laboratory, or the new settings and techniques vital for the History Workshop movement. The question becomes which settings are most conducive to an epistemology which realistically focuses on 'trained judgement' and involves experiment. To illustrate this point, I will provide an example from my own 'practice' as a historian. It involved membership in a research council-funded network set up by the Renaissance art historian Evelyn Welch in London. It included a literary scholar interested in theatre, an economic historian interested in consumption, museum curators, textile conservationists, costume designers, and doctoral students. We met to work out how clothing and appearances mattered in early modern history, because it has recently become clear just how much men and women across society at this time cared about what they looked like. Vestiary codes in this society visualized order, standing, or emotional sensibilities. I say 'we met to work out' intentionally, because we were not just thinking, but making objects. We made ruffs, for instance, to understand what exactly was involved in their production and in wearing them so as to connect more deeply with the life of these curious objects. We looked at seventeenth-century gloves, an expert telling us how their embroidery was made and what we do and do not know about them. They would have been perfumed, but this scent can only be recovered by remaking recipes. These tell us much about the sensuous worlds sustaining social distinction, cultural connections, and symbolizing refinement in this period. So this set-up provides a good example for the way in which Bloch thought laboratory experiments could be adapted by historians to tell us new things about the past through cumulative, collaborative work, how this involves the pooling of expertise and new techniques which prompt fresh epistemological questions. Should we think of material culture as 'direct evidence'? Certainly not. What can we say about the relationship between making and knowing and the low epistemic status traditionally given to 'making'? Remaking ruffs prompts far wider questions about interpretative problems, forcing us to examine the organizing categories of history as a professional discipline.[52]

If we find new forms of dialogue with different kinds of historical practitioners we open up choice—a choice of what kind of historian we want to be, what notions of 'authority' we hold, of what there is to be done with knowledge about the past. Only then can epistemological curiosity flourish in informed debates and experiments, which point to the future of history and changing understandings of academic achievement and selves, with hopefully fewer models of patriarchal discipleship replicating the tragic narrative of one origin, loyalty and sacrifice, or betrayal and war all over again. Instead, history needs more teamwork, cross-fertilization, through diverse people with different skills in experiment. For historians, as Ernst Cassirer put it, are discoverers and interpreters of past human life. They not only narrate but reconstruct the past, inspiring in it a new life.[53] The past hundred years have seen an extraordinary transformation of many areas of history writing—one only needs to think of the international history of slavery, gender history, history from below, imperial history, religious history, or the history of cultural exchange. Areas of dense expertise—such as Holocaust studies—can still be considerably changed by new data from parts of the subject hitherto believed to be marginal.[54] It is important to emphasize, then, the dynamism the subject has displayed, as its importance across the world has extended. The next step is to debate what a trans-cultural analysis of historical writing should look like which does not isolate ideas from politics and practice, and which proceeds thematically.[55] I have tried to show why such attempts can profitably be based on an analysis of epistemic ideals and practices, such as 'detachment' or 'objectivity', notions of how one regards the archive, learns to read texts, deals with debate, behaves at graduate seminars, or does 'interdisciplinary teamwork'.[56] Such ideals and practices can be shared in similar environments across national boundaries and adapted in multi-centric ways. This approach hence necessarily changes the frame from 'Western' ideas of historical interpretation towards a global ethnography of those involved in presenting the past. The question of how different historians aim to arrive at historical interpretation fully opens up as we ask this simple set of questions: what do historians do, what do they take to be the past, which conventions apply to how they establish their relationship with it, and who evaluates how they go about doing what they do?

4. Hanging scroll. Portrait of the historian Yan Gugu. Painted in ink and colours of silk. Ming Dynasty (1368–1644). © By permission of the Trustees of the British Museum

4 Historians

DONALD R. KELLEY AND BONNIE G. SMITH

Historia was the term used at the outset of 'the publication of the researches of Herodotus of Halicarnassus' concerning his travels and observations in the fifth century BC, and it has been preserved down to the present to designate the genre established by him. Herodotus journeyed as far north as Scythia and into Asia Minor and Egypt, and he recorded and lectured on his findings. He drew indirectly on the tradition of Homer and epic poetry and also the logographers, but added to the narrative the criteria of truth and eyewitness testimony (*autopsia*) as well as utility. History had not only a large pattern, such as Greek liberty opposed to 'barbarian' tyranny, but also smaller lessons, such as that taught to the wealthy Croesus, 'that human happiness never continues long in one stay'. Herodotus followed a roughly comparative method and was critical of the claims of extreme antiquity made by the Egyptians and others. The Athenian moment of glory came with their triumph over the Persians. From a modern standpoint Herodotus' work was *primum in genere* and a model for later historians, who followed him in his curiosity about alien cultures, causes of wars and political change, and the pursuit of liberty.

Thucydides, born a generation after Herodotus, took history in another direction and furnished a different sort of model for his successors. His history of the Peloponnesian Wars, intended as 'a possession for the ages', was based on his own participation and military and political experience. It avoided the traps of myth and treated the conflict between the Athenians in terms of its material 'causes'. It related to questions of economic motivation and political power and enduring features of 'human nature'. In general Athenian success was based on its superior constitution (*politeia*), and he took war as a natural phenomenon.

Writing more than two centuries after Herodotus and Thucydides and in the wake of many lesser historians, Polybius had his own distinctive claim to fame, which was his aspiration to encompass the whole world in his narrative of the rise of Rome. Polybius served as a Greek military commander but then was forced to go to Rome for a number of years, and he wrote his history, of which only books I–V, part of VI, and fragments of the original forty books remain. Avoiding 'archaeology', Polybius (like Thucydides) limited himself to 'a history of actual events', which he called 'pragmatic history', though attending also to questions of geography and climate. For him history was useful in both private and public life; without it man is blind. A knowledge of history allowed man to control fortune, but it remained to be seen whether Rome could withstand the forces of nature and cycles of fortune. In book VI Polybius also proposed the theory of the 'mixed constitution', based on the three forms of the Roman state, arranged in a chronological cycle, an idea which Machiavelli restored centuries later and on which later historians would erect even grander metahistorical schemes.

Like Polybius, Diodorus of Sicily offers a bridge between the old Greek civilization and the upstart power of Rome. In his *Historical Library*, which is the largest work of history that antiquity has to offer, Diodorus gives an account of world history (*koina historia*) from mythical origins down to Caesar's Gallic war. Considering questions of geohistory, mythology, and the cultures of Assyria, India, Ethiopia, and Greece itself Diodorus also insisted on the practical utility of history. Contemporary with Diodorus was Dionysius of Halicarnassus, who hoped to bridge the gap between the Greeks and Romans and whose *Roman Antiquities* has been preserved in fragments. He followed the lead of Polybius, though he also dealt with the earliest legends of Rome, which had not (according to a continuing theme) yet found its historian. Nevertheless, Dionysius cited many earlier historians in his accounts of the foundational activities of Romulus and Numa Pompilius, in which he attempted to combine the virtues of Herodotus and Thucydides, that is, the range and richness of the former and the analytical program of the latter. Ammianus Marcellinus followed both Polybius and Tacitus in his *Rerum gestarum libri* (*Book of Actions*) which Gibbon praised for its avoidance of prejudice and passion.

On the edges of the genre of historiography were other human disciplines, including philology, geography, and (retrospectively speaking) political science. Aristotle's *Politics* presented a developmental scheme of which Polybius' cyclical view was derivative as are many other modern versions. Geography—a principal source of inspiration for most earlier historians—was surveyed by Strabo in its links with history and myth. History was also defined in relation to literary fields, including poetry, rhetoric, philology, and philosophy; and such connections were revived by Renaissance humanists and later 'encyclopedic' scholars. Rhetoric was a major source of the narrative and didactic shape of historical narrative— 'philosophy teaching by example', as Dionysius of Halicarnassus put it.[1] The only ancient treatise on methodology to survive was Lucian of Samosata's 'How to Write History'. The task of the historian, according to Lucian, is to tell what happened—a motto repeated famously by Ranke—and avoid useless praise, while its chief virtues are political understanding and literary power. The 'noble dream' of modern 'scientific history' was thus already enshrined in the Herodoto-Thucydides canon.

Roman historians worked out of a deep and even parochial sense of location and tradition, measuring time 'from the founding of the city' and space from the *pomaerium* (borders) established by Numa and guarded by the god Terminus. They were following 'the fathers', honoring their ancestors and family-centered religion. Titus Livius, the 'founder of history' (*historiae conditor*), was an aristocrat who held no office but spent his life reading and writing. His history recounted the ancient legends without seriously trying to discredit them, and he took up the themes of toga and sword—'arms and the man', according to Virgil—trying to tell colorful stories, though within the bounds of truth. Livy began with what the Greeks called 'archaeology', 'covering matters which were obscure both because of their great antiquity...and because in those days there were few written records'.[2] His text seems to display a cyclical pattern, with recurring founders and crises from origins to Virgil's 'empire without end'. Livy's history was also preserved in a popular summary made by Lucius Annaeus Florus, who was even more enthusiastic about Rome's imperial successes, as if the Roman story was 'the history not of a single people but of the whole human race'.[3]

After Livy the greatest of Roman historians was Tacitus, whose two masterpieces were the *Histories* and the *Annales*, surveying Roman vices, decadence, and 'fall of liberty'. In his enormously influential *Germania* Tacitus found the lost virtues of ancient Rome in the pristine customs of the new barbarians, who 'choose their kings by birth, the generals for merit'. Following Thucydides, Tacitus was concerned with 'not only the vicissitude of events…but also with their relations and their causes', and with the empire 'the state had been revolutionized, and there was not a vestige left of the old sound morality'. The plot of Tacitus' story continues to be the downward drift of Rome, whether 'it is fate and unchangeable necessity or chance which governs the revolutions of human affairs'.[4] The larger trajectory in time which Tacitus saw is what Machiavelli, Vico, and other early modern 'Tacitists' admired him for. Tacitus' most direct follower was Ammianus Marcellinus, an admirer of Julian the Apostate, who lived under Christian rule but who wrote in Latin and in Rome from a pagan standpoint.

Cicero was mainly an orator and philosopher, but he had a great admiration for the art of history, and indeed he gave it a classical and much repeated definition: 'the witness of time, the light of truth, the life of memory, the mistress of life, the messenger of antiquity'.[5] The standard of truth is what distinguished history from poetry, as Aristotle had also said, and as Pliny claimed in his *Natural History*. Another rhetorician who praised history was Quintilian, who identified the orator with the ideal historian. He commented on the ancient historians and compared the Latins favorably with the Greeks: he 'would not hesitate to match Sallust against Thucydides, nor would Herodotus resent Titus Livius being placed on the same level with himself'.[6]

Byzantium prided itself on being the 'second Rome', and its historians continued to write history in the Roman manner. The best known of Ammianus Marcellinus' successors in the eastern empire was Procopius, who wrote his history of Justinian's conquests over the 'barbarians' and a *Secret History*, which chronicled—satirized, thought Gibbon—the scandals and mismanagement of the imperial court under the 'pervert' Justinian and his disgraceful consort and ex-prostitute Theodora. Also in the mainstream of Byzantine historiography was Michael Psellus, who wrote a classical chronography for an elite audience. In the seventh century Theophylact Simocatta created a dialogue between Philosophy and her daughter History, who was revived to act as a guide to life. The preservation of classical ideals can also be seen in the work of Anna Comnena, who wrote about the First Crusade while Niketa Choniates covered the Third and Fourth Crusades. The last historians of the Byzantine Empire lived with the memory of the Latin conquest and the fear of the Turkish one to come, which one of them attributed to desire for revenge for Troy. The last Byzantine historian was Doukas, whose focus was universal and style was classical, though he included descriptions of Turkish customs and religion.

In the West Christianity transformed the classical conception of history, giving it a spiritual valence. History was indeed the 'mistress of life', as Cicero had taught, but in a very special sense: 'The education of the human race, represented by the people of God, like that of an individual, through certain epochs... from earthly to heavenly things and from to visible to the invisible.'[7] For Jews and Christians history was not merely deeds done and recorded but an ordeal carried on within a providential design. The story began with Hebrew scriptures concerning the delivery of Israel out of Egypt according to a god not just of nature but also of history. The Jewish sense of history was sustained by the divine promise, covenant, judgment, and national mission. The Greek theory of the four world monarchies was itself based on the biblical text about Daniel's dream and transferred to the succession of the four great powers—Babylonian, Persian, Greek, and Roman empires. The master historian of the Jews was Josephus ben Matthias, who criticized the conceit of the Greeks and tried to demonstrate the superior antiquity of Israel.

Under the Roman Empire, however, began what Clement of Alexandria called a 'new song'—that of Christ, his disciples, and their Church. The New Testament speaks not of history but of truth and wisdom, defined in contrast to human fables, traditions, and even philosophy. In his *Exhortation to the Greeks* Justin Martyr, invoking the 'archaeological' studies of Josephus and Herodotus, urged readers to reject Homer for the 'true antiquity' of Moses; and other early fathers followed suit. The Christian plan of history was laid out by Eusebius of Caesarea—'the Christian Herodotus, father of ecclesiastical history'—whose work traced the words, deeds, and sufferings of Christians from the first Year of Our Lord to the martyrs of his own day. Based on the work of Julius Africanus, his lost *Chronological Canon*, used in many later chronicles, attempted to synchronize Judeo-Christian with pagan history, aligning the Olympiadic system with biblical genealogy; and this work was continued by many successors, including Jerome. After Eusebius, the chronological tradition persisted to the end of the Byzantine Empire and later. In the West universal chronicles continued to appear in all parts of Europe between the third and the twelfth centuries. In the *City of God against the Pagans* Augustine represented history as a pilgrimage from the city of man to that of God. Although the city of God lived according to justice, the city of man was born of violence and fratricide, and it continued through many wars and persecutions. Augustine's younger colleague Orosius continued this work in his own partisan survey of universal history following the four monarchy theory (mentioned above) and the coming of Christ, who proved the falsity of paganism. Otto of Freising carried on the pattern in his *Two Cities*.

In the mid-thirteenth century the Dominican scholar Vincent of Beauvais produced a gigantic encyclopedia, a *Speculum universale* ('Universal Mirror'), of which the last part was a 'Historical Mirror' (*Speculum historiale*). This historical Summa, which was 'old as to subject and authority, new as to compilation and arrangement', represented the state of scholarship in the age of Thomas Aquinas. It is arranged 'following not only the succession of holy scriptures but also the order of secular history',[8] and invoking the usual formulas promising the benefits of truth and utility. This conflation of opposites, of sacred and profane history set in a context of classical and Christian values, reflected the structure and substance of medieval views of the recent and remote past from the time of Augustine to that of the Augustinian monk Martin Luther, when many new horizons opened up to transform Augustine's conception of the human race and its education.

Below the level of universal history the story of the past followed several proto-national lines, including the Goths, Franks, Angles, and Lombards, each of whom was represented by one major historian. Jordanes told the story of the invading Goths from a Byzantine perspective; Bishop Gregory of Tours (who is commonly called 'the father of French history') wrote about the Franks from his position as high churchman; Bede chronicled the affairs of Britain and the Church; and the monk Paul the Deacon was historian of the Lombards, later arrivals on the European scene. After Bede, almost all British chroniclers—Eadmer, Matthew Paris, William of Newburgh, Roger of Hoveden, and

Henry of Huntingdon—invoked his work; and other authors such as Ordericus and John of Salisbury added other scholarship to their citations. In the French tradition Gregory's work was continued in many books including the 'Chronicle of Fredegar' (which carried the legend of Trojan origins), the writings of Richer, the quasi-official *Grandes Chroniques de France*, and Charlemagne's biography by Einhard. In the German lands Widukind of Corvey produced a history of Saxony in the tenth century; a century later Adam of Bremen brought the Norsemen, Danes, and Slavs into European historiography; and Otto of Freising made the most impressive contribution to imperial history in his biography of Frederick of Hohenstaufen as well as his *Two Cities*. Paralleling the imperial tradition was that of the Roman Papacy, which was covered in the *Book of the Popes* and John of Salisbury's *Pontifical History*. Spain, too, had its official chroniclers, including accounts of the Reconquista and discovery of the New World.

The 'Middle Ages' were themselves a creation of Renaissance humanists, who proclaimed the start of a new epoch, or rather a renewal of classical antiquity, following these ignorant times. 'What is all history but the praise of Rome?' asked Petrarch hyperbolically,[9] and carried on this celebration through his works, especially his *Lives of Famous Men*, his letters in imitation of Cicero, and his *Africa* in imitation of Virgil. In this 'praise' other humanists turned to the study of ancient history, including Leonardo Bruni, Lorenzo Valla, Flavio Biondo, and many others throughout Italy and the rest of Europe who flourished during the early ages of print culture. In the early fifteenth century a woman's voice was heard in France. Born in Italy but brought up in France at the court of Charles V and well educated, Christine de Pizan supported herself and her children by writing verse and prose, her most important work being her *Book of the City of Ladies*, in which she showed the historical falsity of the representation of women by male authorities. For Christine, history was full of heroic women who had maintained high standards of conduct or who had nobly borne misfortune. Polydore Vergil was the great humanist historian of England, and he also published an influential study of cultural origins, *De rerum inventoribus* (*The Discoverers of Things*). In France the leader was Paolo Emilio, whose Latin history was translated into French and who was followed by many vernacular historians. In Germany Albert Krantz, Beatus Rhenanus, Johannes Aventinus, and Jacob Wimpheling represented the new Italianate humanist style in historiography, and the recovery of Tacitus' *Germania* spawned many patriotic commentaries and interpretations.

Increasingly vernacular historians joined the mainstream of Western historiography. In France Enguerrand de Monstrelet, Georges Chastellain, and Philippe de Commynes wrote contemporary history, while Claude de Seyssel translated some of the Greek historians. In Italy Villani's and Dino Campani's chronicles of Florence preceded Bruni's work, while Niccolò Machiavelli and Francesco Guicciardini wrote not only about the history of Italy but about modern politics and statecraft. Machiavelli also produced commentaries on Livy and revived the Polybian theory of political cycles, and his *Florentine Histories* contained many general reflections on the historical process. Guicciardini's pioneering *History of Italy* presented a comprehensive explanation of the Italian 'calamity' beginning in 1494. Guicciardini agreed with Machiavelli that 'past events shed light on the future' because of the regularity of human nature.[10] Together, writing in a Thucydidean and Tacitean mode inspired by the 'wind tossed sea' of history, they created what J. H. Hexter called 'a new vision of politics on the eve of the Reformation'.

In the Middle Eastern tradition, *ta'rikh* refers both to the past itself and to historical writing, and in the early modern period it had mainly philological concerns. The Persian religious philosopher al-Iji (d. after 1381–2) wrote the first Arabic work on the method of history, 'The Gift of the Poor Man', and later Ibn Khaldun developed a theoretical pattern to arrange events of the past Arabic historical tradition developed out of oral practice and focused on genealogy. It continued in a theological context as well. The first such writings concerned Muhammad and his allies and sought accuracy in dating above other matters.

Islamic historiography followed two main forms, the universal chronicle (also found in the European tradition) and the biographical dictionary. Examples are al-Tabari's (d. 923) *History of Prophets and Kings* and Ibn Sa'd's (d. 845) *Grand Book of Generations*. The focus of such works gradually shifted from theological to more secular and specialized concerns as in the writings of such authors as Ibn al-'Adim (d. 1262), Ibn Shaddad (d. 1234), and other authors belonging to elite officialdom. Late in the tenth century there was also the rise of the Persian school of historiography, including Rashid al-Din's (d. 1318)

Collection of Chronicles, which told a universal history not just of Muslims but of people beyond that community. The Persian language became the quasi-official tongue for that historiography. Increasingly Arabic narratives were replaced by national ones, and as Islam spread in Africa the oral tradition of transmitting genealogical and other historical material partially gave way to written histories emanating from centers of Islamic scholarship such as that at Timbuktu.

The conventional view in the West was that history had to do with political and military actions (*res gestae*), and the chronicle form continued to be practiced; but under the influence of humanism people began to open their eyes to other human creations, which came to include all the arts and sciences of the 'encyclopedia'. In 1499 Polydore Vergil surveyed the human 'inventors of things' ranging from literature and laws to myth, philosophy, and religion. One major target was civil law, first represented in Aymar du Rivail's *History of Civil Law* (1515), which built on the work of Pomponius and Livy. Perhaps the most striking contribution to cultural and literary history was Christophe Milieu's *Universe of Things* (1551), which covered the chain of being from nature to human experience and creations. Milieu analyzes five spheres of 'wisdom', including writing and print and political organization. Equally broad views of history were taken by Nicolas Vignier's *Historical Library* (1587) and Louis Le Roy's *Vicissitude of Things* (1575), which praised the inventions of a later age, including that trinity of modern devices celebrated by Bacon: gunpowder, the compass, and printing.

The Protestant Reformation, following the critique of Martin Luther, involved historical revisionism on a grand scale, carrying on the reinterpretation of many church traditions as human—and so historical—corruption. The Conciliar movement of the fifteenth century had opened up several new 'national' ecclesiastical lines, including the Gallican, the Hispanic, the English, and the German, each represented by master historians. The official historiographer of the Lutheran party in Germany was Johann Sleidan, who was also the translator of Froissart, Commynes, and Seyssel. His history was entitled *The State of Religion and Government under the Emperor Charles V*, arguing that political history could not be understood without attention to religious matters, and his theme was 'the history of restored religion' under the initiative of Luther down to 1556. The larger patterns of history were reconstructed by Martin Bucer and especially Philip Melanchthon, for whom history was a record of sin and vice and a tradition of 'pure religion' based on Luther's principle of 'scripture alone'. Melanchthon's opponent Flaccius Illyricus compiled a vast *Catalogue of the Witnesses of Time* to celebrate the tenuous tradition of doctrinal purity since the time of the primitive Church; and martyrologists like John Foxe and Jean Crespin followed one aspect of this proto-Protestant tradition. The longer sweeps of history were covered by the *Magdeburg Centuries* for the Protestants and later by the *Annales ecclesiastici* of Cardinal Baronius for the Catholics. The greatest historian of the Counter-Reformation was probably Paolo Sarpi, a critic of papal power who published a detailed history of the Council of Trent.

Throughout Europe, too, national historians began to trace the official history of the monarchies and republics. In France the successors of Paolo Emilio included Nicolas Gilles, Symphorien Champier, Jean Bouchet, Bernard Du Haillan, Jean Du Tillet (and Bishop, brother also Jean), the brothers Pithou, the brothers Dupuy, and many others into the seventeenth century; in England this included such successors of Polydore Vergil as John Leland, William Camden, John Selden (for whom the first chair of history at Oxford was named), Henry Spelman, John Clapham, John Speed, and Lord Clarendon, and others studied by David Douglas; and counterparts can be found for Spain, Italy, Germany, the Netherlands, and the rest. History figured prominently in the compilations of seventeenth-century polyhistors such as Daniel Morhof and G. J. Vossius. At this time erudition was much prized, as was archaeology, and researches were made into the medieval past as well as classical antiquity; and the practices and theory of historical criticism were initiated.

From the European Renaissance, history became the object of 'method' and attempts to transform it from an art (the classical and Renaissance Italian *ars historica*) into a 'science'. The most famous of these efforts was Jean Bodin's *Method for the Easy Comprehension of History* (1566), which tried to raise the study of history above all other sciences and which prepared the way for his *Republic*, a treatise on modern 'absolute' government and its institutions. His work on historical methodology was the first of many handbooks, such as those of Pierre Droit de Gaillard and Bartolomaes Keckerman, Daniel Heinsius, G. J. Vossius, and Degory Wheare, down to the present time, while Henri Voisin de la Popelinière wrote the first history of histories (1599) from poetic predecessors to sixteenth-century 'perfect history' and its attendant 'art of criticism', which reached a high point in the encyclopedia of the skeptical scholar Pierre Bayle and critic Jean Le Clerc. This new form of history was purportedly 'universal', in the sense of Walter Raleigh's *History of the World*, Bishop Bossuet's *Discourse on Universal History*, and of many eighteenth-century German *Weltgeschichten* and studies of the 'grand design of God'.

Born in erudition, the universal form of historiography intersected with the Enlightenment enthusiasm for philosophy and the theory of history. Indeed 'erudition' lost out in the competition with 'philosophy' and 'pure reason'. In Diderot's *Encyclopédie* science predominated, but there were also articles on chronology, historical method, the auxiliary sciences, and criticism. French scholars followed the ancients-and-moderns controversy with emphasis on the 'history of the human spirit', most famously in Voltaire's *Essai sur les mœurs et l'esprit des nations*, and Condorcet followed with his own study of the 'progress of the human spirit'. Other scholars who aspired to combine erudition and reason were Montesquieu, who sought 'the spirit of the laws', and Giambattista Vico, who took a philological approach to universal history and 'true wisdom'. Vico's final expression of his thought was his *New Science* (1725), which traced humanity cyclically through the age of gods, the age of heroes, and of humanity, which made its own history. This was Vico's *Principia* of universal history.

In Britain the Enlightened initiative was taken by the Scottish school, especially in what Dugald Stewart called the 'conjectural history' of Adam Ferguson,[11] often regarded as the 'father of sociology' (along with Montesquieu), William Robertson, Adam Smith, and others, and the history of England by David Hume and Catharine Macaulay. The leading successor of Hume and the Scottish school was Edward Gibbon, who made himself a master not only of the Roman Empire but also of the Christian Middle Ages. Like Vico but in a more narrative way Gibbon steered between the extremes of Mabillon's erudition and Voltaire's 'philosophy of history' and also creates a bridge between the old learning and modern historiography and between learning and narrative history. Gibbon protested D'Alembert's attempt to raise the faculty of reason above that of memory (philosophy above history). Tacitus and Ammianus remained his major guides, and he used them and other classical historians in his account of 'barbarism and religion'.

In Germany ecclesiastical but especially 'cultural' history was practiced by J. L. Mosheim, J. C. Adelung, J. C. Gatterer, and most notably J. C. Herder, who went on to construct a 'philosophy of history', though in a very different and more theoretical sense than Voltaire's. Herder began with literary and linguistic studies, contributing an essay on the popular topic of the origin of language, and he moved on to philosophical questions. In his 'metacriticism' of Kant he also opposed the overemphasis on pure reason and transferred his focus to language and literature. The new genre that he and Adelung pioneered was *Kulturgeschichte*, expanded by later generations into a university discipline. At the same time handbooks of 'historical method' multiplied, and the so-called 'auxiliary sciences' were added to the historical 'encyclopedia' in the universities. So the humanist 'encyclopedic' vision was used in the long road to cultural history—the *old* cultural history. Herder's pioneering work was continued by Romantic historians in the nineteenth century and afterward.

The entry of large numbers of women into the writing of history only occurred from the late eighteenth century on. The Enlightenment and revolutionary upheavals encouraged a handful of prominent women like Louise Dupin, Catharine Macaulay, Mercy Otis Warren, and Louise Keralio to undertake large projects. Like the men around them they participated in events and debates of the time, with Warren and Keralio enmeshed in partisan politics, taking a stand in their works on behalf of the American and French revolutions respectively. During the French Revolution, Marie de Lézardière had an array of ancient manuscripts conveyed to her chateau so that she could document her *Theory of the Political Laws of the French Monarchy* (1792), a work that had little to do with any grand involvement in the events of her time and that made her famous for her use of sources some decades later. The most famous writer, however, was Germaine de Staël, daughter of Jacques Necker and thus *au courant* of the issues of the day. De Staël's *Considerations on the Principal Events of the French Revolution* relied in part on her own experiences of crowds, speechifying, and flight during the course of events, but she also used written accounts and information available in the high circles she frequented. Her account of life in Germany (*De l'Allemagne*) described cultural and intellectual life across the Rhine, breaking through the Franco-centrism of the times with its romanticism and accounts of philosophical currents. De Staël's method in this case involved travel, interviews, and reading works of the writers she covered.

History in the nineteenth century drew interest from an increasingly engaged reading public that liked its accounts of history to focus on the exploits of heroes like George Washington, Napoleon, and Goethe. From Jared Sparks to Ernst Kantorowicz historians provided an array of quasi-mythical biographies to satisfy public hunger for heroes. Likewise in the universities, the elite public flocked to the rousing lectures of François Guizot, Jules Michelet, and others who could spin out tales of the Middle Ages, the English Revolution, or the protagonists of more recent democratic upheavals around the Atlantic. Some of these entrancing lecturers also made a spectacle out of their own research in the archives: Jules Michelet in his popular lectures professed actually to hear the voices of the dead as he ruffled through their papers in the Archives nationales.

However, professionalization was also in the wind, some of it depending on precisely the plunge into archival sources that Michelet so romanticized. The message was nonetheless different from those early nineteenth-century writers who appealed to a wider audience than before. From within the university arose voices of scholars who denounced the public lecture as well as the thumping narratives of the amateurs. Across Europe and the United States historians shifted the boundaries of their identities, from writers into scholars and from amateurs who used multiple sources of evidence to professionals who relied on documents in archives. Historians increasingly added accounts of their travels to archives to the lore of the profession, which became loaded both with the heroics of research, including the challenges of climate, and with fantasies around the 'rescue' of 'fairy princesses' from their captivity. Despite their identification with towering heroes, as they 'assaulted' archives, in reality many a historian was rooted in the family circle, dependent on wives, sisters, mothers, and even children for researching, filing, transcribing, and even composing their works.

Amateurs, of course, could and did use archival and manuscript sources in their histories, though if they were women they had great difficulty gaining entry to closely guarded repositories. Increasingly being credentialed by scholars in universities was a requirement for admission to archives, and with many universities not allowing women to matriculate access to official sources became difficult if not impossible for women. Moreover, the gendering of historical work as male took place around the seminar table where fledgling professionals not only gained their training in the scrutiny of documents, but also built a masculine esprit de corps. They saw themselves as citizens of a republic, manly more than anything else, who brought truth to light. Following the model of science, which prized itself on the scrupulous examination of evidence, historians in the academy claimed to put aside all national, religious, and other interests to write a bias-free history. Their aim, in the memorable phrase of Charles Beard, was to fulfill the 'noble dream' of objectivity.

Historians also saw themselves less as wide-ranging intellectuals such as Voltaire or Diderot than as specialists in the history of politics. 'History is past politics and politics present history,' as J. R. Seeley so famously put it, a motto adopted by the Johns Hopkins history department. Professional historians counseled politicians—and continue to do so right to the present. Their histories focused on official institutions such as the Church or on political developments of nation states, kingdoms, and empires. Despite the 'noble dream' of objectivity, many historians were unabashedly nationalistic, promoting and participating in wars when they weren't writing about them. Down to the present heated historical debates occur over the course of politics both past and present. Professional historians in the nineteenth century began the practice of touting the value of political history and denigrating other kinds of history, such as the 'cultural history' of Karl Lamprecht, or the history of society as valueless, even feminine.

As Christopher Meiners wrote in 1792, 'There is almost no science, no fine or practical art, which has not found its historian in the past century'; and the trend continued in the next two centuries. Histories of literature, language, philosophy, art, natural science, the law, economics, and history itself were objects of historical research; and of course religion, or 'sacred history', was continued by biblical scholars like David Strauss and read by the general public. Other varieties of popular history were oral, not only the Western variety of family lore but the more practiced one of oral histories by such professionals as the West African *griots* and *griottes* who served as repositories of memory. Despite the conduct of written scholarship across Africa, these practitioners performed histories and epics and in so doing played a prominent cultural and political role. Often trained by their *griot* parents, *griots* were often called upon by rulers to perform war histories, genealogies, and the lives of past rulers for the edification of the king. They also recited histories for special occasions such as festivals. Queen mothers, who also played an important political role, often held power because of their genealogical knowledge, which allowed for the structuring of useful alliances.

But such alternatives were running against the powerful current of historical science in the universities. Barthold-Georg Niebuhr investigated early Roman history through his 'ballad theory', which found traces of primitive history in poetic sources, and which passed to England through the work of Thomas Arnold, while Theodor Mommsen wrote a distinguished survey of Roman history (which won him a Nobel Prize) and went on to found the great collection of epigraphy. Francois Guizot wrote the history of 'civilization' long before Lucien Febvre and the *Annales* School, as did Jacob Burckhardt and Karl Lamprecht. In England ancient Greek history was represented by George Grote and J. B. Bury; Fustel de Coulanges and others for France; and Guglielmo Ferraro and Gaetano de Sanctis for Italy; P. J. Bloch for the Netherlands. Karl von Savigny wrote a masterful study of Roman law in the Middle Ages. Archaeology and the history of Egypt were pioneered by Heinrich Schliemann and those who followed him, then by Assyriologists and students of cuneiform; and this led to the new field of 'prehistory' surveyed by James Breasted and others.

Many historians competed and collaborated to produce national histories as part of their self-definition and expertise. Leopold von Ranke was the master of national history, having written surveys of England, France, and of course Prussia, not to mention the Papacy and Italian territories, and he was the first to exploit the Venetian archives. He was soon joined by Heinrich von Treitschke and others surveyed by Lord Acton in the *English Historical Review*. In France the 'new history' of the nineteenth century was carried on by Michelet, Ernst Quinet, the Thierry brothers, François Mignet, and others; and in the first issue of the *Revue historique* (1876) Gabriel Monod assembled the entire canon of French national historians from the late Middle Ages to the nineteenth century. In England Macaulay represented the great tradition and was joined by J. R. Froude, W. E. Lecky, William Stubbs, E. A. Freeman, S. R. Gardiner, F. W. Maitland, and many others to write their history, at first in a largely 'Whiggish' fashion, according to Herbert Butterfield. In America George Bancroft and Francis Parkman were the leading national historians, while William Prescott devoted himself to Spain and its conquests in the New World, and J. R. Motley to the Netherlands.

Writing national and dynastic histories from archives had a longer tradition in the West but also in China and elsewhere around the world. A seventeenth-century Chinese scholar argued that the historian and the ruler write each other into existence. As illustration in 1696 the Kangxi emperor ordered his secretaries to compile a detailed narrative of his campaigns to the western lands. In 1682 an office was established to write the history of these feudatories, forming a new genre aimed at memorializing Qing achievements. The Chinese had long associated writing and authority and this historiographical office expressed this aim which began with archival documents and ended with narrative history.

The Yongzheng emperor did not want military expansion but he did care for his place in history to justify previous conquests. The emperor argued that peoples were defined by their culture, not territory or lineage, and that the virtuous would rule the world. He sought continuity with his father Kangxi on such Confucian grounds. In 1763 the Qianlong emperor ordered the compilation of Mongol records from the newly conquered areas, that is from the 'outer Barbarians'. Although there were competing histories offered by Mongols and nomads and, as in Africa, the continuing tradition of oral history, the Qing official historians tried to dominate the field of historical writing of the dynasty and of politics. In the nineteenth century Chinese historians of statecraft built on the earlier historical tradition to support ideas of strong national defense and Qing imperial history was interpreted in this spirit.[12]

Amateur historians picked up the reins dropped by these professionals and in the West they unabashedly continued in the tradition of Voltaire, de Staël, and other eighteenth-century writers by studying home life, the home front during wartime, art and architecture, and an array of other topics found insignificant by the professionals.

Justifications for this 'low' type of history were many: Amateurs usually wrote to earn a living, and their popular following among the public also tainted their work in the eyes of academics. In contrast, Chinese historian Wanyan Yun Zhu (discussed below) worked with female members of her family and did her work in part to honor women and bring the family esteem. By the end of the century professionals began to explore similarly non-political topics: J. R. Green collaborated with his wife Alice Stopford Green to produce a social history of England. Indeed, from the time of Chinese historian Ban Zhao in the first century, who completed the work of her father and brother, to the Strickland sisters of the nineteenth century and Philippe and Primerose Ariès of the twentieth, family teamwork and familial subject matter were often part of the production of history.

Far more experimentally than other professionals, the Vassar historian Lucy Maynard Salmon produced a study of domestic service in 1898. Salmon had studied with Charles Kendall Adams and Woodrow Wilson, writing a prize-winning thesis on the appointing powers of the US President. Her study of servants was blasted by the critics as unworthy of her. Salmon was hardly deterred, however, as she melded the techniques of seminar criticism with an avant-garde choice of topics. For her, history could count train schedules, laundry lists, cookbooks, and other apparent ephemera as sources, and she began writing about topics that have only recently emerged as pivotal to contemporary scholarship: the museum, vernacular landscape, and the changing arrangement of interior space. Although far less avant-garde and more accepted than Salmon, scholars like Mary Bateson and Eileen Power wrote about nunneries not long after the amateur Lina Eckenstein had produced her own study of life in this institution.

In fact, one of the striking features of amateur writing in the nineteenth century was the burgeoning history of women, ranging from studies of their participation in wars and revolutions, their lives as princesses and queens, their working lives, and the history of their work in workshops, agriculture, and factories. In 1831, Chinese scholar Wanyan Yun Zhu published *Precious Record from the Maidens' Chambers*, a history of Chinese women from many walks of life, based in part on a large collection of poetry by women in the past, some of it sent by relatives from around the empire. These were the types of studies that were also picked up by professionals trained in the university.

Late in the century, Susan B. Anthony and Elizabeth Cady Stanton published several volumes of primary documents relating to the suffrage movement that they led. The documents were woven together with a thread of historical narrative. It would take more than a century for these histories of women to find recognition in the academy and even then the history of women's politics would rarely be elevated to the category of political history, categorized instead as social (and therefore lesser) history.

The cultural history that women wrote also entered the academic mainstream late in the nineteenth century, although at first this development was seen as avant-garde and sometimes even dangerous. Karl Lamprecht produced his and became the center of a late nineteenth-century *Methodenstreit* or debate over method.[13] Lamprecht's work was wildly popular outside the German university world, especially in his own Institute, but disdained within it for its break with the professional tradition of seeing the state as the motor force in history. As one twentieth-century US historian described it: 'The idea, which was already expressed by older historians, that the progress of culture and civilisation, that laws, art, science, and industry and the life of the people form by far the most interesting side of history, has been realised in some of the later historical works which the nineteenth century has produced. We have now, at least, the beginnings of a history of the popular masses, of their occupations, habits, and interests.'[14] Amateur historians could not have expressed it better, and even as their works progressed, professionals like James Harvey Robinson in the United States were singing the praises of cultural history if they were not exactly writing it. Argentine historian Ernesto Quesada added criticism of the old method to praise of the new—'the fetish of analytical and microscopical investigation to the most extreme ends', he called the old political history of the pioneering professionals.[15] By the 1930s, Charles Beard, professional historian turned amateur, and his wife Mary Beard were producing best-selling histories of American civilization that included large quantities of cultural history.

Another related blow to the dominance of a definition of history as nation-based and dependent on the doings of the state came with attacks on the definition of the historian as beyond personal trials because of his own disembodiment. Italian historian Benedetto Croce found himself 'wearied of filling my mind with lifeless and disconnected facts' and eager to jettison the 'sound studies' that were said to elevate the historian to professional heights.[16] Likewise, Henri Berr, a leading French scholar, focused on the emptiness of scholarship and the sensuousness of life in general that drove out his desire to work: 'embalmed in mauve lilacs' is how he characterized his feelings.[17] The flight from facts that some of these leading lights took was part of the general trend toward 'modernism' in the arts, philosophy, and human historians, leading to a redefinition by some historians of history and its method. Historians felt themselves fragmented by hard work and unfortunately divorced from 'practical life' by their profession, as R. G. Collingwood expressed it. There was a call that the historian become an *Übermensch*, stretching to cover a wider swath of past experience and to learn methods outside of history, becoming geographer, sociologist, critic of the arts and literature, and many other things. In the twentieth century historians came to have contempt for the 'scissors and paste men' who set the earlier professional standards.[18] Like a true superman, Croce longed to 'soar to the heights'.[19] Historians trained in the strictest historical methods found themselves picking up the latest theories in science—the germ theory and relativism to name just two. As Marc Bloch put it in *Apology for History; or The Historian's Craft*,[20] written while in hiding during the Second World War, the historian was 'not only a biologist and scientist but an explorer, criminal lawyer and tireless amateur'.

This prodigious expansion of professional self-definition and historical expertise came to cover fields and methods that were inconceivable and reprehensible to earlier professionals. Bloch himself relied on aerial photography of fields for remnants of feudal agriculture, while many others followed the lead of such early aesthetes as Henry Adams who professed to jettison the world of highfalutin facts for his 'delight in studying what is...debased and degraded'.[21] The low studies that women were once said to produce, studies of furniture and fireplaces by the likes of Alice Morse Earle or of servants, housewares, and the vernacular landscape of Lucy Maynard Salmon, now became the stuff of professional reputation, of 'superman' status. Even the work of nineteenth-century amateur Vernon Lee, who wrote histories of art based on her psychosomatic theories of art appreciation, found echoes in the calls of those professionals—from Karl Lamprecht to William Langer—who urged more psychological analyses by historians. And indeed 'psychohistory'—Freudian and post-Freudian—became a popular specialty after the Second World War.

In the interstices of the historical field there developed from the late nineteenth century on a commitment to studying the experiences of those outside white privilege. Amateurs determined to uncover the African American past experimented with methodologies, developing for example the ethnographic mindset of pioneers like Zora Neale Hurston. One legacy of these writers in the US case was the rejection of romantic myths about the old South and the equally suspect frontier thesis. However, amateurs and professionals who wrote about the African American or Native American past were roundly attacked before the Second World War. Bernard de Voto slammed Grace Hebard's recovery of Sacajawea's story as mere 'sentimentalization'. Angie Debo met real vitriol, even though today her works are considered classics. In particular *And Still the Waters Run* attacked the neglect of Native Americans in history and the general dismissal, even denigration, of their contributions in those rare instances when the topic came up. Debo saw it as her civic duty to right this inaccurate history and paid for it. Her exposé of the greed behind high-minded justifications for the murderous treatment of Native Americans netted scorn from the likes of de Voto as lies. The tireless research of these earlier pioneers pointed history in new directions, a result of working on the margins and in fact being marginalized by both professional and amateur establishments.[22] It was only after the Second World War and especially with decolonization and the Civil Rights movement that the definition of historians and history would come to include people of color and their history.

It was during the heyday of feminism and reform in the 1960s that women's history re-emerged in its fully professional form with all the bravura that admission to the academy—albeit grudging—entailed. 'Women's history—we invented it,' one historian mythologized some decades later. The professional woman historian in the 1970s was often a product of the feminist movement and feminist motivation of those years, but the themes that drove women's history were similar to those of the nineteenth and early twentieth centuries: social and cultural history, the history of activism, and the history of minorities. By the late twentieth century globalization of the world's economies, institutions, and societies led to increasing diversity among historians, as non-Western findings and non-Western professionals were added to the ranks of women historians. A final development among historians of women was their turn to theories of gender derived in large part from postmodern and anthropological ideas. According to the writing of Joan Scott, who herself employed views of Claude Lévi-Strauss, Jacques Lacan, Michel Foucault, and Jacques Derrida, to name a few, masculinity and femininity were binaries, developed in relationship to one another, and redolent of power. Those historians of women who adopted Scott's and other writing on gender could be historians of men as well as women. Indeed, Scott stated that her use of gender and theory yielded a new 'critical history'. The history of gender also helped the standing of women in the profession because they could be seen as doing important investigations of men, which ranked higher than studying women. The profession in general became more accepting of women in its ranks, though there remained countries where the history of women even in the twenty-first century was barely developed and where women were only scantly recognized as competent.

If modernism yielded a more encompassing and polymorphous form of history early in the twentieth century and allowed men leeway in the pursuit of historical scholarship, the advent of postmodernism, which historians like Scott fostered, brought still further questioning and redefinition of what history and historians were. The decline and eclipse of Marxism and Marxoid schemes again brought linguistic and literary modes into prominence—the 'revenge of literature' Linda Orr calls it[23]—often in the guise of 'postmodernism', which defied chronology in the (still chronological) quest for novelty. To read literary texts as history and history as a literary text became the goal of scholars like Hayden White and Dominick La Capra, and the 'new historicism' attempted in effect to institutionalize this style, as did Lynn Hunt's 'new cultural history' and the more recent 'new philosophy of history', which also advanced under the banner not of 'reality' but—awakening from the 'noble dream'—of 'representation'. This was a belated sign of early twentieth-century arguments that in science there was no object without a subject and the relativism, if not relativity, was built into perception, analysis, and interpretation.

What is remarkable today is the attempt of historians and literary scholars to fulfill not the 'noble dream' of Beard but the superhuman dream of Braudel to achieve the 'history of everything' from microhistory to macrohistory, and the history of the senses and the emotions as well. Postmodernism had not, despite Lyotard's claims, ended the search for 'macronarratives', and the recent investigations in global history had revived this, as well as much older efforts at world history, going back not only to Ranke but also to Herodotus and Diodorus Siculus.

Not only must historians be ready to study everything, superman style, the ranks of historians today have expanded to include public historians who curate for and direct museums, serve as guides in historic sections of cities, and lead preservation efforts. Journalists often write the most well-received (by other journalists) historical accounts, while film-makers have also entered the ranks of historians since the heyday of film. From the 1920s, biographical films such as *Napoleon* have given depth and color to historical figures and their background. Film-makers also seek to solve historical mysteries and present the history of everyday life. On the other hand quantitative history, after its first spurt of popularity, has resumed with a vengeance in the proliferation of databases and bibliographies, which have intensified the old problem of 'information overload'. So have webnet tools like wikipedia and other less questionable computer 'sources', which have rendered representation not only secondary but also tertiary, or more. The electronically adept can thus join the ranks of scholars, moving the identity of the historian of today another step away from the 'source'. All this suggests that historians will remain as varied a group as ever, with a range of practices and sources variously shaping the field in the future as they have in the past.

Part II
Themes and Structures

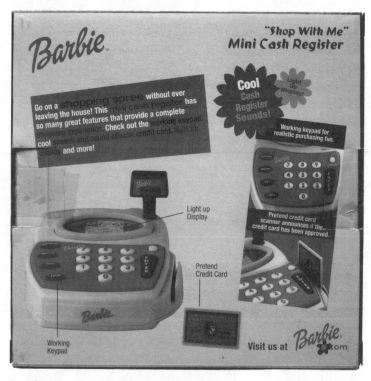

5. KI Designs, Barbie registers, China, 2003. © By permission of the Trustees of the British Museum

5 Commerce

KENNETH POMERANZ

Defining 'commerce' in history

'Commerce' can be surprisingly hard to define. Conventionally, it is the exchange of goods, either for other goods or for money (itself sometimes ambiguous), between parties who are in some economically meaningful sense separate (excluding, for instance, most exchange within families, or wholly owned divisions of the same company). There can be commerce in services, too; this chapter will concentrate on goods, though that distinction can also be blurry.

If defined loosely, commerce appears in numerous places at very early dates—leading Adam Smith, for instance to claim that a universal tendency 'to truck and barter' was as old and fundamental to humans as speaking.[1] Some goods moved very long distances even in the remote past, making it very unlikely that each exchange along the way was between socially connected parties.[2] Amber was traded all around the Baltic Sea as far back as the early Neolithic (c.9,000 years ago); some is found in Egyptian tombs (roughly 2,000 miles away, mostly overland) from 5,000 years ago.[3]

Archaeological evidence from both South Africa (c.75,000 years ago) and West Asia and Eastern Europe (c.35,000 years ago) suggests that 'the appearance of extensive and organized exchange systems for the distribution of both raw materials and decorative prestige items', including evidence of various raw materials found at least 20 km from their place of origin, was roughly contemporaneous with 'the emergence of highly sophisticated and varied forms of both abstract and "naturalistic" art'.[4] (We do not know about simpler messages or even more local goods exchanges.)

But not all exchange of goods is commerce. Some occurs between people who do not have clearly separable economic interests; some may be so powerfully conditioned by coercion as to be more like tribute taking than trade; some may be so shaped by ritual and social propriety that we might best think of religious obligation or reciprocal gift giving. The boundaries of all these categories are vehemently contested, whichever time and place we are discussing.

Exchange must also be distinguished from production. This is sometimes straightforward: Toyota makes cars, your local dealer sells them. Indeed, many scholars (especially but not exclusively, Marxists) place an epochal divide between a long period in which large-scale, profit-seeking, capital investment was mostly confined to commerce, and a more recent period in which production also became a site for capitalist investment and organization. That divide is usually associated with an 'industrial revolution' featuring new technologies which created unprecedented economies of scale in manufacturing, making it far more profitable to buy equipment for production and have wage laborers—who would not own what they produced—operate it than it had been before large-scale manufacturing plants became more efficient than artisanal production.[5]

The generalization that pre-modern commerce often featured economies of scale, but pre-modern production generally did not is crude, but has considerable truth to it. But precisely because of that, vast stretches of history are populated by farmers, artisans, and others who united producer and merchant in one person, greatly complicating any analytical separation of commerce and production. Other mostly modern cases blur the distinction in another way. Today a t-shirt with 'Abercrombie and Fitch', 'New York Yankees', or 'Harvard University' on it may sell for several times the price of the same shirt without words; in that sense the owners of trademarks and logos 'produce' more of the shirt's value than those who transformed cotton into a shirt. Yet common sense still suggests that the textile mill and sewing company are engaged in 'production', and the marketers (who hire no millhands or needle-workers) in 'commerce'. To put it another way, merchants may *produce* markets, rather than just selling to markets that were always there waiting to be satisfied. This is most obvious in our world, which for slightly over a century has had a profession called advertising, but to some extent it has always been true. In fact some of the most interesting questions about commerce in history involve how the demand for and value of certain goods have been created.

There are also questions about how commerce should be sub-divided by geographic, social, and economic scale. 'Formalist' scholars generally see the behavioral principles of classical economics as valid at any scale, though different practical problems may arise; however 'substantivists'—most famously Karl Polanyi, trained as a philosopher, and anthropologists such as Marshall Sahlins, but including many historians and sociologists—have argued for more basic differences.[6] To oversimplify, substantivists see people as always embedded in communities, which condition exchanges at different scales in dif-ferent ways. In the most intimate communities (such as conjugal households) exchange tends to be governed by general reciprocity—members both contribute and consume all sorts of goods and services without keeping accounts, much less expecting them to be balanced out. A second realm of 'balanced reciprocity' governs exchange among members of relatively small-scale communities who expect to have continuing social interaction with each other. People are not indiffer-ent to unequal flows within this sphere in the way that members of a family might be; they expect equity and may bargain hard to secure it. However, they also see the maintenance of the community and cer-tain principles thereof as limiting how much anyone can legitimately press their advantages. Thus, for instance, a person with surplus grain should not be allowed to charge whatever she or he can get during a famine, or sell to outsiders if there are insiders offering a fair price.[7] Debates over to what extent such a 'moral economy' actually existed in particular times and places have been vigorous, and vital to histori-ography on protest, class formation, state building, economic change, and popular *mentalités*.[8]

Consequently, some substantivists argue that the impersonal, *caveat emptor*, exchange that formalists see at every spatial scale was origi-nally restricted to trade with strangers, which mostly occurred across long distances.[9] Thus this view accords certain cases of *long-distance* commerce special historical significance as the cutting edge of a new, more impersonal type of trading that was originally aberrant, but has gradually become normative for much of the world. That many of the societies assigned to anthropologists by the conventional (though now disintegrating) academic division of labor became much more involved in long-distance trade at the same time that they experienced the vio-lent disruptions of colonialism made this association all the stronger.

Some scholars have even insisted that the appearance of impersonal trade marks a distinct 'stage' in the development of society, though the apparent antiquity of some long-distance trade makes this questionable. Certainly the relative amounts of different kinds of exchange have shifted over time, but none is restricted to any particular period;[10] nor is their frequency necessarily correlated with geographic scale.

Other historians also see long-distance trade as requiring a distinct analytical toolkit, but for different reasons. In his massive *Civilization and Capitalism, 15th–18th Centuries*, Fernand Braudel distinguishes three spheres of economic activity: daily life, market economy, and capitalism. 'Daily life' is the sphere of economic activities that rarely enter markets, and in which exchanges are deeply embedded in broader relationships: the various labors by which families or manors produce goods they consume themselves, or the neighbors who 'always' exchange ox labor for eggs. Such relationships may feature sharply opposed interests and even profound exploitation, but what is going on is still non-commercial. 'Market economy', on the other hand, is the sphere of mostly small-scale, mostly local commerce, where anybody who cares to can come bargain: e.g. a local grain, livestock, or cloth market with dozens of buyers and sellers, none of them so privileged (or desperate) as to create lopsided bargaining conditions.[11]

Unlike the substantivist vision, this argument does not assume powerful community norms—it relies instead on competitive haggling—but it reaches some similar results: local markets allow people to meet their needs through commerce, but without large profits being accumulated. For Braudel, most accumulation occurs in the sphere of 'capitalism': exchanges in which merchants have used political connections, credit, violence, information asymmetries, or superior skill to exclude most alternative intermediaries between producers and consumers of some good. Thus, while many people see 'market economy' and 'capitalism' as synonymous, for Braudel they are near-opposites.[12] And while this kind of high-profit intermediation could occur in local commerce—exercised by merchants who bought monopoly rights from the government, or who could seize such rights themselves, for instance[13]—its preferred home ground is long-distance commerce. There, distance, barriers of language and custom, and/or political boundaries preclude face to face contact between buyers and sellers, thus limiting potential intermediaries to those with significant resources, and insuring high profits. As Braudel sees it, it was the profits accumulated in this restricted-access, high-profit area of commerce that financed overseas exploration and colonization, and that required new institutions to make transactions with strangers more predictable.[14] It was also profit from this sphere that was lent to states which wanted to spend future revenues immediately—mostly for warfare—extracting in return rights and privileges for owners of capital that gradually changed the nature of at least some of these states. Later still, Braudel suggests, it was some of this capital which, when new opportunities appeared, abandoned the fluidity and constant reallocation of commercial ventures to become the large-scale fixed capital of technologically modern industry.[15]

Had Braudel lived to see it, he would have found confirmation for his guess that the shift of the largest capital concentrations to industry has not been the final turn of the wheel. For about a century, the largest industrial firms—General Electric, Siemens, Toyota, British Petroleum, etc.—towered over purely commercial firms, but no longer. Wal-Mart and other retailers that make none of the goods they sell are now among the world's largest firms; they often have higher profit margins than their suppliers, and greater power to shape the commodity chains leading to their shelves.[16] Many of the world's leading brands—Apple, Dell, Nike, Liz Claiborne, etc.—own no factories, mines, or farms. (Relatively few people, for instance, have heard of FoxConn, Apple's main supplier, which also makes goods for Motorola, Sony, and other famous firms. Its gross revenues exceed Apple's, though its profits are far smaller.[17]) Many analysts of the industrialization of East Asia—probably the biggest economic story of the last five decades—argue that one key reason why this industrialization has produced very different institutions and effects than the industrialization of Europe and North America is that it has been driven to a great extent by 'backward linkages' from purely commercial (and often foreign) firms.[18] As these cases, and the earlier discussion of branding and the creation of 'value', suggest, commercial capitalism did not simply give birth to industrial capitalism and then become subordinate to it—though some earlier theories expected that.

Thus Braudelians (including adherents of world systems theory) and substantivists both see long-distance and large-scale commerce having a special logic, impact, and historical status. For both, local exchange, even when monetized, often works to reproduce a fairly stable social order, or to change things slowly; long-distance trade is more likely to be destabilizing and transformative. Despite their different explanations of this difference, these two approaches are often woven together, with the Braudelian emphasis on how new relationships between states and capitalists altered formal institutions combined with substantivist arguments about changes in local 'moral economies'.

Neoclassically inclined economic historians, on the other hand, are more likely to see long-distance trade as a scaled-up version of local trade, with greater profits per volume offset (both as a matter of justification and in terms of historical impact) by greater risks and smaller volumes. After all, if all human beings are essentially *homo economicus*, then the longer distances and cross-border nature of some commerce may raise interesting questions about how the obstacles involved are overcome, but there is no particular reason to think long-distance trade requires different modes of analysis or has had a special role in changing economic attitudes.[19] Still, few historians deny that long-distance trade has often had a special relationship to political power, or that the new people, things, and ideas it can introduce to a society have sometimes had enormous social and cultural impact.

Indeed, Adam Smith himself argued that exotic 'baubles'—goods that were unnecessary but appealed strongly to the senses—played a crucial role in motivating elites to shift from maintaining as many human retainers as their income allowed (thus maximizing their influence) to instead acquiring *objects* that struck their fancy. Smith argued that this increased the profitability of lords' estates (getting rid of unneeded laborers/dependents), undermined their political power, and created a new group of poor who were free but had no protectors. The sociologist Werner Sombart later called the same phenomenon the 'objectification of luxury', and likewise saw it as the origin of capitalism.[20] Both Smith and Sombart had Europe in mind, but Smith's argument reads as if it could also be a universal scheme of historical change; the same ambiguity runs through much other stylized history and social theory. While one can find somewhat similar sequences in some non-European societies,[21] they often probably represented reversible movement within a range of possible emphases. Even in Europe, there is no reason to assume that once such a process began, it had to produce modern consumerist society. (Imagine, for instance, what might have happened without the industrial breakthroughs of the last two centuries, which made possible an almost endless supply of new, minutely differentiated products—or without the efforts of dependents who took steps to free themselves.)

Such baubles were, of course, often made nearby. But many were exotic, and/or seemed more desirable because elites elsewhere were known to value them. (In societies with strict sumptuary laws, exotic goods often had a further advantage: being previously unknown, they were not yet assigned or forbidden to any group.) Moreover, products with remote origins were more easily mystified, potentially giving them 'value' far greater than better-known goods with similar functions. Onions and garlic, both readily available throughout medieval and early modern Europe, are actually much better than pepper for preserving meat, but the mysterious origins of pepper led it to be classified as something semi-magical, rather than as an ordinary plant.[22]

Moreover, long-distance contacts often stimulated other major changes. Sogdian merchants brought Buddhism to China; Arab merchants brought Islam to various parts of Africa and South-East Asia, and so on.[23] Going back still further, some prehistorians argue that it was merchants who spread the alphabet around the Mediterranean.[24] So even historians who doubt that trade with strangers imparted a new economic logic to previously self-contained societies still have reasons to give long-distance commerce far more historical weight than its share in total exchange might seem to warrant. The rest of this chapter will do so as well.

Understanding the long-run growth of commerce

Quantities and measurement

Measuring and explaining the changing extent of commercial activities is quite different from studying their impact on other historical questions—and almost as uncertain, especially for remote times and places. It is a reasonable generalization—though with many exceptions—that it is easier to make accurate measurements as we move closer to the present; easier for cross-border trade (which states usually monitored and/or taxed, leaving archival traces) than for trade that remained within borders or occurred where states' territorial control was weak; easier for valuable than cheap goods (since they are more worth keeping precise track of); and easier for legal trade than for the massive smuggling that we find throughout history. Yet even the gold transfers among European states in the 1920s and 1930s cannot be fully reconstructed: the total of all reported exports does not match the total of all reported imports.[25] For other times and places, the challenges are often far greater; but because the issues tend to be technical and specific to particular cases (the problems with seventeenth-century Dutch East India Company records, those with nineteenth-century San Francisco port records, eleventh- to thirteenth-century merchant correspondence found in a Cairo synagogue, or eighteenth-century Huizhou (China) account books) we will omit them here. Still, enough reasonably reliable data exist to support some useful generalizations.

'International' trade is not exactly what we are looking for—especially not before national states became predominant. Trade from Belgium to the Netherlands crosses a national border, but is not long-distance: trade from Maine to California or Sichuan to Heilongjiang is long-distance but not international. But cross-border trade gets counted, and offers a rough proxy for the scale of long-distance trade, at least in recent centuries.

According to Angus Maddison, the (inflation-adjusted) value of exported goods grew roughly 115 times (11,500 per cent) between 1870 and 1998.[26] (Annual growth since then has probably been even faster.[27]) This reflected about 300 per cent growth in 1870–1913; modest growth (perhaps 40 per cent) from 1913 to 1950; 470 per cent growth circa 1950–73; and just under 350 per cent 1973–98. As a percentage of global GDP (an even more uncertain number) merchandise exports were not much bigger in 1950 (5.5 per cent) than in 1870 (4.6 per cent), but reached 10.2 per cent by 1973 and 17.2 per cent by 1998.[28] Consequently, cross-border trade matters much more today, to more economies, than it did 100 or even 25 years ago: not that surprising since fewer and fewer goods are too bulky to be worth shipping long distances, and the wages that make up much of the production cost of many goods differ more across countries than ever before. If we also counted trade in services, which was tiny a century ago and has grown rapidly recently, the accelerating trend would be even stronger. Meanwhile, international migration has not grown nearly as much: the percentage of the world's people living outside their country of birth is only very slightly higher today than in 1913.[29] This difference has important implications for how the relative bargaining power of labor and capital, the nature of cultural change, and other large issues may differ between today's 'globalization' and that of 1870–1914. With goods moving more easily than workers—and, in recent decades, capital moving much more easily than either—workers are likely to have less bargaining power. That more of the songs, stories, etc. moving around the world today move as goods, rather than accompanying migrants, than a century ago probably also creates significant intertemporal differences, though these are harder to gauge.

Before c.1800, growth had to be much slower; production grew slowly before the mid-nineteenth century and transport technologies changed even more slowly. For most inexpensive goods, long-distance trade only made sense if the destination price was *much* higher than the production price. In the 1600s, taking a cask of wine from Beaune to Paris (about 300 km) cost 2.5 to 3 times the value of the wine.[30] For a cheaper good in rougher country, the costs were prohibitive: one Chinese source says the price of coal quintupled if it moved overland 50 km.[31] The contrast with luxuries like caravanned silk, discussed below, or with some water-borne trade, was stark. (And in a world where few people lived concentrated in cities, cheap waterways had limited reach; the few overland miles from a dock to a rural market often cost more than hundreds of riverine miles to that dock.) So despite some exceptions—the massive rice and timber for cloth trade along the Yangzi River, for instance—most ordinary goods did not travel far. Given the handicap this imposed on bulky imports, those that did well were often goods that the importing area could not produce in any quantity: the ancient Phoenicians, for instance sent cedars for construction and boat building to the almost treeless Nile Delta and received grain their rocky homeland could not grow.[32] Such trade does not directly undercut many local producers, and so may broaden the importing society's technical and cultural options without very much social disruption.

Meanwhile most Europeans and East Asians—relatively well-studied populations who probably had the world's highest per capita incomes circa 1750[33]—still spent over half their incomes on bulky, low-cost basic foodstuffs.[34] Thus the percentage of their consumption that came from afar must have generally been quite low. For most of them, it is *very* unlikely that it had even doubled since Roman times.[35] Of course, many basic goods came from local markets, and scattered but plentiful data suggests a slow, non-linear, but unmistakable long-term growth in such markets over the few centuries before 1800. But for a long time, growth in long-distance commerce mostly depended on luxury trades. In early modern times, as we will see, much of that growth came from goods that were previously little known in their destination markets, or even completely unknown. They began as luxuries, but became much more affordable once the consuming societies either produced them at home (as with tobacco in much of Asia, or porcelain in Europe) or gained power over remote producing areas (as Europeans did in the Americas and island South-East Asia).

The last quantitative measurement issue we will consider is market integration, which can have profound effects on members of trading societies, even if they themselves do not buy or sell the traded goods. But measuring it is complicated.

To understand market integration historically, it may be easiest to work backwards from today's world. A great many standardized goods are used similarly in many places, can be shipped for a small percentage of their final price, and do not face significant legal obstacles (high tariffs, embargoes, etc.) to their movement. Those goods obey what economists call 'the law of one price': the price difference between, say, crude oil in Yokohama and Rotterdam cannot exceed the cost of moving oil between them. If it did, it would be profitable to move oil one way or the other, until this situation disappears (which, with electronic trading, can happen in seconds). For this good, the two cities are part of one integrated market, not two separate, local ones; this has many consequences. An integrated grain market including places A, B, C, and D means that a harvest failure in A causes price increases in all four places, but famine in none; separate markets could mean desperate hunger in A with absolutely no effect in B, C, and D. Integration also means that if the cost of producing some good in A rises, residents can buy imported substitutes, and producers from A will lose business; this creates very different constraints on governments, workers, entrepreneurs, and others than if markets were separate. At the extreme, very strong market integration might force business practices, government policies, and even social systems to converge, as some people argue contemporary globalization does.

Likewise, one can speak of markets for two goods being integrated—if enough people can switch between beef and pork as their relative prices shift, they become part of an integrated market for a more abstract commodity 'meat'. The two goods need not have the same price or (perceived) quality; there need only be enough people willing and able to switch that it limits *how far* prices can diverge. Likewise, the consequences of integration are similar. If beef prices soar, some people switch to pork until beef falls. By contrast, if the price of insulin soars, consumers cannot switch to aspirin; some would suffer horribly, while aspirin buyers would be unaffected.

But many markets remain weakly integrated, even between the world's most 'globalized' cities. This is especially true for many services—few people will go from London to Delhi for a haircut, no matter how much cheaper it is—but it is also true for many goods. Shipping milk, for instance, is still expensive enough that a sudden shortage in New York will not induce shipments from Dallas, much less São Paulo. Other markets are not strongly integrated because of government policies (e.g. high tariffs), tastes, or other factors. As I write this, world prices for the major food grains—rice, wheat, and corn—are up more than 150 per cent over the last two years, causing severe and widespread hardships. Yet the price, output, and international trade volume for fresh potatoes—nutritionally speaking, a good, cheap, substitute for grains—have changed only slightly.[36]

Far more markets used to be weakly integrated even across fairly short distances, and fewer goods were sufficiently standardized and/or widely known to be mutually substitutable. Given the many implications of having more (or less) integrated markets, comparing market integration across different times and places can be very revealing.

One method for doing so looks at trends in price differences. In a famous study, Braudel and Spooner showed that between 1450 and 1750, grain prices in grain-importing Western Europe moved much closer to those in grain-exporting Poland: while the largest price differential was 7:1 *c.*1450, it was down to 2:1 *c.*1750.[37] By contrast, prices for pepper and various spices in South-East Asian and European ports barely converged *c.*1580–1800, despite major improvements in seafaring[38]—strongly suggesting that the often-violent competition among Europeans seeking to monopolize Asian–European trade did not greatly constrain the mark-ups (and taxes) assessed on pepper and spices, or make these markets much more integrated than when they had been mediated by long chains of Muslim and Venetian merchants.

But converging prices alone do not distinguish between, say, a one-time, technology-induced fall in shipping costs which a middleman chose to pass along to his customers, and institutional developments which leave middlemen no choice but to pass along all such savings or be undercut by competitors. Often, then, a better measurement of true market integration is the correlation between price *movements*: the degree to which prices in different markets (or of different goods) move up and down in sync with each other.[39]

Unfortunately, we often lack the data needed for these measurements. But where they are available, they suggest important patterns.

Prior to about 1830, inter-continental market integration was very limited—even between major ports[40]—although the volumes of spices, precious metals, porcelain, sugar, tobacco, slaves, and cloth traded soared, and shipping costs on some inter-continental routes fell dramatically even before steam. The eighteenth-century North Atlantic saw particularly large savings: as the British Navy reduced piracy, insurance rates nosedived, and merchant ships that no longer expected to face armed raiders could use far smaller crews, saving on wages and liberating space for cargo. The sixteenth- to seventeenth-century fall in shipping costs for Baltic grain had also depended on changes that reduced merchants' security costs.[41]

Piggy-backing on growing volumes of long-distance commerce were substantial transfers of ideas; faiths; tastes; technologies; plant, animal and germ species; weapons; and so on. The enormous consequences of these movements justify the arguments of scholars who see c.1400–1800 as an era of 'proto-globalization'[42] in the loose sense of a world with much more frequent and influential intercontinental connections. But insofar as 'globalization' refers to what is central in debates over *contemporary* political economy—the strait jacket allegedly imposed by tightly integrated markets on governments, labor movements, environmentalists, and others whose preferred policies might raise costs for local businesses—we will find few examples or even 'proto' examples in this earlier period.[43]

Early modern market integration was more marked on regional scales, but still very spotty. Nor was it necessarily further advanced in

Europe, often imagined as the homeland of open, competitive markets. A study of eighteenth-century grain markets shows that market integration across vast expanses of China—areas larger and more populous than any European country—was better integrated than any in continental Europe, and almost as integrated as those in the much smaller space of England. Only after railroads were built did several national markets in Europe clearly surpass Chinese levels of integration.[44] And since numerous tariffs and other barriers to cross-border trade remained, high levels of integration for most trans-national European markets came much later still.

Explaining growth

How do we explain the magnitude and timing of commercial growth? One family of explanations emphasizes a long succession of technological changes, especially in transportation: from the wheel and the domestication of pack animals to the railroad, refrigerated ship, and internet. Along with these dramatic breakthroughs, subtler changes made over long periods also had important effects. A study of *amphorae* in which wine was shipped to Rome, for instance, shows that decade by decade, their walls grew thinner and lighter, indicating a slow but steady trimming of transport costs.[45]

Nonetheless, the most dramatic changes belong to modern times, with the harnessing of fossil fuels (especially revolutionary in overland transport) and electricity (especially for communications). In the late nineteenth century, the cost of transatlantic shipping fell by one-half to two-thirds in forty years; shipping rice from Burma to Europe went from costing 74 per cent as much as the rice to 18 per cent; cotton, which cost 63 per cent more in Liverpool than Alexandria *c.*1840, cost only 5 per cent more *c.*1895.[46] In 1900, tiny Delaware and New Jersey were two of the four biggest US states for agricultural output (along with New York and Pennsylvania), because only those close to big East Coast cities could tap their lucrative fruit and vegetable markets.[47] Within a few decades, though, railways helped make California dominant; today Chile, South Africa, and New Zealand sell fresh fruit to northern hemisphere consumers.

Also vital—and often forgotten—has been a gradual and far from linear decline in the costs of protecting goods in transit. Protection costs for long-distance trade have often been even more important than those of physical carriage—especially where pre-railroad overland routes took expensive goods across sparsely populated areas, as on the Central Asian Silk Roads and trans-Saharan gold-for-salt routes. Crossing land not continually occupied, the caravans' animals could eat freely whatever grass they found, making the energy for transportation cheap. But the same low population density (and slow speeds) made travelers vulnerable, and whatever government there was often had few revenue sources aside from the caravans. Thus in 1600, the physical cost of moving silk from Isfahan to Aleppo was only 4–5 per cent of its acquisition cost (just over 2 per cent of the Aleppo price), but payments to officials along the way cost considerably more. One merchant's journal lists customs payments between Isfahan to Gombroon (entirely within one empire) that were five times the physical transport costs.[48] Adding the losses from caravans that never arrived, protection costs could exceed transport costs per se by large multiples even in stable times; when governments became particularly ineffective and/or predatory, they could become prohibitive. (When such problems caused luxury traders to avoid a territory, government revenue declined, often further worsening insecurity, in a downward spiral; this is yet another reason why long-distance trade has often played a disproportionate historical role. Local trade was more likely to be in bulky necessities that were less tempting to steal, bore lighter taxes—especially compared to its physical transport costs—and had fewer short-term options for changing its routes.)

Seaborne protection costs could also dwarf actual costs of carriage. About 20 per cent of sixteenth-century Portuguese shipments to Europe never arrived; as warfare intensified late in the century, that number approached 50 per cent.[49] Such high and fluctuating protection costs are one major reason why Europeans operating across the Indian Ocean took centuries to defeat caravan traders, finally triumphing when strong navies limited piracy while the breakdown of major land-based empires made overland security costs soar.

Long-distance commerce also involved other transaction costs—for gathering information about distant markets, specifying and enforcing contracts between people who might meet only once and have different ideas about responsibility for unexpected problems, etc. The changing mechanisms for minimizing these costs have spawned a large, contentious, literature.

Early studies of these issues emphasized state activities, and made the evolution of Western European states normative. Douglass North's very influential work argued that until states began vigorously enforcing unambiguous Western-style private property rights and commercial contracts (at little cost to the transacting parties), what would otherwise have been profitable transactions were too risky to complete, specialization (which requires interdependence) was inhibited, and growth lagged.[50] While North's argument was not particularly focused on long-distance trade, the issues it highlights loom especially in such transactions. In North's model, the main force for change is a selective pressure on states themselves: it predicts that since states which preside over larger economies will have more revenue with which to pursue inter-state competition, history will gradually select for regimes that foster free markets, and trade will grow apace.[51]

But even if one accepts this teleology as having some validity over the very long haul, it is hardly sufficient to explain the workings of trade—or its halting but real expansion—over the many centuries and vast areas where there was very little resembling a liberal state. Consequently, attention has increasingly focused on how merchants themselves created and enforced reasonably reliable rules for long-distance trade.

Many such analyses have focused on one of several 'ethnic' minorities (an unstable term in its own right—see Chapter 11) which organized a disproportionate amount of long-distance trade, often dealing preferentially, though not exclusively, with fellow group members: Armenians, Jews, Gujaratis, Hokkienese, Genoese, and so on. (Conversely, patterns of exchange sometimes created or changed ethic boundaries.) These groups (with a few exceptions) rarely had a state they could rely on for help, much less one with a long reach. So how did they control the risks of receiving defective goods, or of their own overseas agents mis-reporting a sale price and pocketing the difference?

In many ways, of course. Traveling merchants sometimes relied on local justice, or on courts that various empires (especially Muslim ones) had 'minority' communities establish for themselves. In some particularly interesting cases, no sovereign formally delegated power to ethnic communities, but merchant diasporas self-organized to enforce commercial rules anyway. (It is important to note here that kinship or shared ethnicity alone do not automatically make trading partners reliable.) Maghribi Jewish merchants from Spain to India, for instance, apparently agreed that if any of them cheated another who had entrusted him with business, the entire group would boycott the cheater until he made restitution.[52] Armenian merchants from New Julfa (Persia), spread across the seventeenth-century world from Amsterdam to Manila, agreed to blacklist any member who acted dishonestly when employed by another New Julfan. Ad hoc on-site assemblies could issue judgments (generally relying on an orally transmitted code) which would, if necessary, be reviewed and executed by a central assembly in New Julfa. Non-mercantile networks, such as the Armenian Church, sometimes helped transmit information about merchant behavior, but judgment and enforcement seem to have usually been handled by merchants themselves.[53] Other examples appear in many locations.[54] Furthermore, contrary to 'stage' theories which see such institutions as imperfect substitutes for a state enforcing modern commercial law,[55] they function even in the heartlands of contemporary capitalism: orthodox Jewish diamond merchants in New York are a striking example.[56] But they work only within bounded groups.

Fair dealing was sometimes enforced on trading partners from *outside* a particular trade diaspora through collective economic punishment. In medieval Europe, a Florentine merchant could (for instance) complain about a Pisan to Florentine authorities; if they agreed he had been wronged, they would present the complaint to their Pisan counterparts. If the Pisans did not make their member pay up, the Florentines might confiscate the goods of *any* Pisan merchant they could get their hands on (up to the amount of the debt) and/or boycott all future trade with Pisans. (The authorities in question might be explicitly licensed by the state or not.) Since members of a group became de facto guarantors of their colleagues, the system made membership potentially quite costly, but it provided security that facilitated trade; and by making trade with affiliated merchants much safer than trading with unaffiliated ones, it gave group members a compensating competitive advantage.[57] The Maghribi or New Julfan systems helped insiders work with each other and get information about *individuals* that protected against being cheated; the medieval European community responsibility system meant that an outsider who could verify a potential partner's *identity* (as, e.g. a Florentine) did not need to discover his personal reputation.

Such mechanisms could potentially regulate a much more open and varied commercial world than those that only enforced within-group discipline; but they developed problems as trade volumes grew. With enough transactions, even a small percentage of unresolved disputes would lead to many boycott and confiscation orders being in force at any given moment; and since such orders would freeze trade between the groups, even when that trade far exceeded the amount in dispute, this kind of system could easily become wildly expensive.[58] But such institutions did play a significant regulatory role for many years. Avner Greif has suggested that collective responsibility nurtured commercial growth that eventually made collective responsibility unworkable, thus helping to create demand for the modern Western state; he thus reverses North's emphasis on improved state performance as the precondition for commercial expansion.[59]

All these systems raise important questions about the relative roles of cultural values, individual economic incentives, coercion, and non-commercial social consequences (e.g. exclusion from religious activities or marriage networks) in inducing cooperation when uncooperative behavior (e.g. breaking a boycott) might have been profitable. The answers—which naturally vary across cases—matter both for history and for analyzing the effects of legal systems and other institutions on contemporary economies.

Unfortunately, informal enforcement mechanisms leave us few documents to examine: until quite recently, many Armenian historians were not convinced that New Julfa's Assembly of Merchants even existed.[60] Moreover, relations between institutions of, by, and for merchants, and ones for people from a certain place more generally (with other possible sanctions and sources of cohesion), can be blurry. Many Chinese merchant guilds, for instance, began as associations of (for instance) people from Huizhou residing in Beijing, including officials, scholars, and others—and though some were eventually transformed into pure occupational organizations, others remained hybrids.[61] Greif, who has worked on medieval merchants in Europe, North Africa, and the Middle East, argues that on both sides of the Mediterranean, institutions were established that regulated trade without depending on extra-economic social sanctions or bonds.[62] But these 'coalitions' differed: those formed within the Muslim world were closed, non-anonymous, groups that built upon extended kinship, while European coalitions relied more on individualistic models of bilateral contract and the creation of voluntary, self-governing corporations. The latter system, he argues, was perhaps less efficient in the short run,[63] but began an institutional evolution that eventually led Europe to more open and efficient institutions.

Unlike many economic models, this formulation makes culture matter—and Greif makes a plausible case that several observed differences in how medieval Muslims and Christians handled partnership, agency relations, and other aspects of long-distance commerce are consistent with a single original difference between more and less communal solidarity. But it makes culture matter *only* as an initial condition shaping institutions for policing business dealings; once these institutions exist, the argument has them function and evolve through the interplay of culture-free profit-seeking strategies. (This very parsimonious invocation of culture is part of what makes this model more appealing to many social scientists than arguments in which culture *continually* complicates the *construction* of interests.) These claims can probably never be proved, especially given the limited evidence available; my own sense is that the reciprocal conversions of economic, social, and cultural capital in every society are such that truly effective privately generated enforcement in which non-commercial networks and sanctions play no ongoing role must be rare. But the role of various extra-economic props in creating the trust needed for commerce clearly varies in type and degree across time and space—and debates stimulated by Greif's hypotheses have generated a great deal of interesting research on particular cases.

Beyond counting: commerce, society, and culture

The enormous expansion of commerce and division of labor has helped bring a large minority of the world's population vastly more material goods than was previously possible. Controversy remains, however, over whether this is simply improved fulfillment of material desires which are naturally infinite or whether much stronger desires to consume have been a necessary concomitant of commercialization and economic growth. Economists tend to take the former view, anthropologists the latter; historians and sociologists scatter across the spectrum. The history of early modern commerce plays a special role in these debates.

One striking fact about the long-distance trade boom of 1500–1850 is that the major commodities—sugar, tobacco, tea, coffee, cocoa, opium, pepper and spices, silk, and silver—were not basic necessities, nor remained luxuries; while they all began as prestige goods, all (except perhaps silk) became items used by many ordinary people in various societies. Most of them are at least mildly addictive, and were gradually incorporated into basic rituals of domesticity and/or hospitality even among fairly poor people. (Opium, which was usually illegal, never became so ordinary. But even it became normal in certain Chinese social circles—and by one accounting, 'the world's most valuable single commodity trade of the 19th century'.[64]) In a landmark study of sugar, Sidney Mintz has argued that the history of these 'drug foods' tells us a great deal about capitalism in general.

Mintz notes that desire for sugar has a physiological basis, but he emphasizes social reasons why sugar imports soared in early modern Europe. (English consumption was almost nil in 1500, and 90 pounds per person circa 1900.) Its early use as a luxury exchanged among elites, he argues, marked it as a good which could confer status, and made it something that socially ambitious people might show off on special occasions (holidays, weddings) long before it was cheap enough to consume every day. Moreover, it was something that no European family could produce for itself: thus, like other 'tropical groceries' and little luxuries, it could only be acquired by working for cash.[65] Shared consumption of these market-derived working-class luxuries became important to plebeian sociability—and thus, paradoxically, important to the formation of lower-class communities that often opposed the further advance of capitalism.[66] As prices for these goods fell—and as they were promoted by various parties with interests in this commerce[67]—they became increasingly common, and perceived as 'necessities', which any respectable family should have. In England, tea with sugar became a cheap stimulant that could be brewed quickly, helping wage workers stay alert through long working days marked by a much more rigorous time-discipline than had been usual in earlier times. And by the late nineteenth century, sugar became a cheap source of calories for poorer Britons which nonetheless provided some variety in a diet still largely dominated by starches. (Mintz emphasizes the extremely exploitative labor conditions on sugar plantations in explaining this price decline. Without in the least doubting that, one might add that the price of moving sugar from Java to Amsterdam fell by over half just between 1870 and 1914.[68])

Thus Mintz sees in sugar—and tobacco, tea, etc.—something new and extremely important: goods which were not necessities, but which people could be induced to continue working for after they had earned enough to meet their basic biological needs. This made them essential steps toward modern consumerism and modern work culture.

Mintz's work owes much to Marx, and to structuralist anthropologies of food;[69] yet it also offers a plebeian echo to Smith's 'bauble' theory of elite social transformations. For Smith, medieval elites tended to turn surplus grain received from tenants into hospitality and dependents, and thus power. But as unnecessary but attractive 'baubles' replaced large retinues as markers of elite status, the pursuit of money with which to buy such goods made elites less willing to pay for more workers than they needed, while pushing stricter discipline on their remaining workers. Mintz's complement to this story begins with non-elites who may have had low material living standards, but often had quite a bit of leisure; as they began to imitate elite consumption of 'drug foods' and other little luxuries, they had to turn what had once been 'extra' time into the focused labor that procured their version of status-marking 'baubles'.

These more general (and greatly oversimplified) inferences from Mintz's case of sugar are supported by some basic facts about early modern Europe (which, I would argue, have close analogues in China and Japan):

1. Average work hours per person seem to have increased very significantly between about 1450 and sometime in the nineteenth century.[70]
2. The amount of starchy calories (the most basic necessity of all) that a day's labor could buy nosedived in the sixteenth century, and generally did not return to 1450 levels until well into the industrial era.[71]
3. Despite (2), death inventories suggest that ordinary north-west Europeans slowly but steadily accumulated more possessions

across the early modern period, made possible by the increased working hours of (1).[72]

These and other facts suggest that late medieval Europeans ate as well as their eighteenth-century descendants with fewer hours of labor, and 'consumed' more of their remaining time as leisure, and less as purchased goods, than their descendants did. This does not seal the case for Mintz's explanation of how these changes occurred. Changing demography (younger marriage and thus larger families to feed, plus worsening labor/land ratios), relative prices (real cloth prices, for instance, declined considerably while real food prices rose), and religiously inspired changes in the 'work ethic' are other possible factors.[73] There are also important definitional and evidentiary ambiguities regarding 'leisure'.[74] But it seems plausible that newly available goods helped create the patterns of worker and consumer behavior that some now call the 'industrious revolution',[75] and see as a foundation of the modern world. Not all these new goods were imports, by any means, but it seems logical that formerly unobtainable goods with falling prices would play an important role in such a story.

Commerce also made itself felt in other ways. That newly wealthy merchants became important patrons of the arts, scholarship, and high culture generally is a familiar story in every society where such merchants appeared. But meanwhile, growing involvement with markets—and particularly with long-distance markets, which could fluctuate for reasons invisible to most people (e.g. a crop failure hundreds of miles away), also left its mark on early modern popular culture. Some very interesting examples, reflecting profound ambivalence about commercialization, come from China's Lower Yangzi Valley—one of the first places in the world where the livelihood of a large percentage of a large population was strongly affected by long-distance trade.[76] A survey of the relationship of commerce and popular religion in this area may suggest some of the complexities, both there and elsewhere.

During the Song dynasty (960–1276), unprecedented commercialization in this region was accompanied by striking shifts in popular religion. Popular gods became increasingly anthropomorphic, while human–animal hybrids and gods of natural phenomena (rivers, diseases, etc.) with no other bodily form declined. Stories and rituals in which ordinary people bargained with deities—making an offering while seeking a specific favor, or promising a future offering contingent on some favor—also became more common. More people seem to have approached deities without clerical mediation or with the aid of religious specialists that they chose to hire (rather than giving to the local temple and having them make the ritual choices). These phenomena have convinced some scholars that people experienced commercialization as allowing them a new efficacy, which was mirrored in their relations with the cosmos; a few even argue that negotiating to make offerings in return for concrete future assistance from a god represents a deeply held positive view of investment for profit, unlike the view encountered in many cultures that capitalist growth is 'unnatural'.[77]

Yet closer inspection makes the story more complex. At the same time that more people were bargaining directly with supernatural beings, we also find the torments of hell depicted in far greater detail than before; moreover the tortures people suffered there were often described as payments on a debt incurred through undeserved good fortune in this world.[78] Slightly later, we see the emergence of Wutong, a god of wealth who epitomizes many popular anxieties about commerce.

Wutong was most definitely a god of commerce and money, rather than of wealth in general—he did not make crops grow, for instance, but provided adherents with silver and gold directly, or tells them how to make huge profits in trade. Often this involved capitalizing on freakish events. In one relatively benign example, he told a devotee to buy up umbrellas although the rainy season is over; a huge storm follows, bringing windfall profits for disregarding the natural order. More importantly, stories about Wutong almost always show him demanding more and more in return for his favors—this usually included exclusive sexual access to a man's wife and/or daughter (often manifested as possession, sickness, and/or death for the woman), increasingly lavish sacrifices, and morally degrading forms of worship, culminating in complete ruin and post-mortem agonies for the family that he had briefly made rich.

Yet despite this grim pattern—and efforts at suppression by the state—Wutong worship spread very widely in the lower Yangzi, especially its towns, probably peaking in the sixteenth–seventeenth centuries. This was a period of especially rapid commercialization in the

Lower Yangzi.[79] But it was also a period of exceptionally volatile markets: partly due to political instability which frequently interrupted long-distance trade and partly because clumsy government monetary policies and huge influxes of silver (first from Japan, then from the Americas) made prices fluctuate wildly. This god of wealth/commerce, then, seems more like a demonic force to be placated than a constructive one to be celebrated.

During the eighteenth century, amidst much more stable markets, Wutong was gradually replaced by the god of wealth familiar in Chinese communities around the world today: a basically beneficent figure and pillar of order.[80] The newer god of wealth generally helps his devotees make steady, moderate, profits rather than a sudden killing, and makes no excessive or immoral demands upon them. Yet wealth that one gains with his help is still seen as a loan from an otherworldly capital stock, which the borrower must repay or face serious consequences. In 1970s Taiwan, people could take home offerings that had been left in certain temples for a god, asking for a blessing that would make their capital especially productive (in some cases this was accompanied by an actual loan); but they had to return a larger offering the next year, with the 'interest' determined by a dice throw, or face both the failure of their venture and public embarrassment (the names of defaulters are posted in the temple). The procedures resemble those of rotating credit societies—once a major source of capital in China, Taiwan, and many other places and still quite significant among certain groups today.[81]

Many contemporary Taiwanese (and, to some extent, mainland) commercial practices also reflect a preference for a mixture of instrumental and affective ties over purely arm's-length transactions. Many globally successful sectors consist of networks of small firms rather than a few big ones; while the component firms compete fiercely for large orders, the winner usually sub-contracts parts of the resulting work to other network members, who repeatedly switch roles from contractor to sub-contractor. Entrepreneurs in these networks say that they feel compelled to make some investment in any new firm formed by a network member, and do not create vertically integrated firms (which would eliminate sub-contracting) because that would make enemies. Interviewees often explain that individual firms (usually family-run) are governed by filial piety (*xiao*) and the network by 'human feelings' (*renqing*);[82] relations with outsiders, however, can be purely instrumental, and the same business people often operate quite differently (e.g. creating vertically integrated companies) when they invest abroad.[83] Even, then, in a capitalist society which has seen enormous growth with relative equity, and in which small-scale commercial entrepreneurship is often seen as a more secure though no more lucrative option than wage labor (rather than as a gamble on hitting it big),[84] profits gained from exchange rather than production are arguably still seen as slightly magical, and need to be re-socialized through ritual to become fully acceptable. Moreover, we see business groups that are undeniably successful in the modern global economy calling on the full range of exchange modalities cited by substantivists, rather than a purely 'capitalist' logic. Formalists might argue that this merely reflects what the participants *think* they are doing, but so far nobody has successfully analyzed these activities without reference to people's stated intentions.

This is, of course, a superficial sketch of just some attempts to understand and live with commerce and the changes it has wrought within what might be crudely considered one culture—and just as it shows considerable change over time, there are also vast differences across space. Yet certain responses surface repeatedly (albeit not universally) in widely divergent settings. (For instance, a 1990 survey of economic attitudes among New Yorkers and Muscovites—asking about the fairness of practices such as charging more for flowers on holidays—found remarkably similar attitudes, despite very different economic experiences.[85]) The ambivalence evident in these Chinese stories reflects anxieties as contemporary as a small shop-owner suddenly competing with a Wal-Mart, hopes as old as those that brought amber to the tombs of Pharoahs, and a history in which commercial exchange—which, by giving both sides something they want, might seem to promote the status quo—has been both a consequence and source of ceaseless change.

6. Toy gun carved of wood; two rectangles of wood nailed together at right angles; black rubber band wrapped around length of barrel of gun; handle painted yellow, barrel painted red. Made in Papantla by Totonac. © By permission of the Trustees of the British Museum

6 Power

CHRISTOPHER CLARK

Power is at once the most ubiquitous and the most elusive theme of historical writing. Questions of power lie at the centre of most historical narratives, but the concept is rarely interrogated or analysed as an autonomous category. There are studies that aim to clarify the differences between various types of power, but they tend to be written by sociologists or political scientists rather than historians and no consensus on definitions has been reached.[1] Even in the field of political and diplomatic history, pre-eminently concerned with the exercise of power, the term is almost always deployed as a transparent signifier whose meaning requires no separate elucidation. By contrast with 'gender' and 'culture', 'power' has never provided the focal point for the kind of sub-disciplinary formation that might have licensed a concerted theoretical and comparative engagement with the problem of power across the full spectrum of historical practice.

Why is this so? The reason may lie partly in the nature of power itself. It is, as one medieval historian has put it, 'so conceptually vast and so inscrutably inflated, that one instinctively seeks to pluralise the word'.[2] 'Power' is not an identity that can be said to inhere in groups or individuals; rather it expresses a relational state of affairs. The capacity of a powerful person or organization to secure compliance may be sustained through the threat or actual exercise of violence, through the invocation of norms traditional or otherwise, through persuasion, reward, protection, or by other means contingent upon the particularities of the specific social and political constellation. Power is thus neither a substantive entity, nor an institution, nor even a possession, but rather an attribute of the relationships within which it is exercised. It was in recognition of this feature of the phenomenon that Michel Foucault, the most influential post-war theorist on power, refused to treat it under a separate rubric, choosing instead to embed his reflections in an analysis of specific institutional and disciplinary contexts and practices.[3]

From this flows the difficulty of power as an object of synoptic historical contemplation, for the relationships within which it makes itself felt are as varied as the entire field of human experience. As a purely relational concept, it is often difficult to localize. The perennial debates that are fought across academic history over the extent of the power wielded by specific sovereigns and regimes suggest a persistent uncertainty about how and where power arises and resides in complex systems and whether its exercise depends more upon coercion or the consent of those over whom power is supposedly wielded. The bundling of meanings within the term 'power' is a further difficulty. The English word has at least three German synonyms: 'Gewalt', with its strong connotations of violence or force, denotes power in its most coercive form; 'Herrschaft' refers to the personal dominion exercised by a feudal lord, monarch, or dictatorial executive; and 'Macht'—at once a more functional and a more abstract term—denotes the capacity of a powerful individual or entity to make decisions or achieve outcomes. 'Power' and 'influence', though used interchangeably, are not necessarily synonymous, hence what the international relations theorist Robert Keohane called 'the cruel and ridiculous paradox' of the 'influence of small allies'.[4] The boundaries between power and authority are often blurred, despite the long European tradition of theorizing the relationship between secular and priestly authority in terms of the distinction between *potestas* and *auctoritas*. Making sense of power has thus often involved disentangling the different kinds of asset that may be invoked to sustain it. To complicate matters further, the relationship—especially in Europe—between discourses of power and its actual practice has always been far from straightforward.

This chapter therefore makes no attempt to chart chronologically the evolution of historical 'power studies' (since no such thing exists). Nor does it categorize the various ways in which historians have deployed the term or tried to define it. Rather, it examines some of the configurations in which the operations of power have attracted the attention of historians: the 'powers' and 'superpowers' of the international system, power and personal dominion, the power of states, the ultra-concentration of power in the totalitarian regimes of the twentieth century, its place in pluralist democratic systems, and its supposed diffusion in the era of 'late capitalism'. Power is not, of course, a reality external to the historical sources that document it. The sources that historians use are themselves often artefacts of power. The associative life of medieval villages and valleys, Thomas N. Bisson has observed, 'are all but invisible to us, figuring in writing as a rule only when activated by the pressures of kings and other powers'.[5] Historians are not immune to the attractions and repulsions of power and many of the archives historians labour in are the fossilized remnants of once-powerful bureaucracies. Bearing this in mind, I close with some brief thoughts about the operations of power upon the writing of History.

The power of the powers

The rise and fall of states and the struggle for power among them is among the oldest themes of historical narrative. Until the early modern period, the habit of imagining history as a succession of regimes of power was underwritten by the logic of biblical prophecy (derived from the Book of Daniel and Revelation, which foresaw the return of the Messiah after the rise and fall of four world monarchies, to be followed by a 'fifth kingdom' or 'fifth monarchy' that would last for one thousand years. There was controversy over the precise meaning of the prophecy, but it was widely understood to refer to the Babylonian, the Persian, the Greek, and the Roman empires, the last of which continued after the fall of ancient Rome, in the form of the 'Holy Roman Empire of the German Nation').

Despite the continued currency of such prophetic scenarios among millenarian sects, the idea of a foreordained sequence of powers was gradually displaced in sixteenth- and seventeenth-century European historical thought by a secularized 'historia humana', in which the competition among (European) states was perceived as a force in its own right, driven by the ambition of rulers and the exigencies of 'reason of state'. A paradigmatic figure in this respect was the seventeenth-century political theorist and historian Samuel Pufendorf, who denied that the Holy Roman Empire was the continuation (in the prophetic or any other sense) of the ancient Roman Empire and thus challenged the hold of Revelation upon History. The relations among powers, Pufendorf argued, were inherently chaotic and unpredictable, since the interests of each territorial state constantly changed in accordance with shifts in the balance of power among them.[6] In this sense, the idea of powers jockeying for supremacy or at least security within a competitive multi-state system helped to establish 'human history' as an autonomous discourse, distinct from the 'historia divina' underwritten by prophecy.

Separated from prophecy, the history of powers could unfold under the rubric of disruption and change. 'Fragility and instability are inseparable from the works of men,' wrote Frederick II of Prussia in 1751. This was just as well, the king thought. For if there were no great upheavals, 'there would be no great events'. The arc of ascendancy and decline described by the great powers of world history reminded the king of the regular motion of the planets that, 'having traversed the space of the firmament for ten thousand years, find themselves at the place from which they departed'.[7] The study of the careers of great states was thus a study in the mutability and elusiveness of power. The hegemony of any one state was always temporary. The mighty empires of the ancient Near East and of Greece and Rome were now mere ruins. Today's great potentate was tomorrow's Ozymandias. The Spanish Habsburg hegemon of the sixteenth century, with its bullion and mercenary armies, made way for the Dutch Empire of the Golden Age; the hegemony of late seventeenth-century France made way after long and bitter struggles for the British Empire of the nineteenth, a vast naval enterprise sustained by industrial might and unparalleled financial resources. But British imperial hegemony was also temporary; it would not outlive what Henry Luce famously called the 'American century'.[8]

Hegemonies have tended to be temporary in Europe because the emergence of very strong states has usually called forth hostile coalitions of lesser states. Whether the United States, whose relative lead in terms of military power is unprecedented in world history, will succeed in maintaining its leadership position without provoking the emergence of such a coalition is one of the interesting questions asked by contemporary American political science. The former US Secretary of State Joseph Nye has argued that the tools of 'hard power' (superior weaponry and the resources needed to finance it) are most effective when they are supplemented by the 'soft power' generated by the dominant state's association with a universalistic culture, attractive values, and a liberal and/or multilateral engagement with other states and with trans-national organizations.[9]

'Soft power' is important because it has the potential to bestow the appearance of legitimacy upon the enterprises of the hegemon. And legitimacy is precisely what is often lacking when powerful states seek to apply force beyond their own borders. Herein lies one reason for the fact that even the United States, notwithstanding its clear global superiority in 'hard power', has sometimes failed to achieve the objectives it set itself. Projecting power in an environment where the locals do not accept it is an enterprise fraught with difficulty. The historian Arthur Schlesinger recalled that at the height of the Vietnam War, President Lyndon B. Johnson 'found it viscerally inconceivable that what Walt Rostow kept telling him was "the greatest power in the world" could not dispose of a collection of night-riders in black pyjamas'.[10] Even military conquests—the most decisive and conspicuous application of 'hard power'—tend to be undermined over time unless the majority of the conquered population comes to identify with the values of the new rulers.[11] Power remains the arbiter of the international system, but its effective exercise in pursuit of durable solutions may depend, even in highly asymmetrical settings, upon a paradoxical intertwining of coercion and consent.

Power, lordship, and government

Not all power is governmental. But the emergence of governments and later of state executives as the holders of a 'monopoly of legitimate violence' (Max Weber)[12] has been one of the central stories Europeans have told about power. There have been eras of fragmentation and eras of consolidation. In a classic account of the emergence of 'feudal society', the French medievalist Georges Duby described how the encompassing structures of the Carolingian Empire broke apart, first into comital polities, and later into even more localized entities centred on the fortifications and military might of castellans, men who controlled castles, horses, and weapons. In the process, the meaning of power changed; its exercise became less 'public', more closely associated with relations of proprietorship. It took on more aggressive and exploitative forms.[13]

But this period of fragmentation was followed, according to some scholars at least, by the rise of new forms of 'government'.[14] Out of a world in which all power was exercised in the form of lordship, close up and personal, there emerged new forms of government driven by the need to contain the excesses of exploitative and violent forms of local dominion. The insistence on lordly rights gave way to 'the recognition of collective interest', in which government could begin to mean not just coercion and punishment, but also 'office, accountability, competence, social utility'.[15] In England, the century between c.1160 and c.1250 saw the state become 'arguably more powerful than at any other time in English history'.[16] And these developments paved the way for the 'institutionalised territorial state' of the late Middle Ages (Theodor Mayer) in which the power of the sovereign pertained increasingly to the entire surface of a specific territory, a development supported by the increasingly 'spatial' orientation of later medieval legal discourse.[17]

We need not concern ourselves with the details of these arguments, or with the scholarly controversy over their veracity. More important from our point of view is the underlying logic of the narrative. Power is in flux, it disperses, becomes localized, and in doing so changes its character. Then it is refocused on a higher plane. A steady state is never achieved; all relationships are subject in the longer term to renegotiation and social upheavals and wars can always intervene to recalibrate the balance. In England, for example, as Christine Carpenter has suggested, the dynastic civil wars known as the Wars of the Roses (1455–85) produced a structural shift in the provincial relationship between gentries and nobilities that refocused authority on the monarchical state and prepared the ground for the era of muscular Tudor kingship that followed.[18]

These changes were accompanied by a deepening interest in the contrast between legitimate and illegitimate forms of power. Those who ruled illegitimately were called 'tyrants'; in the discourse of medieval clerical moralists, they served as 'antitypes to the good ruler' (though John of Salisbury confused matters by positing that the tyrant could be God's way of punishing sinful subjects).[19] The idea of legitimate human power posed difficulties in a universe in which all power came from God. 'Who does not know', Pope Gregory VII wrote to Bishop Hermann of Metz, 'that kings and princes derive their power from men ignorant of God who aspired to lord over their fellow men by pride, plunder, treachery, murder and lastly by every kind of crime, at the instigation of the devil, the prince of this world?'[20] Coming from a pope at the height of his own power struggle with a German emperor, this was a partisan argument, to be sure. But it touched on a deep vein of medieval thought on the problem of sovereignty, a tradition that reached back to Augustine. Thomas Aquinas conceded that relations of dominion were a natural social fact, given the proclivities of human beings, but he too, like many of the most influential clerical authorities, believed that it was an institution rooted in sin.[21] Even as the structures of princely and governmental power were rationalized and consolidated in the eleventh and twelfth centuries, Philippe Buc has argued, the biblical commentaries of northern France saw a revived emphasis on the negative aspects of *potestas* and *dominatio*.

The distinction between coercive force and the authority bestowed by right remained one of the animating problems of early modern political discourse. 'Princes oft want power, they have . . . right oft without might', wrote the Puritan divine Thomas Gataker in 1620. 'And tyrannous Usurpers have power more than is meete; they have . . . might without right.'[22] The very expectation that power should have to 'legitimize' itself implies, as David Sabean has observed, that it is in some sense always arbitrary, that its exercise requires justification or masking.[23] It is striking that the two most influential early modern students of the problem of secular power, Machiavelli and Hobbes, largely sidestepped (or reframed) the issue of legitimacy, the former by narrowing the rationale of princely power to the pursuit of glory and the 'maintenance of one's state' by whatever means appeared expedient, and the latter by justifying sovereignty in functional terms as the best possible safeguard for public order and the protection of life and property. In this way, the rationale for the exercise of sovereign power was separated—emancipated, one could say—from questions about the personal godliness or virtue of the prince.

The power of the state

For a long time 'absolutism' was a concept that helped historians to characterize the transition from the highly mediated and personal forms of power that prevailed in the medieval world to the abstract, impersonal power of modern states. It was thought that modern centralized states emerged—on the European continent at least—from a long struggle for power between princely executives and provincial elites. Forced to meet the growing costs and burdens of warfare with other states, they swept all before them in the quest for new revenues—the collision of powers thus favoured the concentration of power, and vice versa. Seventeenth- and eighteenth-century princely governments shut down the organs of corporate representation (Estates, Cortes, diets), replaced locally run and financed militias with standing armies, disabled supra-territorial jurisdictions, and imposed new taxes and territorial law codes. Princely executives grew larger: in 1715, Louis XIV had ten times as many *officiers* as Francis I (1515–47) to rule a population that was only slightly larger.[24] In the process, the diverse provinces of 'composite monarchies' were drawn gradually into a closer and more homogeneous association.

Contemporary political theory offered eloquent support for the aggrandizement of princely executives. For the jurist Samuel Pufendorf, the most influential German reader of Hobbes, the legitimacy of states derived from the need to forestall disorder through the concentration of authority. But since it was impossible in peace or war to conduct the affairs of a state without incurring expenses, the sovereign had the right to 'force individual citizens to contribute so much of their own goods as the assumption of these expenses is deemed to require'. Here was a powerful rationale for the extension of state authority. Against the 'libertas' of the Estates, Pufendorf asserted the 'necessitas' of the state.[25]

But how far did the process of consolidation go? Even in the later eighteenth century, most historians would now concede, the powers of monarchical states were still quite limited. Estates may have ceased to convene in territory-wide assemblies, but the nobilities, organized along corporate lines, still ruled the roost in the provinces. Central executives grew, to be sure, but they remained small, by present-day standards. In 1715, the central administrative departments of the French state counted no more than 1,000 men, and a population of just under 20 million were supervised by a corps of only 2,000 police officers. Kings still needed the support and know-how of provincial elites, not to mention their patronage networks.[26] If Peter the Great of Russia attacked and undermined the privileges of the Russian nobility, Catherine the Great reversed the polarities of the state-building process, choosing instead to reinforce the nobilities as pillars of the autocracy. Something broadly analogous happened in Prussia between the reigns of the Great Elector and King Frederick II. An uncertainty thus remains about how exactly power was distributed, given that relations of power so often masked relations of interdependency. The problem penetrated to the heart of royal executives, for even the most powerful monarch depended upon those who advised him—indeed his dependency deepened as the workings of the expanding state became more complex—this issue caught the attention of Carl Schmitt, one of the subtlest twentieth-century writers on the workings of political power.[27] There is something, it seems, about power that resists concentration, at least over the long term.

The concentration of power in processes of state building—'absolutist' or otherwise—is not a uniquely European preoccupation. In China, one scholar has suggested, the state was large and endured through the centuries because rulers succeeded in forging an alliance with the landed warrior nobility of the regions.[28] Here too, however, the relationship between the imperial state and the wielders of local power in peripheral areas changed markedly over time. Until the 1720s, the Chinese state exercised limited political control over the non-Han peoples on the empire's southern periphery. Under the Ming dynasty (1368–1644), this problem was solved through a system of 'native chiefs', who ruled in the localities and received investiture from the central state. This arrangement at first continued under the Qing (1644–1912): the native chiefs coordinated the payment of land and labour-service tax, played a key role in borderland defence, and were expected to render tribute to Beijing every three years. But the Yongzhen emperor, who came to the throne in 1723, was resolved to do away with the chiefdoms. 'His vision of the state as a centralised entity, in which...the emperor extended unmediated benevolence to his subject, was offended by the imposition of native chiefs between himself and some of the people.'[29] Legitimacy was still important: the emperor's officials claimed that in extending their power in the border regions, they were protecting the 'natives' from exploitation by their chieftains. Nevertheless, there were areas, such as Guangxi, where powerful chieftain families continued to defy Qing control.[30]

In Japan, too, we can tell a story of alternating concentration and diffusion that in its general outlines closely resembles the European narrative. The early eighth century AD saw the establishment of a 'centralized polity' that displaced the independent clan chiefdoms that had previously dominated the Japanese islands. The diverse local ancestor cults of the chiefdoms were replaced by a territorial protocol of worship focused on the semi-divine status of the Yamato monarchy. New law codes of 705 and 757 affirmed that authority derived solely from the 'Heavenly Sovereign' in Kyoto. In the thirteenth and fourteenth centuries, however, powerful regional chiefs repeatedly challenged the authority of the court and its military government, the shogunate. By the end of the fifteenth century, rebellions and inter-clan warfare had destroyed the authority of the centralized polity—the court was an 'empty shell'.

Only in 1603 was Japan reunified under Shogun Iyeyasu of the House of Tokugawa, who established the foundations for 'a new and vastly more powerful kind of government than had existed in the past'.[31] Under the Tokugawa shogunate, the Edo administration built up a formidable bureaucracy encompassing 17,000 officials; this was the first regime in Japanese history to 'draw and maintain clear physical boundaries for itself'.[32] The Tokugawa dynasty remained in power until 1867, but long before its political demise, its power too had been undermined by the growing independence of the daimyo, regional magnates who conceived of their landholdings as 'autonomous principalities'. The early Tokugawa shoguns had kept the daimyo under a tight grip, but by the later seventeenth century, the daimyo had begun to behave like little shoguns, issuing their own legal codes and local currencies, imposing taxes, and establishing new administrative systems, while assiduously maintaining the fiction of loyalty to the shogunate.[33] Here again we may discern the familiar dialectic: the daimyos were in the first instance the beneficiaries of the Tokugawa supremacy and the instruments of Tokugawa authority in the regions, but with time they began to suck power out of the centre and accrue it to themselves; indeed, it is precisely these growing limitations to shogunal rule that explain the longevity of the Tokugawa dynasty.[34] The pendulum swung back towards 'concentration' with the Meiji Restoration (1868), a bloodless coup against the Tokugawa system that aimed to reverse the process of devolution and extend central authority over the 280 independent daimyo domains.[35] The appeal to legitimacy was secured through the claim that the new regime would re-establish the centrality and authority (though not the political power) of the 'Heavenly Sovereign' (emperor).[36] As so often in European history, a transfer of power shrouded itself in the mantle of continuity with an ancient tradition.

The paradigm of state power as the attempt to project onto a bounded territory a more or less homogeneous field of authority cannot be universalized. It has been observed of Mexico, for example, that the state's capacity to wield power varied with the landscape: hills and mountains were associated with 'wildness, violence and political freedom', while the plains carried connotations of 'docility, pacification and susceptibility to repression'.[37] In the states of South-East Asia, historians have noted a steep gradient of decreasing power and control from the centre to the periphery of the territory; borders were relatively insignificant, the polity was concentrated in the court or 'capital' city.[38] For the eighteenth- and nineteenth-century United States, the 'Frontier Thesis' was premised on the assumption that state power was not sharply delineated in space, but rather petered out by degrees as the density of white settlement declined.

Above all, the 'great but incomplete drama' of African state formation, as one historian has called it, reveals a pattern quite different from the European. Across most of the African continent, low population densities posed an insuperable obstacle to the concentration of power in large state executives. Only in 1975 did Africa reach population densities comparable with those of Europe around 1500; in 1900 Africa accounted for 18 per cent of the world's surface but only 5–7 per cent of its population. These conditions hindered state-building processes in various ways. First, it was prohibitively expensive to impose control over large areas. This was the case, for example, for the nineteenth-century Ibo in what is today Nigeria, who were organized in a highly decentred manner because, on the one hand, the imposition of authority over a large region would have imposed grievous costs, and, on the other hand, no other polity in a neighbouring region possessed the means to impose their authority on the Ibo.[39] For these, as for many other Africans, it was not at all clear that the state was a desirable or necessary institution.[40] Secondly, climate and geography combined to ensure that land as such was rarely a highly valued commodity—the struggle over access to specific demesnes that was so characteristic of Europe and Japan was much less important here. Finally, in the absence of well-policed political boundaries, any groups upon which an incipient centralized polity wished to impose its will could vote with their feet by means of 'protest migrations'. In many parts of Africa, Jeffrey Herbst has pointed out, 'people have traditionally manifested their discontent with the existing political community by migrating where they can live unhindered by their former rulers'.[41]

One of the exceptions that proves the rule was Ethiopia, an area of relatively high population density. The era of 'Ethiopian absolutism' (1855–1913), one scholar has suggested, witnessed 'the rise of a centralised state power' that displaced older and more dispersed forms of authority. Here, as in many parts of Europe, it was the growing scale, frequency, and organization of military campaigns that strained traditional systems of resource management and propelled the emergence first of a 'centralised regional power' and later of a centralized state.[42] Buganda is another case in point. Situated in the resource-rich and densely populated Great Lakes region, Buganda developed from around the turn of the nineteenth century into a powerful state, in which the intensive exploitation of local resources was integrated with the control of regional trade, buttressed by the military power of the state. But if Buganda was powerful, it was not necessarily centralized. Recent studies have suggested that although the court of the *kabaka* determined the level of taxation and oversaw the use of draft labour on infrastructural projects, it depended on powerful local clan heads and *ssaza* chiefs to implement these policies; commerce, though crucial to the state's prosperity, operated largely outside the control of the central authorities. Here as in early Tokugawa Japan, the centre was only powerful to the extent that it successfully co-opted the local holders of power over people and resources. And in Buganda, as in Tokugawa Japan, the military chiefs (*batongole*) created by the *kabakas* to reinforce their power subsequently mutated into political rivals capable of mounting a concerted challenge to the central authority.[43]

Total power

In 1934, a Jewish doctor living in Nazi Germany had a startling dream. He dreamt that he was lying peacefully on the sofa in his apartment reading a book about the sixteenth-century artist Matthias Grünewald when all of a sudden the walls of his room and apartment disappeared. Appalled, he looked around to see that the walls of all the other apartments within view of his building had also disappeared. Hardly had he taken this in when a metallic voice was heard bellowing into the streets through a loudspeaker: 'in accordance with the decree of the seventeenth of the month on the prevention of walls...'. The dream ended there, because the doctor woke up.[44] This small fragment, drawn from the most private of all the domains of human existence, conveys something of what it meant to experience the power of a terrorist state that claimed the right to see and know everything about the individuals under its sway. In his dystopian fable *Nineteen Eighty-Four*, George Orwell evoked the same nightmarish spectre of the all-seeing state in eerily similar terms. Seated in a detention cell filled with terrified 'suspects', Winston Smith covers his face with his hands. At once, a harsh voice is heard yelling from the telescreen on the wall: 'Smith! 6079 Smith W! Uncover your face! No faces covered in the cells!'[45]

The rise of political regimes with the ambition to shape and control the totality of the life of the citizenry was one of the most remarkable features of the twentieth century. For the Fascist, Benito Mussolini wrote in 1932, everything was 'within the state' and 'nothing human or intellectual' existed outside the state. In this respect, he declared, Fascism was 'totalitarian' and the Fascist state, as the 'summation and unity of all values', interpreted, developed, and dominated the entirety of life.[46] Liberal critics of the Italian regime were quick to see the family resemblance between the Mussolini system and the Communist regime in Russia. 'One can distinguish between Russia and Italy only in one single respect', wrote the Catholic political activist Luigi Sturzo in 1926, 'namely that Bolshevism is a communist dictatorship, or a Fascism from the left; whereas fascism is a conservative dictatorship, or a communism from the right.'[47]

Observing the new European regimes—Stalinist, Fascist, and National Socialist—from across the Atlantic, American political scientists recognized a qualitatively new form of politics, a new 'basic model' of dictatorship in which an extremist party dominated by an all-powerful leader seized control in the name of an all-embracing ideology and replaced the existing parliamentary system with a reign of terror, merging party and state and bringing all means of communication under the 'total control of the regime'.[48] In the 1950s, the US émigré scholars Carl Joachim Friedrich and Zbigniew Brzezinski developed a powerful elaboration of this analysis. Their 'totalitarian' model emphasized the generic structural features that allowed such regimes to achieve an extreme concentration of power, including the deployment of terror, the imposition of an ideology focused on mobilizing the population against real or imagined enemies, control of all aspects of the economy, and the exclusive control of communications.[49]

The result was an awe-inspiring concentration of power in one man, or, in the case of post-Stalin Communism in the Eastern Bloc, in a vast gerontocracy of political guardians known as 'the communist party'. These regimes exploited all the instruments of administrative and technological modernity while at the same excising the power-diffusing armature of *political* modernity—legislatures, pluralist mass communications, and the liberty of expression and association.

Even of these dystopian worlds, however, there are interesting questions to ask about where power resided, and the extent to which its exercise depended upon patterns of consent or acquiescence. Italy, it is now widely conceded, was totalitarian by aspiration only; the Catholic Church, which was never absorbed or fully co-opted by the regime, remained an immensely influential presence: when the government opened its blockbusting Mostra della Rivoluzione Fascista in 1932–3, the Papacy responded by declaring an *Anno Santo* for 1933–4 that attracted more visitors to Rome than the Exhibition had done.[50] There was a still a semi-autonomous Italian monarchy and state structure (including the state police force, whose officers were sent to arrest Mussolini after his deposition by the Fascist Grand Council—a situation unthinkable in Nazi Germany). The Fascists, as Richard Bosworth has shown, unfolded a public culture of leader worship and vainglorious nationalist pomp, but despite their best efforts, they never succeeded in remoulding the beliefs, memories, expectations, or loyalties of most of their subjects. The Fascist movement was diffuse in both thought and structure. Powerful local bosses (known as *Ras*, a term borrowed, interestingly enough, from the regional chieftaincies of Ethiopia) ran the big cities and local party agencies became intertwined—as the tax agents and 'intendants' of would-be 'absolutist' polities had done before them—with a nationwide thicket of local patronage networks that predated the advent of the regime and would survive its demise.[51]

Fascism, perhaps, is a soft target. The Nazi regime was clearly far more lethal, both in its domestic and external projections of power. But even here questions have been asked about whether the regime derived its power over the German population more from coercion (including the threat of violence) or from the consent or acquiescence of citizens. Some historians have stressed the former. In the first volume of his authoritative trilogy on the Third Reich, Richard Evans highlights the role played by terrorist violence in the early consolidation of the regime. The torture, beating, and murder of Communists, prominent social democrats, and other inconvenient persons by the SA during the first six months of 1933 made it clear that this was a regime prepared to enforce its power using the most brutal means.[52] On the other hand, as Robert Gellately has noted, the organs of domestic political policing (Gestapo) were numerically small and beyond the ken of most Germans. Tip-offs and denunciations from the public were crucial to its day-to-day operation. For the bulk of the population, Gellately argues, the terroristic side of Hitler's Germany was 'socially constructed by what was passed along by word of mouth, by what they read of it in the press or heard on the radio'. Terrorist measures took place, but they were 'selective and focused'; Hitler never set out to 'confront large segments of his social world and to break them to his will, as Stalin did'. It follows that consent or at least acquiescence stabilized the regime, rather than the direct application of coercive power. A substantial portion of the German public, Gellately suggests, accepted the new regime because they liked what it was saying and doing.[53]

Even Stalinism, which in terms of its domestic lethality far outperformed the other 'totalitarian' states, is susceptible to a degree of nuance in the matter of regime power. When the regime proceeded with mind-numbing violence to terrorize the 'kulaks' who supposedly stood in the way of the socialization of agriculture, huge brigades of urban volunteers, many of them factory workers from peasant families, streamed out into the countryside to assist in 'dekulakization'. Recent studies of the Stalinist terror have drawn attention to the selectivity of regime violence and the complex synergies between state-sponsored coercion and voluntarist pressures within the population. In some areas, denunciations from the public helped to focus terrorist reprisals against specific groups of party and police personnel.[54] This does not in any sense diminish the breath-taking power of the Stalinist regime over its subjects; it is merely a reminder that even in an ultra-coercive system, the currents of power flow in more complex patterns than a simple, top-down model will allow.

In the ground-zero environment of the Nazi concentration camp, where armed guards could beat, maim, and kill defenceless inmates with impunity, the balancing of coercion with consent is clearly out of place. But even here, as the memoirs of survivors suggest, there were complex hierarchies and power differentials—between 'criminals' and 'politicals', between Kapos and 'ordinary' prisoners, between inmates with valuable skills and those with none. Even in those ultra-circum-scribed systems—concentration camps, the gulag, slavery—where captive humans were reduced to the *nuda vita* of a rightless existence, gradations of power stealthily insinuated themselves.[55]

Nothing, it would seem, about the shared condition of subordination prevents subalterns from dominating or brutalizing other subalterns. In the eighteenth-century Caribbean, slaves newly arriving from Afri-ca were taunted as 'savages' by island-born black slaves, in a process of 'micro-differentiation in which members of oppressed groups strove to carve out what spaces of dignity they might within the framework of white domination'.[56] In social systems where slaves were employed in large numbers and a variety of functions, huge power differentials emerged. A striking example is Ibadan, a military state in nineteenth-century Yorubaland (in today's Nigeria). Founded in the 1820s, this military republic required immense reserves of labour and military manpower, far exceeding what the warrior lineages of the region could supply. The need was met through the use of large numbers of slaves. Highly coercible and exploitable, not to mention cheap to maintain, slaves served as soldiers in the private armies of war chiefs, as farm-workers on the domains of warriors, as traders, porters, craftsmen, and household servants. With time, however, status differences deepened within the slave population. Some slaves took on administrative roles within the compounds of powerful war chiefs, others became diplo-mats or toll collectors, and these privileged slaves were themselves able to acquire property, including slaves, over whom they exercised power in their own right. Indeed, the slave-holding slaves were known for their ruthlessness towards their human chattels, who frequently complained of beatings, under-feeding, excessive labour, and rape.[57] In this setting, we may see more clearly the meaning of Michel Foucault's observation that the individual is both 'an effect of power' and 'the element of its articulation': 'The individual which power has constituted is at the same time its vehicle.'[58]

Power in pluralist systems

In 1969, after the election of Richard Nixon to the White House, President Lyndon B. Johnson gave his successor the following warning:

Before you get to be president, you think you can do anything. You think you're the most powerful leader since God. But when you get in that tall chair, as you're gonna find out, Mr President, you can't count on people. You'll find your hands tied and people cussin' at you. The office is kinda like the little country boy found the hoochie-koochie show at the carnival, once he'd paid his dime and got inside the tent: 'It ain't exactly as it was advertised.'[59]

How is political power configured in a pluralist, democratic society? Do the representative bodies, federal structures, interest groups, and constitutional checks of a large national democracy mute and diffuse the power of the leader? Or does the popular consent manifested in electoral success permit an awe-inspiring concentration of power in the hands of one man or woman? It has been a feature of democratic societies, with their multicameral legislatures and strong judiciaries, that power is continuously renegotiated; it gathers and disperses, or migrates from one node in the system to another.

No office better illustrates the fluidity of power and the difficulty of specifying its locations and quantity in democratic political systems than the presidency of United States of America. When the British essayist and political journalist Walter Bagehot looked across the Atlantic in 1866, he saw a system of 'Presidential Government' so overwhelming that it threatened to 'weaken the legislative power'.[60] When the constitutional lawyer and future President Woodrow Wilson published a major treatise on the same political system nearly twenty years later, however, he called it 'Congressional Government'.[61] The difference was not a function of divergent theoretical perspectives (Wilson was a warm admirer of Bagehot), but of changing historical circumstance. Bagehot had written during the American Civil War, when President Abraham Lincoln conjured out of the constitutional title 'commander-in-chief' the power to impose a blockade, raise a volunteer army, expand the regular military and naval forces, sweep aside civil liberties, and impose conscription and issue the two Executive Orders known as the Emancipation Proclamation.[62]

By the time Wilson published his *Congressional Government*, on the other hand, America had passed through the era of Reconstruction and the legislature was now dominant. Indeed, the President was no better placed to shape legislation, Wilson suggested in 1898, than 'any other influential person who might choose to send to Congress a letter of information and advice'.[63] And yet, when he revisited the problem ten years later in a further major study, Wilson took a different line: Americans, he wrote, now viewed the President as the 'unifying force in our complex system'.[64] This appraisal bore the imprint of the activist presidency of Theodore Roosevelt (in office 1901–9), under which the President not only exercised his constitutional right to make legislative proposals to Congress but also used the unique prestige of his office to rally public support for them. Above all, it was America's expanding role in the early twentieth-century world that revealed new potentialities in the office, since the President's control of foreign policy appeared virtually 'absolute'. 'Our President', Wilson wrote, 'must henceforth be one of the great powers of the world, whether he act greatly and wisely or not.'[65]

One might thus speak of 'cycles' in the relationship between the presidency and the legislature, in which periods of presidential dominance have alternated with periods of congressional resurgence. There was a reassertion of congressional power after Watergate, for example, when the scandals surrounding President Nixon tarnished the standing of the office and produced a mood of determination to thwart suspect initiatives from the White House through deployment of the 'legislative veto', a statutory provision that permits one or both houses of Congress to disapprove or stall an action of the executive branch.[66]

But these oscillations have occurred against the background of a steady growth in the power of the presidential office. War has had much to do with this consolidation of authority, just as it did in the 'absolutist' states of seventeenth- and eighteenth-century Europe. The 'Imperial Presidency' (Arthur M. Schlesinger) of the twentieth century witnessed a dramatic growth in the war-making powers of the presidency and a corresponding shift in the constitutional balance between

Congress and the President.[67] President Harry Truman intervened on his own initiative in the Korean civil war, ordering troops into hostilities without asking either for a declaration of war or for a congressional resolution of support; during the Cuba Missile Crisis, President John F. Kennedy deliberated in 'royal seclusion' with his three closest advisers rather than with the formally responsible Executive Committee and even authorized his brother Robert to make negotiations with the Soviet Union that were not cleared with Congress.[68]

These and other such interventions might appear to reinforce the view that there are two quite distinct presidencies, one focused on the domestic scene and the other on foreign affairs. But in the domestic arena, too, there has been a steady aggrandizement of the office. Even President Gerald Ford, a relatively modest President in the post-Watergate mode, made use of his presidential veto on no fewer than sixty-nine occasions during his period in office; on fewer than one-fifth of these occasions was the veto overruled. As for the 'legislative veto' wielded by Congress, it was struck down by a Supreme Court ruling in 1983. The use of the presidential veto remains an area of contention between the legislative and the executive branches. Some political commentators argued, for example, that the deployment or re-activation of various veto powers by President George Bush Sr. over quite minor issues represented an attempt to 'exert prerogative government' by stealth, even in areas bearing no relation to national security.[69]

That presidents lead within the modern American system seems clear; *how* they lead and where the power to lead comes from is still a matter of debate. A classical analysis of the post-war office-holders by the political scientist Richard E. Neustadt argued that, notwithstanding the plenitude of formal powers vested in them, presidents obtain results not by issuing orders, but by persuading other actors in the system to support and share their objectives. 'Presidential *power*', he wrote, 'is the power to persuade.'[70] Others have argued that the 'persuasiveness' of the man in the White House (i.e. his capacity to achieve outcomes in Congress and secure favourable adjudications from the judiciary) is in fact a function of other variables, such as his electoral success, strategic alignments in both houses of the legislature, the relative strength of opposition, and his performance in opinion polls.[71] Whichever view we favour, it comes down to the same thing: power and consent are endlessly intertwined—at least in the domestic exercise of presidential authority.

The American presidency is doubtless a highly distinctive institution, created as part of a unique attempt to build a new kind of political order. But power exhibits the same slipperiness and ambiguity in all modern democracies. After a period of wartime concentration and growth, the powers of the British government were challenged from the 1950s to the 1980s by a judiciary increasingly willing to scrutinize and even overturn government initiatives and by a House of Commons that was growing new teeth in the form of the Select Committee System and Parliamentary Commissioners charged with the investigation of 'maladministration'. Under Margaret Thatcher and again under Tony Blair, the system passed through phases of 'presidentialization' marked by high levels of prime-ministerial activism and declining deference to Parliament. And yet in recent years the incorporation under Tony Blair of the European Convention on Human Rights and the EU social chapter into UK law have, some would argue, diluted the powers of the executive, while bolstering those of the judiciary.[72] Challenges to executive secrecy under the Freedom of Information Act are a further development with the potential to loosen one of the traditional struts of executive power.[73]

In France, too, the 'hybrid' nature of the Fifth Republic, in which elements of presidential and parliamentary government coexist, permits power to concentrate and disperse in different locations, depending on political relations between the President and the Prime Minister. The power of the French President, David Bell has suggested, depends not upon his formal prerogatives, but upon his skill in 'making the presidency the point of reference in French politics'; in this sense the Fifth Republic presidency is a feat of 'political levitation'.[74] In Germany, the authority of the President of the Federal Republic has tended since 1949 to recede before the growing power of the Chancellor, but this was the outcome of historical contingency (above all the unhoped-for stability of party and parliamentary life after 1949), not of constitutional planning.[75] It is a feature of all these systems that the relationships between state executives and the other power centres in modern pluralist states—judiciaries, bureaucracies, legislatures, lobby groups, the media—are in constant flux.[76]

Nowhere, perhaps, is the determination of power relations more contested than in the multi-state environment of the European Union. 'Intergovernmentalist' accounts emphasize the control exercised by the member state over the process of integration; power, by this reading, is exercised primarily by the member states, but is dispersed between them.[77] By contrast, 'neo-functionalist' analysts of the EU stress the role of supranational institutions, especially the European Commission and, in more recent times, the European Parliament.[78] 'Institutionalist' and 'network' approaches emphasize the limited potential for the concentration of power in such a complex system; power, they argue, can only be exercised when large coalitions involving actors of different kinds (member states, supranational institutions, societal alliances, or 'advocacy coalitions') flow together in support of specific objectives. Power relations are thus played out in the context of a 'multi-level game' involving many different forms of state and private actor and structured around informal, network-like relationships.[79]

The oscillation in the balance of power between competing agencies is not confined to the sphere of government; it replicates itself across all the domains of economic, social, and political life in capitalist countries. A study of the relationship between consumers and big corporations in the automobile sector in the twentieth-century United States has shown that while there were certainly attempts by the 'big three' automakers (Chrysler, General Motors, and Ford) to manipulate consumers and efforts by consumer groups to confront them, the evolution of the auto market was not driven by this stand-off alone, but by the intervention of a plethora of state and non-state actors—the courts, the Justice Department, insurance underwriters, State research entities and motor vehicle administrations, the Federal Reserve Board, and many others. All of these possessed sufficient leverage to contribute to shaping the outcome; none had the power to shape it alone.[80]

This fractal iteration of power relationships suggests a wider fragmentation and decentring of power in modern democratic societies, whose consequences are difficult to think through. In a lyrical, often perverse diagnosis of late capitalism published in 1980, the French post-Marxist leftists Gilles Deleuze and Félix Guattari fixed their eyes on the United States and saw there a new kind of social order in which power did not flow from a single centre and was not anchored in a single core structure. In place of arboreal tropes that opposed centre and periphery, roots and branches, Deleuze and Guattari imagined the 'thousand plateaus' of capitalist society, a world of 'multiplicities, lines, strata and segmentarities, lines of flight and intensities'. They metaphorized the postmodern social order as a 'rhizome', a capillary network in which every point was connected to every other point, an array in which 'power centres' were 'diffuse, dispersed, geared down, miniaturized, perpetually displaced'.[81] The same train of thought can be traced—in a less exalted register—in Francis Fukuyama's Hegelian reflection on the meaning of the European revolutions of 1989. In *The End of History and the Last Man*, Fukuyama speculated that the passing of authoritarian Communism might herald the definitive triumph of liberal capitalism over its various antecedents, alternatives, and adversaries. By this reading, the future was a prosperous suburb, in which sharp power differentials had all but vanished, and with them the revolutionary energies that have hitherto driven history on its course.[82]

Power and history

Power shapes what we have and know of history. This is why the palace of Sans Souci in northern Haiti, completed in 1813 to serve as the residence for Haiti's first and only king, Henry I, is today a ruin, while its namesake in Potsdam, the charming summer residence Frederick II of Prussia built in the 1740s, shines as if it were built yesterday. Even after the abdication of the last Hohenzollern king, power remained close to the Prussian Sans Souci. Frederick's summer lodging was administered as a 'state palace' under the Weimar Republic and later under the Communist government of the German Democratic Republic. The foundation that currently looks after it is administered under a state charter and generously financed from public funds.[83] But power swiftly abandoned the huge edifice of the first and only Haitian king. Its first resident, King Henry, a former slave and hero of the revolution that forced France to acknowledge Haitian independence in 1804, committed suicide on 8 October 1820 when he learned that republican forces were approaching from the south. His son Jacques-Victor, Prince Royal of Haiti, was bayoneted to death in the palace ten days later. There was no succession. The republican government that ruled thereafter from Port au Prince took no interest in the upkeep of this memento of Haiti's ill-fated monarchy. Disfigured in the early years by civil war and neglect, the palace was partly destroyed in the earth-quake of 1842 that wiped out nearby Cap-Haïtien. Today it remains a wreck, despite its status (since 1982) as a Unesco World Heritage Site. Whether it is inscribed in stone or on paper, historical narrative, as Michel-Rolph Trouillot has observed, 'involves the uneven contribution of competing groups and individuals who have unequal access to the means for such production'.[84]

Historians register and accommodate this asymmetry in different ways. Some are attracted to the spectacle of power and the social locations where it is exercised—cabinets, antechambers, military head-quarters, ministries, and boardrooms. They admire the skilful use of power, they baptize it in approving rhetoric. Others work against the gradient of power, 'from the bottom up'—this was the aspiration of much social history in the 1960s and 1970s, which placed at the centre those individuals and groups who had previously figured as the anonymous 'objects' of policies devised by the powerful. In some such narratives, conceived in the paranoid mode, it is power that is anonymized: the textured portraits of leaders make way for faceless 'elites' and 'ruling classes'. But some historians who focus on subaltern actors find, on the contrary, that power pools around the object of contemplation: the more they know of their protagonists, the more power—at least over their own destinies and immediate environments—these appear to wield.[85] They find wit, strategy, determination, autonomy, and resistance among peasant women, Soviet steelworkers, forest-dwellers, slaves, prostitutes. Writing in this mode may come to seem a retrospective act of empowerment, or perhaps it is just that narratives require protagonists, who in turn demand agency and with it a small share of power.

The reasons for making such narrative choices doubtless lie—leaving aside the trends that push historical writing this way and that—within the realm of what Judith Butler called the 'psychic life of power'. We are accustomed to thinking of power as something that presses in on us from outside. But what if we ourselves are actually 'initiated through a primary submission to power'—the power, for example, of our parents? If, Butler suggests, we understand power as a force in our own formation as *subjects*, 'then power is not simply what we oppose, but what we depend on for our existence and what we harbour and preserve in the beings we are'.[86] In *The Trial*, his dark parable on the mysteries of power, Franz Kafka reflected on the impossibility of grasping power at its source, of rendering its foundations visible. The quest of the forlorn protagonist 'K' for authoritative clarification of the progress of the 'case' proceeding against him leads down the endless corridors of administrative buildings into broom closets, basements, and a rooftop shed full of dusty tools, but never into the central chamber where decisions are made and destinies decided. Indeed, it remains unclear whether such a chamber exists, and whether, if it does, there is anyone inside it. We could read this as a lucubration on the impersonal power of modern bureaucracy, but Deleuze and Guattari were surely right to see in it something more visceral and fundamental: Kafka's intuition, unsparingly explored in his *Brief an Meinen Vater*, that the power of his own overbearing father was merely the deferred expression of the father's own subordination to *his* father.[87] The 'line of flight' that stretched back from father to father to father was a long corridor plunged in deepening shadow, at the end of which there could be no definitive reckoning with power.

7. Maori women standing outside exchanging traditional greetings, New Zealand, late nineteenth century. © By permission of the Trustees of the British Museum

7 Communication

PETER BURKE

The media of communication—orality, writing, print, radio, and so on—are technologies, but they are not neutral. They are not pure 'conduits' of information. In the words of Marshall McLuhan, exaggerated for rhetorical effect but containing an important insight, 'The medium is the message' (it is more exact though less ear-catching to say that the medium is part of the message).[1] Such an emphasis on the media does not necessarily imply technological determinism. We might look at different media as presenting different opportunities that individuals or groups may grasp.

As for cultures, we might view them as distinctive packages of technologies and 'communicative resources'. In contrast to a normal package, though, the contents interact. Cultural history is the story of both tradition and innovation (innovation as resistance to tradition and tradition as resistance to innovation). A simple model of the 'replacement' of one medium or genre by another does not do justice to the tradition side of the equation. It is more illuminating to work with a model of the cultural 'coexistence' of orality and writing, manuscript and print, print and radio, radio and television, television and the internet. When new media are introduced, old ones survive, although their place in the package and the functions that they perform are generally more limited or specialized than before.[2]

Communication in history

To write a chapter about communication in human history is a challenge. The origins of language go back a minimum of 50,000 years and a maximum of 5 or 6 million years. The cave paintings of Lascaux are about 20,000 years old, while writing has a history of 5,000 years or more. In order to present such a long history and to discuss many parts of the world in a few pages, it will obviously be necessary to be somewhat schematic.

Any history of communication is inevitably concerned with what the American political scientist Harold Lasswell described as 'Who says What to Whom through What Channel with What Effect'.[3] In what follows I shall privilege the 'channels', in other words the 'media' of communication. The schema chosen to organize this chapter, the red thread through the labyrinth of communication, is that of the successive dominance of four media, which may be described for the sake of brevity as the oral, the written, the printed, and the electric systems. There are of course others: communication by *qipu*, for instance, in Peru under the Incas (discussed below), or by *chapatti* from village to village in Hindustan in 1857, the year of the great 'Mutiny', a rebellion against British rule, as well as communication by gesture and especially by ritual.

The epic of Milman Parry

As a reminder of the importance of interaction between media it seems appropriate to begin this account with a story, the story of a scholarly adventure. For centuries, scholars had engaged in debate about the Homeric poems. Among the questions that they debated, two were particularly important: were the *Iliad* and the *Odyssey* the work of the same poet? Were they composed in writing or were they originally sung? In the 1930s, a young Harvard Professor of Classics, Milman Parry, who was to die tragically young, had the idea of testing the oral hypothesis in the field.

Obviously unable to visit ancient Greece, he decided to work in Bosnia, knowing that oral poets were still active in that region and that they continued to compose epics about battles between Christians and Turks and heroes such as Marko Kraljević. Like an anthropologist, Parry went to live in the region, armed with a phonograph recorder and accompanied by an assistant, Albert Lord. Analysing the poems they heard in coffee houses, at weddings, and elsewhere, recited to the accompaniment of the *gusle*, a one-stringed fiddle, Parry and Lord discovered that the epics were never sung in exactly the same way twice, especially when the poet was as gifted as one of their informants, Avdo Međedović.

More exactly, the epics were semi-improvised, full of recurrent 'formulas' (stock lines or half-lines) and recurrent incidents or 'themes' such as the arming of the hero, the sending of a letter, and so on. With the aid of these formulas and themes, a *guslar* was able to improvise a narrative for hours at a time. Comparing the poems recorded in Bosnia with the Homeric poems, equally full of formulas and themes, the two scholars concluded that the *Iliad* and the *Odyssey* were originally oral poems, semi-improvised at each performance, so that the texts that have come down to us must record special 'command performances' for scribes.

This memorable story has itself an epic quality and indeed one of the Bosnian poets narrated it in verse as 'the epic of Milman Parry'. The conclusions, published in French in Parry's doctoral thesis and in English, by Albert Lord, in a book called *The Singer of Tales* (1960), cast a good deal of light on the creative process by which narratives are produced, combining or developing schemata and thus producing something new.[4]

All the same, some of the conclusions of these remarkable works remain debatable. Some later scholars have noted, for example, that in other parts of the world, such as Rajasthan in India, sung stories keep much closer to fixed texts.[5] The weakest point in the argument is the authors' emphasis on purity. Parry and Lord were in search of an oral culture that was uncontaminated by writing or print. They found what they wanted to find. They ignored evidence to the contrary. Bosnia in the 1930s still had a low literacy rate but it was not a purely oral culture. Printed versions of epics were in circulation, and they were known to some at least of the oral poets. The two scholars failed to notice interaction between media, perhaps less obvious in Bosnia in the 1930s than in (say) the north-east of Brazil, but present all the same. Today, scholars are familiar with the Parry thesis via print and some of them study the Bosnian epics by listening to the old phonograph recordings, thus illustrating once again the interaction between media.

The oral system

At first sight, it might be thought that oral communication has no history, as it is a permanent feature of life in society. It is indeed difficult to imagine any culture in which conversation, rumour, and gossip does not play an important role. But at different times and in different places, oral communication has been supported by different institutions, performed different functions, and played more or less important parts in the media system.

Until relatively recently, about 5,000 years ago, writing did not exist. The system of communication was predominantly oral, although speech was supplemented by ritual and by image making. The great problem of studying the period before writing is the lack of sources. We can still view the cave paintings but we are ignorant of the cultural context that would allow us to interpret the images of hands, wild beasts, and so on. The oral culture of that long period can only be reconstructed indirectly, by analogy with later oral communications recorded in writing or in post-scribal media such as discs and tapes.

What we can say, thinking of the last 5,000 years, is that oral communication has never lost its importance but only its former centrality. In the sphere of religion, for instance, besides Christian services, prayers, and sermons, one might mention the Hindu Vedas, which were transmitted orally long before they were written down, and also the regular recitation of the Qur'an in the Muslim world (the Arabic word 'Qur'an' means 'recitation'). Indeed, Muhammad himself was illiterate, and must have dictated the text to a scribe.

The number and the variety of institutions and forms of material culture that supported oral communication in different cultures, even in the ages of writing and print, deserve to be noted. Think for instance of the pulpits constructed in churches for the use of preachers, or of the balconies of town halls from which speeches were made (the Town Hall of medieval Bologna was called the *Arengo* or 'Speech' for this reason). Think of taverns, barber's shops, and pharmacies, all three notorious—among early modern elites—as places where ordinary people discussed the affairs of the world and criticized the authorities. Think of theatres, built specifically for the purpose of performing plays: a few in the sixteenth century, more in the seventeenth century, many more in the eighteenth. Again, one of the functions of coffee houses, clubs, and *salons*, three institutions that flourished in Europe in the eighteenth and nineteenth centuries, was to facilitate different kinds of oral communication, especially conversation. Bookshops too were centres of oral communication, illustrating the interaction of talk and print—like coffee houses, where newspapers were often available to clients.

These examples come mainly from Europe, but the Islamic world also had its pulpits and its coffee houses—after all, coffee drinking originated in the Middle East. Traditional China and Japan had their tea houses, while in nineteenth- and twentieth-century Bengal, *adda*—a place for conversation, often accompanied by food—was an important cultural institution.[6]

Ancient Greece and modern Africa have been selected as case studies of cultures in which an oral system of communication was dominant.

In the ancient Greek city-states, politics—the very word is derived from 'polis'—depended to an unusual extent on public oral communication. Discussing the optimum size of the *polis*, Aristotle argued that it had to be small enough for all the citizens to be able to hear public speeches. Speeches in assemblies such as the Athenian *ekklesia* (open to all male citizens over the age of 18) were essential to the functioning of the ancient Greek public sphere. So were plays, raising fundamental moral problems and seen and heard by large numbers of people in open-air amphitheatres. So was the reciting in public of poems such as the *Iliad* and *Odyssey*, long viewed not as mere entertainment but as guides to conduct. Today, ancient Greece is studied on the basis of texts by poets, playwrights, and philosophers, but those texts were the products of a largely oral culture in which writing interacted with speech.[7]

A similar point might be made about African cultures after the introduction of writing and printing, often by Muslim or Christian missionaries, in the nineteenth century. Even today, when writing and print have been overtaken by the electric media, oral performances remain unusually important. Storytellers continue to entertain the public, allowing them to participate by using opening and closing formulas to which the audience will reply. In West Africa, oral poets, known as *griots*, are still active. For a long time, knowledge about the past was handed down orally. In Ashanti, there was a special genre known as drum history, in which the drums simulated speech, making use of formulas to avoid the ambiguity of drum language, with its relatively small 'vocabulary'.

It would be a mistake to view these oral cultures as poor in communicative resources, like the oral cultures of the modern West that have been impoverished by competition from alternative media. To describe the African situation, including the diasporic cultures of African Americans, we therefore need to use terms such as 'verbal art' or the oxymoron 'oral literature', drawing attention to the complexity and sophistication not only of individual performers, African equivalents of Avdo, but also of a variety of 'speech genres'.[8]

This oral system has been modified by three revolutions in communication: the rise of writing, printing, and finally of what we might call for convenience the electric media, including radio, television, and the internet.

The writing revolutions

Oral performances, especially lengthy ones like sermons, speeches, or the singing of epics, require a good memory. Hence the so-called 'art of memory', associating the things to be remembered with vivid images located in an imaginary structure such as a theatre or a palace, flourished in medieval and Renaissance Europe.[9] More generally, there was a search for mnemonics. The formulas and themes discussed by Parry and Lord may be regarded as a form of mnemonics. Another form is that of the *qipu* of Peru, the Quechua term for 'knot', referring to coloured strings with knots in them. These 'talking knots' were used to keep accounts of transactions concerning a variety of days, numbers of people, goods, donors, receivers, and so on.[10]

It has also been argued that some at least of the world's writing systems originated as forms of mnemonics. For example, the cuneiform writing system of ancient Babylonia seems to have begun in this way, the marks on the clay tablets being used, like the *qipu*, to record the giving or receiving of various goods. Writing, in the strict sense of signs employed to represent language, developed later.[11]

The first writing systems, in this more precise sense, developed in the Middle East before 3000 BC and include both Babylonian cuneiform and Egyptian hieroglyphics. They were followed by Chinese ideograms, in use before 1000 BC, and the pictograms of the Mayas, which date from round 500 BC. Since that time the number and variety of writing systems has vastly increased, as well as the material on which they have been written (palm leaves, birch bark, animal skins and bones, silk, papyrus, parchment, paper, wax, clay, stone or metal, using styluses, brushes, reed, quill, or metal pens, and so on). Writing systems used to be divided into two groups, the first (including hieroglyphics, ideograms, and pictograms) remaining closer to the mnemonic origins of script and representing ideas or things, while the second, alphabets, represent words or sounds. However, recent research has undermined the importance of this binary distinction and scholars now speak in terms of the predominant organizing principle of a given script.[12]

For historians, the great question or questions to answer is surely that of the manifold effects of writing on culture and society in different parts of the world. Two answers to these questions have become particularly famous, one of them being associated with the Canadian economic historian Harold Innis, in the 1950s, and the other with the British anthropologist Jack Goody, from the 1960s onwards.

Innis suggested that the use of heavier and more durable materials led to what he called a 'cultural bias' towards time and so to religious organization. The clay tablets used in Assyria, for example, were difficult to transport but they were well suited to the keeping of permanent records in an archive. On the other hand the lighter media, such as paper and papyrus, which are relatively ephemeral but may be moved quickly over long distances, led to a bias towards space and political organization. In a sense, then, Innis anticipated the idea associated with his younger colleague at the University of Toronto, Marshall McLuhan, that 'the medium is the message'.[13]

The Goody thesis (originally formulated in collaboration with the literary historian Ian Watt) emphasized the social effects of writing in general and the alphabet in particular. Contrasting ancient Greece in the age of 'alphabetic culture' with the fundamentally oral culture of West Africa (where Goody had carried out his fieldwork), the two scholars argued that writing encouraged abstract thought, a critical attitude to ideas, and the development of political democracy. The thesis has been criticized for paying insufficient emphasis to the various contexts in which different literacies have developed, while Goody himself has revised his views, qualifying but not abandoning them.[14]

Other consequences of writing, and especially of the spread of literacy, have been identified, especially in two domains, religion and politics. In the case of religion, attention has focused on the rise of authoritative 'scriptures': Buddhist, Jewish, Christian, or Muslim.

Writing aided the spread of Mahayana Buddhism, for instance, around the first century AD.[15] Again, in Western Europe in the thirteenth and fourteenth centuries, writing assisted the spread of Christian heresies among what have been described as 'textual communities', groups of literate laymen and laywomen meeting to discuss a book, perhaps the Bible (and so illustrating the interaction between speaking and writing). The Lollards, followers of John Wyclif, are a famous example of such groups.[16]

In the domain of politics, the consequences of literacy were at least equally profound. The famous contrast drawn by the German sociologist Max Weber, between traditional 'patrimonial' or personal forms of government on one side and modern 'bureaucratic' or impersonal forms on the other, depended on the issuing of written orders and the keeping of written records.[17] 'Paperwork', which we associate (like the 'red tape' used to tie the papers into bundles) with bureaucracy, depends on endless supplies of cheap paper. Paper had long been regularly employed in China, it was in use in the Islamic world from about 800 AD, and it was increasingly available in Europe around 1400. Hence it was in the early modern world that the effects of writing on the practices of government became particularly visible, in Europe and the Ottoman and Mughal empires as well as in China under the new dynasty of the Qing.

There were two sides to this rise of writing, two opposite consequences. On one side, it made information about the society they were administering available to the ruler and the central government. This was why Jean-Baptiste Colbert, for instance, one of the most powerful ministers in the service of King Louis XIV of France, spent so much energy collecting, arranging, and retrieving information.[18] Qing China was another example of what has been described as the 'archive state'. The flow of information from the provinces to the centre was carefully organized, with two tracks, the routine track and the confidential track (leading from high provincial officials to the emperor himself, who would add his comments in vermilion ink).[19] Cosmopolitan written languages such as Sanskrit, Latin, and Arabic have long helped to hold multilingual empires together.

There was also a negative side to the rise of writing. King Philip II of Spain became known as the 'paper king' (*el rey papelero*), chained to his desk and so missing the opportunity to become as well acquainted with his empire at first hand as his father the constantly itinerant Charles V. From Spain to Sweden, critics spoke and wrote of 'the rule of the secretaries' rather than that of the monarchs for whom they supposedly worked. In similar fashion, in the early modern Mughal Empire, the regime of Akbar was known as 'government by paper' (*kaghazi raj*) and the administration became more and more 'paper-bound' in the late seventeenth and early eighteenth centuries.[20]

Medieval Europe and the Islamic world have been chosen as two short case studies of cultures of writing. In medieval Europe, one of the major social distinctions was that between the clergy, defined as able to read, and the laity. The Church and the state kept records, generally written on expensive parchment. They were less extensive than they would be in the age of the 'paper state', but the chancery, the place where secretaries wrote and filed letters to and from the prince, was already an important organ of government.[21]

The knowledge of the learned was collected into treatises, available in their hundreds in libraries, especially the libraries of monasteries. Monks copied manuscripts, and so did students in universities, but the multiplication of manuscripts took place above all (at least in the late Middle Ages) in commercial *scriptoria*, where groups of scribes would write down the same words from dictation and thus allow the 'publication' of a text before the age of print.

Medieval Europe may also be described as a 'notarial culture' in which, especially in the cities of the Mediterranean region, a substantial proportion of the population had recourse to notaries in order to record wills, contracts, transfers of property, and so on (thus providing what archivists describe with a mixture of pride and complaint as 'kilometres' of sources for today's historians). It was not necessary for the client to be literate: in the Middle Ages, and indeed much later, people who could not themselves write or even read made use of writing through intermediaries.

In later centuries too, in major cities there were particular places where clients knew they could find public writers who would both compose and write out letters and other documents for them. In eighteenth-century Paris, there was the cemetery of the Saints-Innocents, where graves were used as desks, and in Mexico City, even today, there is the Plaza de Santo Domingo in the old city centre, where the scribes now use electric typewriters.[22] In villages, priests or pastors might perform this function for their parishioners. The importance of what is known as 'mediated literacy' should not be forgotten.

In the Islamic world, until about the year 1800, printing was generally banned, so that scholars have spoken of the 'calligraphic state'.[23] One might even speak of 'calligraphic culture' since, in response to the prohibition of the public display of images, writing, in a variety of scripts, angular or cursive (Kufi, Naskhi, and so on), was used on a variety of surfaces, stone, metal, wood, wool, or ceramics, to decorate walls, weapons, pulpits, rugs, plates, and so on. Good handwriting in the Arabic alphabet (also used to write texts in Persian, Turkish, Urdu, and other languages) was a much appreciated skill. It was necessary for the scribe (*warraq*), who spent his working life producing magnificent manuscripts of the Qur'an and other texts for wealthy patrons. It was equally necessary for the secretary (*katib*), working in the chancery (*diwan*), who both composed and wrote letters on behalf of sultans and shahs. Libraries of manuscript books were founded by rulers in Baghdad, Córdoba, and elsewhere and the numbers of books in them, even if the estimates were exaggerated, far surpassed the holdings of medieval libraries in the West.[24]

However, even more stress was placed on written communication in medieval Europe than in the Muslim world at the same time, at least in the domain of higher education. Muslim students literally sat at the feet of the master, listening to his words.[25] In Europe too universities were centres of oral communication—as indeed they still are—but speech was supplemented by writing. Lectures, for example, expounded texts, while students often took written notes and copied texts in manuscript. The coming of printing would add another element to the mix.

The print revolutions

It has become commonplace to refer to the invention and spread of printing with movable type as a revolution, even though it was still presented as 'the unacknowledged revolution' thirty years ago, by the North American historian Betty Eisenstein in 1979.[26] However, in this context it might be wiser to use the term 'revolution' in the plural, referring to separate revolutions in China, Korea, and the West.

In China, in the seventh century, the age of the Empress Wu, recently described as 'The Woman who discovered Printing', it was already possible to print on a massive scale, using wood-blocks carved with ideograms, a block for each page. The technique was used at this time to print short Buddhist spells, but it would later be employed to print images and also a wide range of texts from the Confucian classics to novels such as *The Romance of the Three Kingdoms*.[27]

Printing with movable type made of clay, wood, or metal was also in use in China and Korea in the thirteenth and fourteenth centuries, but it does not seem to have been taken up widely for obvious reasons. For alphabetic cultures, movable type makes printing simpler and possibly cheaper (though this point has been contested), but for China, with about 2,000 basic ideograms (and another 30,000 in use by educated people), its advantages are, to put it mildly, not obvious. It is surely no accident that the development of printing in Korea coincided with the invention of an alphabetic script in the middle of the fifteenth century.[28]

The similarities between Korean printing with movable type and Gutenberg's 'invention' are obvious enough, and it is quite possible that Gutenberg had heard about the Korean technique (just as Galileo had heard about a Dutch telescope before constructing his own). What was new in Europe was the development of this technique for commercial purposes, thanks in part to the arrival of relatively cheap paper and also to the spread of literacy among the laity (including some women) in the late Middle Ages. In contrast to the West, where printing was commercialized from the start, in both China and Korea printing was controlled by the government. Books were given away rather than sold. By the sixteenth century, however, commercial printing was flourishing in China too, and by the seventeenth century in Japan as well.[29]

Printed images were an important form of communication in all these parts of the world, whether they were used to illustrate texts or sold by themselves. In the West, from the Renaissance onwards, leading artists such as Sandro Botticelli and Albrecht Dürer produced 'prints', originally woodcuts, then copperplates, and later etchings, mezzotints, aquatints, lithographs, and so on, using different techniques to create images that could be reproduced by machine. In China and Japan, by contrast, the woodcut continued to dominate production, using the same method as wood-block printing but refining it to produce colour prints, as in the famous Japanese genre of *ukiyo-e*, 'pictures of the floating world' (the world of the urban pleasure quarters), to which artists of the calibre of Hokusai, Hiroshige, and Utamaro all contributed.[30]

Gradually, the new medium took over the world. Presses were established in Spanish America in the sixteenth century, in both Mexico and Peru. By contrast, only four printers were at work in North America before 1680, while presses were forbidden to be established in Brazil before 1808, so that books had to be imported from Portugal.

The years around 1800 are a watershed in the history of printed communication in many parts of the world. It was in 1810 that the German printer Friedrich Koenig patented a new invention, a press operated by steam power and so capable of printing many more pages per hour than was possible for a press operated by hand.

In Brazil, permission to print in 1808 was followed by the rise of short-lived political and polemical journals such as *O maribondo* (1822), *Bússola da liberdade* (1832), and others, mainly from Recife.[31] The *Mercurio peruano* was founded in 1791, and a famous Mexican newspaper, *El pensador mexicano*, in 1812. Following the revolt against Spain, the first printing houses were established in Buenos Aires and a newspaper in English, the *British Packet and Argentine News*, was founded in 1826.

In Africa, writing and printing arrived at more or less the same time in the nineteenth century, along with missionaries (both Muslim and Christian). The *Cape Town Gazette* and the *Sierra Leone Royal Gazette* both date from the year 1800.

In the Islamic world print, long banned (apart from an abortive experiment in Istanbul at the beginning of the eighteenth century), began to be permitted. In 1795, for instance, the French embassy in Istanbul was allowed to print a newspaper, the *Bulletin des nouvelles*, followed in 1825 by the *Spectateur oriental*, edited by the Frenchman Alexandre Blacque, a merchant in Izmir. Blacque was subsequently asked by the sultan to edit the official Ottoman gazette, the *Takvim-i-Vekayi* (1831). Meanwhile, in 1821, in Cairo, a newspaper in Turkish and Arabic, *Jurnal ül-Khidiv*, had begun publication.[32]

Like writing, the introduction of printing had important consequences, both intended and unintended, for the cultures that adopted it. For one thing, it encouraged the spread of the 'paper state', including its multitude of official forms. Literacy campaigns were organized by churches (in Protestant Germany and Sweden in the eighteenth century, for instance), so that ordinary people would become better Christians by reading the Bible. Similar campaigns were organized by the state in twentieth-century Russia, Cuba, and elsewhere, in order to make ordinary people better citizens, or at least more receptive to official propaganda.[33] Some democratic governments, from the United States to Brazil, have made voting in elections conditional on literacy.

One might say that these governments agreed with the German philosopher-sociologist Jürgen Habermas, who has argued that the rise of what he calls *Öffentlichkeit*, usually translated as the 'public sphere', was encouraged by changes in communication such as the reading of newspapers in coffee houses in the eighteenth century and led—like literacy, according to Goody—to the rise of critical attitudes and democratic culture.[34] This insight is a valuable one. All the same, it might be more useful to employ the term 'public sphere' in the plural than in the singular, distinguishing between male and female, bourgeois and working-class, or religious and secular spheres. It would also be illuminating to distinguish different media of communication, noting the importance of the traditional oral public sphere, associated with public squares, taverns, and other centres of sociability, as well as the newer spheres associated with radio, television, and the internet.

Despite earlier literacy campaigns, reading remained a minority skill in most countries until the twentieth century. Around the year 1850, half the adult population of Europe could not read (around 75 per cent in Italy and Spain, and over 90 per cent in the Russian Empire), while 84 per cent of the Brazilian population was officially described as illiterate in 1890.[35] These illiterates were often familiar with books at second hand, listening to others read aloud. The importance of the oral communication of printed texts must not be forgotten. To take a striking example from Cuba in the nineteenth and early twentieth centuries, workers in tobacco factories, where hands are busy but ears have little to do, used to club together to pay the wages of a colleague who did not work but instead read aloud to the others from a pulpit constructed for the purpose.

The unintended consequences of the arrival of the printing press have probably been even more profound. Print helped to standardize and fix the formerly fluid vernacular languages—especially in their written forms—in order to sell books outside a single region. The press also undermined monopolies of knowledge, allowing readers to share the secrets of many crafts, from mining to cooking. As the rise of advertising in seventeenth-century European books vividly illustrates, communication gradually became more and more commercialized.

Both the religious and the political consequences of printing were profound. Printed pamphlets attacking the Catholic Church, printed translations of the Bible, and printed catechisms all played an important role in the Protestant Reformation, confirming the fears of Catholic clerics that literacy led to heresy and leading to the publication of the notorious *Index of Prohibited Books*, an attempt to fight printing with its own weapons. In the domain of politics, as in that of religion, print, especially printed newspapers, encouraged criticism and even revolution, as in the case of England in the 1640s and France in 1789.[36] Benedict Anderson has argued that what he calls 'print capitalism', and especially the printed newspaper, aided the construction of 'imagined communities', especially the nation, though it should be remembered that only a minority of the population had access to newspapers before the second half of the nineteenth century.[37]

Slowly but surely, printed texts reached wider and wider circles of readers in Europe, Asia, Africa, and the Americas, especially in the form of the booklets known in English as 'chap-books' because they were retailed by 'chapmen' or pedlars. France, for instance, had its *Bibliothèque Bleue*, booklets with blue covers that were distributed in the countryside as well as the towns by itinerant pedlars from the seventeenth century onwards. Spain had its *literatura de cordel*, so-called because the booklets were sold in marketplaces hung on a string. Japan had its *kana-zōshi*, stories written in a simple syllabic script (rather than the Chinese characters used by the elite) and sold in the street.[38]

Brazil had its *folhetos* from the later nineteenth century to the late twentieth (or even later, though this form of literature is in decline), texts that illustrate once again the central theme of this chapter, the interaction between media. *Folhetos* were short texts, ranging from eight to thirty-two pages, printed in small numbers on hand presses in small-scale establishments in a style that was amateur rather than professional (for example, the typeface might change from one page to another). There was often a woodcut illustration on the cover. The texts were traditionally divided into genres such as prophecies, 'stories of suffering', and 'bold exploits', associated with heroes ranging from medieval knights to modern bandits, notably Lampião.

However, these printed texts remained close to oral performances. They were written in verse in a traditional form, *sextilhas*, verses of six lines with seven or eight syllables to the line. The poets, known as *cantadores* or *trovadores*, not only wrote the texts, but also performed them, reciting the verses aloud (often accompanying themselves on a guitar or other stringed instrument), usually at weekly markets, before selling copies of the text to the audience. The printed text was not able to produce many features of the performance, but it may well have functioned as a kind of mnemonic, facilitating re-enactments by the buyers and their friends.

This hypothesis helps explain the paradox that the public for *folhetos* was most extensive in an area of particularly low literacy, the rural north-east. The *folheto* was in a sense a book for the illiterate, a text which they bought so that literate friends or relatives could read it to them. Towards the end of the twentieth century, the *folhetos* were modernized. They discussed contemporary themes, from AIDS to Brazil's foreign debt. The woodcut on the cover was replaced by a coloured photograph. The poets used microphones for their recitations, and sold not only texts but cassettes as well. Where the booklet used to function as a souvenir of the performance, the performance turned into a commercial for the cassette.[39]

Elsewhere in the twentieth century, the rise of 'comics' in the West and *manga* in Japan both continued and transformed the tradition of the chap-book, while Nigeria in the 1950s and 1960s developed a 'market literature', entertaining or improving stories with appealing titles such as 'Mabel the sweet honey that poured away'. The booklets were sold in markets, especially in the town of Onitsha, until the Nigerian civil war.[40]

Scholars have often linked commercialization to mass production and even to 'mass culture'. However, the rise of journals and magazines produced for different groups of people with different interests suggests that the market for print has long been diverse. The first magazines for women date from the late seventeenth century, the *Mercure galant* in France, for instance, and their editors had already discovered the combination of fashion information, romantic stories, and competitions that long remained a key to commercial success. Individual variety is also demonstrated by letters to newspapers and magazines, another tradition that goes back to the years around 1700 (to the *Athenian Mercury* and the *Spectator*) and is not yet exhausted.[41]

What we call 'print culture' is actually a mix of oral, written, and printed communication. The interaction of orality and print may be illustrated by the *folhetos* discussed above and their equivalents in other cultures. Manuscript and print also interacted. Printers produced hybrid books with blank spaces for readers to add information and comments, thus personalizing the text.[42] The production of handwritten texts continued in the age of print but a certain division of labour was established, with intimate and clandestine communication becoming the domain of the manuscript. Handwritten newsletters, for instance, continued to provide the news that was not allowed to be printed.[43]

The electric revolutions

'Electric culture', a convenient shorthand phrase to refer to a sequence or package of nineteenth- and twentieth-century media, is actually 'oral, written, printed, and electric culture'. The phrase is something of a mouthful—but a mouthful with the advantage of reminding us of the variety of cultures of communication in which we continue to live. The age of globalization and cultural homogenization is also an age of fragmentation and heterogenization.[44]

The electric age may be divided into stages dominated by the telegraph, film, radio, television, and the internet, but the earlier stages have survived into the later ones and once again interact with them, as in the case of the technological 'convergence' that has recently produced mobile phones that are also cameras and give access to the internet.[45]

To begin with the telegraph, in 1850, a German journalist, Paul Reuter, who lived in Aachen, began using the new telegraph line to send news to Berlin. This marked the beginning of what became Reuter's Telegram Company, founded in 1865 and based in Britain. The consequent acceleration of the transmission of information about crops, prices, and so on made a considerable impact on the economy. The telegraph also made an impact on politics: the outbreak of the Franco-Prussian War in 1870, for instance, followed Bismarck's publication of an edited form of a confidential telegram, deliberately provoking the French to declare war.

Where the telegraph might be seen as an ally of print, assisting the newspaper, film and radio have undermined the print revolution, encouraging the return of the image and also the return of the oral. However, the cultural and social effects of film and radio have been very different.

The film can of course be used to present news. In France, Pathé Frères began to issue 'newsreels', as they came to be called, in 1908, while in London a news cinema opened in 1909, the Daily Bioscope. All the same, the future of the film was in drama, especially popular dramas of the kind produced in Hollywood and later in 'Bollywood' in Bombay. This future also turned out to be international, especially after the rise of dubbing and subtitling. Hollywood made an unexpected contribution to the globalization of culture, making Third World audiences aware of North American patterns of clothing and behaviour (from kissing to eating with a knife and fork) and encouraging imitation thanks to the 'glamour' of the 'stars'.[46]

The new medium helped to create these stars. Some actors and singers had achieved fame in earlier periods, but film allowed far more people in many places to develop enthusiasms for a relatively small number of performers, creating fanatics or 'fans' as well as stars. One unexpected consequence of the star system has been its impact on politics. Glamour, or charisma, can be translated into votes, launching the political careers of actors such as Ronald Reagan and Arnold Schwarzenegger as well as a number of Bollywood actors in India such as Sunil Dutt and Vinod Khanna, who joined the Bharatiya Janata Party and became Minister of Culture and Tourism in 2002.

In contrast to film, radio turned out to be an ideal medium for presenting the news, especially at the level of the nation. Indeed, one important effect of communication by radio was to encourage the standardization of spoken language, just as print had encouraged the standardization of written language. In Italy, for instance, when the country was united in 1861, less than 10 per cent of the population spoke Italian (as opposed to regional dialects). It was only in the age of radio that the majority came first to understand and then to speak the national language.

By the 1930s and 1940s, a number of governments had become aware of the value of the new medium as a means of generating popular support. Leaders as different as Adolf Hitler and Winston Churchill, with their radio speeches, and F. D. Roosevelt, with his 'Fire Side Chats', grasped the opportunity. Lázaro Cárdenas of Mexico, with his annual New Year broadcasts, and Juan Perón—not to mention his wife Eva—also made use of the radio for political purposes. Again, in the Brazil of Gétulio Vargas, who became a dictator in 1937, there was a daily hour of radio propaganda, the *Hora do Brasil*, from seven till eight in the evening, which all channels were obliged to broadcast.

All the same, the importance of radio as a medium of entertainment should not be forgotten. In England in the middle of the twentieth century, for instance, popular programmes included serials such as *Mrs Dale's Diary* (which ran for more than twenty years, 1948–69), and *The Archers*, featuring a farm family, which began to be broadcast in 1950 and is now the longest-running serial in the world.

Television, invented before the Second World War but launched commercially afterwards, soon overtook both film and radio, combining their advantages, since the medium is well adapted both for spreading the news and for telling stories, for domestic and foreign markets. It brought the world into the living-room and saturated everyday life with images. One of its central genres, the 'soap opera' or *telenovela*, imitated serials on the radio (which had in turn imitated the serials in magazines), but enjoyed much more popular success in countries as different as the USA and Egypt. *Novelas* produced in Mexico and Brazil (most famously *The Slave Isaura*, 1976) have been particularly successful internationally, not only in other parts of Latin America but in Europe and China as well. Like films, they have contributed to globalization by making different styles of life better known all over the world, even if a soap opera such as *Dallas* has been 'read' or interpreted in very different ways by audiences who are culturally as well as geographically distant from Texas.[47]

In our age of accelerating technological innovation, television has in turn been overtaken by audio- and videocassettes, by DVDs, and above all by the rise of the internet from the early 1990s onwards, when a network originally developed in order to support academic research was opened to a wider public.

Some at least of the many economic, political, and cultural consequences of this rapid sequence of changes in the media are visible enough. One of the more obvious trends might be described as the end of the paper state (dominant for the last five hundred years or so) as governments come to keep more and more information on disc. The survival of the newspaper is also threatened, although at the moment paper versions and electronic versions of the same newspaper continue to coexist. The printed book is often said to be an endangered species, but at the moment at least it is holding its own, with something like 200,000 new titles a year published in Britain today, far more than a generation ago.[48]

Another highly visible trend is the tendency to 'unfix' communication, thus reversing the 500-year trend that followed Gutenberg. The new interactive media do not resemble print so much as the oral and manuscript modes of communication, when singers responded to the wishes of their listeners or scribes modified the text they were copying for their own purposes.

In the case of other social and political consequences of the recent round of changes in the media, there are forces pulling in different directions and it is far from clear which, if any, will be victorious. On the one side, the ownership of newspapers and television networks by multinational corporations encourages globalization. On the other, it is now possible for an increasing number of diasporic communities not only to keep in almost daily contact with relatives thousands of miles away but also to conserve their separate culture, for example by viewing television programmes from their country of origin via satellite.[49]

Again, on one side, governments have more access to information about their citizens than ever before, fuelling fears of dictatorial rule by a 'Big Brother' state. Media 'moguls' who control empires of communication are no new phenomenon: they go back at least as far as the Englishman Alfred Harmsworth (1865–1922) and the American William Randolph Hearst (1863–1951), but they have acquired more and more influence on what people see and hear every day from their screens, including the way in which the news is presented. We therefore have some reason to fear what might be called 'Cyberdictatorship'.

On the other hand, leaks of information are increasingly common. Hackers reveal economic, political, and military secrets, while investigative journalists are able to bring down governments, as in the case of 'Watergate', when President Richard Nixon was forced to resign in 1974. In the Islamic world, videocassettes have not only allowed Osama bin Laden to publicize his denunciations of the West, but also permitted a debate about the principles of Islam that some scholars have compared to the Protestant Reformation, with the cassette taking the place of the printing press.[50]

Most spectacular of all, the rise of the internet, a centrifugal medium, is widening the public sphere and supporting civil society and democracy. Like earlier letters to newspapers or telephone calls to television stations, 'blogs' or web-logs, which became popular at the beginning of the twenty-first century, allow individuals to express their opinions in public, but on an even wider scale. The spread of email has encouraged networking and the activism of groups of citizens, especially important when a political regime is authoritarian and controls other media, as in the case of China today (though the Golden Shield project, inaugurated in 2003, is intended to erect a great wall against the internet). For these reasons—although bloggers in some countries risk prison if they criticize the government—there is hope for what some commentators call 'Cyberdemocracy'.[51]

In short, new media bring new opportunities with them as well as new dangers. If anything future is certain, it is that people will have to learn to adjust still more rapidly to changes in the media of communication than they are trying to do today.

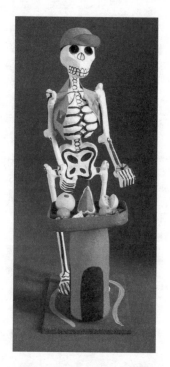

8. Mexico City, figurine in the form of a skeleton fruit-seller with a baseball cap, made from paper-mâché mounted onto a wooden framework. Made by the Garcia family, 1980s. © By permission of the Trustees of the British Museum

8 Population

PAT THANE

The size, structure, and dynamics of change in the population are fundamental to the functioning of any society. Whether it is predominantly old or young, changes in age structure, patterns of births, marriage, deaths, and migration or in its gender balance fundamentally affect a society's culture and emotions, economic, social, and political structures.

Population change is also one of the most mysterious social phenomena. This is partly because, before the comparatively recent past, relevant historical data varies from the patchy and elusive to the non-existent. Also because, even when factual data can be found, it is often difficult to interpret in order to understand why, for example, birth rates rise and fall or why more, or fewer, people marry, or re-marry, or do not, in different times and places.

Origins

We do not know exactly when or where populations we can recognize as 'human' evolved from longer established species, though archaeological findings constantly push the possible origins further into the distant past. These currently suggest that by, at earliest, 250,000–500,000 years ago (indicated by bones discovered in China) and, at latest, between 60,000 and 40,000 years BC, 'humans' lived in what are now Africa, Asia, Europe, and Australia, arriving, probably, by a combination of evolution and migration. At a later point, the date of which is uncertain (perhaps 14,000 years ago), they spread into the Americas, crossing the Bering Strait during the ice age. With the development of new forms of production and of trade and warfare, the extent and complexity of the movements of people and the density of settlement across the regions of the world increased over the millennia.[1]

Indications of the location, size, shape, life expectancy, causes of death (including famines and epidemics), the economy, and cultural practices of populations in the distant past are derived from archaeological fragments such as bones, tablets, tombstones, and other remnants of human existence. Sources, of course, became more abundant over time, though they do not necessarily provide more accurate representations of demographic reality at their times of origin. For example, tombstones from Roman Africa record remarkably long lives: 3 per cent of one collection of 10,697 stones record an age at death past 100. It is most unlikely that these ages can be taken literally. More probably they represent biases both in statements of age and in customs of commemorating older age groups at a time when reaching an advanced age was an indicator of status.[2]

From around 500 BC in classical Greece and the Roman Empire, and rather earlier in Mesopotamia,[3] more documentary texts survive, but everywhere they can provide only a broad approximation of the size and shape of the population. Nevertheless, we can be reasonably certain, from literary and epigraphic testimony, that in the first century AD, and probably earlier, infant mortality was very high (as it is likely always previously to have been) but that those who survived the hazards of very early life lived for as long as survivors did until the twentieth century, when life expectancy in higher-income countries underwent an unprecedented extension. At this early date, evidence from censuses, tombstones, and literary commentaries suggests that around 6–8 per cent of the population of the Roman Empire was aged 60 or above. A very few may have survived to be centenarians.[4]

Gender and population

High infant mortality and relatively long average life expectancy thereafter are continuities of population history until the twentieth century, though with variations across space and time. Another apparent continuity across most times and places is the propensity of females to outlive males at all ages and hence to be a majority of many populations, with the exception of those in which male children are so prized that female babies may be selectively destroyed or abandoned. In the absence of sex-selective intervention, infant mortality is normally lower among females.

Whether or not adult females did outlive males was long debated, in the absence of statistics. Among the great classical writers, Aristotle believed, in keeping with contemporary humoral theory, that it was natural for men to outlive women because the male 'is a warmer creature than the female'. Women were thought to be dry and to wither earlier in life than men. However, Aristotle added that men who fornicated or worked too hard died earlier than most women. It is hard to judge definitively which gender group lived longer because women's ages rarely survive in ancient records—'a reflection of a male world, not necessarily of higher female mortality at younger ages'.[5] For example, women were not routinely recorded in Roman censuses.[6]

The belief in the greater longevity of men continued in medieval Europe, though in the thirteenth century Albertus Magnus, while apparently agreeing with Aristotle that men, by nature, live longer, noted that women, 'per accidens', tended to live longer. He attributed this to menstruation purifying women of harmful humours, sexual intercourse taking away fewer of their bodily fluids, and their suffering less than men from the hazards of work (and, he might have added, warfare). In records of the later Middle Ages, women still figure less than men: 'there is a general tendency to masculinize the data',[7] which tends to bias our picture of the gender composition of the population. Censuses of population were often designed to assess property ownership for taxation purposes, potential for military service or public office. Girls and women were generally excluded from such activities, so were of less interest to census takers than men, especially male heads of household.

At all times, men and women were exposed to different types of risk which influenced health and length of life. Women suffered the hazards of childbirth and were often worn out by work. They cared for the sick and were exposed to infection. Men experienced the risks of hard and sometimes dangerous work, warfare, and casual violence. There is no clear evidence that childbirth was a greater cause of death among women than were work, accidents, and violence among men of comparable age. Until the late nineteenth century tuberculosis was a greater killer of women of childbearing age in Europe than childbirth.[8] Among ducal families in fourteenth-century England, average life expectancy of men at age 20 was 31.5 more years, of women 31.1. This took account of natural death only. When violent death was included, the average for men fell to 21.7.[9] Overall, the gender balance in medieval populations is uncertain and was no doubt variable across social groups, places, and time.

Physicians in Europe were long influenced by the belief introduced by Galen (AD 129–c.200) in Greece that women became more like men when they passed the menopause, becoming leaner, drier, stronger, and healthier than in earlier life and likely to outlive men at these later ages. In later life, women no longer experienced the hazards of childbirth whilst men of similar age were still engaged in work and warfare, though older women worked and tended the sick. Yet physicians in eighteenth-century France still asserted that men had the advantage, though they were puzzled by the consistency with which women 'went against nature' and outlived men.

John Graunt in England in 1662 was the first social statistician systematically to compare mortality differences between adults and children, urban and rural parishes, and between the sexes. He found that, on average, women lived two to three years longer than men, though women resorted more often to medical care. For the following hundred years, Graunt's successors repeatedly found a small but consistent advantage for women, though the conviction survived that this female advantage was 'strange'. Michael Anderson has estimated that of the English birth cohort of 1681, 82 per cent of men and 79 per cent of women were dead by age 65.[10]

Since official registration of births and deaths began in the nineteenth century in most high-income countries (see below) the longer survival rates of females, at all ages from birth, has been undoubted, even whilst tuberculosis remained a scourge of women. The likely explanation is genetic and related to the need for women to be resilient enough to bear and rear children. The fact that among animals, generally but not universally, females outlive males suggests that the difference is not just due to the tendency of males to engage in riskier behaviour. The hormonal differences between males and females appear to influence survival.[11] There have been exceptions, however: women of European origin in North America are estimated to have had a lower expectation of life than men from the mid-seventeenth century to the 1890s, probably due to the rigours of migration and settlement in often inhospitable territory.[12]

In the twentieth century, in most higher-income countries including North America, the female advantage grew, though later in the century the gender gap in adult life expectancy began to narrow in some countries, possibly due to the participation of women in a wider range of occupations and in hazardous pastimes such as smoking. Women also still tended to suffer more ill health in late life, perhaps partly due to their greater propensity to poverty. On the other hand, in some countries, notably Russia and some other former Communist countries of Eastern Europe in the later twentieth century, it widened as male life expectancy fell, perhaps due to increased unemployment and falling living standards for some. In 2005 Russian male life expectancy at birth was 59, below that of such a poor country as Haiti, while that of females was 72—probably the largest gender gap in the world at this time.[13]

In the UK in 2005–7 average life expectancy at birth (at a time when infant mortality was extremely low) was 77.2 for males, 81.5 for females.[14] Comparisons of life expectancy across countries are hazardous even in the early twenty-first century because the quality of data varies and is least reliable in the poorest and most strife-torn states. Also life expectancy at birth is strongly influenced by high infant and child mortality rates, which of course reduce averages (see below) and are also highest in the poorest countries. We can say with confidence that life expectancy at birth in 2005 was greatest in Japan, at 79 for males, 86.1 for females. Iceland came second, with a narrower gender gap: 80.2 and 83.3 respectively. It was lowest in sub-Saharan Africa: in Swaziland 39.8 and 39.4 (one of very few countries where males outlived females, though only marginally); in Zimbabwe, 44.1 and 42.6; in South Africa, 48.8 and 49.7. As well as high infant and child death rates, AIDS raised adult death rates in these countries at this time, together with poverty and poor health care. The gender gap tends to be narrow in these poorer countries, but with women normally having an advantage. Notably, another poor country, but with a good health care system—Cuba—had life expectancy in 2005 of 76.2 for males and 80.4 for females, marginally above the US average at 75.6 and 80.8.[15] These trends and differentials are ongoing. In all but the poorest countries, life expectancy for males and females at all ages improved especially in the second half of the twentieth century, though lack of data makes long-term trends hard to assess for many countries.

The gender balance of local and national populations was not only influenced by survival rates. Migration was also important. Again, statistics are more uncertain the further back we go in time and the poorer and less bureaucratized the society. However, listings for a number of European towns from the seventeenth to the nineteenth centuries show a female majority due to migration from the countryside for work as domestic servants, and, increasingly, for industrial employment.[16]

On the other hand, the populations of white in-migrants to the 'New World' of colonization from the seventeenth to the late nineteenth centuries were predominantly male. In Australia for example, New South Wales and South Australia had a male majority through the nineteenth century into the early twentieth century.[17] About the gender balance, or any other precise details, of the indigenous populations of these countries we have little knowledge until the very recent past because they were long excluded from official statistics or imperfectly counted. For example in Australia Aboriginal people were counted not at all, or inconsistently, in the censuses of the Australian states through the nineteenth century. An incomplete census for New South Wales in 1891 found 4,559 'full-blood' Aboriginal males and 3,721 females; 1,663 male and 1,520 female 'half-castes'.[18] In the first Australian national census in 1911 only 'aboriginal natives' living close to white settlements (as very many did not) were enumerated. The 1971 census was the first seriously to try to improve enumeration of Aboriginal dwellers in 'remote areas' following Aboriginal people finally being unequivocally granted the vote in 1967. Yet still in 2004, the Australian government Bureau of Statistics commented that 'satisfactory data on births, deaths and migration are not generally available' for the Aboriginal population.[19] In the same year the Bureau estimated that Aboriginal females had life expectancy at birth seventeen years below that of non-Aboriginal Australian women.[20] By contrast in New Zealand, Maori people were earlier integrated into the state and its statistics. Civil registration of Maori marriages became compulsory in 1911; previously only marriages between Europeans and Maori were required to be registered. Maori births and deaths had to be registered from 1913, though registration remained poor until at least the 1930s. Censuses of the Maori population took place periodically from 1845. The 1867 Franchise Act made this mandatory following their being granted parliamentary representation. Combined enumeration of the entire population was introduced in the census of 1951.[21]

Ethnic groups within nation states have had differing life expectancies and gender balances. In the USA, for example, in 1900 a white male at birth could expect, on average, to live 46.6 years, a female 48.7; black African American people, 32.5 and 33.5 respectively. By 1950 the gap between ethnic groups had narrowed but not disappeared, the numbers being 66.5/72.2, 59.1/62.9 respectively. In 2005 they were 75.7/80.8, 69.5/76.5. In 1950 the gap in life expectancy between ethnic groups at age 65 had narrowed to 12.8/15.1, 12.9/14.9, but it widened by 2005 to 17.2/20.0 and 15.2/18.7, due perhaps to increasing poverty and diminishing access to health care for poorer people who were disproportionately black.[22]

Censuses and other statistics

Head counts or 'censuses' (from the Latin *census* meaning 'register') of populations, local, regional, or national, have a long history, though ancient censuses do not, of course, always survive.[23] In the ancient world, the Babylonians and Chinese collected statistics about their people for reasons of taxation or military recruitment. The Egyptians used head counts to help plan the building of the Pyramids. According to St Luke, a Roman census ordered by Caesar Augustus brought Mary and Joseph to Bethlehem. Within the British Isles, Scotland seems to have led the way in the seventh century with the Gaelic *Senchus fer n'Alba*.

Where early (and later) census data survive they must be read with caution. For example, Pliny and Phlegon cite figures apparently derived from the Roman census of AD 73/4. Again, these report incredible numbers of centenarians for one region of Italy, some as old as 150. Significant differences between the two authors make the weaknesses in their reporting especially evident.[24] As well as the valorization of advanced age referred to above, the temptation of individuals to misrepresent age and other information may have been strong when censuses were collected for reasons of taxation or military recruitment, since age could bring exemptions.

Record keeping in Roman Egypt appears to have been especially extensive. A census every fourteen years, theoretically, collected and stored comprehensive information about status, origin, age, and financial standing of all inhabitants, including slaves. Those who failed to register in the census were fined. Accuracy may have been harder to police. The incentives to inaccuracy may have been considerable since, again, the primary purpose of the census was tax collection and the records were also used for military recruitment. In this highly bureaucratized culture, probably unparalleled in the ancient world, notices of births and deaths were also recorded.[25]

Over the following centuries there were many local and regional listings of people taken for various purposes, including taxation, which survive in increasing numbers over time. Laslett analysed 100 such listings from various parts of England between 1574 and 1821.[26] Gregory King (1648–1712) was a public servant who pioneered in England the collection of national statistics, including of wealth and poverty, and in 1696 produced his *Natural and Political Observations upon the State and Condition of England*, which attempted, based mainly on tax data, to estimate population size, its distribution between town and countryside, household size, age distribution, marriage patterns, and birth and death rates, plus estimates of income and expenses per head for twenty-six social groups, from peers to vagrants. The estimates are imperfect but are unrivalled in England until the nineteenth century.[27]

The earliest systematic national censuses were taken in Quebec in 1666, Iceland in 1703, Sweden in 1749, Finland 1750, Denmark 1769, Spain 1768/9, followed by some German and Italian states.[28] The United States followed in 1790 and Britain in 1801, preceded in both countries by decades of debate. In both there was some opposition induced by fear among devout Christians that a census would incur the wrath of God because a census of the Israelites ordered by King David was followed by a plague which killed thousands. More influential were fears that a census would intrude upon individual liberty, or that it would reveal to foreign enemies the small size and relative weakness of the country. Such opposition was overridden by uncertainty and curiosity about the actual size of national populations, in particular by awareness that numbers were growing, and concern as to whether population growth might outstrip food supplies. In Britain these fears were fuelled by Thomas Malthus, whose *First Essay on the Principle of Population* (1798) argued that, left unchecked, the population would grow faster than the supply of resources, especially food. He suggested that two kinds of check on growth could follow: a 'preventive check', limiting population growth by delay or avoidance of marriage, reducing births, which required human compliance; and a 'positive' check that limited population growth by raising the death rate due to the effects of scarcity. Demands followed for the measurement of actual population growth and assessment of its causes, to assist judgement of the scale of the risk and the measures required to minimize it.

Everywhere, it was some time before censuses provided reliable head counts, due to inadequate bureaucratic resources, difficulties of communications, including of travel, and resistance and evasion. The first reliable census in Britain was in 1841 when, for the first time, a force of enumerators was employed throughout the country to visit each home and collect information. Little is known about practices in previous censuses which appear to have received little central guidance and to have varied in the completeness of their returns.[29] Until 1850, US censuses enumerated only the head of each household. Probably no census has been wholly accurate. It was, for example, difficult to count the teeming, often impoverished populations of nineteenth-century inner cities and today there are similar problems in lower-income countries and in counting the shifting inner-city populations even of wealthy countries. Some people have always had reasons to evade enumeration, because they feared that it would lead to taxation or because they were illegal immigrants in the many places in which, in all times, there have been restrictions on migration.

As we have seen above, in the countries of white settlement in the 'New World' indigenous peoples were slow to be included in censuses, and recording may still be imperfect. We do not, therefore, have precise information about their undoubtedly high death rates following colonization due to disease, warfare, and persecution, or about other aspects of their demographic histories, though the evidence above of the differing life expectancy of ethnic groups indicates the extent of inequality between their experience and that of the colonizers. While slavery survived in the Americas, slaves were not enumerated in the USA or in European colonies in the Caribbean.

In Britain, as elsewhere, from the time of the first census, the census takers did not just count heads, but asked questions about population characteristics which have changed in each successive census, reflecting the concerns of each place and time period about social and economic conditions.[30] British censuses from the beginning asked about occupation, since this was believed to be linked to patterns of sickness and death which were a central concern of the census. Questions changed as knowledge and cultural assumptions changed. For example, it was decided in the 1851 British census to count women engaged in unpaid domestic duties as part of the working population, and no longer as 'inactive', on the grounds that, as the then Registrar-General put it:

It requires no argument to prove that the wife, mother, mistress of the English family discharges duties of no small importance. The most important production of a country is its population. And under the institution of marriage...this country has a population of much higher character than countries where polygamy prevails [and] where the management of the household belongs to the husband.[31]

The British census in 1891 included a question about the number of rooms in each household, in response to fears of overcrowding in cities and consequent disease. A question about religious adherence was included in 2001 in response to the increasing cultural complexity of the British population due to immigration, and uncertainty about the extent of secularization. A similar question was planned in 1851, to determine whether there were sufficient places of worship to meet demand, especially in growing towns. It was decided to hold, instead, a separate, voluntary, religious census, also in 1851, on the grounds that people should be entitled to withhold such information, as they could not in the regular census without incurring a fine. The results showed levels of non-attendance at religious worship which were thought alarming; only about half of the population in England and Wales judged able to attend religious worship (in terms of age, disability, etc.) did so. The religion question was voluntary in 2001 also but was incorporated in the census.

Because governments in the late eighteenth and early nineteenth centuries were concerned to explain the growth or shrinking of populations, they increasingly sought information about numbers of births, marriages, and deaths and cause of death. Records of baptisms, marriages, and burials had long been kept by religious institutions and, where these survive, they provide valuable historical data. But they did not provide complete information about populations, especially where there were substantial numbers of non-believers, or, more commonly in eighteenth- and nineteenth-century Europe and America, growing Protestant sects which did not practise infant baptism. To provide more precise data, compulsory civil registration of births, marriages, and deaths (including cause of death) was instituted in France at the time of the French Revolution and in England and Wales in July 1837, then in Scotland in 1855 and Ireland in 1864. Again, everywhere—and as we have seen in the cases of minority and indigenous populations— it was some time before complete and accurate data was collected; in England and Wales not before the 1860s.[32] In the USA, again, there was resistance to compulsory registration. Registration began in many cities and some states in the later nineteenth century but was not complete for all states until 1933. Birth and death data were less vital to understanding patterns of population in North America and other countries and regions which were hosts to large-scale immigration and internal migration than in more settled populations.

The rise of demography as a field of study

Modern demography—the scientific study of population—originated in London in the seventeenth century when John Graunt studied the lists of people who had died in London—the 'Bills of Mortality'—in order to estimate life expectancy. Dutch and English mathematicians then developed the concept of forecasting the length of life of members of a specified group, based on information about the lifetimes of other members of that group. In particular, Edmund Halley (who also predicted accurately the return of what is still known as Halley's comet) developed this approach, enabling the calculation of life tables, which estimate the average number of years left to members of a defined group at a certain age. This calculation remains important for insurers and providers of annuities and pensions. It is a more useful measure than average expectation of life at birth in times of high infant mortality—i.e. all times in all countries before the early/mid-twentieth century; high death rates in early life pull down such averages. In most times and places before the twentieth century, those who survived the hazardous early years of life had a good change of living into their fifties, sixties, or beyond. As the insurance market grew in the more developed economies in the seventeenth century, followed by the emergence of commercial annuities and pensions, then of state pensions from the later nineteenth century, more refined calculations of life expectancy became essential for the activities of business and the state.

The term 'demography' was coined by the Belgian statistician Achille Guillard in 1855. Improvements in understanding mathematics and statistics in the twentieth century led to further advances in the scientific study of population in the 1930s and more extensively after the Second World War. It was driven at this time by the apparently unprecedented changes in population occurring in higher-income countries. In particular, a sustained fall in birth rates, discernible from the later nineteenth century, combined with falling adult death rates and rising life expectancy, gave rise to fears of the social and economic effects of the ageing of populations which was resulting. These were fuelled by extremely pessimistic projections of future population size by demographers experimenting with new techniques, especially in Britain and France, where scientific demography was most developed.[33] These fears were stimulated by the high and apparently rising birth rates of less developed regions, which some Europeans saw as a threat.[34] Other demographers were driven simply by the desire to understand these changes and their effects. Early demographic work often made explicit or implicit assumptions about historical population norms and trends, which by the 1950s drove historians to try to investigate population history with more precision.

The 'demographic transition'

Particularly influential in this process was the theory of 'Demographic Transition', most comprehensively formulated in 1944 by F. W. Notestein, Director of the Princeton Office of Population Research.[35] This proposed that a historically new phase of population growth had occurred during industrialization, when, it was believed, fertility remained uncontrolled and high (as, Notestein assumed, it had always been previously) while mortality declined due to improved food supplies and living standards, due to economic growth and improvements in transport, food output and supply, public health, and medical practice. This, Notestein argued, led populations for the first time to find ways to limit births—Malthus' 'preventive checks' preventing 'Malthusian crises', as they became known, as population outstripped resources. According to this theory, mortality decline preceded fertility decline by several decades. The theory was based on observations that birth rates in Europe were generally high in the early nineteenth century, when death rates appeared to be falling during a period of economic growth, and that European birth rates began to decline only at the end of the century. Notestein argued, without benefit of evidence, that 'the whole process of modernization in Europe and overseas brought rising levels of living, new controls over disease and reduced mortality…meanwhile fertility was much less responsive to the process of modernisation'. He assumed that high fertility was a deeply embedded cultural norm in 'pre-industrial' societies, compensating for the high mortality which was assumed also to be an unchanging norm. Ultimately, it was believed, fertility levels adjusted to the new economic and social conditions of 'modern' industrial society. The model shared Malthus' theory of population dynamics.

Historical demography

In the 1920s and 1930s, as economic and social history was emerging as a sub-discipline, historians such as Margaret Buer, A. M. Carr-Saunders, and Dorothy George in Britain sought to explain past population changes, in particular the observable eighteenth-century population growth. They did so primarily in terms of mortality decline, ascribed to economic growth, increased food production, improved medical knowledge and practice, improved public health and social administration, and decreased alcohol consumption.

In the 1950s and 1960s, a prominent and prolific contributor to the debate was the British medical researcher Thomas McKeown,[36] who argued strenuously that population growth in the eighteenth and nineteenth centuries was driven above all by mortality decline due to economic improvements and, particularly, improved diet, rather than to medical advance, which he rightly believed was limited before the twentieth century. He derived this interpretation from data on causes of death reported by the British Registrar-General from 1837, arguing that the diseases whose decline had contributed most to the fall in mortality in the nineteenth century—mainly those associated with airborne micro-organisms, especially tuberculosis—could not be treated effectively by medicine at this time, hence the decline must be due to other causes. He also played down the role of sanitary and public health measures, on the grounds that these were effective mainly from the very late nineteenth century, long after he believed the mortality decline to have begun. McKeown relied almost entirely on the published reports of the Registrar-General, from which he extrapolated backwards to the eighteenth century, assuming that mortality decline began during the economic growth of the nineteenth century.

There were other views. In 1955 Karl Helleiner undertook a survey of European population trends from the fourteenth to the eighteenth centuries, which was not published until 1967. He attributed the falling mortality he assumed to have fuelled eighteenth-century population growth not to improved food supplies due to economic improvements, but to a lessening in the intensity of epidemic disease, which, he argued, occurred autonomously of economic and social changes. He thought it significant that Europe experienced sustained population growth at the time when bubonic plague finally disappeared. Its incidence could not be correlated with the availability or price of food. More recent analysts have suggested for the nineteenth century the importance of public health improvements such as sanitation, pure water, and milk supplies.[37]

Also in the 1950s, historical demographers using parish register evidence were suggesting other interpretations of mortality decline. A new school of demographic history was emerging in France. In the 1950s Louis Henry (1911–91) devised the technique which became known in the English-speaking world as 'family reconstitution': reconstructing the demographic history of an individual or family by linking different sources of data, in particular church registers of births, marriages, and deaths. Only a minority of parish registers are complete enough to reach the precise standards required for the technique to be applied and it is obviously most effective in large, relatively static communities with little in- or out-migration which can provide substantial amounts of information comparable over time. It is also slow, time-consuming work, which has been greatly speeded by advances in information technology which has stimulated the growth of historical demography especially since the 1980s.

One of Henry's contributions was to establish systematic rules to minimize distortions and assist comparability among populations. Henry first applied his technique to the registers of the Normandy parish of Crulai.[38] His work suggested patterns which challenged aspects of demographic transition theory. He and others demonstrated that a sustained fall in fertility began in France in the early nineteenth century and elsewhere in Europe later in the century, whereas mortality began its significant sustained decline in higher-income countries only in the twentieth century.[39]

From the 1960s in Britain the technique of family reconstitution was applied by E. A. Wrigley to the registers of the Devon parish of Colyton. This became the foundation of the pioneering work in long-run historical demography of the Cambridge Group for the History of Population and Social Structure, founded at Cambridge University by Wrigley and Peter Laslett in 1964. The Group assembled 404 high-quality registers from the almost 10,000 Church of England parishes in order to reconstruct national demographic trends from 1541, after the establishment of the Church of England, to the beginning of civil registration in 1837, the longest uninterrupted data series to which the techniques of family reconstitution and back projection have been applied.[40] In England, however, reconstruction of the entire life history of a family is rarely possible, due to high migration rates at most times. Indeed one major discovery resulting from the work of the Cambridge Group was the high level of mobility in pre-industrial England, which was previously assumed to be largely static. Another important contribution was Laslett's finding, again based on parish register evidence, that the entrenched sociological orthodoxy of the time that families in 'pre-industrial' societies lived in large 'extended' kin units, which were later replaced as norms by small 'nuclear' units better suited to the assumed greater geographical mobility of industrial society, was inaccurate, at least in respect of England. Rather, it was clear that for centuries before industrialization, in English parishes, relatively small 'nuclear' households predominated.[41] This was later found to be true of other parts of north-western Europe and assumed to be specific to this region, whilst more complex households characterized southern and eastern Europe.[42] Recent research, however, indicates more diverse patterns in these regions of Europe. Such research is in its infancy, but it is becoming clear that, for example, the characterization of a Russian family type exhibiting complex households, high marriage rates, and early age of marriage, which rested upon a single study of a single community,[43] do not hold true of another region of Russia, where households were smaller and less complex, and marriage ages later, though with variation over time.[44] Studies of Upper Silesia, the Czech Republic, Slovakia, Hungary, Slovenia, and elsewhere similarly call in question simple typologies of family structure in 'East' and 'West' and also in the north and the south of Europe.[45]

Also, historians and demographers tended to assume that family proximity breeds intimacy, that relationships among co-residing relatives are closer than among those who live apart. However, Michael Anderson pointed out some time ago that 'kinship does not stop at the front door'.[46] Qualitative evidence, from diaries, memoirs, etc., and survey evidence in the more recent past indicates the extent of emotional and material support that can be exchanged among family members who do not share a household, though this does not invariably occur; and the tensions that can arise from shared living arrangements.[47]

Increasingly sophisticated techniques of 'back projection' and 'inverse projection' enable intelligent estimates of past population movements in England to be made from relatively scanty data, but they are, of course, estimates.[48] Use of such techniques combined with family reconstitution suggests strongly that almost three-quarters of the population growth in England in the seventy to eighty years after 1750 was due to a rapid rise in fertility rather than a fall in mortality.[49] There appears also to have been a reduction in mortality, in particular in its volatility from year to year, but this does not seem to have been clearly associated with high food prices or harvest failures.[50] English estimates suggest a weak relationship between wheat prices and mortality from 1548 to the 1830s,[51] weakening further after 1750. Indeed there were many periods when English mortality appears to have been quite unresponsive even to serious rises in food prices, e.g. the 1690s, when Scotland, France, and other parts of north-west Europe were less fortunate. Similar reductions in volatility in this time have not been found in countries with comparable data, i.e. France and the four Scandinavian countries, though there are indications that in these countries mortality became less responsive to food prices in the late eighteenth century. Data from other countries are sparse, but there are indications of continuing mortality associated with food crises, including severe epidemics, in southern Europe well into the nineteenth century.

Everywhere, we should be cautious about over-reliance on often sparse wage and price data, but there is not clear evidence of a synchronized pan-European stabilization of mortality as suggested by demographic transition theory. The English experience is likely to be due to increased prosperity in a more productive agricultural system, producing a better-balanced and more varied diet, less dependent upon wheat, underpinned by a system of poor relief which a relatively prosperous society could afford in order to protect the most vulnerable.[52] The evidence points also to the importance of climate change as a cause of mortality fluctuation everywhere. Extremes of temperature, especially very hot summers, increased mortality though with generational differences. Older people were more vulnerable to respiratory diseases, such as pneumonia and influenza, in cold winters; hot summers killed infants and young children through digestive-tract diseases.[53]

The rise and fall of epidemics must also be considered. Arguably, quarantine controls in England and elsewhere made a major contribution to the disappearance of plague as a major killer in Europe from the later seventeenth century.[54] However, Landers's work on seventeenth-century London has demonstrated the complexity of influences on diseases, including the effects of migration, whereby people moved into sickness regimes against which they had no immunity, and of urban overcrowding which encouraged contagion.

It has also been suggested that the fall in mortality in England from c.1750 to the 1830s was in fact a recovery from an equivalent rise in mortality in the preceding century and a half. Family reconstitution data suggests that the death rate rose mainly among infants and children, even among the higher classes, and that this went into reverse in the second half of the eighteenth century. This calls in question whether the fall from c.1750 truly was a secular trend.[55] A similar pattern appears in the only other similarly lengthy dataset available, for Geneva. Nutrition is unlikely to account for these trends. Falling mortality from smallpox may be important. The improvement in infant (and also maternal) mortality at this time may be due in part to improvements in obstetrical practice and management of the newborn. There are indications from France and Scandinavia that declines in infant and, probably, child mortality were important, perhaps dominant, components of overall mortality decline, though they started from higher mortality levels than those prevailing in England. England then lost some of its advantage over other countries by the mid-nineteenth century due to the effects of its exceptionally fast and large-scale urbanization. It was the first country in the world in which a majority of the population, by the mid-nineteenth century, became urban dwellers. Urban overcrowding especially exacerbated infant mortality.

There is evidence from the seventeenth century onwards of wide regional variations in mortality at any given time. Family reconstitution from English parish registers shows differences in infant mortality among parishes amounting to variations of almost fifty years in life expectancy at birth, which were still detectable across the same localities when civil registration began in 1837. These cannot easily be explained in terms of contrasting nutritional levels. Parish registers do not record cause of death, which is not available in England until civil registration was established.

Family reconstitution from parish registers has been most extensively applied in France and England. Other countries have other sources. Klapisch-Zuber has used the very detailed Florentine tax records vividly to recreate Tuscan households in the fourteenth and fifteenth centuries.[56] Also for Italy, Giovanni Levi has reconstructed details of everyday life in the seventeenth and eighteenth centuries from legal, parochial, and administrative records.[57] Alongside parish registers, Swedish historical demographers can use unique periodic, often annual, listings of inhabitants and records of such phenomena as individual migrations and levels of literacy, which began locally in the late seventeenth century and were taken over by the state in 1740.[58] German scholars have made use of the *Ortssippenbücher* (genealogies), long-run family reconstitutions assembled by parish clergy for the Nazi regime in the 1930s to enable them to establish the 'racial purity' of individuals.[59]

Parish registers have increasingly been used by historical demographers in Italy, Spain, and Portugal and more recently in Hungary, Poland, and other parts of Eastern Europe, though in all of these countries survival of registers is even patchier than in England and France, especially before the eighteenth century.[60] In some countries difficulties arise due to the non-survival of records, or problems in interpreting them, for cultural reasons or due to religious fragmentation. In the Netherlands some Reform Church registers exist before the mid-seventeenth century but there are few Roman Catholic registers before 1700; also, before the nineteenth century, difficulties in identifying individuals arise from the lower-class practice of not using surnames. The survival rate of parish registers in Scotland and Ireland is low. The growth of Nonconformity in England after 1700 reduced the utility of Church of England parish registers, though some Nonconformist communities kept good registers.[61] Also, the rapid growth of towns after 1750, and the difficulties of the parish system in keeping pace, increased the proportion of the population lost to parish registers. By the early nineteenth century fewer than 75 per cent of all burials and deaths were recorded by Anglican clergy. Hence the records become less reliable at precisely the time that population was seen to be growing rapidly and controversy was arising as to whether this was due to rising fertility or falling mortality. In France, by contrast, registers are significantly incomplete before the late eighteenth century, then become more comprehensive.

Fertility

Another major finding of historical demographers in Cambridge and elsewhere was that the assumption of unchecked fertility growth in 'pre-industrial' societies was mistaken, at least in Europe. Especially in northern Europe, from at least 1500 (data for earlier periods are especially scanty) until at least the early twentieth century, men and women married relatively late in relation to the age of puberty (men at age 25 to 28, women aged 23 to 25) and a large proportion (15–20 per cent) never married. Most children were born to married couples; the later the age of marriage, the fewer children born. Communities were found to be capable of limiting the rate at which they grew—consciously avoiding the 'Malthusian crisis' of population outstripping resources—by discouraging marriage when economic conditions were poor. This 'European marriage pattern', as it has been called, was first reported by demographer John Hajnal in 1965[62] and has since been confirmed, in particular by the work of Wrigley and Schofield for England. However, Hajnal assumed that this pattern was true only of Western Europe and that 'Eastern Europe' had different patterns, with high marriage rates at early ages and a high proportion of complex households. As suggested above, this has been questioned in the light of research in Eastern and southern Europe.[63] The study of historical populations in other parts of the world has developed more recently and slowly than that of north-western Europe but is expanding and extending our understanding of historical demography.

Historical demographers also established that the desire and capacity to limit fertility was not a product only of industrial society and Malthusian crisis. In various times and places, social groups, including the middle classes of Geneva and large proportions of the populations of northern French cities, practised birth control from at least the late seventeenth century, either by sexual abstinence or *coitus interruptus* (the withdrawal method). From the late nineteenth century, in Europe and North America, such behaviour became a sustained mass phenomenon, in all social classes, though with so far unexplained regional differences,[64] and fertility entered a long-run decline. From around the same time, infant mortality also entered a sustained decline in higher-income countries. Hence completed family size declined more slowly than fertility. In late nineteenth-century Britain 15–20 per cent of deaths still occurred to those under the age of 1 year and about 25 per cent to those under 5 years. Infant mortality was probably declining in rural areas from the mid-century, and there were important differences by social class, but the national averages were affected by the high level of urbanization. The sustained urban decline which followed was due to improved public health and child welfare measures, which were also evident in France and other European countries.[65]

New artificial methods of birth control were introduced, assisted by technological change: condoms, caps, from the 1960s the birth control pill and IUDs. At all times abortion played a role in the limitation of fertility, though it was illegal everywhere in Europe and North America until the 1960s when it was gradually legalized in most European countries, though controversial in many of them. It remains wholly uncertain how large a role abortion played in the European fertility decline.

The decline in fertility in higher-income countries in the early twentieth century caused fears of declining, ageing, weakened populations. This led to attempts especially in authoritarian states, in particular Nazi Germany and Fascist Italy, to stimulate fertility by rewarding parents of numerous children and penalizing the childless. This was less effective than measures taken by the French state, which was first to experience substantial fertility decline, from the beginning of the twentieth century, to assist parents with improved child care and welfare.[66]

Another response to fertility decline was the search for means to improve the quality of surviving populations by increasing health and fitness, and the more extreme response of trying to eliminate what were seen as weaker and less desirable human specimens. Eugenic theory emerged in Europe in the late nineteenth century, arguing that public health reforms were enabling the weak to survive alongside the robust, bringing physical deterioration to their 'races' as they perpetuated their weak genes through the generations. The answer was said to be selective breeding to eliminate the sickly, the deformed, the 'mentally defective' (as they were then described), and others thought undesirable, through marriage regulation, sequestration of the mentally deficient, and sterilization. Such measures were sometimes promoted by otherwise progressive social reformers, such as Gunnar and Alva Myrdal in Sweden, as part of a package of social reform designed to eliminate severe inequality, which included improved maternal and infant care.[67] In the USA, compulsory sterilization laws were passed in forty-four states and strict immigration controls were implemented. A Supreme Court ruling in 1927 upheld a statute instituting compulsory sterilization of the 'mentally retarded' 'for the protection and health of the state'.[68] This led to an estimated 65,000 Americans being sterilized without their consent or that of a family member. Sterilization 'of persons suffering from grave hereditary characteristics and incapable of consent' was practised legally in Sweden from 1934, leading to the sterilization of some 250 people per year. It was practised more covertly, on some occasions at least, in Britain and other European countries. The most extreme practices occurred in Nazi Germany in the attempt to build the 'master race' by eliminating the racially undesirable (such as Jews) and the physically weak.[69] In general, especially after the Second World War and the discovery of the extent of the Nazi atrocities, environmentalist solutions to physical and social inequality were preferred, in particular improved health and welfare measures.

Conclusion

Research on, mainly European, experience from the late nineteenth century called in question the assumption of demographic transition theory that major demographic shifts were necessarily primarily closely linked to economic change. It showed that nations at very different stages of economic development—e.g. England and Bulgaria—underwent similar changes at around the same times.

Patterns elsewhere have been different. Whereas mortality declined slowly in Europe and North America, it fell much faster in other regions due in some places to rapid economic growth, in others to the application of 'Western' medical and public health knowledge, especially after the Second World War, though with wide variations due to differing levels of wealth and poverty. Fertility fell more slowly, but fastest in East Asia, especially in Japan and Taiwan from the 1960s, followed by other countries, due to rapid economic growth; in China initially due to compulsory restriction of births to one per married couple from 1970s, and increasingly from 1970s in South-East Asia and Latin America. Average total fertility rates fell between 1950/5 and 2000/5 from 5.71 to 1.66 in East Asia, 6.58 to 4.98 in Africa, 6.03 to 2.52 in South-East Asia, 5.89 to 2.55 in Latin America and the Caribbean, 6.22 to 1.7 in China, 2.56 to 1.4 in Europe, 3.43 to 1.99 in North America.[70] However, there were differences within these large regions. In some north European countries, particularly the UK, Sweden, Denmark, and Finland, total fertility rates have risen since around 2000, in the UK from 1.63 in 2001 to 1.90 in 2007.[71] Since these were among the first countries to experience significant falling fertility, the turnaround may suggest that low birth rates will not be a permanent feature of experience elsewhere.

The twentieth century, especially the second half of the century, saw dramatic changes in the structure of populations worldwide and dramatic increase in the demographic information available. However, variations in demographic experience and in the availability and reliability of information continue to be extreme and our understanding of the drivers of population change remains imperfect.

Historians have come to pay increasing attention to supplementing the valuable work we have on the structure of populations and households with closer attention to the even more elusive relationships and emotional experiences of families and communities in past times. Often drawing upon ideas and methods from anthropology and cultural history which pay attention to the diversity of individual experience, they have increased our understanding of the differing experiences of different age and social groups, diverse attitudes to incest, sibling relationships, and unmarried motherhood among much else.[72] This rich field, of fundamental importance to all historians, continues to move forwards.

9. Kite made from plastic, Japan, 1997. © By permission of the Trustees of the British Museum

9 Gender

DOROTHY KO

In 1950–2, former American GI George Jorgensen prevailed upon pioneering doctors in Denmark to give him a sex-change operation. After receiving extensive shots of estrogen and two subsequent surgeries that removed his testicles and penis and reshaped his scrotum into labia, Jorgensen adopted the name Christine, applied for a new passport, and sailed back to New York and into the limelight of history. Trying to convince the public that she was not a freak in the media frenzy that ensued, Jorgensen presented herself as a true American—a rugged individualist who dared to oppose prevalent norms that mandated 'there are men and there are women'. Departing from this common-sense model of sexual dimorphism, or the assumption that one's sex is a matter of 'either-or', Jorgensen reiterated in interviews and on stage that sex is a spectrum or a continuum, whereby '[p]eople, both men and women, are both sexes. The most any man or woman can be is 80 percent masculine or feminine.'[1]

In hindsight, this statement was as odd as it was prophetic in the 1950s.[2] In insisting that a woman is (and indeed, has to be) made, not born, Jorgensen and others who clamored for sex changes helped loosen the grip of biological determinism in the minds of the American public. In so doing, they anticipated a seismic shift in social and historical consciousness that gave rise to a brand new concept of 'gender' as social and cultural construction, a key concept that inspired an explosion of research on women's history and gender history in the 1970s–1980s. In recounting some of these efforts and those of their successors in the 1990s–2000s, especially in fields outside Euro-America, this chapter takes stock of the new knowledge opened up by those scholars and activists who refuse to accept the world as it is or as it may seem. Struggles over the meanings of 'gender' are both symptom and effect of this process of contesting and rewriting history.

Gender is not sex

Psychologists and endocrinologists striving to comprehend the challenges to established medical terminologies posed by Jorgensen and other 'transsexuals' like her coined the term 'gender'—as part of the compound 'gender role'—with the intent of short-circuiting people's instinctive conflation of sex with biology. The term 'gender role' first appeared in 1955 in studies by John Money, a Professor of Medical Psychology and Pediatrics at Johns Hopkins University Hospital who was to become *the* authority on transsexualism. By gender role Money meant: '[a]ll those things that a person says or does to disclose himself or herself as having the status of boy or man, girl or woman, respectively. It includes, but is not restricted to, sexuality in the sense of eroticism.' Later, he added the notion of 'gender identity', or 'the sameness, unity, and persistence of one's individuality as male, female, or ambivalent…gender identity is the private experience of gender role, and gender role is the public expression of gender identity.' According to this behavioral definition, the gender of a person has less to do with hormones, gonads, or chromosomes but is largely a function of one's 'outlook, demeanor, and orientation.'[3]

Introducing the ambiguous word gender, which in its Latin roots *genus* means 'kind' or 'sort', was an ingenious move. Although writers since the fourteenth century have used gender to refer to femininity and masculinity as types, its primary usage had been confined to grammatical distinctions.[4] When the referent was transferred from nouns to human beings, gender became an unfamiliar word. To make sense of it, the reader had to ponder what exactly made a person male or female: is it the body, the psyche, the environment, or social teaching? Although the word 'gender' does not dictate an answer—therein lies its usefulness—its very appearance in this guise calls into question the immutability of sex as a fact of biology.

In the 1970s, social psychologists and anthropologists made explicit distinctions between sex and gender: sex is a function of nature or biology whereas gender is a function of the social environment or culture. Hence Money and a collaborator wrote in 1972: '[T]he evidence of human hermaphroditism makes it abundantly clear that nature has ordained a major part of human gender-identity differentiation to be accomplished in the postnatal period.'[5] Social psychologists

Suzanne J. Kessler and Wendy McKenna echoed Money in speaking of 'gender attribution' as largely a matter of culture.[6] Other social scientists, notably anthropologists in Britain, also developed theories of gender not grounded in sex.[7] In the remaining decades of the twentieth century, this definition of gender-as-social-construction would revolutionize the study of sociology, psychology, and science, not to mention history.

From women's history to gender history

Feminist historian Joan Kelly was the first to articulate the impact of the new stirrings on women's history. In her pioneering essay 'Did Women Have a Renaissance?' first published in 1977, Kelly argued that 'events that further the historical development of men, liberating them from natural, social, or ideological constraints, have quite different, even opposite, effects upon women'.[8] Although she did not use the term gender, in advocating a 'doubled' or bifocal vision of history that encompasses male *and* female perspectives, Kelly anticipated the turn to gender history in the subsequent decade.

Four years after Kelly's untimely death in 1982, Joan Wallach Scott published her now classic manifesto of gender history, 'Gender as a Useful Category of Historical Analysis'. Highlighting the semantic ambiguity surrounding the word gender, Scott opened her article with a dictionary entry that reads: 'Gender. n. a grammatical term only. To talk of persons or creatures of the masculine or feminine gender, meaning of the male or female sex, is either a jocularity (permissible or not according to context) or a blunder.'[9] Yet feminist scholars were committing the blunder in increasing numbers in the 1980s. Summarizing their usage, Scott reported that 'gender' was being used in two ways, as a more respectable synonym for 'women' *and* to designate social relations between men and women (31–2).[10]

This seeming contradiction was the source of productive tension for Scott, who formulated her own definition of 'gender' as an analytic category resting on two interconnected propositions: first, 'gender is a constitutive element of social relationships based on perceived differences between the sexes'; second, 'gender is a primary way of signifying relationships of power' (42). She elaborated that historical enquiries into local meanings of 'gender' should focus on four aspects: culturally available symbols (for example, Eve or Mary); normative concepts expressed in religious, educational, scientific, or legal doctrines; politics and social institutions; subjective identity (43–4). Conceived in this broad frame, gender works in tandem with other categories such as race and class to create and naturalize social difference.

Scott's essay and the book in which it was anthologized two years later were treated with skepticism if not alarm by some pioneers of women's history. The newness of the term gender caused misunderstandings. In a heated exchange with Scott, Linda Gordon, the author of a history of birth control in the USA, took gender to be a *vice*, as a synonym of women's oppression: 'Scott's deterministic perspective emphasizes gender as "difference," marked by the otherness and absolute silencing of women.'[11] Such reactions were symptomatic of the intellectual and political ferments in the 1980s in and out of the US academy. Scott's daring resides in her introducing the poststructuralist theories heralded by Derrida and Foucault into feminist historiography, thereby encouraging historians to re-examine their premises not only about women, but also about experience, human agency, causality, and, above all, language as a signification system.[12] As such, her formulations challenge the epistemological assumptions of Marxism, which was prevalent in labor history (Scott's own field), and those of liberalism, which permeated political and social histories but were seldom articulated.

But it was the practitioners of women's history who felt that they had the most to lose. Having labored gallantly since the 1970s to reverse the invisibility of women in male-centered accounts of wars and revolutions, feminists have been successful in recasting the historical gaze on women—in the family and the workplace—as legitimate subjects of history. They have also made institutional advances, as sex discrimination in hiring practices was challenged in court, and women's studies programs gained popularity on campuses. It was feared that shifting to gender could negate the hard-fought battles and render women invisible yet again. Joan Hoff, prolific historian of US presidencies and women, did not mince words in her attack on Scott, warning of the erasure of 'woman as a category of analysis and as a political agent'. The culprit is poststructuralism, which 'by highlighting linguistic signs of difference among women...destroys any collective concept of women needed to organize and sustain a feminist movement'.[13]

If Hoff's accusations of poststructuralism as 'ahistorical and misogynist' are misguided, her visceral distress signals a deeper truth she correctly intuited—gender *is* an artificial theoretical construct (as all theoretical constructs are); a history which takes women-as-collective as its subject *does* differ from gender history in epistemological assumptions; the use of gender *would* change the face of history (and politics) beyond recognition. Twenty years after the publication of Scott's essay, the concept of gender—as a social category imposed on bodies—has become common sense.[14] But women-as-collective did not disappear.

Seldom has a single word been so powerful in altering both the terms of professional history writing and public discourses. The success is not Scott's alone; it rests in large part on the efforts of historians who took gender, a category born of linguistic contrivance and transgression, into the textual, visual, and material archives in Latin America, Africa, Asia, the Middle East, and elsewhere, probing its discursive limits while refining its meanings in time- and locale-specific studies.[15] Neither Scott nor her detractors could have foreseen how divergent yet coherent the global project of gender history would turn out to be.

In search of patriarchy

In the 1970s–1980s, feminist historians adopted several strategies to rescue women from historical oblivion. One humorous observer has called it the archaeology project, 'digging women out of the dust'.[16] To combat the biased belief of 'biology as destiny' which consigned women to the private spheres of family and motherhood, some historians celebrated such public figures as Catharine Beecher, Christine de Pizan, or Jiang Qing (Madame Mao Tse-tung.) Others sought to show that the women's habitat of home and domesticity is just as worthy of historical attention as the male-centered public spheres of politics, industry, and commerce.[17] A shared goal is to probe the historical formation of male domination instead of assuming that it was rooted in biology. As Gerda Lerner declared in her ambitious history of patriarchy in ancient Mesopotamia from 3100 to 600 BC, 'patriarchy as a system is historical: it has a beginning in history. If that is so, it can be ended by historical process.'[18]

Patriarchy to Lerner has a specific and a broad meaning. The former, as stipulated by Greek and Roman law (and Confucian Chinese, although Lerner did not mention it), refers to the 'absolute legal and economic power' that the male head of household enjoyed over his dependent female and male family members. But in its wider meaning of 'the manifestation and institutionalization of male dominance over women and children in the family and the extension of male dominance over women in society in general', patriarchy pre-dated Greek law and lingers in the modern world (238–9). Lerner's project serves as a reminder of the enduring influence of Engels's *Origin of the Family, Private Property and the State* on feminist scholars who came of age in the middle of the twentieth century.[19] Even as Lerner sought to refine Engels's grim prognosis of women's defeat at the dawn of history, her analytic focuses on the rise of private property, slavery, prostitution, and the archaic state bespeak the extent to which Engels dictated the terms of analysis of the history of female sexuality and the family in the 1970s–1980s.

Nowhere is the influence of Engels more keenly felt than in Japan, where Marxism dominated the historical field in the twentieth century. Engels and Lewis Henry Morgan, whose *Ancient Society* inspired Engels, had an indelible impact on the shape of women's history in Japan since the turn of the last century. Part of the appeal of Morgan and Engels stems from their evolutionary framework (from Savagery to Barbarism to Civilization) that allows historians to write meta-narratives, correlating changes in the family system with stages of political and economic development. But a deeper attraction is that Japanese scholars have found in their ancient archives traces of the matriarchy that Morgan and Engels envisioned.

Feminist historian Itsue Takamure (1894–1964), the mother of women's history in Japan, described in her pioneering work of 1953, *A Study of Matrilocal Marriage*, a utopian past in which ancient women on the Japanese archipelago practiced 'visiting marriage' (*tsumadoikon*). A woman could choose her sexual partners (and fathers of her children), who would come to her residence like planets orbiting the sun. This historical picture gave substance to a popular feminist slogan: 'In the beginning, woman was the sun.'[20] Yet as the marriage system changed to a more stable uxorilocal form—historians disagree on when that happened—women suffered a loss of choices over their sexual partners. Their situation worsened as patrilocal marriage became the norm, depriving the wife/mother of even a figment of choice over her sexuality. Japanese history, and the history of women, is thus construed as a paradise lost, a progressive decline in the lot of women as they lost control of their bodies and sexuality to the male head of household.

Unlike in ancient Mesopotamia, the institution of patriarchy had a more traceable beginning on the Japanese archipelago: patrilocal marriage was part of a package of Sinic ideals enshrined in texts that were introduced from China from the late fifth to the eighth centuries. The package, which scholars have termed the 'patriarchal family paradigm', also included the Chinese writing system, poetry, Confucian classics, law codes of the Tang dynasty (618–907), doctrines of political sovereignty, courtly rituals, and an education-based civil bureaucracy. The magnificent model of the Chinese imperial-bureaucratic system shored up by Confucian ethics was attractive to warring chiefs on the archipelago who were in the throes of establishing a stable, centralized polity.

With the Taihō Ritsuryō (penal and administrative) codes promulgated by the court in Nara in 701, Japanese courtiers sought to legislate the Confucian vision of a family-state into reality. Installed in the capital was the Heavenly Sovereign (tennô) who was to be the parent of his or her subjects, and in the realm, a male-headed household with his legal wife and heir that constituted the basic unit of census and taxation. Feminist historian Hiroko Sekiguchi explained the centrality of the family to this political vision: 'First, the foundation [of Confucian ethics] is the patriarchal family; and second, when filiality in the family is extended to the public realm, it becomes loyalty, the basis of public morality. Loyalty to the family patriarch is thus the foundation of state rule.'[21]

The imported ideal of a patriarchal family (born of patrilocal marriage and organized by patrilineal descent) was widely at odds with the marital, residence, and inheritance practices on the archipelago. The census registers and other documentary sources, sketchy as they are, show a complex and fluid situation whereby a couple who lived uxorilocally might eventually move out of her father's to establish a separate residence; in one family some daughters might bring in mates whereas others would marry out. Well into the medieval times, daughters continued to enjoy partible inheritance and polygyny was rampant.[22] Japanese scholars who hewed to Engels's scheme—virtually all who specialized in ancient kinship and marriage—had troubles pinpointing the onset of monogamy which was supposed to coincide with the emergence of private property. Instead of locating the roots of female oppression, the search for the origins of patriarchy in ancient and medieval Japan has yielded a rich and nuanced picture about the ways whereby daughters, wives, prostitutes, nuns, spirit mediums, merchants, novelists, and court officials negotiated with the presence or absence of male authority figures in their lives.

The male breadwinner

The limitations of the Engels-inspired tradition of analyzing women and labor under the rubric of patriarchy become clear when compared with recent works that use gender as the key analytic category. By examining the prodigious career of the 'male breadwinner paradigm' in the USA, Latin America, and Africa, these works show how the concepts of 'gender' and 'labor' construct each other; we cannot fully understand one without the other.

In her study of the gender of waged work and standards of fairness in twentieth-century America, for example, Alice Kessler-Harris has discerned a biased 'gendered imagination' that shaped policy debates and public sentiments, especially during the crucial struggles over social security and tax codes in the 1930s that laid the foundation of the American welfare state. The bias, or the assumption that 'economic citizenship' is gendered male, comes with its corollary, that citizenship for women could only be realized in motherhood and family life instead of the workplace. When activists argued that men deserved to be paid a decent wage because they had to provide for the wife and children, few found it problematic. When mainstream feminists sought citizenship for women, they rallied to the ballot box instead of contesting the presumed maleness of economic citizenship. So pervasive and naturalized was the ideology of the male breadwinner that it had remained hidden in plain sight, and it took a historian as attuned to the valences of language and as committed to a gender analysis that encompasses both masculinity and femininity as Kessler-Harris to expose the bias.

As expounded by the American Federation of Labor, its strongest proponent in the 1930s, the ideology of the male breadwinner was part-and-parcel of the American ideals of self-sufficiency, upward mobility, and individualism. It was rooted in the creed of 'volunteerism' of the AFL since the 1880s, which insisted that real men set their own wages by way of the brotherhood of collective bargaining. 'I want to remain a free man as a wage earner and not become a subject of the state,' declared a delegate to the 1924 Ohio State Federation of Labor.[23] Hence union leaders resisted *any* government intervention in the labor market, including the provision of unemployment insurance, minimum wage, and regulated work hours, even though these measures would benefit the male industrial workers that the AFL represented.

So insidious was this gendered definition of 'worker' as the breadwinner that it was supported by even female reformers and the 'maternalist' feminist groups that lobbied for mother's aid instead of waged labor for women. The real losers, as Kessler-Harris observed, were the large numbers of women and African American *men* who did work, but as part-time or transient domestic and agricultural workers were excluded from union membership and hence economic citizenship. Twice removed from the image of the normative 'worker', African American women swelled the ranks of domestic workers which was in 1939 'ninety percent female, 45 percent African American, with greater proportions married, widowed, deserted, or divorced, and still working in their older years, they simply did not fit the profile of the stable industrial worker for whom social legislation was constructed' (150). The ironic outcome of the workings of the 'gendered imagination' was that those who were most in need of protection were rendered illegible, hence categorically excluded from consideration.

Like the East Asian patriarch who was the linchpin of the Confucian family-state order, the male breadwinner personified the founding ideology of American individualism. Just as a transnational perspective tracing the translation of the Confucian patriarchal paradigm on the Japanese archipelago has exposed its leakage at the seams, recent studies of the male breadwinner paradigm in Latin America and Africa have illuminated the extent to which the liberal male subject could survive the wear and tear of cross-cultural adaptation. In particular, studies of the interpenetrations of state and family in Mexico,

Argentina, and Chile undertaken in the 1990s showcase the analytic power of gender in reshaping a field which had previously approached family and state as separate entities.[24] The problem of the male provider as the subject of family and labor reforms emerged in clear relief as historians began to locate gender politics not only in the familiar spaces of the private and the domestic but also in the heart of public policy, political culture, and state formation.

The breadwinner paradigm was a key objective of the modernization program pursued by the Popular Front state of Chile in the 1930–1940s and women were instrumental to its formation and outcome, according to the recent research of Karin Rosemblatt.[25] The state considered the establishment of a family wage system an important measure of its paternalism, a project that took Congress over two decades to complete. In Chile as in the USA, protracted debates over what constituted fair compensation created a gendered hierarchy of work in rhetoric and in reality: only the predominantly male industrial and mining workers were deemed engaging in 'real' productive work; other male laborers such as the rural *campesinos* were subordinated along with women, who largely took up home-making, domestic service, and small-scale artisanal production at home. Hence 'gender not only structured relations between men and women, and between Left and Right, but also among men', Rosemblatt concluded (50).

But there are crucial differences between the situations in Chile and the USA. The initial champions of family wage in Chile were employers and state agencies who sought a stable labor force to sustain the drive toward industrialization; male workers balked because becoming a breadwinner would entail a drastic transformation of their behavior— they would need to marry, settle down, and be held responsible for their children. In a country where illegitimacy rates were high and what Nara Milanich has called 'non-marrying behavior' widespread, becoming a breadwinner was an *affront* on the workers' masculinity.[26] Although eventually economic calculations won out and the unions rallied behind the family wage system, the ideal type of the breadwinner as a responsible family man could claim only limited success. More than half of the nitrate workers were single men in 1935; in the 1930s–1940s union newspapers were studded with such anti-marriage jokes as 'All that is one's own seems better than one's neighbors, except when it comes to one's woman' (67).

The Popular Front state promoted the breadwinner paradigm with the explicit purpose of reordering family structure by literally domesticating the men. Conforming to what Victoria de Grazia has identified as an early twentieth-century trend of rationalizing domesticity, the Chilean state sought to reshape private life and gender norms as part of its modernization program.[27] Two groups of women, housewives and social workers, became the state's main allies and agents. The housewives' interests in reining in drunk mates and protecting their children from abandonment helped explain their tacit acceptance of the ideology of the breadwinner which excluded them from productive wage labor. Single mothers and sex workers, in turn, were more likely to resist the muddling of the state and its 'bourgeois' agents. Rosemblatt's nuanced analysis has revealed that gender worked in tandem with 'class' to unite and divide. In the end, the breadwinner paradigm and its corollary, maternalism, achieved limited success in Popular Front Chile because of the support of a fragile cross-class alliance among women.

To be a man is more than a day's work

Lisa Lindsay put her finger on the peculiar character of the breadwinner in colonial Nigeria in the 1930s–1960s when she observed that since wheat had to be imported, eating bread was the prerogative of those privileged men who enjoyed access to the colonial cash economy. The urban staple for everybody else was *gari*, a starch prepared from cassava that was the women's crop, 'grown, ground, soaked, resoaked, scrubbed, dried, and usually sold by women'.[28] The British colonial rule that introduced exotic commodities and hierarchies of tastes while emasculating native men, not to mention the thriving networks of women farming, dealing, and selling in the marketplace, presented formidable challenges to the male breadwinner as an ideal type and in reality.

Even more vexing were the native kinship and marriage practices in south-western Nigeria, or Yorubaland, where women routinely worked outside the home after marriage in the first half of the twentieth century. Not only did the majority of households depend on women's income, spouses also maintained separate bursaries—husbands and wives pooled resources only to the extent of meeting household needs. When the colonial regime started to employ Nigerian men as skilled railroad workers in the 1930s, replacing the far more expensive expatriates as station masters and administrative officers, it created a small class of native males who could put bread on their tables. But the affective and economic structures of kinship did not change overnight; women kept on working and the most respectable form of masculinity remained the 'big man' who had multiple wives and even more children and dependents.

The male breadwinner rhetoric arrived in full force in the general strike of 1945, when about 40,000 Nigerian civil servants and railroad workers walked off their jobs. In demanding a rise and a family allowance to offset inflation and to gain a semblance of parity with the expatriates, the unionists strategically deployed the language of the male breadwinner, deliberately downplaying women's contributions (80 per cent of the railroad men had wives who were traders). The colonial administration, in turn, harped on that fact to justify the depressed wages. Ironically, as Lindsay has astutely pointed out, the men managed to stay off their jobs from 22 June to 6 August, eventually winning concessions to their demands, only *because of* the sustenance afforded by the women's income (who presumably put *gari* on the table).

In Nigeria as in Chile and the USA, the male breadwinner rhetoric engendered the image of the normative worker as the waged male head of household, effectively depriving women and non-industrial workers of the most lucrative jobs and economic citizenship. In Nigeria, the rhetoric gained strength in the 1950s even as it flew in the face of the continued economic vibrancy of market women. As 'real' work increasingly became defined as wage-earning work, trading appeared to be a lesser undertaking (less than 2 per cent of the waged employees in 1950 were female). A joke that circulated in the mid-1950s, however, suggests that the masculinity of the male wage earner remained suspect and compromised: 'Said an employee to his employer, "Do you think, sir, I might have a rise?" "But I put a rise in your pay packet last week." "Oh, I'm very sorry sir, my wife never tells me anything"' (112). In south-western Nigeria, where only a minority of *men* held wage-earning jobs (7.8 per cent of the labor force in 1975 were wage earners) the discourse of the male breadwinner rang hollow in spite of its considerable rhetorical power as the shining embodiment of colonial modernity.

These works by Kessler-Harris, Rosemblatt, Lindsay, and others have advanced historical knowledge while refining the apparatus of gender analysis. When read against works of labor history or political history of state and colonial formations that do not use gender as an analytic lens, the usefulness of gender is evinced by its ability to both deconstruct and construct. Narrative viewpoints shifted, stereotypes dismantled, and new connections between previously disparate spheres or phenomena made—the best gendered analyses surprise the reader. Gender writes history in verbs and the active voice, for as Lisa Lindsay has observed, 'it makes sense to think of gender not necessarily as something people *have* but as something people *do* in various ways' (125). The title of her book, *Working with Gender*, conveys an understanding of power that allows for both structural constraints and human agency: gender norms and ideologies are structural but mutable; individuals 'work with gender' by 'acting in particular ways for particular reasons, some of which have to do with existing gender ideologies but some of which can be strategic improvisations' (106, 205).

There are two ways to consider this insight. If one hews to a dualistic framework that presupposes a split between private and public, or between formal and informal power, one may conclude that no matter how disenfranchised, housewives, domestic servants, or male farmhands can be seen to enjoy a modicum of informal power. This is certainly valuable. If one dispenses with the dualistic frame altogether, as some historians working with gender have done, the world becomes a strange and complex place replete with contradictions and local perspectives incommensurable with each other. Out of the strangeness new possibilities of seeing and intervening in the world may emerge.

One of the most articulated proponents of the latter approach is Heidi Tinsman, who in her textured study of women fruit workers in Chile under Pinochet (1973–90) has found that the hiring of young women as temporary wage workers in multinational agribusinesses had unpredictable and contradictory effects on gender relations that defy the standard Marxist feminist critiques of the collusion between capitalism and patriarchy. She called for a 'feminist materialist analysis that insists on the importance of grasping the simultaneity of gender exploitation and erosion of patriarchy without mechanically attributing one to the other'. The complicated relationship between global capitalism and gender that unfolded in the Chilean countryside exceeded the 'false dichotomy' between exploitation and agency or domination and resistance.[29] In embracing epistemological uncertainties and local, situated knowledge, gender history at its best offers new perspectives on the world by subverting the structures of existing knowledge.

That this refined understanding of power and agency has established women (divided by class and other hierarchies) as visible and multi-dimensional subjects of history is not surprising; so absent were they in historical narratives before the 1970s that any gain was significant. More unexpected, at least to some of Scott's detractors, is the realization that new knowledge about women is necessarily new knowledge about men. Studies about the ubiquitous discourses of the breadwinner have revealed, above all, the artificiality and fragility of masculinity. If womanhood is not an automatic outcome of a biological fact, neither is manhood. 'To be a man', as one historian has put it memorably, 'is more than a day's work.'[30]

Of blood and bloodline

If attending to the intersection of gender and class can yield surprising insights on men and masculinity, a focus on the entanglements between gender and 'race' returns the gaze to women as bearers of offspring. By the 1990s, social historians of Latin America and East Asia have made it amply clear that 'the family', previously taken to be a natural conglomerate of people related by blood or marriage and bound by emotional ties, is in fact an artificial unit whose composition and boundary need to be assiduously policed.[31] This realization has focused attention on the politics of fertility and motherhood as well as the important roles played by women in the reproduction of cultural values and racial categories in society. Lynn M. Thomas has proposed an analytic concept of 'gendered reproduction' or 'politics of the womb' to highlight the loaded nature of procreation as a mechanism of reproducing hierarchies in gender, race, class, and age, especially in colonial and postcolonial situations.[32]

Gendered reproduction was at the heart of the Spanish conquest of the New World which, as Kathryn Burns has shown, was accomplished not only by bloodshed but also by careful management of bloodlines. Barely two decades after the Spaniards under Francisco

Pizarro arrived in the magnificent Inca city of Cuzco, Peru, home of 150,000 to 200,000 residents, the conquistadores bought land to build the convent of Santa Clara in 1551, the oldest nunnery in the Americas.[33] Although most of the Spaniards in Cuzco by then had married Spanish wives at the behest of the Crown, they had also fathered daughters (mestizas) and sons (mestizos) with Andean women from elite families. Their concern for the fate of these children was sharply divided on gender lines. The mestizo-sons, some of whom followed their fathers into battles while some others served as translators, were deemed too threatening to the Crown. Although the fathers had wanted to pass on their lucrative entitlements of *encomiendas* (the right to receive Andean labor and tribute) to their sons, the Crown refused to extend these privileges beyond one generation. As if in a self-fulfilled prophecy, the mestizos 'proved' their untamable nature and hatched a revolt in 1567. After its suppression, the mestizos saw their legal rights curtailed and their status in society in irreparable decline.

The mestiza daughters, in contrast, became indispensable agents in the consolidation of Spanish hegemony in Peru, and the cloistered nunneries—at once monastery, orphanage, and boarding school—were key to this process. Santa Clara opened its doors in 1558 with a Spanish widow as its abbess for life; by 1564 it had admitted sixty girls—three Spaniards, one possibly of African descent, and the majority mestizas. Some had taken vows to become nuns but others were boarders plucked from their Indian mothers to learn the Spanish-Christian way of feminine deportment and domesticity. Many of the mestizas' fathers could afford to give the girls a sizeable dowry (100 cattle and 500 sheep from an *encomendero* father, for example) and an annual boarding fee that varied from case to case. Eighteen of the initial entrants eventually professed as nuns, but thirty-three left the convent after their acculturation; among the latter group ten mestizas were deemed hispanized enough to marry Spaniards while some others entered Spanish homes as servants.

At a time when few Spanish-born women found their way to Peru to avail themselves as wives, Burns observed, the mestiza daughters figured as a kind of 'cultural capital' for their fathers. Unlike their dangerous brothers, the mestizas' procreative potential was valued for the biological reproduction of Spanish families, whereas their domestic respectability rendered them agents of the *social* reproduction of

Spanish culture on which Spanish hegemony was staked. The consolidation of Spanish control of Cuzco and its enormous wealth is thus predicated on the conquistadores' 'gendered double vision of their own progeny' (9). Although made into bearers of Spanish culture, the mestiza daughters were by no means equal with their Spaniard counterparts. In the 1560s, when mestizo sons suffered defeat and denigration in Cuzco, the same hierarchy became evident in the convent as the Spaniard nuns—inferior to the mestizas in numbers and size of dowry—started to don black veils whereas the mestizas wore white veils, a sign of servitude.

The different fates of mestizos and mestizas—one deemed untamable and the other readily domesticated—as well as their concomitant marginalization bespeak the making of a nascent racialist consciousness in the colonies in the Inca heartland. In her analysis of the 'gendered dimension to the remote historical antecedents of what we now call race' (8), Burns has found 'race' in sixteenth-century colonial Peru to be a fluid and unnatural category, one that was not predetermined by blood but by a constellation of factors that include gender, religion, and culture. 'Mestizos were not born but made,' she concluded (37). One may venture to add that to be a Spaniard in colonial Peru also required more than a day's work.

The entanglements of gender and race in the European colonies became even more vexing in the nineteenth and early twentieth centuries, when 'race' came to be defined in the stark eugenic terms of generation and degeneracy. On the parts of the European colonizers, the assertion of racial and cultural supremacy often took the form of enforced domesticity of their own wives and daughters, as Ann Stoler has found in the Dutch Indies and French Indochina.[34] Furthermore, to justify their rule and to demonstrate their moral superiority, colonial agents often sought to reform society by outlawing such 'barbaric' native customs as female genital cutting in parts of Africa, sati ('widow-burning') in India, or foot-binding and concubinage in China, thereby intervening in the most intimate affairs of their subjects.[35]

On the part of the colonized, a concern with the sexual purity of their women often became an essential component of nationalism. In British India as in the Japanese colony of Manchuria in northern China, the educated colonial elite's construction of what Partha Chatterjee has called a sphere of inviolability that equated the spiritual with home and the feminine became vital to their imagination of the nascent nation. Lydia Liu, in turn, has found that the inverse—the suffering body of rural woman, bloodied by childbirth, disease, beating, and suicide—was just as important although its presence was submerged in male-centered nationalist discourses.[36]

The body in history

A desire to escape biological determinism has motivated scholars to separate gender from sex and to emphasize gender as social construction, as the discussion thus far makes clear. In the main, early practitioners of women's and gender history presumed 'sex', along with 'nature' and the 'body', to be timeless and stable categories outside the vicissitudes of history. This was true even as Michel Foucault's seminal works on the birth of the clinic and history of sexuality were already available in the 1970s in French and English.[37] Barbara Duden went a long way in reinserting the body into history with her book *The Woman beneath the Skin*, which as the title promised let the reader into the murmurs and fluxes *inside* the bodies of a group of women who lived in the eastern German town of Eisenach in the eighteenth century. That this was possible was due to the industry of Dr Johann Storch, the town physician who treated 1,650 women 1721–40 and later compiled their complaints from his diary with his comments into an eight-volume collection of case histories. By attending to what she termed 'orientational patterns of perception guiding the doctor's practice' as she read the cases, Duden was able to not only discern attitudes toward the body shared by the doctor and his patients but also convey a visceral sense of the embodied experiences of these women from all walks of life.[38]

The practice of medicine and perceptions of the body in the small town diverged from those prescribed in scholarly treatises in the eighteenth century, and they may appear shocking to the reader today. In a 'culture of self-treatment' (75), a patient took the initiative; she consulted neighbors and friends, administered bleeding to herself, sought remedies from a range of healers, and fetched the doctor only when she wanted something from him—a prescription or an affirmation of her own hunch. There were no objective laboratory results to define the ailment apart from the patients' subjective telling, and tell they did. From head to toe they complained of 'a feeling that their hair was falling out...tearing fluxes in the limbs...a closed-in wind running toward the womb', or 'pains in the foot as though the blood itself was trying to force its way out' (89–90). The woman's words constituted the sole basis of Storch's judgment.

The woman's body, so full of fluxes and movement, had yet to be sealed up from its environment. Duden spoke of 'the public nature of the inside' (86) in Eisenach, where a mother delivered 'a large lump' in a bowl to the doctor at midday and the delayed menses of a daughter were the subject of public prayer without embarrassment. The skin, perceived to be full of orifices and poles, was a fragile boundary that did not seal off the body. Instead, it was 'above all a surface on which the inside revealed itself' (123). The bodily fluids did not follow pre-scribed channels; blocked menses could ooze out of a cut on the fin-ger. Cause and effect were connected in even more far-reaching ways: anger suffocated the womb; freckles turned into bad breath; head lice cured white discharge. Clearly, these women experienced their bodies in terms and ways vastly different from the sanitized, objectified bod-ies of the moderns.

It is tempting to lament the ignorance and delusion of these women (and their doctor). But Duden did what any responsible historian is supposed to do: instead of judging her subjects by modern yardsticks, she used the distance between then and now to reveal hidden pat-terns of history. The Eisenach cases 'point to a society in which the concept of a body that could be isolated did not yet exist because an isolated individual did not exist. What did exist were people who were bound into social relations down to their innermost flesh' (145). As the eighteenth century wore on, that individual would gradually take shape and the personal body became increasingly understood (and experienced) as a bounded machine-like entity. The Eisenach bodies appear so strange because they existed in a world *before* the formation of modern concepts of individualism, sexuality, hygiene, and health. The modern body has a history.

The gender of bodies in Eisenach is particularly instructive. Both the doctor and his patients thought that women and men 'have similar corporeal dispositions in terms of periodicity and body regions' (117). Men had breasts just like women although they tended to be different in size; it was unusual but not incredible that one man 'had milked so much milk from himself that he made cheese from it' (117). Men, too, issue periodic menses from their bodies; the only difference was that they discharged blood from everywhere—the nose, the piles, or a wound. Although blood and milk were construed as signs of 'physiological motherhood' (117) in medical treatises in the late seventeenth century, this new view had not found its way into Eisenach in Storch's time. Anatomy was not yet destiny because the body was not experienced in anatomical terms. In such a world, 'a woman was not a "woman" because she was of that biological sex; it was the other way round: she suffered from a woman's disease because she was a woman' (118).

Duden concluded that for eighteenth-century Eisenach, gender is a relational and situational concept: 'Gender [in the sense of male–female difference] was constructed only through diverse relationships to each other and to the environment, but could never be unambiguously fixed in one place or in one flow' (119). In elucidating the strangeness of the pre-modern body, Duden has thus demonstrated that 'anatomy' does not automatically demarcate people into two hierarchical groups, men and women. The facile mapping of anatomy onto sexual difference, or the conflation of 'sex' and 'gender', was in fact a peculiar dynamic in the formation of the modern rational and individual subject. Far from being immutable, the biological category of 'woman' was born only in the nineteenth century.[39]

Flexible systems: disconnect of sex and gender

Two scholars from Nigeria have observed the havoc wreaked by the ideology of the biological woman—as a colonial import—in their native land. As early as 1987, Ifi Amadiume pointed out that a rigid correspondence of gender and sex was the hallmark of Victorian gender ideology that was imposed on her native Igboland. In contrast, the native system was characterized by a 'flexibility of gender constructions in the Igbo language and culture' where biological females could assume such male subject positions as sons.[40] People simply did not assume a one-on-one correspondence between biological sex and gender roles. Hence Nwajiuba Ojukwu, a married woman with no brothers, was recalled to her father's home when he became ill, and he returned her bride payment to her husband (32). This was a common practice in pre-colonial Igboland; these 'male daughters' (*nhanye*) lived in their father's compounds but in a female section, in either her own unit or in her mother's *nypuke* (sub-compound unit).

Furthermore, biological females could become so rich from farming and trading—traditionally the women's jobs whereas men became ritual specialists—that they could become 'husbands' to wives. Okenwanyi, one of the richest women in the rural town of Nnobi in the second half of the nineteenth century, for example, was herself one of two wives of her husband, but she also had nine wives. Both male daughters and female husbands (*igba ohu*, literally buying a slave) could act as the family head, which is designated by the genderless term *di-bu-no* (master of the home). Amadiume concluded, 'The fact that biological sex did not always correspond to ideological gender meant that women could play roles usually monopolized by men, or be classified as "males" in terms of power and authority over others. As such roles were not rigidly masculinized or feminized, no stigma was attached to breaking gender rules' (185). The Christian Church, however, condemned these practices as pagan, and the flexible gender system was eclipsed in the colonial period.

Sociologist Oyeronke Oyewumi launched an even more stinging critique of colonialism in destroying lifeworlds in her native Oyo-Yorubaland in Nigeria. Furthermore, when scholars unthinkingly applied the Western model as if it were universal, it distorted understanding about native practices before the colonial period (1862–1960). In Oyewumi's telling, anatomical differences between male and female were recognized in Oyo-Yoruba culture, but one body type was not deemed superior to the other. She thus coined the terms 'anatomic sex' (anasex in short) 'anatomic female' (anafemale), and 'anatomic male' (anamale) to denote this non-hierarchal understanding of biological sex. Or, in her words, 'to emphasize the nongendered attitude toward the relation between the human body and social roles, positions, and hierarchies'.[41]

Oyo-Yoruba society was hierarchal, but hierarchies were organized primarily by seniority in generational ranking and age. Another factor in the flexibility of the gender–sex system is the lack of essentialized identities. Social identities were not mapped onto individual bodies, but shifted according to specific situations: one's subject position was made in relation to the people with whom one was interacting (p. xiii).

Hence the body was not the basis for the assignment of social roles or identities in any immutable, essentialized way. Both biological sex and social gender were 'real' in pre-colonial Yorubaland—anatomic differences were recognized and anafemales did become wives, mothers, family heads, and traders—but sex and gender were separate realms; there were no linguistic or social mechanisms that automatically mapped one onto the other. In this world, 'woman' (as a biological category) and 'women' (as a collective group sharing certain traits or interests) did not exist.

Oyewumi thus provocatively concluded that Western feminists have erred in assuming that gender is the fundamental organizing principle of all societies and that the subordination of women is universal. Although second-wave feminists made a good strategic move in construing gender as distinct from biology, she continued, 'in spite of all efforts of separating the two, the distinction between sex and gender is a red herring. In Western conceptualization, gender cannot exist without sex since the body sits squarely at the base of both categories'.

Flexibility in sexual and gender identities also characterized the first half of Qajar Iran (1785–1925), albeit the body that mattered was the body of desires instead of economic productivity. The key mechanism of gendering people was a refined 'Persian male homoerotic culture', as Afsaneh Najmabadi has found.[42] Early in the nineteenth century, a transitional period, the people in Qajar Iran were not gendered into male and female according to bodily anatomy, but according to an economy of male desires into adult men, *amrads* (or *ghilman*), and women. *Amrad*s, or beardless young men, were objects of desire of adult males. These three subject positions each prescribed outward forms of beauty: the clean face of *amrads*, with beards barely visible if at all, signaled their sexual availability to adult men; the latter fashioned full-body beards hanging to their waist as emblems of their virility. Demarcated by age, status, and power, these two uneven forms of maleness found unmistakable expressions on their faces. Elite adult women wore a soft down above their upper lips—a thin mustache that was sometimes painted on with mascara—to signal their privileged status and beauty.

This system changed as heightened contacts with Europeans in the course of the nineteenth century brought new sexual norms of compulsory heterosociability. The *amrad* disappeared from sight in a cultural process Najmabadi called 'the feminization of the beloved' (65). Women now frolicked in the arms of men in erotic paintings; female breasts became eroticized. The enactment of a two-sex system was thus part of the modernist discourse that bifurcated homosexuality and heterosexuality while making the latter normative.

The full circle: sex revisited

The dual analytic edge of the category of gender—as social relationships and as power dynamics—has produced a complex understanding about the 'intersectionality' of hierarchies wrought of gender, race, class, age, and generational rank in the 1980s–2000s. From searching for the roots of male domination to exposing the fragility of masculinity, reorienting women in diverse roles as agents of historical change, and eventually undermining the biological foundation of male–female difference, historians of gender have transformed not only the shape and color of history but also loosened some cherished Euro-American notions about being human. Specialists of non-Western and non-modern time-places, in particular, have challenged ethnocentric definitions that had structured previous anglophone scholarship and, in so doing, revealed other possibilities of living in bodies and in culture.

The journey has come full circle. In the 1970s–1980s, scholars codified the category 'gender' to free it from the biased view of anatomy-as-destiny. In her 1990 classic *Gender Trouble*, feminist philosopher Judith Butler questioned the possibility of such a clean separation between sex and gender. 'If the immutable character of sex is contested,' she wrote, 'perhaps this construct called "sex" is as culturally constructed as gender; indeed, perhaps it was always already gender, with the consequence that the distinction between sex and gender turns out to be no distinction at all.'[43] At the beginning of the twenty-first century, historians and sociologists of science are following up on Butler's suggestion in calling for a return to sex—not as a facile equivalent of biology but as in itself a product of culture.

In her study of the politics of molecular genetics of sex determination, for example, Joan Fujimura has discovered that the geneticists' preconceived ideas about binary male–female norms influenced both the design of their experiments and the interpretation of the data gathered. When she switched the frame, Fujimura found that the data could yield the opposite conclusion from the ones drawn by the scientists. 'By reviewing the data without thinking about sex as a binary category, I saw that the last fifteen years of research on "*SRY*" and "*DAX-1*" [the so-called sex determining genes] have produced much evidence for complexity in the genetics of sex determination.' Calling scholars in the humanities and social sciences as well as the public to partake in the making of scientific knowledge instead of leaving it to the natural scientists, Fujimura wrote that, 'instead of treating sex as biological and gender as social, I argue that sex, like gender, is a socio-material product'.[44]

Similarly, feminist biologist Anne Fausto-Sterling has urged her readers to perceive the world from a framework that reintegrates biology and culture on the molecular, personal, and social levels, for 'the changes [in sexual anatomy] that occur throughout the life cycle all happen as part of a biocultural system in which cells and culture mutually construct each other'.[45] In *Sexing the Body*, Fausto-Sterling took Dr John Money to task for building a treatment program for transsexuals on the premise of a two-sex model—that a person could be made into either male or female but should not be left in between. This dualistic thinking also propelled Money to authorize surgery on generations of babies born with ambiguous sexual traits, producing irreparable psychological harm. In the 1990s, when these 'intersexuals' organized into activist groups and pled to be left alone, conservative politicians were scandalized. In calling scientists and the public to embrace a more fluid system whereby one can assume more than one sexual identity, Fausto-Sterling envisions a world of multiple possibilities in the ordering of bodies and sex that had once been natural but has since been forgotten with the onset of modernity and colonialism.

10. Yinka Shonibare, MBE, 'Boy on the Globe', 2008, mannequin, Dutch wax printed cotton and globe. Overall: 175 × 125 × 125 cm, SHO 489. © the artist and Stephen Friedman gallery (London); photography courtesy Stephen White

10 Culture

MEGAN VAUGHAN

In 2003 UNESCO published a Convention for the Safe-guarding of the Intangible Cultural Heritage, some thirty years after the World Heritage Convention had been issued by the same organization. Now UNESCO's stamp of recognition would be extended to include, not only the visible landmarks of 'world civilizations', but also the 'intangible' heritage represented by a song, a dance, a piece of local knowledge. Article 2 of the 2003 Convention defined Intangible Cultural Heritage as:

the practices, representations, expressions, knowledge, skills—as well as the instruments, artefacts and cultural spaces associated therewith—that communities, groups, and in some cases individuals recognize as part of their cultural heritage. The intangible cultural heritage, transmitted from generation to generation, is constantly recreated by communities and groups in response to their environment, their interaction with nature and their history, and provides them with a sense of identity and continuity, thus promoting respect for cultural diversity and human creativity.[1]

As this definition of 'the Intangible Cultural Heritage' implies, the Convention was in part an expression of a recognition of the importance of 'cultural diversity' and of the diverse modes of cultural expression, reflecting a wider shift in the politics of culture and rights in recent decades, to which I will return. At the same time, this represented an implicit move from an exclusive concern with the elitist and material products of 'civilizations' (temples, pyramids, palaces, cathedrals) towards a range of practices that would encompass just about everything human beings engage in. The list includes 'oral traditions and expressions', including 'language', 'social practices', 'rituals', 'knowledge and practices concerning nature and the universe', and 'traditional craftsmanship'. While the emphasis of the Convention is on cultural heritage as a property of groups, whose diverse identities it is important to safeguard, it also implies that under some particular circumstances (presumably those in which the very survival of a group is under threat), a cultural heritage might be the repository of one individual ('and in some cases individuals'). At the same time, through its insistence on the use of the definite article throughout the document ('The Intangible Cultural Heritage') the UNESCO Convention seems to be reminding us that diverse and varied as these practices might be, ultimately they constitute one common 'intangible cultural heritage', which belongs to us all.

In 2005 a UNESCO 'Proclamation' recognized two 'outstanding examples' of Intangible Cultural Heritage in Malawi.[2] One was the 'Gule Wamkulu', a 'ritual dance' traditionally part of a 'secret cult', entirely composed of men. The other was the 'Vimbuza Healing Dance'. Described by UNESCO as 'a useful complement to other forms of medical treatment', which has 'artistic value and a therapeutic function', Vimbuza is part of a wider healing tradition in the region involving spirit possession. Most 'patients' are women, who, having become possessed by Vimbuza spirits, undergo sometimes lengthy treatment by specialists, including a 'dance' during which male drummers employ rhythms identified with specific spirits, 'calling' them and allowing them to be 'danced out'.[3] The UNESCO website includes video and audio clips of one such ritual 'dance', showing a woman entering into a trance, falling to the ground, and being assisted by other women. One clip focuses in on the face of a small child watching as the ritual takes its course.

Few casual visitors to Malawi are likely to be aware of the involvement of UNESCO in this aspect of the country's 'intangible cultural heritage', but in 2007/8 no one in Malawi will have escaped the massive public awareness campaign of another UN agency, UNICEF. Huge billboards on every tarred road in Malawi advertise the UNICEF-funded 'Stop Child Abuse' campaign. Alternating between English and local languages the posters deliver the message to 'STOP' child labour, sexual abuse, child trafficking, and 'harmful cultural practices'.[4] 'Culture', UNICEF reminds us, can have its dark side: one person's 'intangible cultural heritage' may be another's more tangible cultural prison. But the UN has already thought that one through. In a clause in the 2003 Convention on ICH it declares that 'For the purposes of the Convention, consideration will be given solely to such intangible cultural heritage as is compatible with existing international human rights instruments, as well as with the requirements of mutual respect among communities, groups and individuals, and of sustainable development.' In the end, the culture of human rights must trump the culture of cultural diversity.[5]

The UN's dilemma (if that is what it is) is not a new one or even a surprising one. It is central to the history of European thinking on this thing called 'culture'. In the tradition of the French Enlightenment, 'culture' came to mean something akin to 'civilization', embodying a historically specific notion of 'rights' and asserting without embarrassment its superiority to other ways of being and thinking. In the German Romantic tradition, meanwhile, 'cultures', in the plural, were diverse, historically specific, and relative, embodying the 'traditional' virtues of a people. While UNICEF draws on the former tradition, UNESCO draws on the latter. It was a tension inherent in nineteenth- and twentieth-century European empires—between the 'civilizing mission', with all its ambiguities, and the desire to 'protect' the primitive from extermination. Since it is largely people in the former colonial world who are now the subjects of UN attentions, it may come as no surprise to them that their 'intangible cultural heritage' is being offered protection, while their 'harmful cultural practices' are the target for elimination.

In the modern world 'culture' is the subject and object of a vast and powerful industry. This material basis may be viewed as a relatively recent development but it is also an apt reminder of the origins of the word 'culture' in the practice of material transformation (though the 'stuff' to be transformed has changed). The word 'culture' comes from the Latin *colere*, with its original meaning apparently referring to the practice of agriculture or husbandry.[6] As Terry Eagleton reminds us, etymologically 'culture' derived from 'nature', but the two terms are inextricably interdependent, rendering both the Marxist conception of 'base' and 'superstructure' and the split between naturalism and idealism irrelevant:

... nature produces culture which changes nature ... if nature is always in some sense cultural, then cultures are built out of that ceaseless traffic with nature which we call labour.[7]

All human societies depend on some degree of transformation of 'nature', and so, presumably, all have some concept or concepts akin to this early European notion of 'culture' with its dual reference to both material and symbolic production. But in the European tradition(s) the concept made some historically specific leaps in the eighteenth and nineteenth centuries. In the French Enlightenment tradition 'culture' became synonymous with 'civilization', a wide notion embracing political, economic, material, intellectual life and entailing a sense of progress and ethical superiority. In German Idealist thinking, usually traced to the works of Herder, 'Kultur' came to carry a radical and reactionary meaning as a distinctive way (or ways) of life, whose values needed to be defended against the universalism of 'civilization'. In this Romantic tradition, cultures in the plural were organic, traditional, authentic, and embodied the 'spirit' of a people.[8] For Matthew Arnold, culture was the repository of value and order, while 'civilization' entailed anarchy.[9] 'Culture' in this sense was a utopian critique of the imperialistic and repressive aspects of 'civilization', and stood for an entire way of life, but in the course of the nineteenth century, and as one consequence of this dialectical way of thinking, 'culture' also became more narrowly associated with the arts and artistic creation. It was, writes Eagleton, as if the arts were now 'forced to stand in for God, or happiness, or political justice'.[10] 'Culture' was represented, not by the advances of science and economy and industry, but by opera, literary pursuits, painting, and (in a move which has its own trajectory) the 'primitive' pre-modern.

Tracing the genealogy of 'culture' in European thought in the nineteenth and twentieth centuries is inseparable from tracing the genealogy of what Francis Mulhern calls 'metaculture', or a discourse on culture.[11] Culture had become its own topic. In Britain in the mid- to late twentieth century the political 'left' took energetically to the discursive field of 'culture', attacking in the process the by now entrenched association between culture and an elitist artistic aesthetic. The ensuing 'culture wars' reflected wider political and social processes, particularly in relation to the British class system and its material basis, but the debate on culture also became something of an industry in its own right. The critique took a variety of forms. In *The Uses of Literacy* and other works, Richard Hoggart, an inheritor in some senses of the pessimistic Romantic tradition, lamented the passing of an authentic proletarian working-class culture which he saw as under attack from mass marketing. Hoggart's was not just a contribution to academic debates on the meaning of culture—it was a politically engaged and policy-oriented criticism with significant institutional ramifications.[12]

In Britain another central figure in the elaboration of a cultural critique in the twentieth century was Raymond Williams.[13] In a series of works Williams traced the historical development of the concept of culture and constructed his own, cultural Marxist, interpretation.[14] 'Culture is ordinary' is one of Williams's more famous catchphrases, summing up his view that culture was a whole way of life, a product of the creative and non-deterministic relationship between human consciousness and material circumstances. Culture was about to become everything again. In *The Long Revolution* Williams defined it as 'a structure of feeling'. If there were serious problems with this new expansiveness, there is no doubting the creative energy that it helped to unleash. Cultural materialists like Williams brought the economy back into discussions of culture, but in a formulation which moved beyond 'base' and 'superstructure'. Economic relations were themselves cultural entities and it was their cultural qualities which helped embed their inequalities.

By the 1960s this vibrant field of cultural Marxism was being further expanded and informed by new currents of postcolonial criticism and feminism. At the Centre for Contemporary Cultural Studies at the University of Birmingham, Stuart Hall succeeded Richard Hoggart in 1968 as Director (the latter, significantly, leaving for a post in UNESCO).[15] A diffuse Gramscian Marxism still under-girded what had by now become 'Cultural Studies' but it was continually and productively challenged by those who claimed that 'race', ethnicity, and the structural inequalities of gender relations were as central to British society and culture as class relations.[16] Hoggart's somewhat nostalgic lament for the authentic culture of the English working class now appeared rather dated and ethnocentric. Britain was a post-imperial nation and the empire was 'writing back'. The 'writing back' would entail, not simply putting the 'Black in the Union Jack', but insisting that in the diasporic, globalized world of which Britain was a part, it was not enough simply to couple categories such as 'blackness' and 'the nation'—some more radical rethinking of cultural politics was required.[17]

As the work of Stuart Hall and his colleagues reminds us, the subject of culture in Europe, particularly in the nineteenth and twentieth centuries, is also the subject of empire and the conceptualization of difference. Inherent in the Romantic strand of European cultural thinking were two ideas that related directly to European imperialist expansion: the diversity of cultures and primitivism. The Radical Romantics exalted the authentic creative energy and organicism of 'primitive' cultures and in the late nineteenth century the new discipline of anthropology made these primitive cultures its subject. It appeared that for primitive societies culture was everything. In 1871 E. B. Tylor in *Primitive Culture* defined culture 'or Civilisation' as 'that complex whole which includes knowledge, belief, art, morals, law, custom, and any other capabilities and habits acquired by man as a member of society'.[18] For historians of anthropology the fact that for Tylor 'Culture' and 'Civilisation' were synonymous is significant since it indicates that his conceptualization of culture as a whole, organic thing did not necessarily entail complete relativism.[19] For Tylor, it is implied, understanding the internal logic and meaning of a culture did not involve ditching an Enlightenment notion of 'progress'. If Tylor's subject was 'culture', his successors would soon pluralize the noun. Cultures became the subject of twentieth-century anthropology and in some hands these cultures assumed the self-determining qualities of that other great late nineteenth-century invention, 'race'. This is despite the fact that one of the principal founders of cultural anthropology, Frank Boas, constructed his theory of culture explicitly in opposition to race theory.[20]

The political context in which twentieth-century social anthropology constructed its subject is of course critical. Working often in African and Asian colonial contexts, where racial theory had a long life and a deep reach, many anthropologists saw their organic theories of 'tribal' cultures as liberal interventions and critical counterpoints to colonial thinking and, in some cases, as weapons of resistance against capitalist exploitation. Yet their reifications of 'tribal' cultures and their paternalist tendencies also lent their theories a utilitarian function within colonial systems.[21] The dual European heritage of culture as civilization and culture as the embodiment of the spirit of a people permeated European colonial systems. If colonialism was often justified in terms of the advancement of 'civilization', in practice many colonial systems found more useful the alternative version of culture which could be used to justify (often with a paternalistic twist) keeping 'primitive' people firmly in their place. Willingly or unwillingly, anthropologists found that their 'science' of cultural analysis had become a tool of colonial rule and, willingly or unwillingly, colonial subjects found themselves employing the language of culture to press their claims for rights and representation. In the mid-twentieth century as biological racism became discredited and colonial empires sought to justify their existence along liberal lines, 'culture' came in useful. In extreme cases, as in apartheid South Africa concepts of culture not only coexisted happily with 'race', they added intellectual and ideological force to it. Elsewhere 'culture' could be usefully set to work in many contexts in which straightforward talk of biological 'race' had become unacceptable. To take just one example, in the work of a highly influential group of French psychiatrists working in colonial North Africa, Islamic religion and culture (static, all-encompassing) were interpreted as determining the collective 'Arab' psyche through their effect on brain structure—an unusual application of the more general notion that culture is the human capacity to transform nature.[22] Meanwhile colonial nationalists were obliged to employ a dual discursive strategy. On the one hand the leaders of nationalist movements had to demonstrate their commitment to a progressive notion of modernization (culture as 'civilization'), on the other, their claim to self-determination rested on the assertion that they represented a people with a distinctive 'traditional' culture (the 'spirit of the people') which had been unjustly repressed under colonial rule. Frequently this appeal to 'culture' was heavily gendered and women (and 'Woman') became the repositories of an 'authentic' pre-colonial and pre-modern morality and 'tradition'.[23]

It is little wonder that in the period of colonial nationalism and decolonization, anthropology as a discipline came to re-think, and ultimately deconstruct, its concept of culture. But ironically, perhaps, this move coincided, more or less, with the increasing political mobilization of 'culture' in the identity politics of the postcolonial world, as we shall see.

In the 1960s anthropologists, like populist leftist cultural critics, had been expanding the scope of culture until it began to look dangerously like all and nothing. Culture was society, human consciousness, economic structure, religion, politics. It was all these things as manifested in the products of what was now a huge industry of 'popular culture', but it was also all these things as evidenced in our everyday modes of being, down to the way we brush our teeth.

In the 1970s some anthropologists and cultural historians turned to versions of structuralism in a move which promised to rescue culture as a useful concept. The work of the American anthropologist Clifford Geertz was particularly influential and his account of the Balinese cock-fight so widely quoted, in so many different contexts, that it became a fetishized cultural object in its own right.[24] For Geertz, a culture was a 'signifying system', a dense web of symbols and meanings:

The culture concept to which I adhere denotes an historically transmitted pattern of meanings embodied in symbols, a system of inherited conceptions expressed in symbolic forms by means of which men communicate, perpetuate, and develop their knowledge about and attitudes towards life.[25]

In order to 'decode' these complex and multilayered systems of meaning that made up a culture, the anthropologist had to adopt a strategy akin to literary criticism—attentive to style as well as structure, to irony and ambiguity as well as deliberative performance. Though Geertz's theory of culture was essentially a structuralist one, his method ('thick description') implied that the full meaning of a cultural system could not be grasped through a mechanistic structural analysis.[26] The cultural system provided a framework and a set of guidelines within which individuals expressed themselves and acted and the understandings of participants were central to his analysis. His theory allowed a space for human agency, contestation, and the possibility of change, up to a point, but he was criticized for (amongst other things) an apparent lack of attention to power structures. Nevertheless, 'thick description' caught on as a mode of analysis well beyond the confines of the discipline of social anthropology, and Geertz's concept of culture remains influential.

The influence of social anthropology, and of Geertz in particular, was felt very powerfully in the field of cultural history, which was 'rediscovered' in the 1970s, producing a large corpus of innovative historical scholarship.[27] The origins of the 'cultural turn' in historical writing are, however, multiple. In Britain the labour historian E. P. Thompson had been exploring the limits of orthodox Marxism for an understanding of the history of industrialization and class relations.

Thompson contested Raymond Williams's 'culturalist' paradigm, but in his own work he was also concerned to theorize the 'cultural and moral mediations' of class, and to describe the cultural components of class consciousness.[28] This British cultural-Marxist tradition was just one factor influencing the growth of the field of 'cultural history' between the 1960s and the 1980s.[29] The French *Annales* School, with its emphasis on *mentalités*, was another direct influence and anteced-ent. Cultural historians, perhaps sensibly, spent relatively little time trying to define 'culture', but generally took a very expansive view of their field. For some the common ground appeared to be an attention to the symbolic realm and its interpretation, but as Peter Burke (him-self a major figure in the field) points out, even this cannot serve as a general definition.[30] The corpus of work included histories (informed by new modes of interpretation) of topics traditionally defined in the 'Western' tradition as 'cultural' (the arts, architecture, music) but now expanded to include 'popular culture', as well as 'cultural histories' of topics conventionally labelled 'politics' or 'religion'. Meanwhile path-breaking work in gender history led the way in theorizing the rela-tionship between the symbolic and material realms. Gender history has its own history, as Dorothy Ko demonstrates in this volume, but this history intersects at many points with currents in cultural history. Gender historians anticipated many of the debates in the wider field by insisting that gender roles and ideologies could not be bracketed as an aspect of 'culture' but were constitutive of those areas of histori-cal experience conventionally labelled 'political', 'economic', and 'social'. Gender historians also wrestled with an issue that went to the very heart of the definition of 'culture'—that is the construction and role of the biological in human history (see Ko's chapter).

Many of the more heated arguments over cultural history revolve less around the delineation of the field than they do over methods. The cultural historians' interests led them to a much more direct explor-ation of historical consciousness and historical memory than had generally been the case for those who defined themselves as social or political historians. In exploring the dimensions of subjectivity, con-sciousness, and the unconscious, some looked to psychoanalysis, oth-ers to poststructuralist theory, taking a 'linguistic turn'.[31] Critics of the new cultural history feared that entire university history departments would be staffed by scholars whose intellectual energies were directed at proving there was no such thing as history. Predictably, perhaps, critics had a tendency to label every cultural historian a deconstructionist, which was far from being the case. Others bemoaned the fact that, running fast and loose in the terrain of literary theory, historians were losing altogether the close relationship with the social sciences which had characterized much historical investigation in the 1960s and 1970s.[32] While defenders of the new cultural history argued that it continued to provide a more grounded account of the way in which social action was historically constituted, others worried that in the process concepts such as 'identity' were being used without any reference to their theoretical underpinnings.[33]

Despite these doubts, it is clear that some versions of the 'new cultural history' held a powerful appeal, not least in the area of colonial and postcolonial history. In South Asia a new 'school' of history emerged in the form of 'Subaltern Studies', which drew on new currents of cultural analysis to re-examine the histories of the peasantry, of nationalism, religion, and gender. Part of the attraction of this new approach lay in the apparent restoration of agency and consciousness to colonial subjects whose histories had previously either been erased entirely by colonial modes of thinking, or had been subsumed under a mechanistic version of a neo-Marxist 'modes of production' analysis.[34] In my own field of African history a similar trend brought forward new accounts of the impact of colonialism and capitalism which gave room for an appreciation of the ways in which African communities had creatively negotiated these forces and of the role of historical consciousness in this process. Histories of labour migration, for example, were transformed by this approach, as were studies of the impact of Christianity and literacy, while the long-term social and political consequences of the slave trade were traced through studies of social memory and ritual practice.[35] Histories of colonial governance in Africa meanwhile moved beyond the idea of 'invented tradition' (with its stress on the power of colonial knowledge) to an analysis that emphasized the agency of certain groups of African colonial subjects in engaging with colonial rulers in the definition of 'culture', custom, and difference.[36] Cultural history looks different in a postcolonial setting. No histories of cultural production in Africa can avoid the politics of the definition of the cultural sphere and so in the field of plastic arts scholars have examined the role of colonial and postcolonial collecting in redefining artefacts as 'art', and in literary and music studies the enduring effects of the colonial binary of traditional/modern.[37]

Though the influence of Foucault and Said was certainly felt in the area of African studies, 'deconstruction' as a mode of analysis held little appeal to historians on the Continent. The reasons are not hard to find. Whilst we might agree that 'Africa' was discursively constructed, we were not keen to see it disappear. The field of African history had only emerged in the 1960s and that had involved a long hard struggle to prove that the 'dark continent' did, in fact, have verifiable pre-colonial histories. To argue now that these histories were mere 'constructions' was not an attractive option.[38] Neither was it an attractive option for subordinated groups in African societies whose historical experiences were finally being written about and made available in school textbooks.

An examination of 'culture' in African historiography raises the more general question of whether doing 'cultural history' is better described as doing 'history'. 'Culture', as I have indicated, is a particularly loaded term in a postcolonial context, with its implication of the importance of 'difference'. Certainly we need to acknowledge the historical importance of changing concepts of culture in the colonial and postcolonial histories of African societies, but it is not clear that we need to carry on employing the term ourselves, except in relation to specific areas of 'cultural production'. For example, in their recent critique of the field of comparative politics, Patrick Chabal and Jean-Pascal Daloz make a case for the importance of culture (defined as a system of meanings) for an understanding of African politics that goes beyond the ethnocentric models of Western political science. Certainly they have a point when they argue that analyses of the democratic process in Africa need to take account of local meanings of power and might (for example) have to include an examination of the 'occult' in the process.[39] But is it helpful to describe this as taking account of the 'role of culture'? I prefer to read this as an appeal for studies of African politics that are properly grounded in histories of power relations and take account of historical consciousness.

Historians of Africa have long been writing histories which, had they been written of European societies, might well have been defined as 'cultural history', but they have done so largely without recourse to the term 'culture'. The context and conditions of production of African history have always necessitated the use of a range of non-literary sources and an engagement with other disciplines, and this in itself entails an ongoing enquiry into meaning and historical consciousness.[40] Jan Vansina, for example, has been researching and writing on the pre-colonial history of Central Africa since the 1950s. Employing a range of methodologies including historical linguistics and oral history, he has produced *longue durée* accounts of political traditions which are embedded in an understanding of environment and population history, but also in ideologies, concepts, and values.[41] Vansina was certainly influenced by the *Annales* School, and so his work could be described as 'cultural history' in that tradition, but I think it would be better described as 'history'. Vansina's reconstruction of pre-colonial political traditions would be impossible without his use of multiple forms of evidence and an interrogation of the meanings of this evidence that goes far beyond conventional questions of 'reliability'.[42] This mode of historical practice is not confined to work on pre-colonial Africa, however. Two outstanding works on the history of reproduction in the colonial period, by Nancy Rose Hunt and Lynn M. Thomas, demonstrate clearly the centrality of 'cultures' of reproduction to political and economic history, but they are able to do so precisely because they do not employ a concept of 'culture' as a separate sphere of historical analysis.[43] Such strategies of historical writing are not confined to African history, of course. In his recent study of death in Mexican history, Claudio Lomnitz argues convincingly for the centrality of death to any understanding of the political history of Mexico. This goes much further than arguing that 'cultures' of death are politically influential, or politically manipulated in Mexican history. Rather, Lomnitz explores the ways in which death is constitutive of the very idea of Mexico, and of sovereignty.[44] If the concept of 'culture' begins to look redundant in these works of history, nevertheless it is important to acknowledge that they have been directly or indirectly informed by the critical debates on culture that have energized social anthropologists and historians over the last twenty years.

In the 1980s and 1990s social anthropologists seemed intent on deconstructing the subject of their discipline.[45] This self-questioning crisis was induced in part by the influence of postmodernist theory, but also by a postcolonial politics in which the 'native' subject, no longer prepared to be passively observed, was answering back. Social anthropological methods now seemed hopelessly implicated in a representational power system which reified difference and elevated one system of knowledge production over all others.[46] Not only was it now incumbent on the anthropological observer to be aware of his or her 'subject position', but the very acts of observation of and writing about the 'other' could be seen as forms of violent appropriation. Furthermore, there was this thing called 'globalization' and the world itself was changing (it always had been of course), so now cultures were increasingly 'contested', 'contingent', in flux, hybridized, and essentially indescribable.

But if 'culture' had done a disappearing act in anthropology departments, it was far from dead in the real world of late twentieth-century identity politics. Disillusionment with conventional politics and the increasing pace of globalization (particularly in the 1980s) produced the mobilization of 'culture' as 'identity' among minority ethnic and religious groups, feminists, and gay activists. In the United States in particular, where, in the face of neo-liberal policies, the traditional leftist struggle for economic equality looked doomed, the political language of equality was overtaken by one which stressed 'identity'.[47] Rights were now claimed less on the basis of equality (as in the Civil Rights era) than of difference, and an essentialist concept of culture re-emerged in a range of social movements that emphasized the distinctiveness of group beliefs, ideals, values, and styles. Encouraged, in some cases, by non-governmental and international organizations, this pattern of political mobilization also gathered strength in the former colonial world. For social anthropologists there was a certain irony in all of this, for 'just at the very moment in which anthropologists were engaged in an intense and wide-ranging critique of the more essentialist interpretation of the concept, they found themselves witnessing the increasing prevalence of "culture" as a rhetorical object'.[48] Fortunately for social anthropologists, this has produced a productive new field of study and analysis. It is not simply that 'culture' was once again being set up against 'civilization' in the form of 'rights'. Rather, something more interesting and complex was happening. A more generalized culture of rights, encouraged by liberal democratic constitutions and the activism of human rights organizations, was providing a space in which groups were claiming their rights to culture. The assumed opposition between a rights-based politics and one based on 'culture' seemed to have been dissolved, but the field in which these notions coexisted was full of revealing contestations. Global capitalism, meanwhile, seemed to be feeding very productively off this re-invention of cultural difference.

The re-invention of an essentialist version of culture, and the deployment of this idea of culture as a 'right', has significant political consequences. In liberal democracies all over the world 'culture' appeared, in the 1980s and 1990s, to have become the keyword in a range of political debates, with varied results. In northern countries a number of issues consequent on rapid globalization, neo-liberal economic policy, and migration have been glossed as questions of 'multiculturalism'. In some cases the 'right' to culture was appropriated by the Right, as in Britain under Margaret Thatcher, where New Right ideologues productively utilized Gramscian notions of hegemony and anti-racist notions of cultural difference in order to promote an idea of the distinctiveness of a (white) English nation and culture.[49] British Conservative Party leaders claimed that the recognition of cultural difference ('multiculturalism') was divisive and indeed dangerous as likely to provoke racist attacks from white Britons who felt that their 'culture' was under attack. The discourse of 'Culture' had been very effectively mobilized as a euphemism (once again) for racism and as a means of exclusion.

In France, where Republicanism and secularism apparently made formal recognition of 'multiculturalism' a political impossibility, the *affaire foulard* has refused to go away. As Benhabib shows, beginning in 1989, when three scarf-wearing Muslim girls were excluded from their school, the 'affaire' raised difficult issues for the French state, which sees itself as an agent of women's emancipation. The French authorities' interpretation of scarf-wearing as a symbol of cultural oppression was belied by the fact that the girls had clearly been making a conscious though complex gesture, claiming to 'exercise their freedom of religion as French citizens' and on the other hand to exhibit 'their Muslim and North African origins in a context that sought to envelop them, as students of the nation, within an egalitarian, secularist ideal of republican citizenship'.[50] Some see it as 'ironic' that this kind of claim to difference is made possible by the freedoms of expression afforded by liberal political traditions. In the Netherlands this 'irony' has taken a further twist. In the wake of two political murders in 2002 and 2005, some citizens of the Netherlands claim that 'tolerance' is an essential and defining feature of the nation's 'culture', and that groups which do not subscribe to this value have no place in the nation.

The hazards of a politics in which 'culture' is synonymous with 'identity' and forms the basis for claims on rights and resources are particularly striking in the many cases around the world in which indigenous or aboriginal peoples seek legal redress and restitution from states claiming to operate a form of liberal 'multiculturalism'. In Australia in 1992 a court ruling (*Eddie Mabo* v. *State of Queensland*) for the first time accorded recognition to native land title on the part of Aboriginal Australians. Previously, it had been held that at the moment of colonization indigenous Australians had lacked the degree of social organization and cultural evolution necessary for a concept of land title. Now the law admitted the validity of a form of native title, but there were conditions attached to this recognition. Under the Native Title Act of 1994 granting of title was dependent on claimants demonstrating, not only that they were direct descendants of the original inhabitants of the land and had occupied that land continuously, but that there existed a form of customary law relating to the land, a law to which they had shown a consistent allegiance. At the same time, however, it was reiterated that only those native laws and customs which were not 'repugnant' to natural justice and equity would be so recognized. Furthermore, if it could be shown that Aboriginal heritage had been seriously diluted through 'interbreeding' with another heritage, then recognition would not be accorded. As Elizabeth Povinelli argues in her account of this process, it would not be true to say that the Australian government engaged in this process in bad faith. Rather, they engaged in it with an 'excess of optimism' in the possibilities of a liberal multiculturalism. But the position in which it placed Aboriginal communities was an invidious one, forcing them both to re-invent themselves in the image of the primitive, to emphasize 'difference' and at the same time to disavow those elements of 'difference' which offended white Australian sensibilities.[51] It is an injunction that invites an ironic and mimetic approach to 'culture'.[52]

Clearly 'culture' cannot do all the work being asked of it in many contemporary political contexts, where large issues of colonialism, inequality, and racism are at stake. These strains on 'culture' as a language of accommodation and contestation and rights have become all the more evident since the events of 11 September 2001, after which some discussion of religion in its own right has seemed unavoidable. As Slavoj Zizek wryly remarks:

Culture has commonly become the name for all things we practice without really taking seriously. And this is why we dismiss fundamentalist believers as 'barbarians' with a 'medieval mindset': they dare to take their beliefs seriously. Today we seem to see the ultimate threat to culture as coming from those who live immediately in their culture, who lack the proper distance.[53]

Though an essentialist and ahistorical definition of culture appears to be in the ascendant in a world of liberal multiculturalist democracies, this is a world simultaneously marked by an unprecedented degree of mobility. While Australia in the 1980s and 1990s grappled with the historical legacy of the treatment of Aboriginal Australians, it was also faced with the economic and political ascendancy of its East Asian neighbours and the question of how 'Asian' it wanted to be. This posed issues which could not be resolved by recourse to the notions of nativism and continuity of culture which had been applied to Aboriginal communities. 'Globalization', migration, and the development of new technologies have had complex consequences, as I have indicated. Global capitalism, far from eradicating difference, has sought to profit from it, and the internet has facilitated the reinvention of local communities and identifications, even though members of those communities may be physically located on different continents. But it has also produced new identifications and associations. Whilst legislators in liberal democracies struggle to fit people into cultural straitjackets, millions of people are willingly or unwillingly on the move, physically and culturally.

This is not a new phenomenon, of course, and for some the genealogy of modern culture lies in the very circumstances that made authentic 'family trees' (of the sort that would be recognized by legislators according 'native title') impossible to reconstruct. When millions of Africans were forcibly displaced by the Atlantic and Indian Ocean slave trades, their 'cultures' were inevitably disrupted, dispersed, and in some cases brought to the point of extinction. But there is a variety of ways of describing this historical process, which reflect very different understandings of what constitutes culture. Transplanted to the plantation factories of the new world, slaves laboured collectively, and the labour they performed was cultural as well as manual. The work of culture was the work of creating new meanings for their lives. But nothing is completely new. Depending on specific circumstances (death rates, ethnic preferences of slave buyers, and labour practices), to different degrees African slaves brought with them, and passed on to future generations, elements of their former lives or the lives of their ancestors, ranging from ritual practices very consciously re-enacted, to rhythms and bodily praxis more or less unconsciously performed. The circumstances in which these historical elements were practised were radically different, not least because many slave communities consisted of individuals with very multiple origins on the African continent, speaking different languages, and worshipping different gods. How should we describe this process? Is it best described in terms of loss and trauma, or of 'African cultural survivals'? Some approaches to the history of the Atlantic slave trade emphasize the latter and attempt to trace the exact origins of slave practices in the New World to exact locations on the African continent. This is the cultural equivalent of the tracing of one's ancestry through DNA (another popular and not unrelated pastime), and it is easy enough to point out its dangers and shortcomings, which include oversimplification, and a re-invention of 'Africa' as a patchwork of clearly defined ethnicities and closed cultural systems.[54] But the perceived need for and attraction of such an approach are themselves indicative of a very real cultural phenomenon born out of the brutality of slavery. For as long as the dominant narrative of culture is one of origins, and for as long as such a narrative remains integral to claims for recognition, people will be looking for their 'roots'. When historical narratives are too complex, contradictory, or ambivalent to satisfy us, we seek biological evidence to satisfy our desire for cultural continuity.

There is an alternative approach to this history, however, which conceptualizes culture in a very different way. This is one which privileges process over origins, mixture over purity, the creole over the native. This approach is fundamentally at odds with a multiculturalism which conceives of groups coexisting and interacting from their self-contained cultural bubbles, each with its clear narrative of origins, but it comes out of the same history. In his account of the 'Black Atlantic', Paul Gilroy replaced a search for 'roots' with an epistemology centred on 'routes' and webs of diaspora identities from Africa to the

New World to Europe.[55] Slavery, he argued, with its shared experience of terror, was central to the creation of modernity. Violence and displacement are constitutive of modernity.

The Black Atlantic, in Gilroy's analysis, is not a free-floating web of diasporas. It is a real historically produced entity, but one which cannot have recourse to neat genealogical narratives of race or kinship. Gilroy's emphasis is on identifications rather than identities but the processes involved are historically located within fields of power relations.[56] To argue that cultures are made and re-made, mutually constitutive and often in flux, is not to imply that there is not also loss involved in this process or the operation of power. To claim that we are all subject to these processes to the same degree, and all happily embracing our creolized identities, would be a gross misrepresentation of the contemporary world. 'Asian fusion' cuisine is not on everyone's daily menu. Some people would never be able to afford it. Others just do not like it.

This is where 'culture' in one of its more conventional guises comes in. While social theorists, historians, and anthropologists struggle to find words to describe the processes which constitute contemporary global culture, artists are both creating and simultaneously commenting on this phenomenon. The work of British-Nigerian artist Yinka Shonibare explores some of these issues in the conceptualization of a cosmopolitan culture with a specific history.[57] African-born artists are often confronted with the demand, implicitly or explicitly made, that their work should reflect an authentic African cultural tradition. Shonibare's reply to that demand is to reflect it back. Shonibare creates sculptures dressed in the Dutch wax printed cloth that, since the nineteenth century, has been widely adopted by women in West Africa (undermining in the process a vibrant local textile industry) and has come to be regarded as 'traditional' clothing. The story of this cloth's production is part of the history analysed by Gilroy. Produced in Britain and the Netherlands, 'Dutch wax' production incorporated Indonesian technology and was designed to satisfy changing West African tastes, incorporating traditional motifs and signs and symbols of 'modernity'. Shonibare's work displaces the cloth, using it in ways that reflect on the nature of African diasporic identities. In dressing 'English' figures like Dickens and the Brontë sisters in Dutch wax cloth, he goes beyond this, destabilizing metropolitan self-conceptions.

Dickens, read by generations of African schoolchildren, and regarded as the quintessential Englishman, becomes an 'African', in just the same way as Africans have become 'English' by reading him. But describing Shonibare's figures is no substitute for seeing them. These powerful but enigmatic creations are a reminder that we need cultural productions more than we need cultural studies.

11. Yinka Shonibare, MBE, 'Girl on the Globe', 2008, mannequin, Dutch wax printed cotton textile and globe, 220 × 100 × 100 cm, SHO 490. © the artist and Stephen Friedman gallery (London); photography courtesy Stephen White

II Ethnicity

ELIZABETH BUETTNER

Introduction: approaching ethnicity

'Ethnicity' is currently understood as 'a highly elastic concept applied to groups who say they share or are perceived to share some combination of cultural, historical, racial, religious, or linguistic features. Ethnicity also often implies shared ancestral origins; thus there is a thematic overlap with the older concept of peoples and some modern notions of race.'[1] Now a ubiquitous concept within academic writing as well as popular thinking alike, its origins are nonetheless recent, as attested to by its debut in the *Oxford English Dictionary* as late as 1953. 'Ethnic', however, dates back to the ancient Greek noun *ethnos* and is commonly translated as 'nation', or 'people'. This chapter addresses the changing, often ambiguous, meanings of 'ethnic' and 'ethnicity' over time, considering some of the many ways recent scholars have applied them. That groups and individuals long historically conceived along religious, tribal, caste, national, geographical, linguistic, cultural, and especially racial lines are more and more commonly examined through ethnic lenses suggests only some of the diverse tasks ethnicity has been entrusted with performing since the Second World War.

Fredrik Barth, one of the most influential contributors to the emerging interdisciplinary field of ethnic studies in the late 1960s and whose work remains seminal today, defined an ethnic group as a population that:

1. is largely biologically self-perpetuating; 2. shares fundamental cultural values, realized in overt unity in cultural forms; 3. makes up a field of communication and interaction; 4. has a membership which identifies itself, and is identified by others, as constituting a category distinguishable from other categories of the same order.[2]

Within this formulation, a confluence of biological and cultural factors sits alongside the acknowledgement of a particular ethnic identity both by those within and outside it as key features demarcating an ethnic group's parameters. Although biology had a role to play for Barth, culture was paramount and was to remain so for almost all subsequent scholars—many of whom were to downplay ethnicity's biological aspects further, as will be considered below. Nonetheless, despite foregrounding cultural dimensions of ethnicity such as language, religion, dress, and customs that are historically specific, able to be learned, and therefore mutable—in other words, socially constructed—as opposed to timeless, innate, and inborn, many debating ethnicity continue to place considerable importance upon far less negotiable components. Putative common descent, shared historical experiences, and either inhabiting or having ancestral origins in a particular territory also feature prominently in discussions about what connotes an ethnicity.[3]

Barth's cultural emphasis, however, did not revolve around seeking an inventory of specific cultural characteristics and practices; rather, the central issue was 'the ethnic boundary that defines the group, not the cultural stuff that it encloses'.[4] Through imposing boundaries, ethnicity drew a dividing line between different peoples and thereby enabled differentiation between 'us' and 'them'. Time and again, ethnic distinctions and boundaries have served as decisive means of calibrating the supposed superiority of the 'self' vis-à-vis the purported inferiority of the 'other'—a measure repeatedly deployed to justify enslavement, colonization, 'civilizing missions', assimilation projects, attempts to control sexual reproduction, expulsion of populations from a territory, and genocide. Ethnic delineations are never innocent: they signify social hierarchies through providing ideologies of difference and sameness as well as differentiate dominant from subordinate populations.

Indeed, the use of ethnic labels has never been neutral. Malcolm Chapman, Maryon McDonald, and Elizabeth Tonkin have outlined how, from its first appearance in ancient Greece, *ethnos* 'was not a word used for familiar groups of people sharing a culture, an origin, or a language. It was used, rather, to describe large, undifferentiated groups of either animals or warriors', more akin to 'throng' or 'swarm'. Pindar used *ethnos* with reference to people whose behaviour or location placed them outside Greek social norms, while Aristotle applied it to foreigners or barbarians—not, significantly, to the Greeks themselves, whom he called 'Hellenes'. *Ethnos* had deep connotations of 'naturality, of non-legitimate social organization, of disorganization, and of animality', while the derivative term *ethnikos* meant nearly the same thing as *barbaros*—the barbarian thought to lack civilization. 'Ethnic' long connoted an otherness that took religious as well as other forms, a theme addressed further below. As Chapman, McDonald, and Tonkin perceptively conclude, 'ethnicity' remains 'a term that half-heartedly aspires to describe phenomena that involve everybody, and that nevertheless has settled in the vocabulary as a marker of strangeness and unfamiliarity'—and frequently an implied inferiority.[5] In more recent times, it has commonly been applied to immigrants and minority groups within larger collectivities, particularly within modern multicultural nations where it has become an accepted way of describing sub-national groups.

Consistently addressing ethnicity with reference to the 'self' and the 'other' alike—to the ethnic majority 'mainstream' as much as minorities—remains an incomplete, yet pressing, task. The same can be said of race, a theme rarely far away from discussions about ethnicity. While ethnicity only entered the scholarly lexicon and, later, popular parlance starting in the mid-twentieth century, race has a much longer history as a means of classifying human difference. What, then, distinguishes the two concepts?

Race, in short, has been said to rest on physical, inherited, biological qualities, whereas with ethnicity cultural distinctions are paramount. While the former has been widely understood as fixed and unchangeable, the latter's social constructedness and malleability is emphasized. Yet as scholars including David Theo Goldberg, Werner Sollors, and Peter Wade have insisted, the line between racial/physical and ethnic/cultural distinctions repeatedly proves imprecise, shifting, and a matter of perception rather than an undisputed natural phenomenon. 'Assigning significance to biological or physical attributes, in the way required...by race, is a cultural choice,' Goldberg stresses; moreover, some physical characteristics (particularly visible ones such as skin colour, facial features, and hair) have repeatedly been singled out as racial indicators while others (such as height or weight) have been ignored.[6] Physical features are also prone to considerable alteration through surgery, exposure to the sun, and cosmetics—all of which are undergone, or not, in accordance with cultural preferences and the degree of importance accorded them within particular societies.

Similarly, a person classified as 'white' in one society at a given time, for example, might be considered 'black' or 'mixed race' in another—with the difference often reflecting socio-economic and other status attributes and wider historical circumstances. Describing his relatives in mid-twentieth-century Jamaica—then still a British Caribbean colony with a prior history of slavery—Stuart Hall recalled his mother's middle-class uncle as someone 'you would have thought...was an English expatriate, nearly white, or what we would call "local white"'. While his father's family was darker-skinned and lower-middle-class, both sides of the family 'were opposed to the majority culture of poor Jamaican black people: highly race and colour conscious, and identifying with the colonizers'.[7] As will become clearer below, those who were 'local white' in Jamaica on account of their mixed ancestry, class, and cultural proclivities almost certainly would have been labelled 'black' had they lived in the United States—or if they relocated to Britain. Barack Obama, who became the United States' first African American President in 2009, recounts searching for a 'workable meaning for his life as a black American' as the son of a white mother and a Kenyan father whose mixed ancestry long created feelings of being an outsider slipping 'back and forth between my black and white worlds'.[8]

What is more, while ethnicity emphasizes cultural over 'natural' qualities, it has never completely neglected the latter. Ethnic identities today are often treated as though they were objective 'facts' and determined by biology and ancestry, even when they take largely symbolic forms—a point Mary Waters persuasively makes with respect to present-day white ethnic groups in the United States.[9] Barth's definition of ethnic groups as 'largely biologically self-perpetuating' marks only one of the innumerable instances where descent and ancestry are invoked in relationship to ethnicity, just as they have been with reference to race.

That ethnicity continues to overlap with race in public understanding and academic work alike—sometimes being used as virtual synonyms—is unsurprising, given how much the former's current status owes to the compromised fortunes of the latter. Ethnicity's history and rise to prominence occurred in tandem with race's international disrepute starting in the mid-twentieth century, largely on account of the atrocities committed by Nazi Germany in the name of racial science. Discussed further below, discrediting the scientific racism that had prevailed in one form or another since the eighteenth century made ethnicity the framework of choice in many political, academic, and cultural discourses—albeit far more reluctantly and belatedly in racially structured arenas like South Africa under apartheid or the United States before the Civil Rights movement. One of many turning points came with UNESCO's declaration on race in 1950, in which scientists stated there was no biological foundation to racial categories. Like ethnicities, races also came down to distinctions imposed by society and culture. Nevertheless, while it is all well and good to proclaim that 'races don't exist' and are simply constructs, racial ideas retain immense power until the present day. For individuals and groups whose life experiences, choices, opportunities, and identities have been racially configured—either in ways that empower or disenfranchise them—race maintains an undeniable social reality if not a biological one.

New approaches to the study of both race and ethnicity correspond closely with developments within gender studies since the 1970s. Identifying and determining the boundaries of racial and ethnic groups, not to mention the recurring anxieties about the reality of boundary crossings and porosity which underlie ideals of group purity and an absolute divide between 'self' and 'other', have repeatedly assumed gendered contours. Historical work on the distinct roles women and men have played in sexual and cultural reproduction within, and across, such imposed 'lines' has moved themes such as hybridity to the top of many scholarly agendas. Yet the connections between these fields do not end here. In recent decades, historians of gender have challenged the biological determinism implied by 'sex' and 'sexual difference', arguing against traditional assumptions of the fixed, unchanging, and essential qualities of 'men' and 'women'. As Joan Scott powerfully asserts, 'gender is a constitutive element of social relationships based on perceived differences between the sexes, and gender is a primary way of signifying relationships of power'—a formulation strikingly similar to the arguments concerning race and ethnicity discussed above.[10] Rejecting that notion that 'biology is destiny' and the naturalization of social inequalities, scholars engaged with issues of race, ethnicity, and gender have made deconstructing languages of purportedly innate and timeless differences, categories, and boundaries an urgent task.[11]

Historically situated analyses of ethnic groups and, by extension, those that have been variously called peoples, nations, religions, tribes, or races before the rise of ethnic paradigms, point the way forward. The following pages consider ethnic issues as manifest at distinct moments and places, emphasizing their flexibility and historicity and arguing against their universality. The examples highlighted here are inevitably selective, but indicate how the history of ethnicity might be approached in other contexts unable to receive attention. What will become apparent throughout the discussion is that ethnic groups are invariably understood in relation to others with which they interact and are considered to fall outside their confines. Encounters between populations through migrations, the diasporas and multi-ethnic societies resulting from these, and other forms of cultural contact such as conquest and colonization thus emerge as central themes.

Medieval and early modern applications

Historical examples charting the fluidity and dynamic nature of groups and categorizations that might be understood as 'ethnic' exist for every time period.[12] Peoples who were defined as coherent groups by others, and who understood themselves as collectivities, emerge and disappear throughout history, with particularly pertinent incidents occurring at times of upheaval. Social and political change alongside large-scale migrations provided the historical conditions for new groups and identities to take shape, with ideal conditions for the reconstitution of ethnic identities arising in Western Europe between late antiquity and the early medieval era. The late Roman Empire ruled over wide swathes of territory inhabited by various peoples who, while not united, were collectively labelled 'barbarians'—a term deriving from *barbarus*, one speaking an incomprehensible language. A 'Roman' identity could overlay, and coexist with, other local or regional affiliations. *Romanitas* derived from specific modes of behaviour and political loyalty; it could be learned—and performed—and did not depend on being born with it. The decline and political fragmentation of the Roman Empire and the barbarian migrations during the fifth and sixth centuries saw new identities take shape. Peoples who may have counted as Roman in *c*.350 AD were largely reconfigured as Frankish, Gothic, or Saxon 200 years later. Not for the last time, the end of an empire enabled distinct groupings, and understandings of personal and collective affiliation, to be challenged and to evolve.[13]

In recent years, medieval scholars have debated the merits of using ethnicity or race as concepts when assessing pre-modern European societies. The Latin words most commonly found in medieval sources to describe communities of common descent were *gens* (singular—a people), *gentes* (plural—peoples), and *natio* (a nation)—terms often used interchangeably that connoted birth and biological reproduction.[14] Later translators chose terms which invariably reflected the political and cultural ideologies of their times. In the era of nation building and nationalism in the later nineteenth and twentieth centuries, 'race', 'nation', 'tribe', or 'stock' described medieval societies in thoroughly modern ways. Nazi ideologies that rendered groups as diverse as the Germanic-speaking peoples of early medieval times as a unified 'German race' or 'German nation' from which the modern German state claimed its origins provide only one example of the past being recast in tune with contemporary concerns.[15]

Rescued from their modern interlocutors, *gens* and *natio* both suggested collectivities that did not mirror today's understandings of either race or ethnicity. Writing of Latin Europe's frontier regions between the tenth and fifteenth centuries, Robert Bartlett identified descent, customs, language, and law as ethnicity's most salient components. 'While the language of race—*gens*, *natio*, "blood", "stock", etc.—is biological', he noted, 'its medieval reality was almost entirely cultural.'[16] Customs, language, and law—cultural dimensions which could all be altered—proved far more important to defining a community, and one's membership in it, than descent, particularly before the fifteenth century. Thus, although *gens* and *natio* foregrounded birth and blood, *gentes* could prove mutable as different populations coming into contact via group migrations converged or became reconfigured. The British Isles in the centuries after the Norman Conquest of 1066 provide a case in point. Between the late eleventh and the late thirteenth centuries, the number of identifiable major peoples shrank to just four, the English, Welsh, Scots, and Irish, by dint of altered political structures, intermarriage, and cultural borrowing.[17]

Among the most central cultural aspects of ethnic identity was religion. Religious difference and ethnic difference were closely connected in the Middle Ages, although a shared religion was by no means equivalent to a shared ethnicity. Christianity was practised by many peoples in Europe who, by virtue of their distinct languages, cultural customs, geographies or origin and habitation, and political loyalties formed many separate ethnic groups. Although intra-Christian ethnic divisions could be profound, the treatment meted out to Europe's non-Christian minority populations revealed more fundamental faultlines, particularly in the late Middle Ages which saw the decline of political and social tolerance for minority groups. The history of Jews and Moors (Muslims of North African origin) provides a succinct illustration of how groups which might coexist with the majority despite religious, cultural, and linguistic differences in one era could find themselves subjected to extreme persecution in another, with the Jews, for example, suffering a series of massacres and expulsions in England, Spain, and elsewhere between the eleventh and fifteenth centuries.

Spain's changing treatment of its Jewish and Muslim populations exemplifies how a religious identity could shift from being viewed as a cultural characteristic that could be adopted or discarded to being reimagined as an immutable, and more racialized and biologized, quality which remained innate even if an individual converted. With the Christian Reconquest of Spain which culminated in the conquest of Grenada in 1492, Jews and Moors who did not convert were expelled from Spain. Nonetheless, converted Jews and Moors, respectively known as *conversos* and *moriscos*, were the subject of ongoing and intense suspicion by the Christian authorities. Despite conversion, these 'New Christians' seemingly could never be Christian enough. Jewish *conversos*—and, crucially, their descendants—remained marked by their religious descent; so too did *moriscos*, who were ultimately expelled from Spain altogether in the early seventeenth century. Religious identities were increasingly racialized in this era; as David Nirenberg writes, 'categories that had previously seemed primarily legal and religious were replaced by the genealogical notion that Christians descended from Jewish converts...were essentially different from "Christians by nature".'[18] 'Old Christians' were those without the 'taint' of Jewish or Moorish antecedents (however distant) that 'New Christians' could not escape. In short, 'Old Christians' were those possessing *limpieza de sangre*—purity of blood.

Colonial encounters and categories

The year 1492 was a turning point in Spain's racial history, with respect to both the protracted ramifications of the Reconquest and the naturalization of Jewish and Moorish differences at home and Columbus' so-called 'discovery' of the New World alike. Spain's overseas colonization in America saw the concept of *limpieza de sangre* recast on a much larger scale. Concerns about guarding the boundaries of Christianity against Jews and Muslims within Spain took on enhanced racial connotations when deployed in New Spain (Mexico) to construct a colonial hierarchy in which purity of blood separated Spaniards from indigenous American peoples, black slaves from Africa, and persons of mixed descent, with the latter groups never able to be, or become, more than 'New Christians'. Genealogies that were 'stained' in religious terms were similarly tainted in racial terms, with religiously- and colour-coded racism becoming even more indelibly intertwined in the Iberian Atlantic World.[19]

European racial ideologies were thus decisively reshaped by the colonial encounter, a shift already discernible before the American conquests. Not only did prior interactions with Muslim North Africa at home and across the Mediterranean both precede and inform Spain and Portugal's responses to America's indigenous peoples; so too did the history of contact with West Africa and the slave trade, which pre-dated the Columbian era. The evolution of Iberian racism before 1492 had already enhanced the role of specific physical features (especially darker skin colour) as a signifier of supposed human inferiority. Blackness was closely linked to religious infidelity and paganism, and not being Christian came to serve as a justification for enslaving sub-Saharan Africans. As the longer history of African slavery in Spain's, Portugal's, France's, and Britain's American colonies revealed, however, blacks who became Christians were not thereby emancipated. The biblical 'curse of Ham', referring to the 'racial' identities allocated to Noah's three sons whereby Ham became associated with Africa and slavery, gradually developed over the course of the early modern era and the eighteenth century as one of a cluster of ideological defences for enslaving blacks. Ethnicity similarly retained a strong religious dimension in eighteenth-century Britain and its empire, with Dr Johnson's 1755 *Dictionary* seeing 'Ethnick' defined as 'heathen; pagan; not Jewish; not Christian'. Such views long structured responses to Native Americans and blacks alike in British North America.[20]

Colonial encounters and power structures encouraged the physical, biological notions that had coexisted with cultural and theological aspects in the early modern period to morph into the secular racial discourses that became predicated upon science by the eighteenth and nineteenth centuries. The mutable cultural dimensions of ethnicity became hardened into a widespread belief in fixed, hereditary racial categories in tandem with Western Europe's ongoing overseas expansion of the modern era. Scientific racism as developed and espoused by Europeans unsurprisingly positioned Europeans themselves as biologically superior to sub-Saharan Africans, North Africans, Indians, Chinese, and the indigenous peoples of the Americas and Australia, to name but several. The division of humanity into distinct superior and inferior categories served to rationalize Europeans' rights to conquer, colonize, and rule other peoples dismissed as less civilized and unfit to govern themselves. European colonizers assiduously sought means of differentiating themselves from the many 'others' they ruled overseas and simultaneously strengthening their political and cultural authority. In the process, colonialism wrought a series of invented, or re-invented, peoples along what might variously be described as racial, ethnic, religious, tribal, or other lines. The crucible of colonialism enveloped colonizing and colonized peoples alike, as examples from the nineteenth- and twentieth-century British Empire illustrate.

Following Europe's 'scramble for Africa' in the later nineteenth century, many colonies emerged populated by Africans comprising, as John Lonsdale has phrased it, 'a Babel of little ethnicities'—colonies whose 'one unifying principle...was territorial, mapped out by conquest'.[21] Individual colonies were invariably multi-ethnic, incorporating diverse African peoples who have more commonly been referred to as tribes. Indeed, 'tribalism' and 'ethnicity' appear as almost interchangeable terms in much scholarly work. Whatever the nomenclature, in the wake of studies by Terence Ranger, John Iliffe, and Leroy Vail—to name but a few distinguished contributors to the field—most historians agree that tribes and their customs were not the 'traditional', primordial groupings that European colonizers typically portrayed them to be.[22] Rather than pre-colonial social formations, they were early twentieth-century creations first and foremost.

Tribal contours and groupings emerged as a result of colonial administrative policies that looked to conservative societal forms that would facilitate indirect rule via African intermediaries, usually tribal chieftains. Institutionalizing tribal identities and divisions counted among 'divide and rule' tactics meant to hinder the emergence of a colony-wide political consciousness—which, of course, ultimately arose in the form of anti-colonial African nationalism. Yet colonial policy in and of itself fails to explain tribalism, and certainly does not account for its wide popular appeal and its resilience among much of African society—despite the fact that tribes were typically divided from within as opposed to being unified groups. For many Africans, tribes proved as useful as they were for European colonial authorities. At a time of intense social upheaval, Iliffe summarizes, 'Africans wanted effective units of action just as officials wanted effective units of government.... Europeans believed Africans belonged to tribes; Africans built tribes to belong to.'[23] African agency in the invention of tribal traditions helps explain tribalism's survival during and after decolonization, a theme that will be considered further below.

Britain's role in codifying, creating, and bestowing new meanings upon group identities among the peoples it colonized was equally influential in India. As was the case with respect to Africa, Britons did not discuss Indians in terms of their 'ethnicity', nor did Indians describe themselves in this way during the colonial era. By extension, ethnicity is not consistently used by historians of South Asia today, who may instead assess social sectors in terms of their caste, religious, racial, or other forms of group membership. During the nineteenth and early twentieth centuries under the British Raj both caste and religious (or 'communal') identities were typically viewed as unchanging, innate characteristics, signs of India's naturalized social order. Like ethnic categories as well as the African 'tribes' discussed above, however, castes as well as religious identities owed their contours to the historically specific conditions of colonialism. To quote Gyanendra Pandey, British 'common-sense' ideas about India involved 'false totalities of ready-made religious communities—"Hindu", "Muslim", "Sikh"', etc. Ignoring not only the linguistic, regional, and economic divisions within such groups but also the extent to which their members commonly coexisted and their relationships continually evolved, the British instead stressed that religious communities—particularly Hindus and Muslims—were fundamentally exclusive, fractured, and destined to remain forever antagonistic.[24]

Seeing India in terms of its supposedly endemic divisions, British administrators similarly drew distinctions along racial lines in ways that reflected their desire for colonial stability—not least when order was, or seemed, under threat. In the wake of the revolt of 1857–8, often called the Indian 'Mutiny', the British military authorities favoured groups considered the most 'natural', manly soldiers, who were, not coincidentally, those deemed most likely to remain loyal to their British officers. In place of the Hindu, Bengali, and other groups of soldiers prominent among the mutinying troops, Britain recruited those they construed as 'martial races'—Punjabi Sikhs, Nepalese Gurkhas, and Scottish Highlanders—to man its Indian Army and control the subcontinent. In fact, none of these could be said to constitute a delimited 'racial' grouping: Sikhism was a religion, Gurkhas did not hail from a culturally distinct community, and 'Highland' regiments recruited many Lowland and urban Scots as well as English and Irish soldiers. Yet racialized depictions persisted regardless of their fictional quality, depictions given added impetus by their gendered nature. 'Martial races' were 'manly', whereas other Indians, particularly Bengalis, were scorned as 'effeminate'—not only poor military material, but also resented for their increasingly vocal political demands at a time when nationalism was asserting itself among Indians in more insistent tones. The 'effeminate Bengali' was thus unfavourably juxtaposed not simply with 'martial races' (which included Indians and Britons) but also with the 'manly Englishman' deemed fit to continue ruling the subcontinent.[25]

The examples of India's 'manly Englishmen' and the inclusion of British men serving in Scottish Highland regiments among the 'martial races' both suggest how Britons themselves were racialized in ways specific to modern imperial encounters alongside, and in relation to, colonized populations. Like their depictions of colonized Indians and Africans, Britons too were racially stereotyped, whether in ways construed as positive or negative. As Sander Gilman has argued, stereotypes are labels that create 'the illusion of an absolute difference between self and Other...[arising] when self-integration is threatened'. 'We need crude representations of difference to localize our anxiety, to prove to ourselves that what we fear does not lie within,' he concludes.[26] Indeed, fear of the 'within' proved relentless, even when Britain's empire was arguably at its fin-de-siècle zenith. Alongside the self-congratulation and assertions of superiority intrinsic within Britain's colonial rhetoric, concerns were continually voiced about the racial integrity of Britons themselves. Whether they found expression in concerns about Britons in the empire culturally 'going native' or intermarrying with colonized peoples and producing mixed-race communities, cultural and biological hybridity was both an ongoing fear and an imperial reality.[27] Moreover, Britons at home deemed socially worrying were similarly viewed as a source of weakness at once racial, national, and imperial. In the eyes of the more affluent, for example, working-class Britons in urban slums seemed a 'race apart' and inhabited 'darkest England', analogous to the 'darkest Africa' claimed as the nation's responsibility to explore, rule, and thereby 'civilize'.[28]

Race, ethnicity, and modern nations

Concerns about the loss of 'racial strength' and the British population's own 'degeneration' resulted in considerable interest in the eugenics movement at home in the late nineteenth and early twentieth centuries at the same time as efforts were made to categorize and control the colonized 'other' overseas. As a social and scientific ideology that advocated improving the 'quality' of populations by selective breeding and focusing upon the influence of heredity, the eugenics movement within Britain targeted the indigenous working classes as 'unfit' candidates ripe for social engineering to guard against the nation's own 'racial decline'. Yet anxieties also encompassed the immigrant population of Irish and East European Jews whom many considered inferior 'stock'.[29] While eugenicists in Britain were thus primarily concerned with subordinate social sectors (not to mention criminals and those condemned as mentally or physically handicapped), their discussion of white Britons in racial terms and condemnation of immigration as pernicious to the national fibre reveals common grounds with eugenicists, and wider historical developments, in other nations such as the United States and Germany.

The history of the United States since winning independence from Britain underscores the ongoing centrality of race, its changing delineations, and a gradual shift towards the use of ethnic alongside racial categories for certain social groups. In the newly established republic's first naturalization law of 1790, the 'founding fathers' stipulated that those who qualified for settlement and citizenship rights should be 'free white persons'. Whiteness set those of British, 'Anglo-Saxon' origin apart from, and above, blacks (whether enslaved or freed) and America's indigenous 'Indian' population in terms of political rights and socio-economic opportunities. Yet during the course of the nineteenth century, new groups of European immigrants arrived who, while legally able to enter, settle, and be accorded citizenship in the United States as 'free white persons', posed the dilemma of 'whiteness of a different color', as Matthew Frye Jacobson memorably phrased it.[30] The large numbers of Irish followed by Germans, Italians, Slavs, Eastern European Jews, and other groups arriving from the 1840s onwards may have counted as white, but were seen as constituting separate 'races' by virtue of their diverse European geographical origins, distinctive appearances, and linguistic and other cultural differences. Religious difference was often a distinguishing factor, with Catholicism or Judaism separating many newcomers from the largely Protestant white Americans who had settled previously. A commission reporting on immigration in 1910 identified forty-five different 'races' among America's immigrant groups, thirty-six of which hailed from Europe (non-European immigrant groups, particularly the Chinese, also caused concern). Whiteness lost its relatively monolithic character, with 'Anglo-Saxon' Americans viewing European newcomers as culturally and biologically inferior, less civilized, and a threat to the nation's character and future potential. Immigrants became subjected to economic, cultural, and explicitly racial forms of discrimination. Racist opposition to immigration, much of it explicitly eugenic in tone, culminated in the 1924 Johnson Act, which ushered in a quota system that severely restricted the numbers of Eastern and southern Europeans permitted entry.

The 1924 Act, coupled with global and domestic events over the ensuing decades (to be explored further below), heralded a new era in America's racial history. Between the 1920s and the 1960s, differences among Americans of European immigrant origins largely ceased to be discussed in 'racial' terms; instead, such groups were collectively labelled 'Caucasian' and 'white'. Conceptualizations of race on the basis of national origins and religion receded, particularly as the descendants of European immigrants once deemed socially problematic appeared to be assimilating within the mainstream white population. Like other groups, Irish and Jews, once widely represented as racially distinct, 'became white', demonstrating clearly the fluidity of ideas about race and racial categories alike at different historical moments.[31] Race was increasingly conceived in terms of colour difference, with the most salient line dividing American society being that separating black and white.

If those of European origin came to count as white in the twentieth-century United States, who counted as black? Like whiteness, blackness was a historically specific construct. Hailing from many cultures in Africa, forced migration, slavery, and ultimately emancipation forged an African American 'black' population along colour lines whose label defies its ethnically diverse origins. Equally important, individuals of mixed African and European (and other) ancestries were overwhelmingly included within the black population. Regardless of their outward appearance, the 'one drop rule' long meant that persons with even a small fraction of African 'blood' officially counted as black rather than white or any other racial affiliation. As America's dominant and privileged racial identity, whiteness was subjected to vigilant protection from incursions by the 'other', and being partially white meant not being white at all—yet another example of how races are made, and are social, cultural, and political rather than biological or natural 'facts'.[32] Stringent efforts to police racial boundaries and protect white empowerment vis-à-vis blacks involved a range of measures such as legal prohibitions on mixed marriages in many states until the 1960s and 1970s. Thanks to the Civil Rights movement, African Americans have succeeded in overturning many of the racist laws once rampant in the United States, making considerable political and economic gains in recent decades—as the 2008 election of Barack Obama, of both black and white descent, as the first black President attests. Nonetheless, racial inequality remains a social reality for many, and whiteness continues as the often unspoken 'norm' in American culture from which other groups diverge and are accorded specificity. Remarking on a character in an Ernest Hemingway novel, Toni Morrison observed that 'Eddy is white, and we know he is because nobody says so.'[33]

Given whiteness's ongoing hegemonic cultural dominance that habitually renders it invisible, racially unmarked, and, as Morrison stresses, 'unsaid', its history, unstable meanings, and succession of inclusions and exclusions are salutary to bear in mind. If the descendants of European immigrants to America both became white—a path barred to blacks—and, in their own minds at least, lost a racialized identity, they gained ethnicities in its place. Starting in the 1930s and 1940s, scientific racism began its slow—and highly uneven—retreat from respectability, and differences between European populations once seen as innate and biological were repackaged as cultural and ethnic.[34] The political imperative for rethinking the meanings of differences between whites—yet by and large not those erected between whites and non-whites, particularly blacks—within the United States, Britain, and other countries stemmed from a combination of domestic and international circumstances. But more than any other factor, the organized mass murder of millions of European Jews along with Poles and other groups by Nazi Germany caused previously entrenched race-based ideologies to be internationally scrutinized and challenged as never before.

Germany's longer tradition of what a number of scholars have termed 'ethnocultural nationhood' is essential to understand if the tragedy of the 1930s and 1940s is to be fully comprehended. In the wake of the Romantic movement in particular, the nineteenth century witnessed the emergence of a common self-understanding of Germany as a closed, organic, and pre-existing ethnic community of descent—whether or not those who were deemed part of it resided within the newly formed empire dating from 1870–1. Ethnic Germans were scattered across many other Central and Eastern European territories following waves of migration in the medieval and early modern periods, not to mention via the émigrés who had departed for the Americas and elsewhere in modern times.[35] Within the German Empire, meanwhile, lived minorities who increasingly became viewed as a threat to the new nation's strength, integrity, and desired homogeneity—particularly the Jews, who, although never more than 1 per cent of Germany's population, were feared as quintessentially foreign, non-national, or even anti-national. As Saul Friedländer describes, Germans contemplating the 'Jewish question' did so through anti-Semitic lenses that could either be non-racial *or* racial. '[W]hereas for the non-racial anti-Semite [Jewish] difference could and *should* have been totally effaced by complete assimilation and disappearance of the Jews as such, the racial anti-Semite argued that the difference was indelible, that it was inscribed in the blood.' In sum, 'for the non-racial anti-Semite, a solution to the "Jewish question" was possible within society in general; for the racial anti-Semite, because of the dangerous impact of Jewish presence and equality, the only solution was exclusion (legal and possibly physical) from society in general.'[36]

While both non-racial and racial anti-Semites sought the full eradication of Jewish difference, the latter approach prevailed after the Nazi seizure of power. In 1935, the Nuremberg Laws defined Jews not according to the religious faith they practised but rather by heredity and race and denied them the status and protection of German citizenship. To be a citizen meant having German 'blood'—a criterion that excluded Jews and converts of Jewish ancestry born and living in Germany, but included 'ethnic Germans' who had long resided outside Germany's political territory. The Nazi 'racial state' deployed eugenic policies to manipulate Germany's demography via forced sterilizations of the mentally and physically handicapped and other problematic social elements within the community of ethnic Germans as well as via a series of increasingly radical measures to eliminate its Jews. What began as efforts to remove Jews via deportations and expulsions ended in the 'final solution': over six million Jews perished—a shift from what Norman Naimark has delineated as an instance of ethnic cleansing (involving the driving out of a victimized population from a territory) to genocide (the orchestrated murder of a people).[37] As the example of the Nazis' policies towards Jews illustrates, ethnic cleansing and genocide need not be mutually exclusive in either their aims or their effects.

Conclusion: post-Holocaust and postcolonial race and ethnicity

In his *Discourse on Colonialism* first published in 1950, Aimé Césaire, a writer from the French Caribbean island of Martinique, underscored Nazism's importance in relation to the longer history of European racism and colonialism. White Europeans 'tolerated that Nazism before it was inflicted on them...they absolved it, shut their eyes to it, legitimized it, because, until then, it had been applied only to non-European peoples'. What the European, he continued, 'cannot forgive Hitler for...is not *the humiliation of man as such*, it is the crime against the white man, the humiliation of the white man, and the fact that he applied to Europe colonialist procedures which until then had been reserved exclusively for the Arabs of Algeria, the "coolies" of India, and the "niggers" of Africa'.[38] As noted above, the defeat of the Nazis in 1945 and the protracted international assessment of the Holocaust thereafter was a crucial step in the de-racialization of Jews in Europe as well as in the United States and other nations. The end of the Second World War marked the onset of a new era that saw the decline of what had long been major empires, the emergence of new nations, and the reconfiguration of older nations, in part by migrations—all of which had profound consequences for peoples marked out as ethnic or racial communities.

The Nazi defeat may have played a significant role in discrediting racialized or ethnic conceptions of nationhood in some respects, but in others they were reinforced in both the immediate aftermath and the decades following 1945. As Michael Mann summarizes, the end of the Third Reich 'did not end ethnic cleansing in Europe. It redirected it against the losing master race'.[39] Ethnic Germans long settled in Poland and Czechoslovakia were expelled *en masse*, and of the twelve million who either fled or were forcibly driven out of Eastern Europe it was estimated that two million perished. Two-thirds of those who survived resettled in West Germany, thereby enabling ethnocultural ideologies of nationhood to be further strengthened in the post-war Federal Republic.

Population transfers occurring in Europe in the late 1940s were matched or exceeded only by those taking place in South Asia in 1947. When Britain ceased to rule the subcontinent and it was partitioned into two independent nations, India and Pakistan, millions of Hindus and Sikhs left Pakistan for India while many Muslims travelled in the other direction, with over one million slaughtered en route. While both India and Pakistan retained substantial communities of ethno-religious minorities (with over 100 million Muslims still living in India today), the partition migrations reinforced conceptualizations of Pakistan as a Muslim nation and India as a predominately Hindu one—despite the assertive secularism of the Indian National Congress and the Nehru-led governments after independence. Since the 1990s in particular, communal tensions and violence fomented by Hindu nationalist groups have been a recurrent feature of India's political landscape.[40]

Indian and Pakistani independence marked the beginning of the end of the overseas empires in Asia and Africa ruled by Britain, France, and other Western European nations. Gathering pace by the late 1950s and early 1960s, decolonization's legacy was a plethora of new multi-ethnic states which, like the colonies they succeeded, were political territories whose borders rarely contained just one self-identified ethnic community. In Africa following of the anti-colonial nationalist movements that led to political independence, many observers assumed—or perhaps simply hoped—that tribal affiliations would become largely consigned to history as Africans grew to identify with modern nations. Indeed, tribalism was widely perceived as backward and traditional—the enemy of the modern nations meant to take their place. Yet ethnic and tribal consciousness did not recede into the background in independent African nations; instead, these loyalties proved persistent and highly popular within nations that all too often proved weak and failed to generate deep-seated attachments. As considered above, because ethnic consciousness in Africa was very much a modern and meaningful phenomenon and the antithesis of backward and antiquated, it survived with remarkable tenacity into the postcolonial period. So recently codified under colonial rule, ethnic classifications could readily become enhanced after decolonization, as was the case in the former Belgian territory of Rwanda. Ethnic divisions and violence between Hutus and Tutsis recurred in the territory prior to, upon, and well after independence, assuming genocidal proportions when over 800,000 Tutsi were slaughtered in 1994.[41]

Within Europe, ethnic cleansing, violence, and mass migrations have also returned as the twentieth century drew to a close with the collapse of communism and the fragmentation of multi-ethnic states such as occurred in the former Soviet Union and Yugoslavia. In a manner resembling South Asia's partition and the forced departures of ethnic Germans from Eastern Europe in the late 1940s, ethnic violence assumed gendered contours, with the abuse of women becoming central to the ways in which communities took revenge on those perceived as the enemy. Abductions and rapes across ethnic lines were legion. As Naimark encapsulates, 'the ideology of integral nationalism identifies women as the carriers, quite literally, of the next generation of the nation. Not only do women constitute the biological core of nationality, but they are often charged with the task of passing on the cultural and spiritual values of nationhood to their children. The result is that ethnic cleansing often targets women.'[42] While gender issues deserve much deeper treatment than they can receive here, the examples of forced sterilizations under the Nazis, concerns about managed breeding and reproduction that informed eugenicist ideas internationally, anxieties about intermarriage and mixed-race populations in Europe's colonies, and attempts to maintain ethnic boundaries and cultural 'purity' more generally consistently foregrounded women.

Boundaries constructed between ethnic groups were, in reality, repeatedly crossed in the post-war era as before. Migration ensured that this would remain the case, whether this was forced or undertaken voluntarily. Labour migrations into post-war Western Europe count among the latter, with (West) Germany and Britain providing illustrations of how nations, perceived along ethnic and racial lines, faced new challenges upon becoming more diverse. In Germany, the arrival of Turkish 'guestworkers', many of whom ultimately became permanent residents, demonstrated the resilience of ethnocultural traditions of citizenship. Unlike the ethnic Germans welcomed 'home' from Eastern Europe after the Second World War (and again in the late 1980s and early 1990s with the fall of communism), Turks and their German-born children have found it difficult to become citizens. Lacking German descent, most remain outside the nation's boundaries conceived along ethnic lines, regardless of their duration of residence, birthplace, or sense of belonging.[43]

In Britain, the end of empire coincided with high levels of immigration. Strictly speaking, however, persons from colonies and ex-colonies in the Caribbean, South Asia, and elsewhere were not 'immigrants'. The 1948 British Nationality Act aimed to shore up Britain's colonial and Commonwealth relations and thus formalized free access for all colonial and Commonwealth subjects who legally counted as 'British'. But anxieties about the impact of the 'coloured' influx into Britain mounted, culminating in a series of immigration restriction acts starting in 1962. Legislation passed in 1968 and 1971 contracted the definition of British citizenship, largely limiting future new arrivals to those who had 'patrial' (ancestral) ties to the United Kingdom. Significantly, these changes did not explicitly exclude persons on racial or ethnic grounds: as the vast majority who could document British ancestry were white, patriality made direct reference to race, ethnicity, or colour unnecessary.

Currently counting several million people of black and Asian descent among its citizenry, Britain is a deeply multi-ethnic, or multicultural, society. But black and Asian Britons continue to face exclusion from ideological conceptions of the nation that remain culturally and racially homogeneous—a phenomenon Paul Gilroy has called 'ethnic absolutism'. Older-style biological racism may have lost credibility, but 'new racism' has appeared in its place. Race is now widely deemed a cultural issue—for all intents and purposes, race has become ethnicity—but one in which culture is understood as something inherent and rigid—effectively 'biologised', as Gilroy argues. 'The absolutist view of black and white cultures, as fixed, mutually impermeable expressions of racial and national identity, is a ubiquitous theme in racial "common sense"', he summarizes; nevertheless, 'it is constantly under challenge from the activities of blacks who pass through the cultural and ideological net which is supposed to screen Englishness from them, and from the complex organic process which renders black Britons partially soluble in the national culture which their presence helps to transform'.[44]

The transformative quality Gilroy stresses provides as apt a conclusion as any to a discussion of ethnicity which must, of necessity, remain ever a work in progress. Constantly in flux in tandem with wider historical changes, ethnic groups and the geographies they inhabit—both imaginative geographies and actual nations and territories—will continue to evolve. In Britain as elsewhere, 'selves' and 'others', ethnic majorities and ethnic minorities alike, will continue to experience changes and challenges to their current identities which will involve the emergence of a succession of 'new ethnicities', a theme Stuart Hall has explored—new ethnicities to match new times.[45] Though the forms these take will only gradually become discernible, ethnic identities promise to remain socially constructed, subjective as opposed to objective, and obscuring as many characteristics of the individuals and groups concerned as they reveal.

12. Map outlined on a deer skin, North America, c.1770, made by Miami. © By permission of the Trustees of the British Museum

12 Science

PAMELA H. SMITH

One of the most powerful forces in world culture today is science. The human engagement with nature that has come to be codified in the natural sciences has brought into being structures and systems of knowledge, of belief, of education, and of communities, and has come to provide a means of arbitrating competing knowledge claims. Nothing like the system that exists today to produce knowledge of the natural world, a system that includes structures of education and research and a generally standardized method of obtaining and presenting knowledge, ever existed on a similarly worldwide scale in previous ages. Historians view this new mode of producing knowledge as having emerged in Europe in the early modern period during the 'Scientific Revolution' (c. AD 1400–1700). Some components of this 'Revolution' trace their history back to Graeco-Roman antiquity and even to ancient Babylon, but historians have usually regarded modern science as coalescing in the nineteenth century during the 'Industrial Revolution' when scientific research came to be regarded as the basis of material progress and national strength, and then coming to full force with the military sponsorship of scientific research in the Second World War and the boom in industrial and state-sponsored research in post-war society.

Introduction: telling the story of 'science'

In describing the development of 'science', previous historians often privileged those aspects of past world views that still endured in some form in our present view of the cosmos, so that they labeled Babylonian predictive astronomy 'science' although it was part of religious practice, while Native American views of the universe, for example, were labeled as 'belief'. More recently, historians have argued that science should be viewed as simply one more indigenous knowledge system, similar to vernacular potato taxonomies of the Andes,[1] for example, or the building knowledge of medieval European master masons that made them capable of constructing very large and enduring cathedrals over many generations.[2] The hierarchies that classified science and belief at opposite ends of a spectrum emerged in the seventeenth and eighteenth centuries with the growth of European dominance in world trade, and the professionalization of the university-trained group who researched the natural sciences, now known as 'scientists'. This process lasted at least two centuries, however, and rigid demarcation of the sphere of scientific theories and practices from the 'pseudo-sciences' such as astrology and alchemy did not emerge categorically until the nineteenth century. At the same time, the word 'scientist' was coined by William Whewell (1794–1866) in England, and scientific research was institutionalized in new 'research' universities in Germany.

Such hierarchies are often viewed as corresponding to a progressively more complete unveiling of a 'true picture' of nature and/or a greater ability to produce effects and products by manipulating natural materials. Indeed, the system of scientific-technological knowledge production since the first half of the twentieth century has so far proven to be a powerful mode of interacting with nature (although the jury is out on whether some aspects—the atomic bomb, for instance—will ultimately destroy human life on earth), but these rapid developments are not entirely due to a more effective understanding of nature as contained in new theories of the behavior of matter (atomic and particle theory) and of the cosmos (post-Newtonian physics). More important as causes for the rapid scientific and technological developments may be particular geo-political structures, new energy sources, and the state sponsorship of science and technology that came into being during the twentieth century.

The historical narrative about the development of science has usually concentrated on the intellectual aspects of the growth of the natural sciences as we define them today, such as theories about the origin of the universe or the composition of matter, for example. This has left the social and material context of that development less well explored, and, until recently, historians have not examined the many fully articulated views of nature no longer considered 'science', such as astrology and alchemy. The conventional narrative of the growth of science has traced the development of the theoretical and mathematicized sciences (astronomy and physics) from ancient Mesopotamia to Greece to Europe (often neglecting altogether the Roman and Islamicate periods or viewing them as constituting only reproductive 'transmission' and 'translation' or as being overly focused on applied science), and, finally, diffusion out to the European colonies from European metropolises during the nineteenth century. This of course overlooks huge swaths of the world—Africa, China, and the Americas—and it creates hierarchies closely correlated to the ideology of nineteenth-century European imperialists. Moreover, it entirely neglects material factors such as, for example, the centrality of new energy regimes for human interaction with and control over the immediate environment: the shift from wood energy to fossil fuels—first coal in the 1780s and then petroleum in the early twentieth century—and nuclear energy in the mid-twentieth century.[3]

Since the eighteenth century, philosophical positivists have viewed the growth of science as an inevitable process of discoveries about the natural world which allowed increased scientific-technological human capabilities, a greater control over natural processes, and revealed an ever more accurate picture of the natural world. The truth of the world picture was viewed as the result of a unique method which involved a combination of theory, experiment, and observation, that relied upon replication and recording of evidence in unbiased circumstances, often by use of instruments, and from strictly separating the subjective experience of the observer/theorizer from the objective process of the method.[4] The picture of nature that resulted from this method was considered more certain if expressed quantitatively and mathematically. This view has been complicated by the theories of modern theoretical physics, first by the Heisenberg Uncertainty Principle which has been commonly interpreted to mean that the object observed is affected by the process of observation itself, thus complicating the subject/object distinction, and, second, by the principles of quantum mechanics that the laws at macro and atomic levels of matter are not the same. But these difficulties have generally changed neither the views of scientists nor of the public about the 'objectivity' and power of scientific knowledge. While it is right to point to the strength of the scientific method in its ideals of institutionalized skepticism and dispassionate reasoning, its repeated testing and processes of falsification, its distrust of the anecdote, and its cumulative and collective process, historians of science since Thomas Kuhn's *The Structure of Scientific Revolutions* (1962) do not see scientific knowledge as emerging inexorably and progressively from practices commonly labeled 'the scientific method,' but rather see natural knowledge and the methods of obtaining it as contingent upon, and constructed within, particular communities and their place in social and intellectual structures, as people make use of ideas, information, and techniques available in that society.[5] Science is not, then, something apart from human society, but very much a product of it. Relying on this new scholarship in the history of science, this chapter will consider four ways we might understand this new force—science—in human affairs: (1) as human engagement with nature, (2) as a generalized understanding and explanation of natural processes (often called 'theory'), (3) as a *method* for gaining knowledge, and (4) as a means of constructing social hierarchies.

Science as human engagement with nature

All human societies interact in a variety of ways with their environment for survival, and, out of the experience gained through that interaction, certain skills and knowledge emerge.[6] Taking a broad perspective, we can see that this engagement with nature and the resulting accumulation of skills and knowledge has occurred throughout the long human past. The emergence of tool use in the Paleolithic era may have led to the development of language, which took on written form about 5,000 years ago, apparently growing out of commercial exchange and the need for keeping track of trade goods. The discovery of the uses of fire among early hominids allowed the manipulation of materials such as clay and native metals, whereas the ability to control fire itself led to high-temperature furnaces in which minerals could be smelted (e.g. bronze—a mixture of copper and tin—$c.3500$ BC, and iron $c.1500$ BC) and glass produced ($c.1500$ BC), which led to the use of progressively sturdier artificially produced materials. The domestication of plants during what has been called the 'Neolithic Revolution' about 10,000 years ago and of animals further in the past,[7] and their subsequent cultivation and breeding for food, medicine, textile production, and other survival uses, was based on long-term systematic observation of patterns in nature, which led to a significant increase in skills and knowledge. So too did the accumulation of celestial observations evident first in Neolithic grave and religious monuments and then emerging in calendrical form (often pictorial, or monolithic constructions such as Stonehenge) at various times in Africa, ancient Mesopotamia, Asia, Europe, and the Americas, and eventually in written form in Egypt and Babylon. These observations enabled the codification of a planting schedule divorced from immediate meteorological observations, and, by this means, numbers, arithmetic, and the calculation and prediction of celestial events emerged.

Such skills grew out of a collective interaction with the material world, sometimes apparently emerging spontaneously in different places, and at other times traceable as they spread throughout various regions by means of trade (see Kenneth Pomeranz's chapter above). Some see the modern scientific and technological capability of human beings as qualitatively different from these earlier developments, but there is no reason to regard the present development and accumulation of techniques and knowledge by means of the natural sciences as radically different from the very long enduring human engagement with the environment. There may be a difference in the quantity and speed at which knowledge is accumulated, as the system of knowledge production that we call 'science' now involves many people and exists in a highly networked world where information travels very fast. Some observers might point to the recent history of science and the discoveries of individual scientists as evidence of new processes of knowledge production occurring since the Scientific Revolution. Such a view, however, grows out of a limited perspective on human history arising from historians' overwhelming reliance upon the written word. The existence of a written record for the exceedingly short recent present of human history (only about 7,000 of the approximately 200,000 years since *homo sapiens* emerged) gives historians the sense that they can pin scientific discoveries and inventions to individuals. On further investigation, however, those discoveries are found to have been the result of collective and collaborative processes,[8] much like those that produced bronze, writing, glass, and movable type, to name only a few at random. One such discovery was of the Gulf Stream in the eighteenth century, often ascribed to Benjamin Franklin, but actually the common knowledge of whalers (and mariners before them). Timothy Folger, Franklin's cousin and a Nantucket whaleboat captain, informed Franklin of the existence of the Stream and mapped it for him.[9] There is no doubt that the transition of knowledge from oral to written form as happened in this case is an extremely important step, but writing is not necessary to transmit knowledge from one generation or region to another, although it can be more efficient. Innovation, intelligence, and 'creativity' (sometimes labeled 'genius') have often been thought about as located in and manifested by individual brains, but in reality, they emerge and occur within social fields. Of course, individuals can still be important in developing particular aspects of innovations, in focusing ideas and methods emerging out of the social field, and in giving written form to ideas or methods, as we see in the case of the Gulf Stream. Reliance by historians on written records and on identifiable individuals (whose papers or works are still extant) living in the recent human past has had the effect of misleading us about the collective and distributed nature by which all knowledge, but especially knowledge of our natural environment, is produced. Moreover, recent institutions such as the Nobel Prize have reinforced the view that science develops by means of discrete inventions and discoveries on the part of individual scientists.

The results of this perceptual and technical engagement with the environment are often codified, especially in relation to health and the prediction of agricultural or hunting cycles. Such codification has been recorded in texts, tables, and taxonomies in some societies, such as Mesopotamian cuneiform tablets containing the risings and settings of the stars and planets brought together in the library at Nineveh in the seventh century BC. In others, this knowledge has been encoded in myths, songs, or rituals, such as the oral songs and mnemonic devices by which Polynesian peoples transmitted from one generation to the next the knowledge needed to navigate thousands of miles over the open ocean.[10] Human beings are also tool users, and human societies often manipulate natural materials, such as minerals, metals, plants, and animals, in order to produce useful effects and products. The manipulation of natural materials is also codified, although it is more often transmitted from master to apprentice or via rituals and the spoken word rather than by texts. And its transmission is often facilitated or organized by the body politic, as in the case of state intervention in agriculture throughout the two millennia of imperial rule in China (221 BC–AD 1911),[11] or in mining, controlled in Egypt by the pharaoh-gods as early as the third millennium BC. The codification of this knowledge often leads to the creation of certain culturally specific identities, such as shamans, medical doctors, and craftspeople, and, today, 'scientists' and 'engineers'. Such codification has also been used as a marker of more general cultural identity and character, expressed in such contrasts as those often drawn between 'Chinese' and 'Western' medicine, between 'modern' and pre-modern modes of understanding, and between universal and local ways of knowing. Sometimes, problematically, the possession of scientific knowledge has also been viewed as indicating a superior intellectual capacity or way of life (more on that below).

Human engagement with nature has also led to the construction of views of the cosmos, often undertaken as a means of determining agricultural cycles or arising out of the processes of manipulating natural materials. Historians have usually labeled such attempts to understand the cosmos and nature as 'science' and the manipulation of natural materials as 'technology', while the attempt to understand human health and disease has been called 'medicine'. In pre-modern societies, these spheres of culture were generally not separate from each other, and, some historians of science and technology argue that these three realms are still deeply imbricated in each other today. One recent historian sees science, technique, and technology as functioning together as parts of a whole to produce knowledge about the natural world: science, she says, is 'knowledge about natural, material processes expressed in declarative, transmissible form; its representations generally aspire to be authoritative beyond the time and place of their production'. In other words, it is the knowledge about nature usually written down in texts that claims to be valid at all times and places. Techniques are the 'skilled practices that go into the material production of knowledge as well as the production of artifacts'. These are the skills by which nature is manipulated, knowledge is gained, and objects are produced. Technology, on the other hand, can be thought about as an entire system involving a variety of people, practices, machines, raw materials, and institutions by which knowledge is both made and applied. In her view of the production of knowledge, the three areas of science, technique, and technology are 'not separate kinds of activity but rather overlapping phases of an organic process of knowledge production'.[12] Moreover, they are not separable from social relations and human institutions, but rather are embedded within them. Indeed, at a more general level, if we conceive of techniques as arising at the interface of human beings and the natural environment, even nature and human culture cannot be entirely separated.[13]

Understanding and explaining nature: science as world view

The views of the cosmos that human engagement with nature brought forth have been extremely varied and never entirely uniformly held within a society. Indeed, it is one of the remarkable features of modern science that certain theories of the natural world have become widely accepted by many different levels of society. For most of human history, competing and often contradictory theories of nature coexisted even within a single society without a widespread sense that one had to be believed exclusively of the others. But, within this diversity, two widespread and long-lasting foci for observation and investigation of the human relationship to nature have been the connection of human life to the heavens (of microcosm to macrocosm), and the problem of the transformation of matter, especially that which is wrought by human action. Each of these is treated in turn below.

Microcosm and macrocosm

For most of human history many societies recognized what might be called the first universal law of nature, that is, that the heavens have influence over the earth. The motions of the heavenly bodies that correlate to the waning and waxing of the seasons and the agricultural cycles, the setting and rising of the sun, the ebb and flow of the tides in relation to the phases of the moon, all gave common-sense evidence of such a relationship. This was both a lived reality, experienced and subscribed to by individuals, and a theorized relationship codified in religious rituals, megalithic monuments marking the movements of the heavenly bodies, and eventually in writing. Although experience of the natural world could give rise in different societies to similar questions about the human relationship to nature, the ways in which these questions were answered in each society differed significantly. Nevertheless, historians have been able to trace extremely long-lived systems of knowledge which explicated the relationship of nature and humans: two of the longest enduring written examples of such systems that were not tied directly to religious practice (although in both cases they were tied to ethical practice) were to be found in the physical and medical world views put in place in fourth-century BC China and Greece. The codification of a system and the formation of an institutional framework to transmit it began somewhat earlier in China than in the Graeco-Roman world. A comprehensive system was developed and codified in China from the eighth century BC to about the second century AD; the concept of *qi*, denoting both vital energy and mutable matter, was joined by the fundamental forces of yin and yang, in about the sixth century BC. These were then overlaid in Chinese explanations for change by the conception of five states of matter (*wu xing*)—wood, fire, earth, metal, water—that corresponded to qualities of substances in which *qi* manifested itself. In addition to *qi*, natural order or organizing principle (*li*) was also central to Chinese medicine and natural philosophy.[14]

Although some central medical concepts were shared throughout Eurasia, such as that of 'life-breath', common to ancient Chinese, Stoic, and South Asian medical writers (*qi*, pneuma, and prāna), in the interests of brevity, we shall concentrate in what follows on only one of these, the Greek case. In fourth-century BC Greece, what became a remarkably durable (some aspects lasting through the early nineteenth century) and widely disseminated view of the natural world and humankind's place within it was set down in writing by two groups of people: students and others associated with the lecturing activity of Aristotle (384–322 BC) at the Lyceum in Athens and the medical practitioners responsible for what is now called the Hippocratic corpus (after Hippocrates of Kos, c.460–c.370 BC). Drawing on a Greek tradition of speculation about the make-up of the natural world, the Aristotelian view of the cosmos included two realms: the terrestrial, or sublunar sphere (below the sphere of the moon's revolution around the earth), where mixtures of four elements—earth, water, air, and fire—came into being and passed away (while the underlying reality of the elements endured beneath these ephemeral phenomena). Change in position over time occurred as all things sought their natural place, thus a heavy object composed mainly of earth fell to its natural place at the center of the universe, while water floated on earth, air floated above water (as air bubbles rise upward through water), and fire leapt upward toward the heavens, its natural place. Above the sphere of the moon, all things, including the stars, sun, and the planets (or, as they were known, the 'wandering stars'), were eternal and unchanging, composed of a fifth element, or quintessence.

The school of Aristotle formulated this common-sense and experiential understanding of the natural world at about the same time the writers of the Hippocratic corpus codified views about the workings of the human body. The texts of the Hippocratic authors set out a framework for understanding human health consisting of the four humors and six non-naturals. The Alexandrian physician Galen (c. AD 129–210), and those who followed in his tradition, such as Abu Ali al-Husayn or Ibn Sina (Avicenna) (d. 1037), formed this Hippocratic-Galenic system into a canon for teaching and practice. The theory that the human body was made up of a balance of fluids which determined sickness and health was first articulated by the Hippocratic writers and formed into a comprehensive but flexible system by the institutional framework that grew up around teaching this system in which the names of Galen and Ibn-Sina stand out. This view was held in common throughout the Roman Empire and the spheres of intellectual influence that it left behind in the Islamicate and Christian lands.

In the Hippocratic-Galenic system, the four humors—which to a certain extent corresponded to real bodily fluids but were not identical with them, sharing their qualities rather than their substance—made up a person's temperament, either phlegmatic, melancholic, choleric, or sanguine. Phlegm was a colorless or whitish excretion of the body (not including semen and milk); yellow bile or choler could be found in the gallbladder; black bile in the spleen; and the blood in the veins was a mixture of pure humoral blood with a lesser proportion of the other humors. Based on this combination of humors (and ultimately 'elements' because the humors were composed from the four Aristotelian elements), every individual had his or her own innate natural 'complexion'. This complexion (which could be recognized to a certain extent in a person's face, or 'complexion') determined an individual's physical constitution and mental state.[15] A person's constitution also depended on the time of birth, which planets were ruling at the moments of conception and birth, the place of birth—for northerners were generally cooler than southerners (the Scythians, for example, were known to be colder than the Egyptians)—and gender (for women were colder and wetter than men). Age also played a part, for as a person aged she or he dried out and cooled off.

Each individual's temperament, conditioned by these natural factors, could be influenced (by self-treatment or in consultation with a medical practitioner) by what came to be known as the six 'non-naturals', that is, the factors that an individual could control: airs, diet, exercise, and rest; sleep and waking; evacuation and retention; and control of the passions, or emotions. These non-naturals held the key to medical therapy. In this view, the body was viewed as porous not just to the airs around it, and the miasmas that roiled out from under the earth or from bodies of water—which could be released by earthquakes and other natural disturbances—but also to the influences that rained down from the heavens, from planetary bodies, and from comets, which were believed to bring with them new, often dangerous astral influences. The illness we know today as flu or 'influenza' under this paradigm was ascribed to the influence of the planets, while malaria was attributed to 'bad airs' (just as the phlegm-associated illness that we still call a 'cold' was viewed as an imbalance that could be rectified by drinking hot liquids sweetened with 'hot-dry' substances such as honey).

This belief in the influence of the heavens over the human body gave rise to a view that the microcosm (human body) and macrocosm (the cosmos) were linked together in such a way that the signs of one could be read in the other, and the effects of the cosmos could be felt minutely in the human body. Moreover, bodily processes replicated the processes of nature. This idea was held in common across Eurasia, although it was never monolithic and it came to be differentiated at various times and places. One example of this differentiation is the pulse as a measure of health, which played a major role in medicine in both the Greek and Chinese spheres in the second century AD, but had ceased to have a central importance in Greek medicine by the European Middle Ages, as Europe's doctors (Islamic and Christian) came to emphasize blood and breath, rather than pulse.[16] This understanding of the cosmos (the macrocosm) and the human body (the microcosm) shaped how individuals at all social levels and over a very wide swath of the globe viewed themselves and their place in the universe. These theories about the workings of macrocosm and microcosm thus formed the most widely disseminated codified engagement with the natural world from about the second century BC up through at least the seventeenth century.

Astronomy and astrology came to be linked closely to medicine, and by the European Middle Ages, astrology had come to comprise the specialized knowledge of physicians throughout Eurasia. The position of the stars and planets (including the sun) at a person's conception and birth influenced his or her temperament, and the movement of the planets determined sickness and health in groups and in individual body parts: as bodily organs, limbs, and systems were associated with specific planets and constellations.

Astrology also involved highly sophisticated applications of mathematics to natural phenomena: geometry and the trigonometry of sines and chords were needed to trace the courses and to find the positions of the planets. The mathematical model on which astrology relied was formulated by the Alexandrian mathematician Claudius Ptolemy (*fl. c.* AD 129–41) in a work he titled 'Mathematical Construction' that came to be known via Arabic as the *Almagest*. In the Chinese sphere of influence, the *Chou Gnomon*, a work of mathematical cosmology set down in the first century BC, played a similar role.[17] In the model of the universe Ptolemy describes mathematically, the earth is at rest in the center and the rest of the universe revolves around it once every twenty-four hours. In addition to sharing this diurnal motion of the 'fixed stars', the sun, moon, and planets, known as the 'wandering stars', moved irregularly against the background of the constellations, and Ptolemy describes this mathematically as combinations of perfect circles. Ptolemy also wrote a work of astrology, the *Tetrabiblos*, which predicted events and temperaments based on the movements of the stars and planets. It continued to be used throughout the Graeco-Roman sphere of influence (Europe and the Muslim world including Mughal South Asia) up to the seventeenth century.[18] The *Tetrabiblos*, presented as the second part of the study of astronomy of which the *Almagest* was the first, was concerned with the influences of the celestial bodies over the sublunar sphere. Ptolemy's astrological outlook was practical: astrology was like medicine, conjectural, because of the many variable individual factors to be taken into account. The uses of astrology were many, not just predictive, but also as a means of talking about personality. It was a way of thinking about oneself, in order to come to 'know thyself', the principle at the base of all Socratic philosophy and Hippocratic medicine. Philosophy was a means of seeking the good life, which meant a life of self-discipline and self-knowledge; philosophy was thus a discipline of life, and astrology could function as a kind of self-therapy in this discipline, a way to understand the relationship of one's body and soul to the cosmos. Astrology still retains a vestige of this function in South Asia, where astrological medicine is an accepted part of the medical marketplace, and also in the modern West, where most people are aware of their astrological birth sign, as if it were a part of identity even when they see in it no scientific merit or personal significance. Certainly, given the horoscopes printed in newspapers, any historian of our present era could conclude that some value was attached to astrology in this day and age.

Perhaps the closest analogy among the disciplines today to these aspects of astrology is economics:

Astrologers...carried out the tasks that twentieth-century society assigns to the economist. Like the economist, the astrologer tried to bring the chaotic phenomena of everyday life into order by fitting them to sharply defined quantitative models. Like the economist, the astrologer insisted, when teaching or writing for professional peers, that astrology had only a limited ability to predict the future. Formally speaking, after all, astrology concerned itself with the interplay of general forces rather than the outcome of a single configuration of them....Like the economist, the astrologer proved willing in practice, when powerful clients demanded it, to predict individual outcomes anyhow. Like the economist, the astrologer generally found that the events did not match the prediction; and like the economist, the astrologer normally received as a reward for this confirmation of the powers of his art a better job and a higher salary.

Like the economist...the astrologer became the butt of universal criticism—and still proved indispensable.[19]

The fact that predictions could always be contested did not necessarily demean the science itself.

Although there were skeptics about the predictive ability of astrologers from at least the period of the Renaissance in Europe, and the Aristotelian two-sphere, geocentric picture of the universe came to be questioned in Europe following the publication of Copernicus' 1543 *De revolutionibus orbium celestium*, and was destroyed by the Newtonian synthesis of terrestrial and celestial physics, the belief in the influence of the heavens over earth almost never wavered. Astrology might need to be reformed, most people believed, but it was in general outline still useful. It was not until the late eighteenth century that satirists began to ridicule it, not so much for its lack of scientific principles, but rather because it was deemed a lower-class and vulgar belief. Astrology retains its hold in popular culture (even relied upon by recent US presidential households), but it is no longer accepted as valid by the scientific community and thereby is not subjected to its collective system of scientific testing and falsification.

The tenacity of this belief in the influence of the heavens over earth was buttressed by the three monotheistic religions. Well into the nineteenth century, natural theology—finding proof or evidence of God through his natural Creation—held sway even among scientists. William Paley's 1802 *Natural Theology; or, Evidences of the Existence and Attributes of the Deity* was simply one attempt in a millennia-old tradition in Judaism, Christianity, and Islam of proving the existence of God through Nature. Indeed, natural theology still finds adherents today among Christians and Muslims who profess a belief in 'intelligent design'.

In the pre-modern period, this providential picture of an earth-centered cosmos, in which all things were made up of mixtures of elements and the human body was governed by its humors, was embedded within an organic understanding of change: all things came into being, grew, and passed away. Death and putrefaction led to renewed growth and regeneration, just as winter led inexorably to spring and summer. Such a view found evidence in the visible growth and change of all things (including metals in the earth) and especially in the cycle of the seasons. All the monotheistic religions incorporated older agrarian festival cycles of sowing and harvesting into their liturgical calendars, thereby enshrining the cycles of nature within their own sacred trajectories, imbuing nature with portentous spiritual significance, and consolidating the place of institutionalized religion within the natural order. In general the mundane and everyday objects and events of nature gave evidence of and had meaning for the sphere of the sacred. Until the twentieth century, the majority of the population of Europe and the Near East experienced, engaged with, and 'theorized' about nature in these terms. This view of the relationship between sacred and natural history began to crack in the eighteenth century, as French *philosophes* argued for a 'scientific' analysis of organized religion. François-Marie Arouet de Voltaire (1694–1778) asserted that Isaac Newton's method of drawing truth from observation could be extended to all areas of study, even to religion. In his 1748 book *Man a Machine*, the physician Julien Offray de la Mettrie (1709–51) announced that he was applying the methods of observation and the mechanical world view of the new science to the soul and morality. The link between sacred history and natural history further disintegrated in the nineteenth century, first as geological investigation showed the age of the earth as much older than previously believed (increasing from c.4000 to c.4.6 billion years), and as concepts of an infinite universe developed. When Charles Darwin (1809–82) put forward the theory of evolution in 1859, it spelled the end of this providential and teleological world view. The mechanism of natural selection as the motor of the evolution of species not only contradicted the instantaneous creation of all life on earth, it also asserted that life on earth developed in accordance with impersonal natural laws in an ultimately purposeless manner. Although ideas of natural law go back at least to the Greek philosophers, the cosmos and nature as a whole have come to be seen in modern science as operating in accordance with impassive forces which behave regularly and are capable of prediction. With industrialization, increasingly urban populations, and the growth of secularism, humans have come to see themselves as separated from the greater cycles of the natural world, even as biologists have located them ever more firmly within the sphere of nature and its laws. There is much more willingness in the last two decades, for example, to blur the line between humans and animals, not only in medical research and as a result of the study of genetics, but also in the investigation of language and communication, and even in ethical thought. Interestingly, the essential similarity of humans and animals, and the concept of personhood as the endowment of all living beings rather than the sole preserve of humans, are features of Native American Cree views of the world as well.[20] Perhaps the current crisis of global warming will revive a perception of the interrelatedness of nature and human life, and the participation of humans in the larger cycles and changes in the natural world.

The transformation of matter

The transformation of matter has also been an enduring area of investigation and a productive site of natural knowledge, as craftspeople struggled to produce goods from the variable materials of nature and they and others sought to explain how such transformation and metamorphosis occurred. In general, for the pre-industrial craftsperson, the manipulation of materials was not simply about the handling and transformation of inert materials as we might think of it today, but rather allowed the artisan to engage in life forces, even to investigate and imitate the deepest mysteries such as death and resurrection, the relationship of matter to spirit, and creation. On the one hand, artisans engaged in mundane and hard-headed practices that produced useful goods, but on the other, these artisanal techniques gave access to these greater powers of the universe. The same held for agricultural production—it was productive of the necessities of life, but it also gave a view into the profound forces of coming into being and passing away. Again, this was the manner in which an ordinary person 'theorized' about the cosmos and took part him-/herself in the greater cycles of the universe through which matter was transformed.

Across Eurasia, the transformation of matter was explained by alchemical theory. Like astrology, alchemy was widely accepted at all levels of society and only came to be regarded as 'unscientific' late in the eighteenth century. In both China and Egypt alchemy appears to go back to technical processes for alloying and coloring metals and fabricating gems of the sort also found in alchemical recipes. Material evidence of these practices is documented already in Egypt in the third millennium BC, while extant written recipes for dyes, pigments, and artificial gems date from the third century AD. Alchemical theory and practice is documented in China in a first-century AD text dealing with elixirs of health and longevity,[21] although ideas about transformation and longevity go back at least to the fourth century BC and Taoist thought.[22] We can trace European alchemy back to the amalgam of Egyptian and Greek cultures that emerged in Alexandria and other Near Eastern cities in the first centuries of the Common Era, influenced by the spread of techniques and ideas back and forth across Eurasia, and incorporating theories of transformation from China. Alchemy as a pursuit concerned with both the practice and theory of the transformation of matter began to give rise to a body of texts in Hellenistic Egypt in the second century AD. As it emerged in these texts, it contained a theory of matter based on Aristotle's four elements and the belief that all metals can be reduced to a homogeneous prime matter and then transmuted into one another. Also, all three realms of nature—mineral, vegetable, animal—operated on the same principles of conception, birth, growth, digestion, evacuation, growing old, drying out, and so on. But alchemy at this time also included a remarkable accretion of other components that came out of religious and gnostic concerns with the relationship of matter and spirit, as well as a discussion of qualitative change, color, weight, and malleability as indicators of transformation; in all, a remarkable amalgam of ideas from the Near and Far East. As Arabs moved out over the Hellenistic world and conquered Alexandria in the seventh century, they took up this body of alchemical literature, referring to it as *al-chemeia*. By the eleventh century, Arabic authors had greatly expanded this corpus both in practical operations, such as distillation, and theoretical speculation, and, beginning in the twelfth century, it was in these Arabic texts that alchemy entered Western Europe.

European alchemical theory described the most basic manifestations and transformations of active matter. Alchemy also sought the vital principle—the Elixir—and this bound it up intimately with medical theory and practice. In addition, alchemy was seen as the essence of craft or art because it was the best imitator of the processes of nature. Thus it became the focal point of a debate about the power of art to imitate nature which influenced conceptions of the human ability to replicate and control the processes of nature.[23] At the same time, alchemy was also a powerful practice, productive of valuable material goods. This interaction between productive and contemplative knowledge would prove exceedingly fruitful in the development of a new scientific method in early modern Europe (discussed below).

The transformation and production of materials continues to be of central importance in science today, with chemists, physicists, and materials scientists among those who investigate matter theory and attempt to apply the insight that it provides to bring material products into being. While the production of knowledge in this area still involves both theorizing and producing material goods, the study of transformation has shed its connection to religious and spiritual domains as the professional boundaries of science have been drawn more sharply in the course of the last two centuries.

Science as method

While the process of interacting with nature and the building of theories about natural processes have been constant from the advent of recorded history to the present day (although the resultant practices and theories have varied markedly), the development of a method through which nature is investigated and understood by means of the exercise of reason and practice can be traced to a quite specific beginning point: Europe in the fifteenth through nineteenth centuries. During this period, various individuals put forth a 'new method of philosophizing' that was intended to bring both material, spiritual, and intellectual reform. While elements of this new method can be found in earlier times and places, it was consolidated and spread across the globe with European political and institutional hegemony. The construction of this new method of science has conventionally been viewed as purely European, but this is mistaken, for it was a cosmopolitan process: it was through diverse routes of world trade that novel ideas, techniques, inventions, scholarly manuscripts, and books entered Europe.[24]

Arabic numerals (actually Indian numerals) began to be used by European merchants in the fifteenth century and sophisticated mathematics and astronomy entered Europe from the Islamic world. Gunpowder, paper making, and the use of the compass, among other crucial technologies, endured complex routes of transmission which stretched back to the Far East, while tales of marvels that helped to legitimize curiosity as a motor of discovery were transmitted by literature from South Asia. New modes of collecting information in unfamiliar environments by means of observation and testing were fostered by the movement of peoples and the search for commodities.[25] New attitudes to nature arose as a result of viewing natural objects as commodities convertible into monetary values that could be sent around the world. In the process, these natural goods were decontextualized and shorn of their original religious and cultural significance. World trade also brought about the dominance of Europe by the nineteenth century, as European nations established colonies, in which cultural forms, such as the pursuit of science, were constructed as superior modes of knowing that distinguished the modernity of the European colonizer from the 'primitive' colonized subject. In colonial India, for example, the pursuit of science functioned as a dividing line between colonizer and colonized, as individuals of Indian extraction were not allowed to be members of the Asiatic Society in Mumbai (founded 1830), the premier scientific institution in South Asia.[26]

The new practices of making knowledge that arose in the early modern period were characterized by a new relationship between 'mind' and 'hand', and they brought about the increasing intersection of vernacular and scholarly culture. But this new connection between mind and hand also brought with it a stark division between 'science' and 'pseudo-science'. The view of the relationship between what we might call the 'mind' and the 'hand', seems to have emerged from Greek culture, exemplified by the epistemology of Aristotle, although it was also expressed in China in the fourth century BC, when the Confucian Mencius stated that, 'Some labor with their hearts and minds; some labor with their strength. Those who labor with their heart and minds govern others. Those who labor with their strength are governed by others.'[27] In his ethical writings, Aristotle divided up the pursuit of knowledge about the natural world into *episteme, praxis*, and *technē* (see Figure 12.1). *Episteme* (also called *scientia* or *theoria*) was absolutely certain knowledge based on the model of geometrical deduction from principles.[28] Less certain knowledge was gained by the collection of instances, exempla, or experiences. This *pragmon* was modeled on history, in which nothing can be known by deduction or by syllogism, but a great deal of useful knowledge can be amassed for the use of the citizen and the ruler in leading an ethical life. The last type of knowledge was *technē*, by which people produced valuable goods, but which possessed no certainty because its practitioners had to deal with the uncertainties and idiosyncrasies of changeable matter. Unlike the other two forms of knowledge, *technē* was rife with potential for both ill and good. Good because it was the source of valuable and useful goods, and it held the key to manipulating and transforming matter. On the other hand, the labor of the craftsperson was a source of physical deformity, and in Greek culture this translated into moral deficiency. In addition, the goods made by the artisan engendered 'unnatural' commercial speculation and could bring about destabilizing social mobility.[29]

Aristotle was scathing about the unsuitability of the manual worker for citizenship in the republic, and this prejudice would be carried forward with the rest of the Aristotelian corpus into European conceptions of science, in which engineering and the 'applied' sciences are still ranked below those deemed 'theoretical', such as theoretical physics. This prejudice was reinforced as the medieval university system in Europe grew, especially with the integration of medicine into the professions taught in the higher faculties at university. Initially, this view of epistemology had been partially countered by the practice

Episteme, theoria, scientia

- absolutely certain
- deductive
- models: geometry and syllogistic logic

Pragmon, praxis

- things done, human actions, active knowledge
- never absolutely certain
- possessed moral certainty, i.e. certain enough to act
- accumulate and collect experiences and exempla (can be inductive)
- examples: history, oeconomics, politics

Technē

- things made; productive knowledge
- has nothing to do with certainty
- manual, not appropriate to the free Greek citizen
- useful
- examples: beehives, birds' nests (knowledge of brutes), the manual work of the *banausos* (craftsman) and slave

Figure 12.1 The Aristotelian schema of knowledge

of medicine, which was seen as a *technē* by the Greeks and Romans, but in the medieval European universities, medicine emerged as one of the three professions—law, medicine, and theology—and thus came to be seen as both a science and an art. As science it possessed theoretical prestige, but it continued to possess practical aspects. The bifurcated character of medicine was further emphasized by the fact that medical theory aimed at attaining a deeper knowledge of the causes of health while medical practice sought to collect all possible individual particulars or cases, the causes of which could not be divined by syllogistic reasoning, but rather had to be teased out of the collection of particular experiences and observations. Because medical theory dictated that each individual had a unique complexion, constitution, and regimen of health, this collection of particular instances of disease became paramount, and even the patient's own collection of experiences about his or her own body was part of medical care in a way that is largely alien to the practice of scientific medicine today because that self-knowledge is viewed as subjective and unreliable. The observing and 'case study' practices of the early modern physician would prove very influential in the development of this new scientific method.[30]

In most parts of Eurasia, a medical marketplace reigned in which the university-trained physician, the barber-surgeon, apothecary, midwife, kidney and bladder stone-cutters, and other medical practitioners all competed for market share, and the patient took part in and directed his or her own healthcare. This began to change in Europe as medicine became increasingly professionalized, a process that began in the Renaissance and was not completed in Europe until the twentieth century. In the rivalry occasioned by the marketplace, practitioners could be distinguished by their university degree, their literacy, their access to written texts, and their knowledge of the authorities of their discipline; in short, by their ability to employ *scientia*, or certain knowledge, as defined by Aristotle. *Scientia* in the Middle Ages through the seventeenth century had come to be seen as textual, and to be 'learned' was to have mastered the corpus of the texts of authorities. At the same time, geometry and arithmetic remained models of certain knowledge as well, especially as they had come to play a central role in the *quadrivium*, the second half of the course of study followed by young men at European universities. The seven liberal arts included the *trivium*, comprising (Latin) grammar, dialectic, and rhetoric, and the *quadrivium*, composed of arithmetic, geometry, music (theory of chords), and astronomy. The mathematical nature of the training in the *quadrivium* was important because it reinforced the idea that higher-order knowledge was connected to mathematics, and medical doctors exploited this connection in their astrological calculations.

Certainty continued to be associated with geometry into the seventeenth century, and, in their work in astronomy, both Johannes Kepler and Galileo Galilei declared that geometry was the language in which God wrote the book of nature. The expression of natural knowledge in mathematical terms and the attempt to quantify that knowledge, at first in physics but increasingly in all scientific domains, became predominant in the twentieth century as statistics and probability theory developed.[31] At the same time, however, the level of absolute certainty believed to be obtainable through the scientific method decreased, and by the beginning of the twentieth century both the theories of theoretical physics and philosophical pragmatism viewed the human observer as of central importance in determining the content of the knowledge that was produced. The dream of positive, objective knowledge resulting from a strict separation between subject and object proved to be fleeting.

But to return to the construction of a new epistemology in early modern Europe: the idea that learning was obtained only at university by means of reading texts began to be challenged in Europe from about 1400, as new arenas opened up for practitioners of all kinds who had not been trained at university. The rapidly growing cities and territorial courts throughout Europe from the fifteenth through eighteenth centuries became places to which claimants to natural knowledge, such as craftspeople, alchemists, architects, and practitioners of all sorts, came to assert new standards of proof and make new claims about their ability to obtain certainty in natural knowledge.

As cities in the global backwater that was Europe in the twelfth and thirteenth centuries burgeoned, a new group of people emerged in European society—city dwellers. These urban dwellers, making their living as craftspeople and merchants, gained power in city governments throughout Europe. As their social and political power increased, it raised their intellectual status and that of their de facto epistemology, in which practices such as observation, repeated trial and error testing, and demonstration and proof by producing things that worked often counted for more than texts and textual authorities. Craft could not generally be taught by texts, as observation and experience were more important in building the skills required to respond to the variability of materials and forces involved in producing goods. Similarly, the merchant required news of markets, information about goods, the ability to discern among products, and a working knowledge of mathematical functions. As for knowledge of natural things, merchants viewed knowledge as a product that could travel and be converted into units of value, and their natural commodities were treated in this way. Historians have recently argued that this created a new type of 'objectivity' in the early modern period because natural objects were stripped of their polyvalent meanings and religious significances to become interchangeable units of information and value, a reductionist and non-religious approach to nature that became typical of modern science.[32]

This attitude to natural knowledge became especially prevalent as the commercial and territorial expansion of Europe and the Ottoman Empire and the formation of long-distance trading networks in East and South-East Asia in the early modern period led to an unprecedented movement of individuals, objects, and trade goods. The search for commodities and the investigation of nature went hand in hand on the European voyages of navigation and conquest. These voyages, often joint enterprises between merchants and the emerging territorial powers of Spain, Portugal, the Netherlands, France, and Great Britain, certainly encouraged the viewing of nature as the source of material gain and even the material improvement of society. Moreover, navigation itself, which had brought knowledge of a new continent to Europeans, was seen by them, along with the printing press and gunpowder, as proof of the moderns' superiority over the ancients. This novel idea of progress took hold from the seventeenth century, and the knowledge of nature was viewed as a motor of that progress. In the mid-seventeenth century, societies imbued with these notions of material reform and progress, such as the Royal Society of London for the Improvement of Natural Knowledge and the Académie Royale des Sciences in Paris, were established and began to sponsor information gathering of all kinds. These institutions were allied directly with the centralized territorial powers and proclaimed their method as a means to arbitrate disputes about natural questions.

The model of knowledge making promoted by these societies was collective and cumulative, and it involved the gathering and partial testing of particular facts rather than posing general theories. They advocated both skepticism in the face of received wisdom and textual authorities, and empirical work of observation and hands-on 'experiments' in the laboratory. Indeed, the laboratory became the hallmark of the 'new method of philosophizing' promoted by these societies. The laboratory, as a space where nature was investigated by engaging with the materials of nature themselves and getting the hands dirty, can be traced back to the workshops of craftspeople and to the hands-on activities of alchemy.[33] Laboratories existed in noble courts in Europe and medical faculties up through the late eighteenth century, and, although they were a centerpiece of a new model of knowledge making, they were mainly used for the demonstration of already-established facts of nature rather than for research into the unknown. It was not until the early nineteenth century that scientific research was instituted at the most elite universities, first in Justus von Liebig's (1803–73) chemical laboratory at the University at Giessen in Hesse-Darmstadt and then in the French and Anglo-American sphere. The presence of original scientific research continues to be a measure of academic quality today. Since the mid-twentieth century, scientific research has been carried out in industry- and state-sponsored institutions, including universities and corporate laboratories, for the purposes of war, medicine, and commodity production. Natural philosophy, once of interest to a very limited group of individuals, has come to be of intense interest to the entire body politic, and it is viewed as possessing great national importance.

By the end of the seventeenth century, the knowledge of nature, mediated by European men who called themselves new experimental philosophers, was becoming a tool of centralizing territories seeking wealth through commercial projects, including colonies and manufactories. In distinction to past ages, these natural philosophers viewed knowledge of nature as cumulative, and continually refined and improved by new methods rather than contained in a fixed corpus of texts. In other words, natural knowledge was active, not contemplative: a way of 'doing' that involved manual work in the laboratory. It was as certain as human knowledge could be, but it also produced effects, thus turning inside out Aristotle's schema of knowledge that had endured for a millennium. Natural knowledge was believed to be capable of bringing into being useful inventions and knowledge that would contribute to a limitless progress of the human mind and human society. Its adherents claimed that the new method of gaining knowledge was removed from controversies of religion, literature, and politics, as is evident from the by-laws of the Royal Society of London, which forbade the discussion of religion or politics in the meetings of the society.

Not everyone agreed with the claims of the new philosophy. Thomas Shadwell, in his 1676 play *The Virtuoso*, pilloried the new experimental philosophy because its protagonists cared more for the minute details of the plant and animal kingdoms than for what the playwright saw as the true goal of human contemplation and concern: the human world and ethical behavior within it. Shadwell's view reflected the predominant vision for the aim of knowledge over recorded human history. Taoist thought—the concept of living in accordance with the *tao*, the Way—in China emphasized this aim, as did the ancient Greeks. Aristotle, whose copious writings on physics, astronomy, natural history, and most other natural subjects largely shaped the understanding of the cosmos and nature for almost two millennia, gave an ethical framework to all natural knowledge, for he believed that each natural entity had a *telos*, which must be understood in order to truly have knowledge about that entity. All things strive towards their individual *telos*, and this striving toward functional excellence defined moral goodness or virtue. Lucretius' second-century BC *De rerum natura* (On the nature of things), which first put forward in writing a view that all matter was composed of atoms, was not primarily a work of natural philosophy, but rather an attempt by a follower of Epicureanism to understand how a person could pursue ethical action in a world of random motion and cause. Similarly, eighteenth-century Egyptian scholars showed interest in the natural science being pursued by their French occupiers, but regarded such studies as trifling and ephemeral as compared to the investigation of human history.

Thomas Hobbes (1588–1679) criticized the Royal Society from another perspective, believing it to be seriously and dangerously misled. He maintained that the only certainty to be found in natural knowledge was *scientia*, taking as his paradigm the self-contained axiomatic system of Euclidean geometry. That the Royal Society thought they could obtain certain knowledge by experiment with instruments, such as the air pump, and by the senses, he thought absurd and hubristic. Hobbes called for natural laws, mathematically expressed, which were deduced from principles, rather than induced from faulty sense experience. In its claim to be an arbiter of true knowledge, the Royal Society seemed to him to be declaring itself an exclusive and dangerous guild.[34]

Up through the seventeenth century, it was only a small group of scholars who were interested in philosophical reflection about the natural world, but as the new philosophers became propagandists for the power of the study of nature, the practice and ideology of science set in motion the formation of a new intellectual regime with consequences for religious belief, social structure, and world order, as discussed in the next section.

Science and distinction

Bernard le Bovier de Fontanelle (1657–1757), secretary of the Parisian Académie Royale des Sciences, outlined the persona of the new philosopher and the ideology of the new science in the eulogies he wrote for members. In these eulogies, he portrayed science as neutral, without ethical content, and not subject to the hold of tradition or the winds of fashion because it was concerned only with certain and unchanging knowledge, with the real and eternal laws of nature. As such, it did not contribute to the controversies of religion, politics, or literary style. Not religion, especially in its institutionalized form, but science was viewed as the search for truth by many individuals calling for the reform of society. The importance of nature as an authority and of the investigation of nature as a way to settle even social disputes took hold in the eighteenth century, especially under the influence of the *philosophes* of the Enlightenment. These writers, scholars, and professionals believed they could transform the minds of men by teaching them the scientific method. Science became a universal remedy for ignorance and prejudice. The philosopher was supposed to be a man immune from popular preoccupations and error, stripped of vanity, devoted to a transcendent ideal of truth, and destined to be the instructor of all humankind. His knowledge would revolutionize the material aspects of life as new inventions and arts brought better living. But it would also free the popular mind from superstition, belief in magic, and deception by charlatans. Advocates of the new method and the new society began to exclude various areas of knowledge from the domain of science: for example, herb women, midwives, and other female seekers of natural knowledge who previously had possessed an established place in medical practice, and, in the case of midwives, an important official function and status, came to be seen as the possessors, not of knowledge, but of nonsensical 'old-wives tales'. Colonizers and budding ethnographers began to report on the ways in which peasants and extra-European inhabitants engaged with nature, often labeling these practices as 'superstitions'. Ironically, some of these indigenous practices are now the target of bio-prospectors. During the same period, in the dialectical give-and-take between Europe and its colonies, the so-called 'human' and 'social sciences' began to take shape to explain the forces governing peoples and societies,[35] and the scientific method came to be seen as a means of passing judgment on knowledge claims in any field, whether dealing with nature or with human behavior.

With European expansion and colonization of large swaths of the world in the eighteenth and nineteenth centuries, the epistemology and ideology of science enjoyed an unprecedented global reach. For example, in the great mapping projects of the South Asian continent beginning in the 1760s and culminating in the 1801 Ordinance Survey of India, the British employed many indigenous surveyors and inform-ants, as well as using Mughal road maps and local modes and units of measurement.[36] Thus, even in asymmetrical colonial conditions, knowledge making could be collective and reciprocal both vertically and laterally in the social hierarchy. Despite the collective nature of this knowledge making, it often reinforced traditional social hierar-chies and inequities, and could even create new ones.[37] In nineteenth-century India, the possession of science was employed as a marker to distinguish between European and Indian, and it quickly became a way that elite Indian society attempted to distinguish itself from lower castes as well.[38] In the twentieth century, colonial officials in the British colony of Rhodesia used a powerful but nebulous notion of 'science' to justify their policies and just as clearly to demarcate themselves from their colonial subjects:

What 'science' actually was remained unclear. It could mean anything from the ability to predict eclipses in order to save Our Hero from death at the hands of ignorant savages, to the ability to grow crops more productively. Whatever it was, however, 'science' served as the marker of difference between whites and Africans. While Africans might appear to speak like Shakespeare, or even like Biblical characters, it seems that they were never deemed to speak as experts on the material world.[39]

In the nineteenth and twentieth centuries, as historians began to search for the causes of Europe's alleged 'modernity' in relation to the rest of the world, they identified science as one of the most impor-tant factors that propelled Europe to its pinnacle of political and social power. Recently, economic historians have debated whether science contributed to the economic 'take-off' of Europe in the nineteenth century, and, although most historians now doubt a straightforward link between the new philosophy of the seventeenth and eighteenth centuries and the rapid industrialization of Europe after 1850, it seems clear that the use of science as a means of distinguishing between 'modern' and 'primitive', between 'rational' and 'superstitious', and between 'knowledge' and 'belief' exercised great power as social ideology in the policies of colonial officials and the attitudes of Europeans in the process of colonization. Science was central in the assertion of European superiority that upheld the hierarchies and ideology of the colonial regime, a system that worked materially to enrich and strengthen European nations at the expense of the rest of the world.

Historians and sociologists of science have striven in the past thirty years to revise this automatic association of science and (European) modernity (as, indeed, historians in general have questioned the very concept of 'modernity'), in order to make clear other dimensions of modern science—its global origins, the contingency of its formation, its commercial ties, for example—but their efforts have had little effect on the view of science held by much of the scientific community or the general public. Scientific expertise continues to exercise dominant intellectual authority in society, and public and corporate funding for the natural sciences remains far higher than for the similarly empirical pursuit of historical understanding. Investigation by the quantitative and reductionist methods of the natural sciences is accorded a greater level of trust even in the study of such multifaceted and complex subjects as human behavior, society, and culture. Because the modern scientific view of nature presupposes a separation between nature and human culture, science has appealed to the authority of nature to assert the 'natural fact' of the inferiority of women, the 'primitive' faculties of non-Europeans, and even the virtues of aggression and selfishness. On the other hand, it has also asserted the 'brotherhood' of all human 'races' and the equal mental capacities of men and women. In the wake of the atomic bomb and environmental catastrophe, science is looked upon both as the destroyer of humanity and the source of a 'technological fix' that will save it. As a mode of making knowledge about nature, science is epistemologically powerful: it can encourage skepticism about received wisdom, it provides broadly accepted and relatively standardized methods and metrics to examine knowledge claims, it can settle disputes and compel assent, it is productive both of the means by which humans can better control the material conditions of their lives as well as the means to unleash appallingly destructive forces. As such, it is an essentially human and social activity, value-laden and fallible.

13. Rivane Neuenschwander, 'Continent-Cloud' 2007–8, installation with Correx, aluminium, Styrofoam balls, fluorescent lighting, electric fans, timers, Neuen 221. © the artist and Stephen Friedman gallery (London); photography courtesy Stephen White

Environmental History

J. R. MCNEILL

What is environmental history?

Like every other subset of history, environmental history is different things to different people. My preferred definition is: the history of the relationship between human societies and the rest of nature on which they depended. This includes three chief areas of enquiry, which of course overlap and have no firm boundaries.[1]

First is the study of material environmental history, the human involvement with forests and frogs, with coal and cholera. This entails study of the evolution of both human impact on the rest of nature and nature's influence upon human affairs, each of which is always in flux and always affecting the other. This form of environmental history puts human history in a fuller context, that of earth and life on earth, and recognizes that human events are part of a larger story in which humans are not the only actors.[2] In practice, most of the historical work in this vein—as with most historical work—concerns the last 200 years, when industrialization among other forces greatly enhanced the human power to alter environments.

Second is political and policy-related environmental history. This concerns the history of self-conscious human efforts to regulate the relationship between society and nature, and between social groups in matters concerning nature. Thus efforts at soil conservation or pollution control qualify, as perhaps do social struggles over land and resource use. Political struggle over resources is as old as human societies and close to ubiquitous. I would not use the term environmental history to refer to contests between one group of herders and another over pastures; but I would use the term to refer to struggles over whether a certain patch of land should be pasture or farmland. The difference lies in the fact that the outcome of the struggle carries major implications for the land itself, as well as for the people involved. (Mind you, others see this differently than I.) In practice, policy-related environmental history extends back only to the late nineteenth century, with a few exceptions for early examples of soil conservation, air pollution restrictions, or monarchical efforts to protect charismatic species for their own hunting pleasure. This is because only in the late nineteenth century did states and societies mount systematic efforts to regulate their interaction with the environment generally (as opposed to regulating irrigation water, for example, which states have done for millennia). Because these efforts were spasmodic and often modest in their effects, most of this sort of environmental history deals with the decades since 1965, when both states and explicitly environmental organizations grew more active in their efforts.

The third main form of environmental history is a subset of cultural and intellectual history. It concerns what humans have thought, believed, written, and, more rarely, painted, sculpted, sung, or danced dealing with the relationship between society and nature. Evidence of a sort exists from tens of thousands of years ago in Australian Aboriginal rock shelter paintings, or in the cave art of south-western Europe. But the great majority of this sort of work is drawn from published texts, as with intellectual history, and treats the environmental thought contained either in major religious traditions or, more commonly, in the works of influential (and sometimes not-so-influential) writers from Mohandas K. Gandhi to Arne Naess.[3] This sort of environmental history once tended to focus on individual thinkers, but increasingly it extends to the study of popular environmentalism as a cultural movement.

More than most varieties of history, environmental history is an interdisciplinary project. Many scholars in the field trained as geographers or historical ecologists. In addition to the customary published and archival texts of the standard historian, environmental historians routinely use the findings culled from bio-archives (such as pollen deposits which can tell us about former vegetation patterns) and geo-archives (such as soil profiles that can tell us about past land use practices). The subject matter of environmental history is often much the same as the subject matter in historical geography or historical ecology, although the sorts of sources emphasized normally differ. An illustration is the field of climate history, which is pursued by scholars from at least half a dozen disciplines, including text-based historians.

The origins and institutionalization of environmental history

Like every twist and turn within intellectual life, environmental history has countless and tangled roots. Some of the earliest extant texts, such as the Epic of Gilgamesh, deal with environmental change generated by human action (cutting cedar forests in this case). Many scholars of long ago found in the variations of the natural world, of climate especially, a key to human behavior and fortunes. Ibn Khaldun and Montesquieu were notable in this regard. Historical geographers since the 1870s charted landscape change.[4] Among professional historians, awareness of geographical constraints and influences has long been a hallmark, although not a universal. Fernand Braudel, in what was probably the twentieth century's most influential book among professional historians, devoted a large chunk of *La Méditerranée* to geography and environment.[5] He and his followers aspired to what they called total history, but some have seen in their sensitivity to geography a harbinger of environmental history.[6]

Environmental history as a self-conscious undertaking dates only to about 1970 and, like so much in intellectual life, drew its energy from society at large. Around the world, of course, the 1960s and 1970s witnessed the coalescence of popular environmentalism as a cultural and political force. It was stronger in some places than in others, and took different shapes in different contexts. In the United States it helped a few historians, initially almost all scholars of US history, to come together both intellectually and institutionally to launch environmental history. Among them were Americanists[7] Roderick Nash, John Opie, Donald Worster, Susan Flader, and a historian of the ancient Mediterranean, Donald Hughes. By some accounts Nash, author of *Wilderness and the American Mind*,[8] an intellectual history of an environmental subject, was the first to employ the term 'environmental history'.

Between Nash's book and 1985 a small handful of books acquired status as foundational texts in US environmental history. The first was Alfred Crosby's *Columbian Exchange*,[9] one of the few books whose title became part of nearly every historian's vocabulary. Revealingly,

Crosby had great difficulty finding a publisher for a book that explained the extraordinary ecological consequences of the regular crossing of the Atlantic after 1492. Worster's *Dust Bowl*[10] took an iconic subject in US history and gave it a new twist. William Cronon's *Changes in the Land*,[11] which explored the transformations of the southern New England landscape between 1600 and 1800, enjoyed great success and inspired direct imitation. Worster and Cronon soon became the most influential figures in US environmental history, joined by Richard White, who like Cronon featured Amerindians prominently in much of his work, and Carolyn Merchant, who put women front and center. Martin Melosi and Joel Tarr pioneered American urban environmental history.[12]

These US scholars, who continued to produce influential work, attracted international attention too. Historians around the world contemplating taking an environmental turn often read them, especially Worster and Cronon, while formulating their own projects. Worster's work on droughts and irrigation in the American West, for example, seemed relevant in many settings outside the United States.[13] The themes of cultural clash and colonization, developed in Cronon's, Crosby's, and White's work, found interested readers among those writing about colonial encounters in Asia and Africa. White's concept of a 'middle ground' seemed helpful to scholars of medieval Central Europe and to Tokugawa Japan.[14]

Part of the influence of the US authors must be attributed to institutional factors rather than intellectual sparkle. The first generation formed the American Society for Environmental History in 1976–7 and by the early 1980s held regular conferences. Most importantly, the ASEH began publishing a journal, now called *Environmental History*, in 1976. Moreover, as in all fields of history, the Americans enjoyed advantages in the form of the general vigor and (comparatively) generous funding of US academia, and in the fact that so many historians around the world could read English (this, obviously, boosted the fortunes of all anglophones).[15]

The intellectual prominence of the Americanists' examples soon waned. Scholars elsewhere quickly found their own voices and confronted the limits of the relevance of American precedents. The Americanist environmental historians' emphasis on wilderness, for example, had minimal resonance in most of the world. Beyond that, while almost everyone in the field could read the work of the Americanists, they could not (or chose not to) read the work of scholars elsewhere. Over time the proportion of environmental history written in tongues other than English grew, and most Americanists ignored it. A few prominent works, such as Joachim Radkau's *Natur und Macht*,[16] which will be discussed below, were translated for anglophone audiences, but only a few.[17]

Thus as the enterprise of environmental history globalized, the intellectual exchange expanded but not evenly: by and large everyone around the world read the prominent Americanists, but the Americanists, for reasons of language and inclination, mainly read only one another. This is not quite as blinkered as it sounds: Americanists were numerous enough that keeping up with their production alone became a full-time job by the 1990s.[18]

Critiques of environmental history

Questions of language, training, and inclination also inform one of the three main weaknesses of environmental history. First is its awkward compatibility with the nation state as a unit of analysis. Most historians for more than a century have defined themselves in national terms, as historians of Japan, Russia, Canada, or Mexico. The publishing industry and the job markets reinforced this socialization. The investment in linguistic skills made it seem unrewarding for someone who had learned Turkish to study the history of China. Moreover, many archives are kept by national governments and record the behavior of a single state. Very few historians see themselves as specialists in a given time period, e.g. 1600–50, around the world, and indeed most would find this ambition absurd, as they would the idea of specializing in, say, the history of plantations or monasticism or smallpox throughout the ages and around the globe. The main reason these things seem absurd to most historians is the importance of reading texts in original languages—and there is a great deal to be said in favor of this preference. However, it is a preference that fits poorly with most forms of environmental history. The natural phenomena that form part of environmental history's subject matter pay no heed to political borders. Elephants, manatees, and sulfur dioxide plumes migrate across political boundaries with impunity. The cultural and intellectual trends concerning human views of nature migrate internationally with almost equal ease, as the rise of modern environmentalism as a popular movement around the world in the 1960s and 1970s attests. Only in the realm of policy and political environmental history does the historian's preference for national units of analysis make much sense, and even here it carries less logic with each passing year, because in recent history international organizations and environmental diplomacy have grown in significance. The long-standing, although weakening, fetish for national-scale history is problematic for many genres of history, but especially so for environmental history.

The second problem for environmental history is that it consists (allegedly) of a single dreary and repetitive tale of woe.[19] Environmental historians grandiosely call the tendency to write in this vein 'declensionism'. In the 1970s and 1980s, many scholars found in environmental history an opportunity to critique the environmental record of societies, their own or others, writing what are now sometimes derided as 'degradation narratives'. With varying degrees of plausibility, they located in the past societies which behaved with ecological prudence and restraint, or at least a better time when ecosystems were intact. Since those halcyon days, it seems, all has gone relentlessly downhill.

The weight of this critique has diminished over time. Since the 1980s, environmental historians have lost some of their political commitment and moral certitude, especially in Europe and North America, and are ever more apt to write about environmental change rather than 'loss' and 'degradation'. Their stories have grown more complex, in recognition of the likelihood that most environmental change is good for some people and species and bad for others.[20] The beguiling formula of Aldo Leopold's 'Land Ethic' ('A thing is right when it tends to preserve the integrity, stability, and beauty of the biotic community. It is wrong when it tends otherwise'[21]) seemed progressively less suitable as a guiding principle as layer after layer of complexity emerged from ever more researches. Moreover, historians found encouraging stories of environmental change that could scarcely be seen as degradation, such as the reduction in urban air pollution in many cities since 1965, or the diplomatic protocols that led to bans of chlorofluorocarbon use in parts of the world, thereby sparing the ozone shield a quick death and perhaps giving humanity time in which to save it.

Related to the impatience with declensionism is a critique of degradation narratives as either intentional or unwitting accusations of improper ecological conduct on the part of others, especially Africans. Environmental history that found degradation as a result of African land use was suspect, complicit with colonialism, because it implied that Africans ought not be allowed sovereignty over African ecosystems.[22] Normally this view carried weight only when applied to European and American authors writing about formerly colonial, or Amerindian, societies.

Third among the chief faults found with environmental history is environmental determinism. Scholars in the social sciences and history have been highly sensitive to environmental determinism for more than half a century, as a result of early twentieth-century over-enthusiasms (e.g. the geographer Ellsworth Huntington) and the efforts to justify Nazi racism by recourse to biological determinism. Hence any effort to explain matters with emphasis on environmental or biological factors arouses objections. Alfred Crosby's *Ecological Imperialism* is a case in point.[23] It argues that the success of European imperialism in the temperate Americas, in Australia, and New Zealand owed a lot to the unconscious teamwork of pathogens, plants, and animals that paved the way for the imposition of imperialism, the removal and near-extinction of indigenous peoples, and the creation of settler societies. To some readers this seemed to go much too far, serving to exculpate Europeans for crimes against humanity (which a proper reading of Crosby rules out). To others, it seemed remiss to locate agency and causation not in human choice and social structures, but in viruses, sheep, and bluegrass (which Crosby unapologetically did). Jared Diamond's enormously popular and much admired *Guns, Germs, and Steel*,[24] which I do not consider a work of environmental history but which Diamond and others do, aroused sharp criticisms for its efforts to explain the long-term distribution of wealth and power around the world in environmental terms.[25]

A quick around-the-world tour

Critiques and complaints about the genre notwithstanding, since the 1970s environmental history has appealed to thousands of scholars around the world. However, the degree to which environmental history has made inroads in professional history varies tremendously from place to place and era to era.[26] About eras I will only say that in general the further from the present the less interest environmental historians have shown. The chief exceptions to this are the ancient Mediterranean, where comparatively abundant sources and other attractions have invited historians and classicists to take up the theme;[27] and the 1960s–1970s, where the tumult of popular environmentalism cast a spell over historians' imaginations.

Regionally, matters are especially uneven. Here I will touch down quickly on several world regions, and dally only in South Asia and Latin America. Historians of Australia and New Zealand have taken to environmental history with gusto since the early 1990s. The theme of ecological change brought by settler colonialism, especially the extinction of native species and the spread of exotics, predominated in both countries. The brevity of the settler period and the pace of ecological change made this theme irresistible, although subjects such as the (politically sensitive) ecological impact of Aborigines and Maori, and the meanings of modern environmentalism, have also found their historians.[28]

Jeyamalar Kathirithamby-Wells, Greg Bankoff, and Peter Boomgaard led the way in bringing South-East Asian environmental history to international audiences. Kathirithamby-Wells's history of forests and forestry in Malaya resonated with other studies of imperial forestry, in India for example, but also devoted detailed attention to postcolonial developments such as the inroads upon Malay forests made by the international timber trade since the 1960s. Bankoff was among the first to bring the scholarly literature on natural disasters (often not so natural as the term implies) into history, specifically into the modern history of the Philippines. That archipelago has long felt more than its fair share of typhoons, floods, droughts, and earthquakes. But what these events became, in human terms, depended on social and political patterns and preferences such as where people settled, what sorts of homes they lived in, what economic investments they made, and how the authorities responded when disaster struck. In many respects economic development as practiced there made Filipinos more rather than less vulnerable to natural disasters. Boomgaard's detailed work on the environmental implications of Dutch colonial rule in what is now Indonesia and in British Malaya involved many standard themes of imperial environmental history, but some distinctive ones as well, such as the fate and cultural role of tigers.[29]

East Asia presents a contrasting picture. If my informants are correct, Chinese, Japanese, and Korean historians were as of 2000 little interested in environmental history, but foreigners working on China had made excellent use of the approach. Here the majority of work came from scholars closer to economic history, and themes such as agriculture, irrigation, and state management predominated.[30] Soon after 2000, however, Bao Maohong, originally an Africanist, led the development of environmental history within China, focusing mainly on modern Chinese environmental policy.[31]

Leaving South Asia aside for the moment, the rest of Asia remains almost *terra incognita* for environmental history—in other words, a beckoning opportunity. While historical geographers have done excellent work on south-west Asia, Central Asia, and Russia, environmental historians have scarcely set to work.[32]

Europeanists since 1990 have excelled in producing provocative environmental history. A landmark early work, *The Silent Countdown*, edited by Peter Brimblecombe and Christian Pfister,[33] set a fine example, showing some of the variety of possible subjects and how to make use of a comparatively deep documentary base. A set of detailed studies written by both historians and natural scientists, the book taken as a whole suggested a new angle of vision, explicitly ecological, on European history of all periods from the medieval to the contemporary. Scholars working on Germany, Scandinavia, Scotland, and the Netherlands led the way in the 1980s, originally concentrating on forests and water issues, but the strong traditions of agrarian history in Italy and especially Spain soon led to a fruitful exploration of environmental themes in the rural history of southern Europe. East Europeanists got off to a late start, perhaps because environmental perspectives did not fit easily with the state's approved approach before 1989. Since 1989, Hungary and Czechia have developed small but lively environmental history communities. Perhaps because of the supply of suitable records, Europeanists have done more than others with climate history as it affected human affairs. The prominent French historian Emmanuel Le Roy Ladurie in a 1967 landmark study of French and (to some extent) Western European climate concluded that climate change since AD 1000, while real, held only modest importance for historians or for history. A later generation led by Christian Pfister, armed with fuller data, found more robust connections between the vagaries of climate and agrarian fortunes. Indeed, Le Roy Ladurie modified his views somewhat, recognizing a stronger role for climate change in the rhythms of harvest crises.[34] European environmental historians are sometimes inclined to lament the state of their field, partly on the grounds that mainstream historians seem uninterested in what they do (an interesting contrast to the fate of US environmental historians), but from an outsider's perspective, the Europeanists have done and continue to do well in almost every sphere of environmental history.[35]

Africanists showed an early inclination to adopt environmental history perspectives. The famous challenges of African environments— aridity, disease—helped Africanists keep ecological matters in view. More than any other, the theme of colonial alteration to the environment has dominated, partly because of the availability of suitable sources. Of necessity, Africanists have gone further than anyone else in making the techniques of oral history serve the interests of environmental history. This allowed research into the environmental thought and practices of Africans, as opposed to the better-documented subjects of the doings of colonial states, science in the service of empire, and the resource conflicts between Africans and settlers. Lately it seems that work on South Africa pours out faster than that on the rest of the continent put together.[36] The persuasiveness of Africanist environmental history is reflected in the fact that John Iliffe, one of the leading lights of African history since the late 1960s, chose to put environmental themes at the center of his conspectus, *Africans: The History of a Continent*.[37]

While historians of one region or another may have made an earlier start in adopting the perspectives of environmental history, by the time of writing environmental history had traveled almost everywhere, from the polar regions to the equatorial latitudes, from ancient Mesopotamia to the day before yesterday. Almost every world region by 2008 had an environmental history survey.[38]

Before turning to more detailed remarks on South Asia and Latin America, a few remarks are in order about global-scale environmental history. This enterprise has the obvious intellectual merit that many ecological processes are global in scope, and many of the cultural trends concerning the environment have been nearly so. But it has the equally obvious practical problem that mastering the relevant information is out of the question, and bringing coherence to the subject much more difficult than, say, to the history of asbestos regulation in Osaka or Omaha. For decades the only global syntheses came from authors who were not professional historians, but geographers and in one case a former mandarin of the British Foreign Office. Sociologists too joined the fray, unencumbered by the documentation fetish that historians acquire during their apprenticeships.[39] Eventually natural scientists had a go at global historical treatments of subjects such as nitrogen and soil.[40]

Professional historians began by taking slices of the whole, with books on global fire history by Stephen Pyne, or environmentalism by Ramachandra Guha.[41] Joachim Radkau was perhaps the first to bring the sensibilities of the historian to general global-scale environmental history in his *Natur und Macht: Eine Weltgeschichte der Umwelt*. His was not a survey, but a sprawling series of soundings and reflections on everything from dog domestication 15,000 years ago to modern tourism in the Himalaya. It took up some very large themes such as the proper role of moralism in environmentalism (preferably small), of religion in environmental history, of colonialism, and the problem of periodization within global environmental history. It connects more frequently and more deeply to issues of concern to historians generally than many environmental history books. Radkau drew upon a wide reading of the field and is often comparative in his presentation, if inevitably more at home in some places than others—in other words his book has the weaknesses of all global-scale history. A small flurry of world environmental histories appeared almost simultaneously, some written as surveys, some as portraits of an era.[42] While the practical problems of such efforts will always remain, environmental history probably lends itself to global-scale work more readily than does, for example, labor history, women's history, or intellectual history.

South Asia and Latin America: active frontiers

Two of the most active arenas for environmental history since the 1990s have been South Asia and Latin America. Both appear energized by scholars' investment in current environmental struggles.

Note, however, that my choice to focus on these two regions is arbitrary; Canada, South Africa, and southern Europe have also been lively frontiers for environmental history in the past decade.

Within South Asia, indeed within all of Asia, environmental history writing began soonest and appears strongest in India.[43] Sri Lanka, Bangladesh, and especially Pakistan have come in for much less scrutiny. If this impression is not an illusion resulting from my English-language bias, it is probably a result of Indian scholars' engagement with social and environmental struggles since 1980. As in Latin America, environmental history in India seems to carry more political content, a stronger social commitment, than it now does in Europe or North America, where that sort of engagement has waned since the 1970s.

The vigor of Indian environmental history also results from the helpfulness of the historical records. The gazetteers of the Raj, for example, proved most useful for understanding land use patterns. Its forestry service left behind mountains of memoranda allowing very detailed work on Indian forest management history. The lack of comparably meticulous work on the period 1500 to 1750 suggests that the record base left by the Mughals is not nearly so helpful, but that may be disproven in years to come.[44] The success of Indian environmental historians may also owe something to their having easy access, through English, to work done elsewhere. The Indians too have often read Worster and Cronon.

Environmental historians of India (the great majority of whom are Indians working in India) naturally developed some themes in preference to others. A good deal of early work focused on land use and forests, and issues of access to forests, especially under the Raj when ambitious state forest conservation efforts put officialdom on a collision course with peasants for whom forests had routinely provided much of their daily wherewithal. Another important theme was water manipulation, including canal building chiefly in the colonial era, and dam building mainly since independence (1947). Indeed, one might fairly say that Indian environmental history grew out of the study of forests and irrigation. A third subject, taken up more recently, was the fate of wildlife, especially iconic mammals such as tigers and elephants, and their meanings in different Indian cultural settings.[45] These are rural subjects, appropriate enough in India. But the tremendous urbanization of the last century, the daunting environmental issues of modern megacities such as Mumbai, Kolkata, or New Delhi, has made Indian cities a most interesting and rewarding topic for environmental history, one that as yet has no takers.

Environmental historians of India also tended to focus their work on the role of the state, whether that refers to the Mughal Empire, or more commonly the British Raj, or the post-1947 national state. There is a threefold logic to this. First, since at least the middle of the nineteenth century, India has been home to environmentally activist states. Rulers chose to try to remake nature in India according to (evolving) ideas about modernity, security, and prosperity. Not content with the nature they inherited from the past, they sought to improve it and to manage it, in service of either imperial or nationalist agendas. This is far from unique, and never reached the levels of ambition attained by the Soviet state. But it supplies a rationale for historians (who rarely need encouragement) to focus on the role of the state.

Second, just as states indulge in gross simplifications in order to try to understand the complexities of the societies they rule,[46] historians often focus on the state in order to simplify their tasks. In the Indian subcontinent the situation is especially challenging. Its ecological diversity, from Himalaya to deserts to rice paddies to jungle (and much else besides), is sobering enough. Add to that the linguistic, religio-cultural, and ethnic diversities, and then bear in mind that none of this stays still for long. Indian history, and a fortiori South Asian history, is a kaleidoscopic swirl that, as much as anywhere in the world, drives historians to take intellectual refuge in emphasizing the role of the state.

Third, a focus on the role of the state makes environmental history in India (perhaps more so than most other settings) more interesting and relevant to historians in general and the public at large. The significance of colonial rule has probably been the foremost preoccupation of Indian historians in general in the last half century, and certainly that issue has dominated Indian environmental historiography. While it may be that the import of colonial rule is often exaggerated, it did bring major changes: new plantations, railways (and forest protection to ensure supply of railway sleepers), and far more ambitious irrigation, among other things. The colonial preoccupation, I cautiously predict, will change as the colonial experience recedes in time and memory. Historians of Africa, where admittedly colonial rule came later and lasted less long, have progressively demoted colonialism from its formerly dominant position among historiographical priorities. The same, I suspect, is happening or will happen in Indian historiography, both in general and with respect to environmental history. Against this prediction, it must be admitted, is the convenience of record keeping and archives created and maintained by colonial authorities, which will long make work in this sphere tempting for historians.

Since the pioneering works of two decades ago,[47] Indian environmental history has grown with extraordinary exuberance. Those working in it freely admit that they can scarcely keep up with the spate of publications in the field.

The same happy situation now exists for Latin American environmental history as well.[48] Scholarship on this region included a rich tradition of scholarly historical geography dating back to Alexander von Humboldt. But environmental history as such arrived only in 1972 with Crosby's *Columbian Exchange*, which included a good deal about Latin America and the Caribbean, and in the 1980s, with the work of Luis Vitale and Warren Dean.[49] Leaving aside the question of pre-Columbian Amerindian relations with nature—the preserve of anthropologists, geographers, and archaeologists—the main issues of Latin American environmental history have been connected to colonial conquest (as in South Asia) and settlement (unlike South Asia). More recently, work on industrialization, urbanization, conservation, and environmentalism has emerged, making Latin American environmental history both richer than before and less distinctive because closer in content to that of Europe and North America.

As in India, environmental historians have sought to explore the ecological impacts of colonialism and capitalism. Some of the themes are familiar, such as the installation of plantation economies or the spread of deforestation. Dean took up both these in his final book, *With Broadax and Firebrand: The Destruction of Brazil's Atlantic Forest*,[50] a masterpiece of research and a model of politically committed scholarship. Dean wore his heart unabashedly on his sleeve in chronicling the transformation of the formerly giant forest of Brazil's eastern coast into farms, pastures, plantations, and other uses. He found the waste of timber, the loss of biodiversity and of soil fertility, tragic and at times criminal, and rated independent Brazil as no better than its colonial predecessor, which may help to account for the book's cooler reception in Brazil than overseas. These themes of colonialism and capitalism also predominate in the as-yet thin environmental history of the Caribbean.[51] Settlement of the pampas by people and herbivores naturally looms large in the environmental history of Argentina, summarized in a prize-winning book, *Memoria verde: historia ecológica de la Argentina*.[52] Within the environmental history of the colonial economy, pastoralism, irrigation, and mining attracted attention, although much opportunity remains especially as regards mining. Who will write the environmental history of Potosí? Or Chilean copper?[53]

Lately environmental historians of Latin America have struck out in new directions. While not neglecting the study of colonial transformations, they have begun to work on environmental thought and science in both colonial and independence periods. In terms of research, the standard setters were probably José Augusto Pádua and Stuart McCook.[54] State programs of nature conservation also came in for some treatment, usually on the national scale.[55] Latin America has for centuries been among the most urbanized parts of the world (today nearly 80 per cent of its people live in metropolitan areas), so the early work on rural and agrarian subjects acquired a complementary literature, albeit still small. The first in-depth work was Exequiel Ezcurra's study of Mexico City and its surroundings, eventually followed by works on Brazilian cities such as São Paulo, regarded as an environmental blight, and Curitiba, a southern Brazilian city viewed by some as a bright example of enlightened environmental city planning.[56] Bogotá is another giant city now the subject of an environmental history.[57] Latin Americanists have gone further in the direction of urban environmental history than have the South Asianists (after all their region is twice as urbanized), but plenty of interesting cities still await treatment. Moreover, the environmental history of colonial cities remains little explored. In Spanish America this is an especially inviting theme because of the tradition of rectilinear urban planning that Spaniards imported.

Latin Americanists produced several regional (and national) overviews after Vitale's early effort, taking into account the avalanches of new research. Guillermo Castro offered a compact survey, and Elio Brailovsky a longer one, both well within the declensionist tradition of environmental history. Shawn Miller's *An Environmental History of*

Latin America succeeded admirably as an introduction and conspectus of the field.[58]

But there will soon be need for further overviews, as more research pours forth, and as new subjects find their historians. Climate history, for example, including the impacts of El Niño, has only just begun to figure in Latin American environmental history, and the same may be said of energy history—although Georgina Endfield and Myrna Santiago have shown some of the potential these areas hold.[59] The entire Caribbean region, so prominent in one of the great achievements of modern historiography—the illumination of the world of plantation slavery—remains woefully underdeveloped when it comes to environmental history.[60]

Conclusion

Environmental history as a self-aware field is one human generation old. It has emerged from the shadows to become one of the fastest-growing sub-fields within professional history writing. It has cropped up almost everywhere that historians are at work. In some respects Americanists still predominate, although less so every day. The political commitments of the early days have waned somewhat, especially in North America and Europe, but remain a strong motive for some environmental historians everywhere, and perhaps the majority of those working in India and Latin America.

In the first decade of the twenty-first century environmental history appeared in robust good health. Nearly 700 scholars proposed papers for the first world congress, held in Denmark in 2009. The *Encyclopedia of World Environmental History*, published in 2004, quickly looked out of date.[61] Young scholars in dozens of countries continued to flock to environmental history. Much of this good health, regrettably, was owing to unhappy circumstances, notably the continuing anxieties over environmental problems around the world. As long as global climate change, Beijing's air quality, Brazil's Amazonian forests, and several dozen other concerns remains with us, environmental history will probably maintain its grip on historians' imaginations. Since these issues are likely to grow in salience—although one never knows—the future for environmental history looks distressingly vital.

Sustaining innovation and intellectual excitement is always an issue for a young sub-field. In environmental history two easy routes remain which it can follow in the years to come: more interdisciplinarity and more imitation. While many historians trained to work as individual scholars find it uncomfortable, interdisciplinary collaborations of the sort routine among, say, environmental archaeologists are one way forward. Combining the data and perspectives of environmental historians with those of archaeology, ecology, botany, climatology, and so forth, while not without practical problems, will help push along the frontiers of knowledge. Archaeology, always a historical science, has taken an environmental turn in the last three decades. Ecology, botany, and climatology have taken historical turns. Thus the rewards for interdisciplinary collaboration are greater than ever before, although the practical difficulties of such work are undiminished. With a little effort and cross-cultural patience, environmental historians can work together with scholars whose work entails measuring strontium/calcium ratios in long-dead bones and teeth. And if they do, they can hope to find out about past diets, agriculture, hunting, and even human migration.[62]

Paradoxically, more imitation will also propel environmental history forward. Americanists have as of yet taken virtually no notice of the social metabolism approach used to good effect by many scholars in Europe.[63] Environmental historians have written eco-biographies of at least ten US cities, but no one yet has published one of an Asian or African city. In this respect at least, environmental history in and of the USA still deserves the attention of, and within the limits implied by local variations, imitation by, scholars elsewhere. In short, to maintain its intellectual vibrancy, environmental history as a field needs more integration, both more integration with other disciplines, and more integration within itself, among scholars at work on different regions and different problems.

14. Huejutla de Reyes, plastic bag with image of a multi-storey church 'Recuerdo San Juan de los Lagos' stamped on each side, 1980s. © by permission of the Trustees of the British Museum

 **Religion**

MIRI RUBIN

The study of religion has been diversified almost beyond recognition during the twentieth century. Religious ideas and practices of the past are no longer the exclusive domain of those professing a religious faith. They form part of what the French call *sciences humaines*—the human sciences—like literature and economics. Religion is no longer taken to be a self-evident truth—to be studied by its adherents, or to be derided by its detractors—but rather it is the very terrain of enquiry, the *explanandum*, through the wide array of strategies which historians use in their enquiries. This holds true for all world religions, but it is probably most evident in the study of Christianity, the cultural frame for most academic historical study of religion, and in which a remarkable degree of diversification and change has occurred in the course of the last century. This is not to say that history is not enriched by the insights of scholars who study traditions to which they are deeply attached; it is rather to say that faith is no longer considered a prerequisite for effective and illuminating study of the history of religion.

The move away from the study of religion as a phenomenon outside the realm of the social, one to be treated with tools laid down by its own followers and defenders, has meant that scholars sought new frameworks within which the history of religions might be explored. One of the most obvious was the sociological and anthropological frame, which offered techniques for observation and procedures for explanation. French scholars of the tradition known as the *Annales* School were influenced by the sociology of Émile Durkheim (1858–1917), the anthropology of Marcel Mauss (1872–1950) and later of Claude Lévi-Strauss (1908–2009).[1] Insights gained from the observation of non-European societies offered starting points for the understanding of European societies in the past, and in the present. Émile Durkheim analysed the 'elementary forms of religious life', belief and practices about the sacred which create something of a 'moral community'.[2] French historians were soon using these insights to study Christian rituals. Religion was revealed as a social and cultural phenomenon and thus all skills of understanding human societies could contribute to the work of understanding it. This was not only a move outside of religion, so as to look in, but a strategy aimed at broadening the subject of religion itself, by seeking out experience and participation in religious life. Since the majority of Europeans left no written sources for historical scrutiny, historians imitated economists in employing 'proxies', that is identified categories they could measure or assess, in place of the elusive lives of the many. That elusive religious experience was tracked through activities that could be counted, measured, or weighed; might religious enthusiasm be measured by the quantities of wax candles offered to churches? Or by the numbers of new members who chose to join religious confraternities?[3] Religious cults and the operations of shrines could similarly be scrutinized anthropologically, as well as through the structure of tales they generated. In *The Holy Greyhound*, Jean-Claude Schmitt traced the cult of St Guinefort over seven centuries, combining a wide range of sources to construct a linear ethnography, a continuous history of devotional practices. The saint was a greyhound, who was deemed since the thirteenth century to have been killed by his owner despite the fact that he had saved the life of the family's child. In at least sixty locations Guinefort was treated as a martyr, and attracted the prayers and offerings of anxious parents. The very documentation that recorded the Church's attempts to extirpate this popular cult—deemed superstitious and idolatrous—provided the historian glimpses into religious sentiment in rural France over some 700 years.[4] The anthropological treatment allowed him to interpret and understand better the beliefs which underpinned the cult which had been thitherto treated as an oddity or an aberration.

The insights developed by French scholars were matched by a worldwide interest, and were soon espoused by scholars of religion all over the world. Americans, Australians, Israeli, and Indian scholars revelled in the possibilities of this new history. One of the most frequently cited articles which launched many a historian's turn to anthropology was the American anthropologist Clifford Geertz's 'Religion as a Cultural System'.[5] Here was the suggestion that 'culture' offered a frame for understanding religion. It invited scholars to identify within each religious culture an inner logic, and to trace it through the narratives and rituals which people enacted collectively, in the search for explanation and meaning in all areas of their lives. This definition was broad and inviting. Each and every historian had to figure out for her specific period and with the source material available to her, how this cultural system was to be identified and understood.

Here was a real challenge to historians, for their traditions offered little guidance. True, the history of religion is implicit in a wide range of narratives from the past, from the myths of ancient Greece to the *hadith* of early Islam, but European preoccupation with the history of religion was often prompted by polemic, and thus concentrated on institutions, leaders, and disputes. The Reformation in Europe inspired two vast historical projects: the *Magdeburg Centuries* (between 1559 and 1574), a collaborative history according to a Protestant world view, and the *Historia ecclesiastica* by Cesare Baronius (1538–1607), which soon countered it from the Catholic side. Though dramatically opposed to each other these histories shared a common sense of what the history of Christianity was: an account of the institutions of the Christian Church, its doctrines, leaders, reformers, and teachers. Such preoccupation determined for centuries the shape of histories to come. Historians of religion had traditionally concentrated on theological developments, institutional histories, the study of law codes and their interpretation, as well as the impact of unique persons—Augustine, Luther—or sweeping movements, like Sufism or the Great Awakening.

While acknowledging the power of institutions to formulate creeds, teach and encourage particular practices, persecute dissenters, teach powerfully, and mould perceptions, historians of religion nowadays seek to understand and chronicle *religious cultures*.[6] This has meant that greater attention is now paid to the experience of the multitude of believers, to the ways in which a religious cosmology—an understanding of the world—structures people's lives, and whereby the most obvious social arrangements gain fresh clarity and authority from their expression in religious language.

If the study of religion is moving outwards, this has also been facilitated by the growing attention paid by historians to groups traditionally deemed 'marginal' or 'deviant'. The age-long concentration on institutions, theology, and doctrine meant that histories of religion were usually made by men, about men, and for men. A few rare examples of prominent women—martyrs of the early Christian Church, mystics, or female devotees—had always received biographical/hagiographical treatment, but few others enjoyed such care. Histories of the Church or of religious orders rarely dwelt on the ideas and experiences of women. Such an absence was the effect of the prevailing patriarchy which shaped—albeit with different emphases—all religions and societies.[7] When the French poet Christine de Pizan (1363–c.1434) railed against the misogynistic tone of most poetry of her time, she asked why no author ever wrote about good, exemplary women: historical figures from classical antiquity and the Bible. So she set out to rectify this absence, and wrote her *Le Livre de la cité des dames* (Book of the city of women) (1405), full of examples of female piety and fortitude.[8] These were historical examples of good conduct, proof of what women could achieve in matters spiritual and moral.

It was the sustained interest of feminist scholars—in their various styles—that led to a breakthrough in attitudes to religious experience. Alongside the power of anthropology and sociology to offer frames of observation and interpretation, I consider the interest in women—and then in gender more broadly, encompassing men and women, femininity and masculinity—to be the second most significant intellectual trend to shape the way historians study religion.[9] The treatment of women religious began with studies of the most prominent, and it directed historians' interest to styles of worship and reflection hitherto ignored. A good example of this shift is the case of the nun Hildegard of Bingen (d. 1179). Hildegard grew up in the Rhineland to become abbess, author, and composer, visionary and ecclesiastical polemicist, writer on medicine and the natural world. The diverse body of her written work, critical editions of which were produced only in the late twentieth century, show her operating in several genres: visionary accounts, theology, medicine, poetry, and music. The discovery of Hildegard has been accompanied by several highly instructive historical insights into religious life, and beyond it too. It demonstrated the complex role of the holy person, as a figure that strove to exit the world and its vices, and yet was so often sought out by followers and admirers, for advice, consolation, and healing. The life of Hildegard also demonstrated the power of visual representation in structuring and communicating religious experiences, since the manuscripts of Hildegard's visions were illustrated with diagrams and images.[10] Moreover, Hildegard was a composer too, and her poetry exemplifies the importance of sound to religious practice, but more. In her antiphons devoted to the Virgin Mary Hildegard displayed a unique awareness of the female body, as a conduit to the divine, as a carrier of the divine, a sensibility unrivalled by others.[11] So inspiring was Hildegard that the monk/priest appointed to serve her community became enthralled by the proximity to so powerful a spiritual personality.

This last point is of great interest. The intellectual rigour that has been brought to the study of women religious has led to close investigations of process by which they became—against the odds—authors, and developed their known style, a creative 'voice'. In some cases the relationships between religious woman and mentor—confessor, kinsman, parish priest—was so close as to suggest something like 'shared' authorship.[12] So the probing of women in religion drew historians' attention to new ways of understanding the relationship between mystic/visionary and the recorder of those experiences. Religious friendships of various kinds—with brother, with confessor, with distant kin or friend through the exchange of letters—appear now as constitutive of the religious experience itself.[13] The language of transcendence and of personal freedom so characteristic of mysticism was thus revealed as a field of social relations, with its own dialectic of outpouring and recapitulation.[14] Even the 'free spirit' Marguerite Porete, who was burnt at the stake in Paris in 1310 for insubordination to her bishop's rulings which demanded that she cease preaching and circulating her book, benefited from the approval of the Franciscan master Geoffrey of Fontaines, a scholar who encouraged her unorthodox yet passionate mysticism.[15]

Growing interest in women, and in the effect of sexual difference, gender—on lives in the past, intersected with other formative trends towards examination of religion in practice, religion in daily life and as a language for the making of social relations. By studying women, the household was opened to view, for within households children learned the tenets of their faith, as well as reading and prayer.[16] The role of women in the transformation of religions—from cult to church, from charisma to institution—has directed the study of early Christianity, of Protestantism, and of Islam. The process by which the religious persuasion of a few was turned into the life-world of the many involved the development of new versions of all the central institutions of social life—marriage and kinship, work, mutual help, and death. All these ideas and practices were deeply marked by sexual difference, and they combined to form patriarchal systems, where the rule of men, especially fathers, guided family and civic life.

Within the privileged households of early Christians, often Roman citizens of high birth, women decreed and developed styles of decorum and devotion, within communities of kindred women.[17] They went on pilgrimage together and sought the support of Christian leaders together: like Athanasius, Ambrose, or Jerome.[18] Many Christian households of late antiquity were led by women, while menfolk remained loyal to the traditional cult of emperors, engrained in rhythms of male education, politics, and friendship. Similarly, throughout the Middle Ages preachers and priests guided parents to teach their children the tenets of faith at home, to familiarize them with prayer and the decorous gestures appropriate for attendance in church. Children were taught the ABC at their mother's knee and the very same book taught them to pray. Through the telling of miracle tales mothers imparted knowledge of the working of grace in the world, and a rich oral lore of incantations armed the child for the encounters with malign demons and the temptations of the flesh.

This 'domestication' of religion has been accompanied by a convergent 'embodiment' of religion. There are long traditions in most religions of praising the feats of bodily endurance—fasts, isolation, enduring of pain—achieved by exemplary persons, even unto death. But embodied religion means much more, and it marks the experience of the many: circumcision of Jewish boys, the long fast of Christian Lent, abstention from meat in ancient Greece and India, celibacy of Catholic priests, and more. Tracking the bodily routines, the ordering of such acts by the rhythm of the calendar and related rituals, opens up worlds of actions and experience, of emotion and creativity.

Training the body allowed for the experience of heightened states of awareness, and was a portal for religious contemplation. The medieval Chinese monastery of Shaolin, founded in the fifth century by an Indian Buddhist monk, developed martial arts as a form of disciplined homage to violent Buddhist deities; in turn, its monks also fought for the emperor, and in protection of their own landed properties.[19] Indeed, the approach to the body has been so powerful that it has offered some historians the key to understanding the power of certain religious cultures. Peter Brown's *The Body and Society: Men Women, and Sexual Renunciation in Early Christianity*[20] described the subtle manner in which some of the strands of late antique lifestyle blended with the urge of renunciation of early Christianity to create an ethos that favoured renunciation of sexuality and control of bodily comportment. Celibacy and fasting offered new types of challenges, occasions for personal and conjugal development, attractive both to elite men and to some women. It is this bodily ethos—taught and embellished by early Christian writers—that offered an alternative lifestyle and drew new converts from among the most privileged and powerful. Caroline Bynum found that almost a thousand years later women of many European cities were drawn to the devotional possibilities of immersion in the images and meanings of a God made Flesh, of a male body without power or resistance, suffering and accepting of its fate.[21] The construction of the divine created the possibilities for personal participation in it.

As the study of religion moved from the predominant consideration of leading figures and literate communities, as it moved from orthodoxy towards marginalized groups—so-called heretics, mystics, or other enthusiasts—some historians expected, even hoped, that women might become more visible. Within frameworks that were at odds with prevailing norms and institutions—patriarchal all—it was expected that women might be more prominent, be able to express themselves. A number of interesting historical studies have demonstrated just how untrue this is. Among the Cathars of Languedoc a strict hierarchy privileged a small group of men, the *perfecti*; few could aspire to the heights of physical purity and spiritual rigour that they attained. Inasmuch as the female body was particularly repugnant in this religion which saw all flesh as evil, women were doubly marginalized.[22] They fared little better within the alternative religion that developed in late medieval England—Lollardy—where reading and interpretation of the vernacular Bible was placed within family and kinship groups, with all the attendant hierarchies of gender they endorsed.[23]

Attention to gender and the body also placed at the centre the experience of those ritual agents—priests—set apart in so many traditions by the training, celibacy, ritual purity, and special garb. Here were men empowered with unique qualities: to augur and divine, to enact mysteries—such as the transubstantiation at the altar during the Catholic mass—to advise and console. New questions are being asked about the tasks such men were required to undertake—mission, instruction, correction—and the resulting social situations they inhabited and subjectivities they experienced.[24]

When attending to practices of the body historians have been obliged to engage in new ways with the material environment of religious experience.[25] The setting of collective ritual as well as private prayer was enhanced and shaped by excitation—or indeed deprivation—of the senses.[26] It was easiest for historians to identify and use the visual sources—and in doing so they are guided in fruitful interlocution with art historians.[27] The objects studied were large and monumental, or small, like prayer beads or amuletic jewellery.[28] The contexts of use stimulated all the senses.[29]

Historians of religious cultures have recently begun a dialogue with the rich world of music. Music was the core of liturgies offered up to God or gods; it had the power to form religious identities, old and new.[30] Congregational singing transcended barriers which separated men and women in the space of worship, it was heard by those who did not belong, and is now appreciated as a powerful component of religious experience in its power to integrate and include as well as its ability to separate and exclude.[31]

Persons draw meaning from the spaces they inhabit, and those spaces in turn interact with sensations—sound, smell, sight. As historians of religion sought to understand the experience of ritual, the rhythms of contemplation, the excitement of pilgrimages, the drama of approaching the sacred within a world profane, space became a subject of study too.[32] While churches, mosques, temples, and synagogues have long been treated as manifestations of architectural knowledge and style, historians now oppose questions of a different nature, about the hierarchies created by space, about states of mind induced in specific settings, like a cloister or a monastic cell. The Dervish lodges of medieval Anatolia—home to Sufi mystics—not only housed these ascetic mystics, but were sites of memory around tombs of holy men, which drew pilgrims, but also separated them by sex. During the period of Mongol hegemony, after 1240, these were centres of Muslim culture, beacons of local identity even for local Christians.[33]

Cities were the setting for a great deal of such religious building. In late Roman antiquity great churches—those which were seats of bishops, cathedrals—were built wherever an administrative centre— a *civitas*—existed. Cities possessed wealth and creative know-how; their markets and civic rituals drew crowds, ready to be informed, chastised, or entertained by preachers. Islam was born within the commercial nexus of Mecca; and as it grew and mobilized tribesmen from the *hijaz* and beyond, with the growing of a veritable Islamic empire, cities remained central to its religious culture, from Mesopotamia to Iberia and beyond.[34] In these cities there were not only venerable mosques, but great schools; commerce also attracted a wide range of people of many faiths and cultures. So cities also saw the staging of religious conversation and disputations.[35]

In Christian Europe too cities were centres for scholarship and display of religious message, indeed of its unique mastery over all other religions. Cathedrals and cathedral schools existed in most large cities, and this concentration of priests and clerks meant that cities were the hub for cultural production and for new forms of religious life.[36] The clerks of Notre Dame Cathedral in Paris in the thirteenth century developed a particularly urbane form of music, the motet, in which a Latin scriptural text was intoned alongside snippets of love poetry of the most mundane and racy quality.[37] The possibilities of paid work in cities also meant that women could gain some autonomy, and support devout religious lives within the community, serving its poor and sick and living a communal life. Such were the beguines of medieval northern Europe—not enclosed nun, nor a woman alone—a new creation at the intersection of urban life and the search for the enhancement of religious life.[38] Even more dramatic was the dialectic manifested between urban wealth and the urban movements for religious perfection through poverty, most notably that led by Francis of Assisi (*c*.1181/2–1226). Urban life fostered conventional religion with its wealth, population, and administrative skills; it also inspired periodic waves of disgust with all that the city had to offer.

Yet all religions—even those which directed people away from renunciation and towards settled and productive conformity—also inspired the 'search for the desert', as individuals and communities were drawn away from hubs of settlement and social life and into silence and loneliness. The organization of space is once more a telling trace of the life-world created in isolation. In the Christian European monastery space was organized by function: places of work, places of worship, places of silence. Historians have sought in the silence not only adherence to the monastic rule, but a field for social interaction and even display. Architecture developed for Cistercian monasteries emphasized simplicity in decoration and welcomed silence in the cloister; yet the cloister was also full of life, with its fountain gently bubbling water, and the symbolism of purity and life it embodies. Even in the silent periods of monastic life an intricate system of signs allowed members to communicate, and even to express complex and colloquial meaning.[39] The same is true of the music of religious life; silence was as expressive and important as sound.

The sounds of religious chant, litanies, and hymn continued to echo long after religious life had ceased. People turned to religious authorities for help in making sense of death, this harshest of realities. In studying death historians now find an entry point into the most compelling narratives and the most treasured rituals of all cultures, even those deemed secular. Religious groups marked the difference between them by their death rituals.[40] Historians of the second half of the twelfth century, motivated perhaps by the aftermath of Holocaust and destruction, sought to understand the trails of memory. They developed nuanced ways of tracing commemoration and oblivion, and of relating these to collective and individual identities.[41]

The interest in religious material culture, in the bodily, sense-related experience of religion, also directed attention to memory. Religious ritual left a legacy of memory: the smell and sounds of the sacraments, the hardships and adventures of pilgrimage, and the experience of proximity to holy relics in sacred places. An intense religious experience could be captured in a keepsake—a phial of holy water, a badge from a pilgrimage site, or a piece of stone chopped off a rock.[42] Memory of one religion could create the ground for the reception of a new one. It is no coincidence that the site which became—and still is—one of the greatest Catholic pilgrimage sites, and from which emerged a powerful devotion—the Our Lady of Guadalupe—developed at a holy site on the Hill of Tepeyac.[43] The dramatic, and painful, displacement of one religion by another produced forms of absorption and resistance, and above all an inevitable admixture of elements from both. Historians of religion attend to such now not as 'contamination' or 'residue', but as evidence that the cultural processes of a new cosmology can, even must, be related to pre-existing understandings of the world. Images of the Virgin Mary in the Andes drew upon local and indigenous cultural resources, canons of beauty, and holiness. In a similar fashion a thousand years earlier Christians of Egypt blended the Virgin Mary with the much-loved figure of the beneficent goddess Isis.[44]

Away from overriding commitment to the foundational wholeness of religions, freed from the desire to argue for their coherence or consistency of vision, historians have become increasingly adept at identifying and chronicling the many ways in which religious cultures draw upon others, and often owe a great deal to the very religions with which their relations are most vexed. Daniel Boyarin and Israel Yuval have drawn attention in their studies to the many imprints which the polemic between Judaism and emergent Christianity left upon core values such as martyrdom and celibacy within those religious cultures.[45]

Historians' attention to material culture and social practices has also shown that in the search for health and consolation people readily transgressed official barriers between religions. Protestants persisted in pilgrimage habits to Catholic shrines in Europe and Muslims visited Christian shrines in the Near East. Study of mixed religious communities—'messy' categories which historians have tended to neglect—now shows a great deal of accommodation. A single cave in the outskirts of Jerusalem was imagined by Jews, Christians, and Muslims all as the tomb of a holy woman, Pelagia, and was visited by members of each religion, each with its own narrative on the site's essential holiness.[46] Shrines of the Virgin Mary in the Near East attracted Orthodox Christians, Muslims, and European Christians too.[47] Protestants tolerated the art of Catholics in the churches of great cities, and there was frequent intermarriage between Catholics and Protestants in the Low Countries.[48] Yet historians must be wary, for as they rightly paint the historical landscape full of hues, showing up the blended mixture and mutual fascination between members of differing religious cultures, this worthwhile historical insight should not obscure the different emphases, indeed the polemical emphases, which prevailed and developed in shared sites.

Historians are attuned to the possibilities of shared and interlocking heritages even across official lines of religious and ethnic adherence. Shared sites are methodologically enticing as they offer a neat focus for enquiry, but fields of interaction and interdependence between religious cultures can be broader.[49] There were rules of adherence and competition; there was clearly a social 'cost' to religious *métissage*, the blending and cross-fertilization of traditions, especially when they usually existed in conflict with each other.[50] Laws of marriage, inquisitorial scrutiny, codes of purity, denial of charity or burial to members who exhibited a willingness to cross boundaries, all of these combined as a countervailing force which regimented and attempted to keep identities uniform, and loyalties focused on a single faith. In search of the making of identity historians now pay attention to processes of conversion by individuals and groups. Alert to the effects of proselytization and the threat of violence, but also to the enticement of another's religion, conversion is now deemed not a moment of 'failure' in a religious system, of confusion around identity, but rather a moment that is rich and revealing, even when it is associated with pain and even violence.[51] Conversion is sometimes articulated by the convert in texts which explain the process of inner transformation,[52] but it also prompted reactions from the group abandoned as well as the group joined. The Peruvian writer and soldier (of mixed Inca/Spanish parentage) Garcilaso de la Vega (*c.*1539–1616) described with disapproval an Andean convert at prayer. As he prayed in a Dominican church, which had once been the imperial sanctuary of the Inca Sun God, the convert addressed the sacrament 'Pachacamac', and the image of Mary 'Mother of God'. Gracilaso doubted the sincerity of the convert's prayer, offered in traditional invocations. Such were the questions that had animated debate and suspicion in Spain, where so much conversion followed mass violence. This awareness prompted doubt in the birth of 'new Christians', in the fulfilment of Christian mission; it also sullied those relations which Christians were meant to share, with suspicion and even a palpable disgust.[53]

Political and religious institutions coincided in the dynastic empire of late medieval Spain, and within them a powerful drive towards 'purification' was launched, with the aid of an investigative inquisition, and the tool of mass expulsion of both Jews and Muslims.[54] Similarly, in other dynastic polities, like England, France, or the Japanese shogunates—legislation and propaganda could effectively combine into campaigns of religious purity, which tolerated as lesser subjects those—Jews, Catholics or Protestants in turn, Buddhists—who did not belong.

Historians of religion are also finding ways into the vast realms of action, the *political*. Some thinkers have suggested that modern politics is but the re-expression of what had historically been considered as religion. Many world religions make powerful claims for their location in the public realms: in early Islam the roles of sultan and khalif represented a division of labour but this was a vexed separation, which another Islamic empire, the Ottoman, dispensed with altogether. While European Jewish communities had no political autonomy, their leaders—rabbinic scholars—often combined judicial, diplomatic, ritual, and moral authority. Moreover, the field of *politics* has been redefined by historians to include a wide range of acts and representations of power and authority: from tracts on government to rituals of coronation, from urban processions to the conduct of elections. In many religious traditions and for vast periods the predominant language in which politics was discussed and expressed was indeed the religious idiom. Notions of justice and charity, of reward and punishment—domains of actions by the state or political elites—were articulated in the language of religion.

Historians have been inventive and innovative in identifying sources which allow for an exploration of this nexus. A good example is the *imaret*—the soup kitchen endowed in 1558 by Hurrem Sultan, wife of Süleiman I, in Jerusalem. This institution offered the deserving recipients a ladle of soup and a loaf of bread at each meal, and a meat stew on Fridays. It was a religious charity—*waqf*—and a vestige of Ottoman presence and munificence. Every city with an *imaret* was marked as an Ottoman city, enjoying the charity and effective administration of a Muslim ruler. Here was the making of community and of political loyalty with the charitable soup offered not only to the poor, but to students, officials, and emissaries.[55]

The city has indeed become the forum for discussions of the civic dimensions of religion, and we have already considered its importance for religious creativity and interaction.[56] In cities politics was palpable in many forms: in the monuments of self-governing republics, in the capitals of kings and emperors, and in the places of devotion which brought worship into city squares and neighbourhoods: mosques or chapels, temples or cathedrals. It is also evident that polities drew upon the powerful stock of religious imagery: representations of virtue, of the sacred, of reward and punishment. Indeed, a ceremony like a coronation, or like a thanksgiving after a victory in battle, cannot be defined as belonging to a single sphere—political or religious. These examples demonstrate how supple and open minded the historians of religion must be.

It is significant that historians of religion now aim to understand it in the broadest contexts of politics and collective action on the one hand, and the subjectivity of experience, on the other. It is only when religion is understood as clusters of ideas and practices expressed and embedded within material objects, lived as stimuli to the senses, prompting memory and securing identity, that historians will be able to contribute to the understanding and interpretation of religion throughout the world—near and far, alluring and threatening. The approaches now used by historians help understand religions not as temporal avenues to the divine, not as expressions of sanctity within the mundane world, but as cultural forms constitutive of the identities of individuals and groups. By doing so, historians of religious cultures are contributing to the making and remaking of history in important and inspiring ways.

15. Egyptian blue glazed composition doll (?), 18th Dynasty. © by permission of the Trustees of the British Museum

15 Emotions

EIKO IKEGAMI

> The emotions are all those feelings that so change men as to affect
> their judgments, and that are also attended by pain or pleasure. Such
> are anger, pity, fear and the like, with their opposites.
>
> (Aristotle, *Rhetoric*[1])

Anger, joy, shame, jealousy, pity, fear, and love—whatever you name them, emotions are felt immediately by individuals as realistic internal forces. Emotion-driven human actions, however, often result in serious consequences for an individual's personal or social life. Positive emotions make people feel worthy of life; at the same time, emotions also sometimes push them to desire death. Emotions sometimes induce individuals to perform compassionate or altruistic behaviors. Emotions are also frequently perceived as the causes of all kinds of violence, from small-scale crimes of passion to contemporary instances of collective mob violence and ethnic cleansing. People in the past as well as now know intuitively the importance and danger of emotions in their personal and corporate lives.[2]

I

The English word *emotion* is derived from the Latin verb *emovere*, a compound of the preposition *ex* (out of) and *movere* (to move). *Emovere* can be translated as 'to remove' or 'to move out from' or 'to move away'. In any case, it conveys the sense of emotions as propulsive or leading to action or movement of some kind. In fact, since the dawn of civilization, writers and storytellers have observed the intensity of emotional conflicts in human life, and have been engaged in making sense of the mysterious power of emotions. In ancient Greece, the poet of the *Iliad* sang of the ruinous anger of a warrior elite who sought honor in battle and dared to risk death. At the same time, Homer also underscored the emotional vulnerability of the heroes—their fear and remorse in facing their uncontrollable fates. The *Iliad* painfully depicted the feelings of these Bronze Age warriors confronting their human mortality.

People in ancient times also recognized the existence of quieter and subtle emotional expressions such as manifestations of human longing for love and empathy. The cultivation of passive or compassionate emotions, which might be better called sentiments or feelings, also developed refined forms of expression in ancient civilizations. The oldest Japanese anthology of poetry, dating from the Nara period in the eighth century and known as Manyōshū (Collection of ten thousand leaves),[3] offers us the poetic voices of lowly soldiers—mostly peasants conscripted from the eastern regions of Japan to serve in stations in remote outposts in the south. These poems are known as the frontier guards (*sakimori*) poems. Many *sakimori* lamented their loneliness and sorrow while delicately expressing their emotions of longing for their wives and children left behind. From ancient times, exchanging poetry became an important means of sociability in Japan; it became a method of cultivating the emotions and enriching one's social life. The following famous passage is from the preface (*Kanajo*) to the *Kokin wakashū*, an anthology of *waka* poetry that appeared at the beginning of the tenth century AD.

Japanese poetry has the human heart as seed and myriads of words as leaves. It comes into being when individuals use the seen and the heard to give voice to feelings aroused by the innumerable events in their lives. The song of the warbler among the blossoms, the voice of the frog dwelling in the water— these teach us that every living creature sings. It is song that moves heaven and earth without effort, stirs emotions in the invisible spirits and gods, brings harmony to the relations between men and women, and tames the hearts of fierce warriors.[4]

This passage suggests that within an overall world view shaped by animism, early Japanese people self-consciously developed a sophisticated method of emotional control that used poetry as a medium of cultivating sentiments and sociability. Clearly, the critical importance of emotional life has been a given across human cultures for millennia; cultural methods of channeling emotion may differ across time and place, but they have provided remarkably complex and refined methods to govern emotion.

In fact, it is difficult to state that past methods of controlling emotion are less refined or sophisticated than modern alternatives. There are only different modes of channeling feeling across times and cultures. For example, it is hard to maintain that pre-modern uses of poetry to navigate feelings are less complex than supposed 'modern' methods of controlling emotion through rational/legal regulations and internalization of self-control. Barbara H. Rosenwein, a historian of medieval Europe, is a vocal opponent of the view that regards increasing control of emotion as a sign of modernity while assuming that pre-modern people's emotional lives were simpler and less restrained. She attributes this misconception primarily to Johan Huizinga's *The Waning of the Middle Ages*, first published in 1919, in which the Dutch historian spoke of the childlike nature of medieval emotional life, its exhibition of a perpetual oscillation between cruelty and pious tenderness; Huizinga's view of medieval emotion influenced a number of such prominent historical writers as Lucian Febvre, Marc Bloch, and Norbert Elias.[5]

Norbert Elias's work on the civilizing process[6] is now considered the classic statement of a sociological approach to the transformation of emotional cultures in the West; his work also has been increasingly influential among historians for the past two decades. In his *Civilizing Process*, Elias traced the ways in which post-medieval European standards regarding violence, the discharge or discussion of bodily functions, table manners, and forms of speech were gradually transformed into modern 'civility', with the early modern period as the turning point. Elias attempted to describe the entwined processes of state formation, increasing network complexity, and social expectations of individual self-control of emotion in Western Europe. For example, Elias noted that medieval people usually blew their noses into their fingers; therefore etiquette manuals recommended blowing one's nose into the fingers of the left hand when one ate, while taking meat from the common dish with the right. As a medieval historian, Rosenwein is particularly critical of Elias's description of medieval European emotional culture as unrefined in comparison with that of the early modern period; she also regards his grand narrative of the history of increasing emotional self-restraint in the West as problematic.

In fact, when I studied the polite arts and aesthetic ways of sociability from late medieval to early modern periods, I found that Japanese texts of etiquette instructions in manner books are not very different from each other.[7] In that sense, there was no definite turning point for increasing self-constraint reflected in the text of etiquette books in Japan, unlike Norbert Elias's famous thesis in *Civilizing Process*. In contrast to Elias's description of medieval table manners as rather rough and unsophisticated even among the aristocracy, late medieval Japanese courtiers already served food with individualized dishes and utensils, and they did not have to be advised against blowing their noses into their fingers or onto their sleeves, since such behaviors would never even occur to them. Elias outlined a grand narrative of an increase in self-control and regulation of human interactions in Western societies during the early modern period as the turning point for emotional self-control, but that narrative is not a universal story. Nonetheless, it does not mean that there was no cultural transformation in navigating and controlling sentiments. The whole social and cultural context of transmitting and educating proper ways of conduct was apparently changing in early modern Japan. At that time commercial publishing and various expanding networks of learning polite arts and poetry created distinctive cultural styles and modes for dealing with emotions. As a consequence, new aesthetic ways of socializing and navigating emotions became popularized in early modern Japan. And this development of educating sentiments had a deep political implication in Japanese history. Since emotions are critically related to human bonds and conflicts, power politics naturally enters the dynamics of navigating sentiments. Thus, although it is certainly misleading to assume a simple picture of the past in which people had fewer emotional constraints, it does not mean that a large-scale transformation of emotional culture cannot be a subject for historians.

Nonetheless, compared to political, social, and cultural history, the history of human emotion remains a less clearly defined field. The epistemological difficulty of defining emotion plays a role. Contemporary historians must confront the elusive nature of emotions as experienced in order to write about the emotions of people in the past. In this context, the present chapter will highlight four aspects that are important in order to study the dynamics of emotion cultures in history; (1) the internal and external dimensions of emotions; (2) mind/

body dualism and theories of emotion; (3) emotions and cultures; (4) emotions, politics, and social change. Since these dimensions overlap with one another, I will pay particular attention to the close interconnections among these four dimensions.

II

Although emotions are immediate and obvious as subjective experiences, once we try to define them conceptually, they tend to evade our grasp. One particular question that has arisen concerns the boundary of emotions and not-emotions. One could say that emotions are like the radiant colors of many tropical fish, vivid and immediate while in the water, as the anthropologist Julian Pitt-Rivers once phrased them in regard to sentiments of honor and shame; however, they 'fade once they are taken from the water, the concepts which compose such a system retain their exact significance only within the environment of the society which nurtures them and which resolves, thanks to its internal structuring, their conflicts with each other'.[8] Anthropologists and sociologists as well as historians are inclined to observe emotions 'in water', so to speak, to study them *not in isolation but to observe them within the social, cultural, and cognitive contexts in which they are manifested.*[9] What makes the matter even more complex is that the subject's cognitions and the expression of his or her own emotion are already seen in a looking glass. We can only guess another person's emotion from such external expressions as words, gestures, and actions; these manifestations of emotions are then recognized and translated through the subject's cognitions, values, and culture. Those of us who try to understand the other's emotion also have our own 'water', as we tend to look at ourselves in a mirror in order to understand others. Anthropologists are quick to understand the complexity of this issue because they are constantly obliged to study other cultures. Observations and interpretations of emotions in people of previous generations, however, are also difficult tasks for historians. We are far more at home in our own particular emotional culture; we look through cultural filters of our own.

Emotions also depend on evaluations, and the criteria for such evaluations are defined culturally, socially, and politically. The individual's judgment as to what is important to him or her hinges on the norms and cultural conventions of society. Hence emotions are linked to one's internality as well to one's externality. Echoing the ideas of the ancient Greek Stoics, the contemporary philosopher Martha C. Nussbaum advanced her thesis that emotions are judgments of values ascribed to objects outside one's full control. 'Emotions, I shall argue,' she noted, 'that involve judgments about important things, judgments in which, appraising an external object as salient for our own well-being, we acknowledge our own neediness and incompleteness before parts of the world that we do not fully control'.[10] For example, a person may become angry when a normative assumption, usually taken for granted, is questioned. If we experience a strong emotion when we judge something as critical to our well-being, there will be some assessment of value preceding the experience of the emotion. This type of evaluation occurs within a social environment, including culture. In this sense, emotion is closely associated with society and culture. The culture surrounding an emotion can be seen as a bridge between individual aspirations and social expectations. Therefore, the history of human feeling cannot be studied adequately if it is based on a conceptual dualism that distinguishes sharply between emotion and reason, body and mind, self and society, feeling and cognition, nature and culture, and also internality and externality.

Since these mutually constitutive aspects of subjectivity and objectivity render the social criteria of judgments in part fluid and open, the strategy of the individual also matters. Building on his early fieldwork with the honor-ridden culture of Algeria, Pierre Bourdieu focused on the close connection between emotions/dispositions on the one hand and strategic actions on the other.[11] He emphasized the mutual dependency of subjectivity and objectivity in such emotion-laden social exchanges as making a point of honor; in such social exchanges Bourdieu noted that 'even the most strictly ritualized exchanges... have room for strategies' (15). The individual's strategy—that is, an intentional choice on the subject's part that is usually considered to belong to the realm of practical reason—is in fact closely connected to the realm of emotions. In fact, the unpredictability of social exchanges in which an individual's strategy matters but is never fully able to control the situation gives rise to fear of an uncertain future. This kind of concern led Bourdieu to propose the notion of *habitus*, a mental structure in which ideas, cultural norms, emotions, and individual strategies are mutually constitutive.

Furthermore, a curious aspect of studying human emotion is that an emotion is clearly felt 'inside', but it can also manifest outwardly in recurrent patterns of personal or collective behavior. In this sense, emotion can be considered to have an institutional aspect; put slightly differently, we recognize the presence of various 'emotional cultures'.

III

We should note, however, that emotions have not always been seen and studied in that way. An individualist or isolationist approach to human emotions constitutes an important trend in modernist and scientific views of emotions. Furthermore, there are influential views of emotion that consider it from the perspective of a physical/mental dualism in both scholarly and scientific studies as well as in popular understanding in contemporary Western thinking. Historians should be conscious of the presence of such mental filters, which can unconsciously affect one's views of the past as well as of other contemporary cultures.

From the dawn of classical civilizations in the West, a tendency developed to conceive reason as the opposite of and superior to emotion. Plato's famous hostility to poets is related to this dichotomy; he clearly takes the side of reasoned discourse when he refers to 'an old quarrel between philosophy and poetry' (*Republic*, 607b). Elsewhere, he also says that if a skillful dramatic poet comes to visit an ideal city, 'we should send him away to another city' because of the negative social influence of drama (39 8a). Plato's disapproval of poetry stands in striking contrast to the traditional Japanese conception of poetry mentioned earlier. To be sure, Plato's position did not reflect the dominant view of classical Greece either. Rather it was expressed in a context within which, in the words of Iris Murdoch, the poets 'existed, as well as prophets and sages, long before the emergence of philosophers, and were the traditional purveyors of theological and cosmological information.'[12]

European intellectual history on the studies of emotion also developed under the strong influence of a dualistic view of the relationship between mind and body. From the early modern period in Europe, however, the dichotomous separation of reason and emotion gained renewed strength. The rising scientific view of human feeling attributed emotions to biological functions while considering cognitive functions distinct within the workings of the mind. René Descartes' metaphysical distinction between the physical and mental dimensions in understanding the whole nature of human beings was most influential in this regard. To be sure, philosophical and analytical discourses on emotions in relation to the human body and mind date as far back as the age of Plato and Aristotle. In particular, Aristotle's view of emotions, a remarkably well-balanced set of insights, does not draw sharp distinctions among emotions, cognitive factors, and physical sensations. Since the seventeenth century, as D. M. Gross observes,[13] European theories of emotions beginning with Descartes tend to emphasize the close connection between emotions and the physical aspects of human being. Although the long-standing influence of Aristotle, who emphasized both individual and social aspects of emotions, persisted in the West, a new epistemological break began to create a bifurcation in theories of emotion. Within a dualistic view of mind and body, emotions then became more closely associated with body, the inferior realm, while reasoned cognitive investigations were associated with the mind. Alison M. Jaggar, a feminist philosopher, observes that 'Typically, although again not invariably, the rational has been contrasted with the emotional, the cultural, the universal, the public, and the male, whereas emotion has been associated with the irrational, the physical, the natural, the particular, the private, and of course, the female.'[14]

This bifurcation in studies of emotions had a significant impact on Anglo-American and continental European popular views of emotions. For example, there is a famous nineteenth-century legal case in the United States involving a crime of passion that was intimately linked to this Cartesian dualism and scientific views of emotions, while a more traditional and communal understanding of emotions related to masculine honor and gender relations also remained strong.

On a quiet Sunday afternoon in February 1859, Daniel Sickles, a 39-year-old prominent leader of the Democratic Party, shot and killed his 22-year-old wife's lover, Philip Barton Key, in Washington, DC. Key was a friend of the killer and also a well-connected political figure in Washington society. The Italian opera-like setting among political celebrities in the nation's capital made the case one of the most visible scandals of the time. Several capable lawyers were assembled to defend Sickles.

Sickles's lawyers constructed a powerful argument for the defendant. The main line of their defense was to advance the point that Sickles was a respectable man carried away by an emotional whirlwind. No aspect of his cultured nature could restrain the force of jealousy because jealous rage is an emotion programmed into human males by God. Sickles's lawyer claimed that 'Jealousy is the rage of a man.' 'When once it has entered within his breast, he has to yield to an instinct which the Almighty has implanted in every animal or creature that crawls the earth.... when I examine the characteristics of the birds that move about in the air, I find the jealousy of the bird incites him to inflict death upon the stranger that invades his nest.'[15] Once an emotion has been assigned to the realm of physicality, an instant and irresistible but inferior realm, the defense can make the forceful claim that, first, Sickles's action was not planned; second, a temporary seizure by jealousy does not compromise the respectable quality of his mind. The burst of emotions can drive individuals to forget themselves or to claim to lose self-control. The case of Sickles became widely known in legal history as the first use of a plea of temporary insanity for the criminal defendant and the appeal to an unwritten law to justify homicide. The dualistic view of body and mind combined with the prevailing traditional view of masculinity and community control of family relations, and the elitist masculine code of honor that demanded vindication—all were merged to produce the curious legal defense of this crime of passion.

Peter Sterns in his study of jealousy in American history contends that such a marriage of modernist and traditionalist mentalities was soon replaced, from the late nineteenth to the early twentieth century, by a pure modernist form, in which 'true love' was intentionally separated from straightforward expressions of honorific passions and jealousy and from communal control of family relations.[16] This notion of romantic love was coupled with a new assignment of the highest value to the imagined true or pure selfhood. This alternative view of the self, which introduces a dichotomy between a relatively unimportant external self and an inner 'true' self, began to constitute a new dominant cultural framework for navigating sentiments.

On its surface, the case of Sickles simply looks like a traditional instance of honorific elitist male sentiments calling on the Almighty as the source of justification. Beneath the words, however, the logic of Sickles's defense attorney amazingly resembles Charles Darwin's logic of emotion theory, published a few decades later in his *Emotional Expressions of Man and Animals* (1872). Darwin's theory articulated emotions as valuable mechanisms for self-preservation. In Darwin's account, emotions are instinctive reactions with physical and biological bases. Given the premise of early modern bifurcation, the late nineteenth century saw the rise of scientific studies of emotions. William James—generally considered a pioneer of modern psychological theories of emotion—in his *What Is an Emotion* (1884) advanced an influential formulation that defines emotions primarily as sensations caused by physical disturbances. It was amplified into what is now known as the James–Lang theory: emotions are feelings caused by changes in bodily conditions, as James articulated, 'We feel sorry because we cry, angry because we strike, afraid because we tremble, and not that we cry, strike, or tremble, because we are sorry, angry, or fearful, as the case may be.'[17]

James's theory has already been sharply criticized by more recent psychologists, cognitive scientists, neurologists, brain scientists, and evolutionary biologists. For example, psychologists have found intimate connections between cognition and emotion to such a degree as to consider, as Isen and Diamond remarked, that emotions resemble 'overlearned cognitions', and that the occurrence of seemingly automatic processes may sometimes result from earlier decisions to deploy one's attention elsewhere.[18] In fact conventional perceptions that regard emotions as exclusively individual phenomena leave the study of emotion primarily to philosophers, neurologists, psychologists, psychiatrists, and biologists. Without rejecting biological or medical studies of a physical basis for emotion, historians and sociologists may easily locate distinctive terrains of research in which cognitions, cultures, values, and social institutions play important roles. Contemporary neuroscientists may identify the exact physical mechanisms and the particular loci in the brain that give rise to certain emotions. But while the brain may register and record a human emotion, it is only through the lens of culture that the individual can express that feeling to others. We can study only such cultural manifestations of emotions through the looking glasses of various cultures—those of people in the past, but also those of our own time when we try to observe the past. It is not surprising, therefore, that scholars tend to handle the history of emotions, not in isolation, but within the context of cultural, political, and social history.

The history of bifurcated discourse in the description of emotion presents a challenge to historians in terms of historical imagination in understanding emotion cultures of the past. It is not only ordinary people in contemporary Western societies, but also scholars who may be influenced by this history, as we might be unconsciously wearing a particular looking glass as the product of the post-bifurcation era.[19]

IV

The same problem can manifest even more acutely when scholars with this particular looking glass study the emotion culture of other societies. That was quite possibly the problem behind the anthropologist Ruth Benedict's iconographic description of Japanese emotional culture, *The Chrysanthemum and the Sword*. The book was written during the Second World War with the explicit goal of studying 'the most alien enemy the United States ever fought' (1).[20] In fact, Benedict was trying to study the emotion culture of an enemy. The Japanese soldier looked loyal, obedient, and conformist, but he was perceived as curiously aggressive and violent. She thought it was the Japanese culture of shame compared to 'our' Christian culture of guilt that holds the key to understanding the Japanese emotion culture of the pre-war period. She did interview Japanese Americans who were apparently constrained by the exigencies of the wartime situation. Nonetheless, the result of Benedict's research produced an iconographic book on Japanese culture published after the war that greatly influenced the Western view of Japanese culture. According to Benedict, the Japanese culture of shame conditioned Japanese people to be obedient to social norms and duties while Westerners were taught to develop an internalized sense of sin in a culture based on guilt.

Benedict thought that shame-based cultures rely on external sanctions while guilt-based cultures use an internalized conviction of sin, a totally different way of navigating emotion. Although Benedict never discussed it, she was raised in a culture that valued internalization and individualization of emotional control. Benedict grew up in a post-bifurcation nominally Christian culture in the United States, where the term *shame* was usually associated with a primarily passive emotion external to the true self. She also tacitly accepted the distinction between a core true self and a comparatively superficial social self. The core true self remains in the domain of the internal mind, whereas the more social and interactive self resides in the domain of an external self. The latter self is comparatively shallow compared to the 'true' self. In contrast, shame represented an emotional culture Benedict considered passive and external. Consequently, Benedict automatically assumed that her respondents' reference to shame and duties concerned matters external to the self. But she certainly also encountered more spontaneous, less passive aspects of Japanese emotional expression. She regarded them as expressions of a 'contradictory character' in Japanese people stemming from a shame-based culture; 'the Japanese are, to the highest degree, both aggressive and unaggressive.' Her discourse offers a multilayered set of dichotomies: shame/external/other versus guilt/internal/Westerners.[21] Just like Huizinga's view of medieval people as childlike, simple, and easily angered people, Benedict described Japanese people as inherently contradictory, emotionally passive but also often aggressive and warlike.

Shame in modern Anglo-American usage has a strongly negative connotation. It also often implies a passive emotion as a reaction to external evaluation. To impose this image onto other cultures' usage of shame, however, may obscure the complexity and dynamics of this notion. For example, pre-modern Japanese samurai culture indicates that the notion of shame can be a powerful public concept while it was rooted in the innermost depth of an individual's dignity. By bridging individual aspirations and social expectations, shame in the samurai culture presents us with the complexity of interactive relationships between the self and society. Their honorific sentiments were expressed by the constellation of words such as *na* (name), *meiyo* (honor), *haji* (shame), *chijyoku* (shame), *iji* (pride), and *mengoku* (face). Within this cultural complex of honor, knowing shame (*haji*) meant not simply the external concern of their honorific status, but a matter of pride and dignity connected to an internal evaluation in the light of their own behavioral principles.[22]

'Shame (*haji*) is the most important word in a samurai's lexicon. Nothing is more shameful than not understanding shame,' a young samurai named Yoshida Shōin (1830–59) noted in his prison lecture notes.[23] By this time, Japan had been peacefully ruled by the Tokugawa shogunate (1603–1868) for more than two centuries. Shôin's prison lecture continued in this way; 'On one occasion someone asked me: Which is more serious, crime (tsumi) or shame (haji)? I answered: Crime belongs to the body, but shame lies in the soul.... Now, people at the grass-roots level discuss national politics and criticize office-holders. This kind of behavior is a crime because it is not the job of ordinary people, and it is not their prescribed role in society. However, if you ask about their internal motivation and find that they are worried about the future of the nation, and have tried to ask questions about its legitimacy—their behavior is less culpable.'

Shōin's contrast between shame and crime is not a theory of emotions but an effective political statement in the making that reframed the meaning of shame as an ideology of political activism. Using the highly accepted culture of honor and shame among the samurai, Shōin considered the individual's inner principle as the ultimate decision maker for defining shame—much higher than the societal definition of shame. Shame is by no means external only. Rather, its usage includes an internal dimension close to the connotations of *guilt* in English. Shōin's formulation mentioned above, however, cannot be understood without considering the context of contemporary politics and Shōin's own public 'crime' under the law of the shogunate—namely his attempt to go abroad. In fact Shōin successfully reframed the culture of honorific emotion in nineteenth-century Japan as a cultural justification of political activism and moral autonomy. After his death by execution, his students became political activists against the shogunate in the context of rising nationalism reacting to the threat of Western imperialism. Note the fact that he did not encourage combat with the shogunate, but simply asked his students to be truthful to their inner-felt emotion. Reframing the notion of shame is thus critically related to the navigation of emotion culture that justified political actions based on moral autonomy.[24]

The above examples from Japan should not be taken as differences between East and West, however. Ancient Greece and Rome developed a complex culture of shame and honor as a cultural mechanism of navigating emotion with internal depth. Bernard William observes,[25] 'The silly mistake is to suppose that the reactions of shame depend simply on being found out, that the feeling behind every decision or thought that is governed by shame is literally and immediately the fear of being seen' (81). 'By the late fifth century the Greeks had developed their own distinction between a shame that merely followed public opinion and a shame that expressed inner personal conviction' (95). He analyzed the usage of shame in Homeric society; however, his philosophical analysis also re-examines the notions of guilt and shame in modern usage and claims that shame and guilt are in fact not contrasting notions but are mutually connected in the practice of using imagined others. Although ancient Greek does not have an equivalent word for *guilt*, usages of shame and honor cover inner moral concerns. 'One way in which we can be helped by the Greek conception that brings (something like) guilt under a wider conception of (something more than) shame is that it can give us a wiser understanding of the connection between guilt and shame themselves' (92). By undertaking a complex re-examination of shame and guilt among the ancient Greeks as well as in contemporary moral consciousness, William paradoxically demonstrated a profound similarity between the emotional and moral life of contemporary and ancient Greeks.

These comparative examples show that lexicons of emotion such as 'shame' have manifested different meanings in various cultural contexts. Elitist cultures of honor maintained by exclusive social groups are becoming so rare in the contemporary world that it is rather difficult for us to imagine and to reconstruct any older forms of honor that had explicit internal components and salient political dimensions. In contrast, the analysis of the ancient Greek culture of shame reveals the depth of this culture; it also reminds us to scrutinize our binary conception of shame and honor. In using the practices of different emotional cultures as a mirror, we are able to scrutinize our own looking glass that we are unconsciously wearing.

V

We must also note that expressions, practices, and control methods of emotions may be very different even within the same linguistic and/or ethnic context; for example, the same word that represents emotion might be applied differently to people of different classes, genders, and other social categories; it can also be used differently in various times and places. In the actual interactional process in which an emotion is triggered, the individual's strategic choice of emotional expressions and actions also plays a role toward the outcome of the conflict. In such a strategic action, unequal distributions of power among inter-acting parties are important considerations for the game of emotions. The process of navigating and cultivating sentiments has been located within the political dynamics.

Ethnographers tend to encounter a similar challenge in trying to interpret obscure words and actions of people, and the political mean-ing of emotional expressions in the field. Let me take an example of ethnography of shame and honor from the Middle East. In *Veiled Sen-timents: Honor and Poetry in a Bedouin Society*,[26] Lila Abu-Lughod, an American anthropologist, reports on her fieldwork at a Bedouin com-munity. Awlad 'Ali Bedouin culture is distinctive in its social uses of poetry as a method of navigating sentiments. Abu-Lughod described delicate practices of navigating and controlling sentiments of honor through the use of oral poetry as a medium of expressing emotions. To be sure, the tradition of honorific oral exchanges of Arabic poetry is well known. Clifford Geertz once discussed the intensely political nature of Arabic communal poetry in Morocco in which performan-ces in poetry exchanges are often representing and controlling fights among individuals and rival families.[27] Steven C. Caton's ethnography of oral poetry among tribal men in North Yemen covers an area where poetic exchanges are deeply implicated in the context of challenges and accumulation of points of honor for individuals and communi-ties.[28] However, these examples are primarily of public uses of poetry among male members of communities expressing competitive and masculine sentiments of honor. Oral exchange of poetry often con-cerns not only political competition of individuals but also the honor-ific status of collectivities such as a family and clan.

Abu-Lughod gained an insider perspective as she was taken up in the family of the chief as a daughter of a respected Arab man. Through her socialization with women and men in the community, she found that 'one cannot talk about Awlad 'Ali personal life without talking about poetry, that vital and highly valued expressive form that carries such moving messages about the life of sentiment' (171). She observed evocative, honorific but subtle tender sentiments among people in this community where poetry was used 'to express special sentiments, sentiments radically different from those they express about the same situation using nonpoetic language' (186). For example, an emotion resulting from rejected love might be handled with the pattern of dual responses in tension; public displays of honor ideals in non-poetic discourse, and emotional responses of grief and pain personally expressed by poems.

Abu-Lughod pays attention to social structural dominations and power relations among genders in this community in decoding its emotional culture. There are competing principles of bonds in this community: bonds made by sexuality and marriage and bonds made by the authority and control of elder agnates. Sexual bonds including marriage in principle threaten the existing hierarchy of the community as it provides a competing principle of social bonds. This complicates the relationship between men and women as 'sexual desire is an internal force that is difficult to master, thus representing a potent challenge to one of the keystones of honor, self-control.... Sexuality can lead to dependency, which is inimical to the highest honor-linked value, independence' (148). It is in this context that women support the modesty code, not to show any sexual desire and emotional attachments to the sexual partner, even to one's husband; it would become a strategy of empowerment to increase their respectability and power in this social system.[29] People of Awlad 'Ali used poetry as a means to communicate feelings of defiance against the dominant structure and norms of their own society. Hence, navigating sentiments represents the complex dual political dynamics of this small, tightly connected community. Abu-Lughod's analysis reminds us of the need for sensitivity to social category-specific and context-specific practices of emotion cultures.

The social uses of poetry as interactional rituals are not a monopoly of the Arab world. Peter Burke has reported on the collective dimension of popular poetry in early modern Europe, recited in organizations of craftsmen as an expression of civic solidarities and 'the cultural equivalent of the citizen-militia'.[30] The oral citation of poetry creates a ritual space, which encourages the making of bonds and generates intimacy among members of groups.

In contrast, pre-modern Japanese poetry not only became a means of expressing delicate sentiments but also constituted important tools for socializing with strangers and different kinds of people. A poet of the fifteenth century once described the virtue of participating in sessions of linked verse as follows: 'Even when we are meeting others for the first time, once we get into the seated world of linked poetry together, we feel an intimacy with one another. It is only in this way of linked poetry that older people do not feel uncomfortable socializing with their juniors, and that those of noble birth do not shun their social inferiors.'[31] Poetry creates numerous unofficial publics that permit manifestations of delicate personal sentiments and observations, thus allowing individuals to express their fuller personhoods closer to their own feelings and self-identifications compared to their formal social identities given by the hierarchical order of status distinctions. Keeping an aspect of cultivating and navigating sentiments in the rigidly hierarchical society, poetry circles became an institution for creating 'bonds of civility' without civil society. Poetry has often been seen as a medium for revealing cosmic truth in many cultures; hence, it sometimes generates a ritual sphere that allows discourse against the dominant structures as the case of the Bedouin community exemplifies. In pre-modern Japan, the sphere of sharing poetic sentiments constituted by a powerful literary ritualism set poetic space apart from the rules of non-poetic space. Well-established methods of cultivating poetic sentiments not only became instruments for regulating emotional aspects of sociability, but also provided precious spheres of civilized sociability in the middle of an otherwise hierarchically segmented society governed by the shogunate. During the eighteenth and nineteenth centuries, numerous circles of *haikai* poetry making developed throughout Japan; with the expansion of the nationwide market network and commercial publishing industry, even agricultural provinces were endowed with numerous poetry circles loosely connected with nationwide networks of aesthetic circles. The activities of rural and urban cultural enthusiasts created social spheres that operated totally outside the state's control. Repeated experiences of switching network connections and sharing of poetic sentiments began to articulate the participants' personhood outside of assigned roles in the existing social order. This process began to undermine the foundations of the social order set on the basis of status distinctions and segregation. Consequently, the expansion of poetic publics was critical, not only for understanding, cultivating, and regulating sentiments, but in a wider sense for illuminating the development of political modernity in Japan.[32]

VI

Earlier in this chapter, I referred to the paradox of emotion; although emotions are felt personally as immediate private feelings, they also develop an institutional dimension with recurrent patterns of behavior on both individual and corporate levels. Culture represents one of those institutional mechanisms for cultivating and regulating emotions. Culture, however, is hardly static and unitary. Although the question of how to define culture always entails serious academic debates, culture can be simply considered as a set of shared understandings among people. In a smallest possible setting, a 'working hypothesis' concerning a common understanding may emerge among two interacting persons. As in the case of a small Bedouin community, even though there was an overall code of honor, people constantly attempted to test the waters, and to find ways of revising the details of the code in search of ways to improve their situations. Such micro practices of emotion cultures are embedded in the larger structure of social hierarchy.

Culture also has an aspect of 'tool kits' for actions (Ann Swidler);[33] people can use an idiom of culture freely in order to pursue their own ends. On the downside, if the individual totally neglects cultural conventions and institutional requirements, he or she becomes less effective in finding solutions and in persuading others that his or her feeling is *right*. In order to receive sympathy for one's emotional actions, a clever use of cultural conventions is essential. In this way, people's strategic attempts to solve everyday problems yield various solutions, which can in turn result in a new cultural convention. As the example of Japanese poetry circles shows, sometimes successive actions of problem solving, while tackling issues of navigating sentiments, succeeded in cultivating new institutional frameworks in a bottom-up way. Conversely, the political or intellectual authorities at times took the initiative by attempting to discipline people by prescribing new standards for judging emotions.[34]

Emotions involve judgments about important aspects of the individual's life. We easily get angry when we feel that something which we value is abused or challenged. We feel happiness and satisfaction when our life situation matches the criteria that we cherish. Such a judgment of values is in part personal but also in a critical way socially and politically determined. Hence, it is not difficult to imagine how a serious social change might yield a shift of evaluation criteria resulting in a change of emotion cultures.

The changing patterns of emotion cultures and their relationships with macro social changes form an exciting area of enquiry; many influential thinkers have been tackling this issue. For example, Albert Hirschman's *Passion and Interest*,[35] a masterpiece of intellectual history, examined writings from St Augustine to Montesquieu in order to articulate the process in which the passionate pursuit of glory by ancient and medieval warriors was replaced by the sober calculating mindset of capitalism; the discovery of 'interest' and the view of 'interests' as tamers of the passions during the eighteenth century was the key point of his argument. Hirschman was thereby in fact discussing the transformation of an emotion culture with regard to the rise of capitalism. In contrast to Hirschman's focus on ideas, Nobert Elias's approach was more social structural with a focus on self-regulating one's emotions. He thought that there should be a relationship between the patterns of self-control and large-scale social changes such as state formation and pacification, as well as the rise of a more densely net-worked society. To be sure, as Rosenwein pointed out, Elias's assumption of increasing self-control as a sign of modernity coupled with a simplistic image of medieval people is problematic. Nonetheless, Elias pioneered a new terrain of enquiry by investigating relationships between the micro-level practice of emotional control and the macro-level of political and economic challenges. Conversely, when Michel Foucault was describing social discipline and the technologies of power in his study of the genealogy of Western disciplinary and penal institutions, he was dissecting the process of the penetration of power into corporal discipline and self-control that led to the creation of contemporary patterns of sentiments.[36] Foucault also underscored the institutional control mechanisms that regulate and educate sentiments as forms of embodiment of discipline. For historians as well as sociologists and anthropologists, it poses an exciting intellectual challenge for us to explore shifting modalities of, and control methods for, sentiments in relation to macro social transformation.

Historians generally aspire to develop a detailed analysis to illustrate dynamic processes in which micro dynamics of emotion cultures and macro-political and economic transformations are interrelated.

However, the issues related to identifying and interpreting historical sources will remain important challenges for them. Available sources that allow us to study emotion cultures of people in the past are usually limited, fragmented, and ambiguous. In order to reconstruct the emotional life of people in the past, we have to use various kinds of sources including arts and icons and literary sources down to manuals for behavioral management and state policies and laws. There are usually more prescriptive sources available for historians, which offer rules and norms for emotions. Such prescriptive sources include, but are not limited to, ideas of emotion theories prescribed by intellectuals, religious teachings, school programs to educate sentiments of students, and state regulations as well as laws. Notably, these sources for prescribing rules and norms also reflect the process of producing social categories by and for those who have more power.[37] At finishing schools, the creation of the well-behaved 'lady' who controls her sentiments in a ladylike proper way, for example, is not an apolitical process; it not only reflects gender politics of the time, but it both generates and excludes the category of women of a lower class who are not ladies. We should remain aware, however, that when we only rely on sources that prescribe better ways of managing emotions, no matter how important these are, we might lose sight of the rich lived *practice* of emotion culture. People are not always passive recipients of prescribed norms of emotion cultures. The cultural practices of actors and structures cannot be understood strictly in terms of a one-way causal relationship in which the latter guides the former. We should also pay attention to the agency of the people since emotion cultures are constantly revised and recreated by individual actions despite institutional and structural constraints.

Since the availability of historical sources is so different in each case, historians have to improvise and devise various tactics to handle the difficult task of reconstructing emotion cultures of the past. For example, when I studied the process in which the samurai's passionate and heroic culture was tamed through several centuries of political struggles and state transformations, I at first imagined a rather straightforward process of progressive 'taming' of the samurai. I envisioned a process of transforming the samurai's violent passions with the changing of the samurai's social functions from heroic mounted warriors to quasi-bureaucrats with hereditary stipends. My expectation was only partially right. Although superficially the process of transforming and redirecting samurai honorific sentiments was the direct result of pacification and political integrations, in practice the process of change was far more protracted, messy, and complex. I first studied various different kinds of reports and descriptions related to cases of private fights, quarrels, and revenge in which the samurai's honor and use of violence were questioned. In particular, I focused in depth on one famous case known as the forty-seven samurai vendetta in 1703; the forty-seven masterless samurai killed the enemy of their deceased master. This case allowed me to study primary sources written from different perspectives: private letters exchanged among samurai avengers who discussed their honorific sentiments and their criteria of justice; the state's official position; samurai intellectuals' debates over this famous case; and popular reactions including literary reproductions of the story. I was able to encounter the complex dynamics of politics of honorific sentiments, in which each individual in this vendetta, whether actual participant, regulator, or spectator, agreed that the interpretation of this case was critical to the politics of the time and the articulation of samurai-hood.[38] The elitist culture of honor was refocused and redirected through successive events that forced those actors to make serious decisions, while the actors retained individualistic dimensions of their honor culture.

Historical studies of emotion cultures remind us of the existence of multilayered epistemological difficulties. Intricate and complex sets of interactions among emotion, culture, and politics can be addressed only through a close analysis and imaginative interpretation of historical sources. However, this process of explication is as rewarding for historians as is the process of proving and analyzing the historically located nature of our own sentiments and feelings.

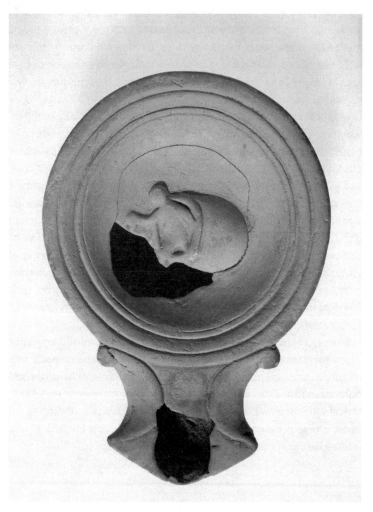

16. Roman pottery lamp from a mould decorated with Diogenes emerging from a storage jar, supporting himself with a staff. Found in Corfu. © by permission of the Trustees of the British Museum

16 The Power of Ideas

ANTHONY GRAFTON

In the bitter fall of 1939, W. H. Auden, who had left Britain for the United States, sat on Forty-Second Street in Manhattan and meditated, 'As the clever hopes expire, | Of a low dishonest decade'. He now saw the Communists and Fascists who had confronted one another in Spain during the Civil War as equally dishonest. Both sides were led by dictators who talked the 'elderly rubbish' that had already been too familiar, millennia before, to the Greek historian, 'exiled Thucydides'. He warned his readers that 'There is no such thing as the State | And no one exists alone,' and urged, 'We must love one another or die.' The politics of ideas, so it seemed, led only to the grave, one large enough to hold millions.

Even as Auden despaired of the political ideas that had meant most to his generation, however, he recognized that ideas could grip and move the minds of individuals. However corrupt Communism had become, its power and coherence as a political program still derived from the theories of Marx and Engels. The crimes of the Nazis stemmed even more directly from ideas and arguments made by earlier generations of Germans, which historians could trace back to those who had framed them: 'Accurate scholarship can | Unearth the whole offence | From Luther until now | That has driven a culture mad,' and identify the 'huge imago' that had created the 'psychopathic god'. The poet was perceptive. His particular vision of Nazism as the culmination of a German intellectual tradition that went awry with Martin Luther in the early sixteenth century and never returned to sanity had more to do with Allied propaganda than historical research. But his belief that intellectual programs—such as the drive to create a biologically pure Germany, with reservoirs of lesser human stock in the East—were fundamental to the creation of the Nazi state has been borne out by historical research over the last two decades.

The Western intellectuals who reached maturity in the 1930s and 1940s disagreed savagely on a vast range of issues. Many responded to the economic crisis of the 1930s, as Auden had in earlier years, by concluding that capitalism was bankrupt, and declared their adherence to one version or another of Marxism. Others, horrified by the purge of Stalin's old Bolshevik rivals and by such news of the Ukraine famine as reached them, rejected Marxism for a commitment to liberal democracy, more or less vigorous. Still others saw in Fascism new energies and a new social order that might yet save the West. Some defended particular programs of ideas, claiming that they offered the key to society and history, and the past and the future. Others, like George Orwell, defended another idea: that freedom of thought mattered most. Ordinary people must be protected from all of the 'smelly little orthodoxies' that contended for absolute adherence. For all of them, ideas mattered existentially.

At the time, though, the majority of historians rejected the notion that ideas played a powerful part in history itself. The most influential historians of the time—Ronald Syme, for example, who revolutionized the study of Roman history in these years, and Lewis Namier, who seemed to do the same for that of English politics in the eighteenth century—insisted that ideas had played no significant part in the day-to-day struggles that actually shaped political landscapes. Historians of ideas were few, and even some of them—for example, the Cambridge scholar Herbert Butterfield—believed that political history formed the core of their discipline. Younger scholars like Christopher Hill often took their methods from the Marxist tradition, which treated the relations of production, not the creation of ideas, as the base that determined the shapes of society and history. As we will see over the course of this chapter, in France, America, and Germany, scholars were already at work crafting new ways of writing the history of ideas, and their new models gradually became part of the professional practice of history.

Ideas: range and variety

The nature and importance of ideas—like the very term idea itself—had been debated since ancient times. For Plato, who first formulated the notion, the idea was the perfect instantiation of the thing it represented. Existing outside time and space, it served as the pattern by which the demiurge, the superior being who brought the material universe into being, actually worked. Ideas, for him, were prior to anything else in the created world, which could not have come into existence without them. Plato also cherished, for a time, a faith in ideas in a more familiar sense. He believed that a sufficiently just and wise ruler could put his views about the state and justice into practice, and went to Sicily to advise Dionysius II, the tyrant of Syracuse.

By contrast, Plato's most gifted pupil, Aristotle, did not agree that ideas had any real existence—as opposed to the four causes that, he thought, explained everything from starfish to states. An empiricist who concentrated on examining and anatomizing actual samples of phenomena from starfish to constitutions, he believed that nothing could exist in the mind that had not entered it through the senses. Aristotle poured particularly cold water on the notion that an idea could affect the world. This disagreement between pupil and teacher was only the start of a long debate in the West about ideas—one that would involve medieval scholastics like Thomas Aquinas and William of Occam and early modern reformers of philosophy like René Descartes as well as many more recent thinkers from John Locke to Charles Saunders Peirce, who would continue to debate such questions as whether all ideas have their roots in experience, or some ideas exist in the mind before it begins to encounter the outside world, and guide its interpretation of phenomena.[1] Similar debates—partly inspired by the Greek philosophical texts translated through Syriac into Arabic—have taken place in the Islamic world. East Asian traditions have their own, quite differently formulated central concepts, in some cases rooted in such classical texts as the Confucian classics, in others formed over the millennia in response to the impact of new visions of the world, such as that of Buddhism, and to contact with Asian and Western peoples. Translating these without distorting them beyond recognition poses the intellectual historian great challenges.[2]

Ideas in history have been as multiple as views of them in philosophy. They range from complex concepts, such as nature and culture, to political ideals, such as liberty and freedom and speech. They can be complex combinations of subordinate ideas, such as constitutionalism, or apparently simpler building blocks, such as atoms; systems of classification and theories of history; unspoken assumptions and popular delusions. Almost anything, moreover, can become an idea, as writers and artists, film-makers and musicians transform objects and individuals, communities, and movements. Ancient Sparta, for example, was a Greek city known for the bravery and prowess of its warriors. In the hands of writers on politics and the proper education of young men, it became an idea in its own right, and the prototype of many later visions of the ideal society. By the same token, the East End of London and the Lower East Side of New York City, both of them neighborhoods that have attracted generations of immigrants, usually poor and culturally distinct from the natives, have metamorphosed over time into ideas of a very different sort: nostalgic visions of a lost past in which close families and supportive neighbors made up for poverty and oppression. Still other cities—Paris in the age of Haussmann and after, Vienna in the years around 1900, Moscow and Berlin in the 1920s—are remembered less for the lives of their ordinary citizens than for their extraordinary cultural creativity: the little communities of painters and art dealers, writers, musicians, and performers stand, by synecdoche, for the whole cities. And such ideas have consequences. Europe itself—now the largest and most powerful economic community in the world—began as an idea that took shape across centuries of population movement, warfare, and the writing and rewriting of history, only to crystallize in the material world of banks, currency, and politics during the decades after the Second World War.

Ideas, in other words, are as varied as butterflies, and the historian who hopes to fix and analyze them must be aware of all of their complexities. In every instance, an idea begins with individual minds, embedded in particular places and circumstances. But individuals change their views. In Plato's *Republic*, the largest and most complex of his books, the philosopher argued that in an ideal society, men and women of special wisdom and virtue, whom he called guardians, would rule and protect the rest of the population. But he also elaborated in a discrete section of the work what has long been known as 'the allegory of the cave': a complex vision of life on earth as a form of confinement in darkness and illusion. This vivid passage suggested that only philosophers, who seek the truth outside the cave, could ever see the world as it is. But they gain this advantage at the price of seeing truths denied to ordinary people. Socrates, in the text, emphasizes both the difficulty that such philosophers would face in trying to live in the ordinary world and their duty to use their knowledge for the good of society.

Did Plato believe that society could reshape the world—or conclude that philosophy would be relevant only to an ideal society? Were Socrates' arguments really concerned with the moral self-government of individuals? Or do the tensions in Socrates' argument—part of the text that Plato presumably composed, as authors of substantial works usually do, over a long period—reflect the fact that he wrote different parts of it at different periods in his life and thought? Did the work in any way reflect Plato's experiences on his two journeys to Syracuse, during which he tried without success to help Dionysius II become a philosopher-king?

As this case shows, even when historians confront an idea at its creation, they face difficult problems. The idea itself is embodied in some sort of text; but texts must be interpreted. In some cases—for example, when trying to interpret the thought of Friedrich Nietzsche—the historian must identify, and find ways of peeling off, layers of irony and sarcasm, without ignoring them. In other cases—for example, that of the Russian agronomist Trofim Lysenko, who rejected genetics, persecuted biologists, and dominated the realm of the life sciences in Soviet Russia—the ideas espoused may seem so alien that the historian must carry out an act of the imagination simply in order to take them seriously—and believe that the author did so as well. Equally difficult is the puzzle of motivation: of identifying the circumstances, intellectual or personal, biographical or collective, which form the context for a particular idea and may help to explain why it was formulated and espoused. Sometimes, surviving personal documents show that individuals formed or changed their opinions under the impact of political events or after the discovery of countervailing evidence; sometimes, however, surviving evidence does not reveal any identifiable external stimulus. No single assumption about the ways in which ideas take shape can do justice to the multiple cases that the historian will encounter.

Ideas in time: continuity and evolution

Ideas affect the world once they are embodied in texts, images, buildings, songs, films, and other media, and adopted by groups or institutions that approve of them and transmit them to their members. When ideas become canonical—are accepted as authoritative by groups and institutions—they can survive for generations, even for centuries. But the ideas that succeed in this way continue to evolve in their new environments, and as new layers of concepts and techniques are overlaid on the original ones, they often develop inconsistencies or fissures. In Shakespeare's *Merchant of Venice*, Lorenzo says to Jessica,

> How sweet the moonlight sleeps upon this bank!
> Here we will sit, and let the sounds of music
> Creep in our ears: soft stillness, and the night,
> Become the touches of sweet harmony.
> Sit, Jessica. Look how the floor of heaven
> Is thick inlaid with patines of bright gold.
> There's not the smallest orb which thou behold'st
> But in his motion like an angel sings,
> Still quiring to the young-eyed cherubins.
> Such harmony is in immortal souls;
> But, whilst this muddy vesture of decay
> Doth grossly close it in, we cannot hear it.

Here the night sky is represented not only as a brilliant display of stars, the 'patines of bright gold' in the 'floor of heaven', but also as a complex, magnificent celestial mechanism. The stars, Lorenzo explains, produce music as they move, a form of harmony so subtle that mortals cannot hear it, with which they charm the 'young-eyed cherubins', the angels who accompany the stars.

As writers often do, Shakespeare partly explains, and partly alludes to, the idea that he has in mind—and that he expects his audience to recognize. He imagines the universe as bounded and spherical. Following the ancient authorities, Plato, Eudoxus, and Aristotle, who gradually devised a powerful model to explain the motion of the heavenly bodies, he sees the stars and planets as fixed to the surfaces of transparent, crystalline nested spheres. Like the planets, these are perfect, and they turn uniformly around their centers. In size, moreover, the spheres are related to one another by the same neat ratios that, when applied to a taut string, yield such musical intervals as the octave, fifth, and fourth. Hence, they produce music as they move: the 'harmony of the spheres'.[3]

This vision of the cosmos, created in antiquity, was offered as the accepted truth in standard textbooks of astronomy and cosmology, taught in schools and universities, and embodied in dozens of works of art and literature. Shakespeare knew it, almost certainly, not from the original texts of the Greek thinkers who created it, but from later works written by Christians, such as the medieval *Sphere* of John of Sacrobosco, which he might have studied at the grammar school that he attended in Stratford. Nonetheless, his vision of the cosmos was genuinely classical in origin. Had Plato, Eudoxus, or the greatest ancient astronomer, Ptolemy, who wrote in the second century AD, come back to life and seen the play, they would have seen the heavens as Lorenzo did and sympathized with his evocation of celestial music. In one sense, then, the passage illustrates the perdurability of ideas: their ability to survive, in recognizable form, translation from one language and culture into any number of others.[4]

Yet Lorenzo's vision also contains one vital element that Ptolemy would not have recognized. Though he and Jessica cannot hear the harmony generated by the spheres, angels—the 'cherubin'—can. In the third, fourth, and fifth centuries AD, the philosophers who served as Plato's successors in the Athenian institution he had founded, the Academy, forged a more elaborate and systematic picture of the universe from elements in his and Aristotle's works. Like Plato himself, many of them held that the universe was populated by celestial as well as terrestrial beings, and they did their best to identify these and work out their places in the heavenly order. Many Christian thinkers believed that the cosmos of the Neoplatonists was largely consonant with their own. They drew analogies between the superhuman spirits that played a role in the Platonic tradition and the angels mentioned in the Jewish and Christian scriptures. In the sixth century AD, an unknown Christian composed a set of treatises in which he laid out, in parallel form, the hierarchy of the nine orders of angels and the hierarchy of the Church on earth. His beautiful treatises were ascribed to St Dionysius (or St Denis), a Greek whose encounter with St Paul is described in the New Testament. They enjoyed immense authority through the Middle Ages in both the Eastern and the Western Christian churches. Even after the Reformation, many British theologians who had rejected dozens of traditional Catholic doctrines and practices continued to accept these texts as genuine and to populate the heavens with the angels, marshaled in their hierarchical ranks. Ptolemy—and, for that matter, Plato and Aristotle—would not have understood the theological system that Lorenzo referred to when he told Jessica about the angels. But the great Puritan poet Milton would have followed the passage with understanding and interest. In this way, ideas—even complex ones whose parts seem to work together as smoothly and precisely as the cogs and wheels of an engine—take on new elements over time, which do not replace, but can obscure and conceal, the original core.[5]

Ideas, finally, develop fissures—especially if they survive over long periods, during which the impact of new questions and new data can make what had originally been hairline cracks widen until they threaten the stability of the whole system. Central to Shakespeare's ordered vision of the cosmos was the assumption, so solid that it hardly needed to be stated, that perfect crystalline spheres must, of their nature, move in circles, with absolute regularity. But already in antiquity, astronomers had realized that the planets, as seen from the earth, do not move regularly. Their angular velocity increases and decreases periodically. At intervals, moreover, the planets (though not the sun and moon) seem to stop, move backwards, and stop again before they resume their normal motion. The only way to account for these irregularities without abandoning the principle that spheres turn regularly around their centers was to nest two or more spheres of different sizes and impart their composite motion to the sun, moon, and planets. While the motion of the bodies in the planetary system was generated by spheres moving regularly around their centers, their actual paths and velocities lacked the musical regularity that Lorenzo evoked in his description.

Worse still, the most accurate model of all, as Ptolemy discovered, was one that actually made each planet's chief sphere move regularly not around its own center, but around a point at some distance from it, the equant—even though doing so contradicted one of the principles on which the whole system rested. In late antiquity, and again in the Islamic world, astronomers objected to this contradiction. Nicolaus Copernicus, who spent the first decades of the sixteenth century working on his treatise *On the Revolutions of the Celestial Spheres*, was one of those most offended by this violation of basic principles, and by his account it helped to motivate his own effort to reform astronomy. (In the end, though, Copernicus found that he could not entirely dispense with the device of which he disapproved.[6])

By the time *The Merchant of Venice* was first performed, probably in 1596 or 1597, a number of Englishmen had read Copernicus, and a few had described his work—as had the Neapolitan philosopher Giordano Bruno. Outside England, astronomers like Tycho Brahe were finding it possible to dispense with the celestial spheres—though others, such as the young Johannes Kepler, still hoped to adapt the spheres and their music to the new astronomy. It is possible that members of his audience knew that Lorenzo's model was both ancient and beginning to show wear—though none of them could have guessed how soon the ancient, harmonious, and orderly world that Shakespeare evoked so beautifully would make way for an infinite and largely empty universe, while John Donne complained that 'the element of fire is quite put out'.[7] In twelve lines, Shakespeare's Lorenzo makes a brilliant mosaic of ancient and medieval, pagan and Christian elements. Every historian of ideas must be ready to find the origins of every separate piece in an assemblage of this kind.

Histories of ideas

Despite the difficulties involved in tracing the history of ideas, scholars have been doing so for hundreds of years. Already in the ancient world, scholars compiled lists of the members of the different schools of philosophy, tried to reconstruct their lives and relations to their teachers, and sometimes even preserved fragments of their teaching. Debate raged—for example, about whether formal philosophy had come into being in Greece, as its name (which means 'the love of wisdom' in Greek) suggested, or in the older countries of the ancient Near East, Egypt and Babylon, whose priests had a reputation for learning and sagacity. In the first centuries of the Christian era, church fathers who had studied the classics tried to show that some of the ancients—both Near Eastern and Greek—had enjoyed vivid inklings of the truths that were fully revealed to Christians by the Old and New Testaments. More than one of them quoted the Neoplatonist Numenius of Apamea, who supposedly asked, 'What else is Plato, than Moses speaking Greek?'

The learned humanists of the Renaissance tried to sort out the several ancient schools of philosophy, each of which had had its own distinctive principles and methods, and began to enquire into the conditions that allowed knowledge to flourish in particular times and places. In the seventeenth and eighteenth centuries, as philosophers like Francis Bacon called for a radical reform of natural philosophy and scientists like Isaac Newton seemed to produce it, the history of learning became a central subject of scholarly enquiry. In the first decades of the eighteenth century, Giambattista Vico argued that the ancient pagans had actually lived in a world more primitive than that of his own time, and traced their ideas about the universe and gods to the natural conditions that had existed after the Flood. Eighteenth-century philosophers acknowledged and developed all of these approaches.[8]

The history of ideas in its modern sense—as a scholarly, documented effort to trace the relations of ideas to one another and their impact on individuals and societies—really began to take shape in the nineteenth century. Historians agreed with thinkers of many other sorts in that heyday of Clio's hegemony, when every Parliament and university that could afford to do so swathed itself in Gothic stone to prove its fidelity to ancient antecedents, that everything in the world, from nature to society, took shape over time, as the result of complex processes of evolution. Ideas must have obeyed this universal rule. In the heyday of liberal optimism, it seemed that Western science would soon unlock the secrets of the physical universe as it had those of the biological world, and that Western technology and power would soon pacify and civilize the entire surface of the earth. Ideas, in short, played an active role in history, and must always have done so. J. B. Bury, the classicist and Byzantinist who became Regius Professor of History at Cambridge in 1902, was a consummate professional scholar in the mode that had been first created in the universities of nineteenth-century Germany. In his inaugural lecture he made clear that he saw history as a science, not an art: a highly technical pursuit centered on politics. Yet Bury also believed that historians must trace the development of ideas. In 1920, he published a massive history of the idea of progress, which he identified as the notion, common in his own period, that human civilization had progressed from simpler beginnings in the past and would continue to do so for an infinite period in the future. Starting in ancient Greece, Bury followed the multiple paths by which, as he believed, the one full and legitimate notion of progress had taken shape. Charles Beard, the historian who presented Bury's work to the American public in 1932, could not have been less like Bury. A radical and an outsider, he fiercely criticized traditional political histories that concealed the secret interests, economic and political, which, he believed, had actually led the 'founding fathers' to create the American Constitution and the Western powers to confront Germany and Austria in 1914. Yet he agreed enthusiastically with Bury about the fertility of intellectual history: ideas, among which he included what he described as the most powerful idea of all, technology, played a central role in the evolution of humanity.

From the start, historians of ideas disagreed on points of method. A. O. Lovejoy, the American philosopher who founded the *Journal of the History of Ideas*, believed that certain complex 'unit-ideas', or complex sets of simple concepts, dominated the Western tradition (he did not make clear whether they had counterparts that dominated non-Western traditions). Like Bury and Beard, he agreed that these ideas generally had a single, coherent, and powerful form, which they reached over time. In a highly influential book, *The Great Chain of Being*, Lovejoy traced what he saw as the basic traditional idea of the universe: a hierarchy with no gaps, in which everything that existed had a single place from which it could not rise or fall. The first task that confronted the historian of ideas, then, was to trace this long-term process of evolution: to show how such ideas reached their definitive form. But there were other tasks as well, equally important or even more so. The historian must show how 'unit-ideas', normally first formulated by philosophers (Lovejoy himself was a philosopher), found expression in works of literature and art as well as in sermons and other forms of popular literature aimed at a non-literary public; and must trace the inevitable process by which internal contradictions and new information gradually destroyed the idea's original unity.[9]

In the histories of the nineteenth and early twentieth centuries, this process—crystallization followed by vulgarization and dissolution— was sometimes depicted as taking place almost independently of time and space, to say nothing of local political and intellectual conditions. That explained how—in Bury's history of the idea of progress—he could argue that certain individuals, such as Roger Bacon, had arrived at ideas so uniquely radical as to be ahead of their time. They were engaging in pure intellection, untrammeled by limits of technology and practicality. Others, by contrast, insisted on finding mechanisms to explain the formulation and perpetuation of ideas. Robert Flint, author of a pioneering history of historical thought, worked, as he said, on the assumption that thinkers always frame their arguments in response to their immediate circumstances. Flint's assumption that the history of ideas must be grounded in historical and political conditions gave his story a richly contextual character, which few other histories of ideas shared at the time.

In the first half of the twentieth century, as the history of ideas gradually transformed itself into a largely academic pursuit, multiple lines of investigation developed. As histories of ideas became more specialized, they also became more grounded in time and place. Scholars examined the development of intellectual and literary movements such as Romanticism. They traced the ways in which intellectuals responded to the discovery of places and societies previously unknown to them, or largely unknown: the ways, for example, in which Chinese intellectuals responded to contact with Viet Nam in the Han Period and with Europe in the Ch'ing, and in which European intellectuals responded to the discovery of the Americas and the regaining of contact with Africa, India, and China in the early modern period.[10] And they debated the question of which ideas dominated the thought of particular periods: for example, the European Enlightenment. In the 1930s, the French historian Paul Hazard and the German philosopher Ernst Cassirer both brought out influential efforts to show that the Enlightenment represented a break with earlier traditions of European thought, in which a new empirical, secular form of thought triumphed. Meanwhile the American Carl Becker insisted that the *philosophes* of the Enlightenment had actually revived, in a secular form, the totalizing theology of the medieval scholastics, propelled by their conviction that a single intellectual system could encompass the natural and social worlds.

Still, the problem of evaluation remained urgent: on what grounds could the historian decide which ideas would most reward study? And the problem of explanation continued to nag. How to explain why certain ideas developed and others did not, and why larger cultural climates and smaller systems of ideas changed? One standard way of solving the problem, as the French thinker Michael Foucault recalled in 1987, was to take refuge in 'concepts that seem rather magical to me, such as influences, crisis, sudden realization, the interest taken in a problem, and so on—convenient concepts that don't work, in my view'. To explain why a particular thinker—for example, John Locke—wrote as he did, the historian pointed out that he had read—and been 'influenced' by—earlier thinkers. Foucault—himself an original and influential writer on the history of thought—was right, in this instance, to point out that the originally astrological concept of 'influence' did not describe a mechanism that could help the historian understand why one writer decided to draw on a second, but simply restated the fact in a way that falsely claimed explanatory value.

Foucault also noted that a second, more up-to-date form of explanation flanked these traditional ones: every time an apparent break occurred, the historian could explain it by reference to conditions external to the realm of ideas, from social and economic change to larger, unexplained cultural transformations: 'When one encounters a difficulty, one goes from the level of analysis which is that of the statements themselves to another, which is exterior to it. Thus, faced with a change, a contradiction, an incoherence, one resorts to an explanation by social conditions, mentality, worldview, and so on.' In the 1930s, scholars tried to show that the new science of the seventeenth century, which they saw as resting on a new experimental method, reflected the rise of a capitalist economy, which had brought into being a new bourgeoisie whose members had a new, empirical view of the world. Ingenious though some of these constructions were, they eventually foundered as new work in social and political history revealed that early modern European society remained tightly bound to older social orders and traditions. A bourgeois revolution that had not taken place could hardly have given rise to the new empirical science.

Equally problematic were a number of constructions that Foucault did not mention, with which other scholars did their best to reverse the arrow of causality. The German sociologist Max Weber, for example, argued in a work that appeared just after the First World War, *The Protestant Ethic and the Spirit of Capitalism*, that the new Protestant religion of the sixteenth century—especially in its Calvinist version— had provided vital support for the rise of capitalism. True, neither Martin Luther nor John Calvin had favored acquisitiveness or approved of such basic capitalist practices as lending money at interest. But they had argued eloquently that every man's work in the world was assigned to him by God, as a vocation, and their beliefs had been treated as authoritative in the new Christian churches that they created. Their re-evaluation of work, including the work of craftsmen and traders, gave secular callings a new value. In their distaste for luxury and excess, moreover,

Luther and Calvin encouraged merchants to invest their profits not in conspicuous consumption, but in their own businesses.

'Inner worldly asceticism', Weber held, powered the rise of Holland, Britain, and the New England colonies to economic supremacy. More important still, it inspired Protestants to realize that they inhabited a universe that lacked angels and other spirits—a 'disenchanted', modern physical world. Religious ideas, thanks to their capacity to shape conduct and feeling, thus helped to create a world that no longer needed to invoke religious categories of explanation. This elegantly paradoxical argument—which was independently developed by Weber's contemporary Ernst Troeltsch and by the British historian R. H. Tawney—failed to convince on multiple grounds. Closer reading of multiple sources showed that Weber had mingled late texts and tenets with earlier ones, and a more precise economic history undermined his geography and chronology of the expansion of capitalism. Most striking of all, scholars realized that both in the sixteenth and seventeenth and in the nineteenth and twentieth centuries, there was no single arrow of cultural development pointing toward secularism. In fact, the seventeenth and the twentieth centuries both ended in periods of strong sectarian loyalty—as is clear not only from the vortex of apocalyptic prophecies that swirled on printed broadsides in the first instance and on websites like RaptureReady.com in the second, but also from the conflicts motivated by religious difference that raged in both periods.[11]

History of ideas in practice: politics and science

Over time, a number of enduring lines of research crystallized, sometimes based in particular institutions. In the decades around 1800, when history took its full place as an academic discipline in Germany and France, its practitioners saw their central task as tracing the history of nations. Leopold von Ranke, the most influential of the first generation, told his students that 'nations are thoughts of God'. Michelet—who disagreed about God—agreed about the central role of the nation in history. So did Macaulay, whose narrative of the Glorious Revolution described in vivid, dramatic terms how the still feudal England of the mid-seventeenth century turned within a century into the core and capital of a modern empire. Even the most obsessive students of archival documents agreed that political thought played a role in the formation of policy and offered insight into the development of institutions.

From the eighteenth century onwards, moreover, political ideas had not only responded to great political changes, but also inspired them. Both the American revolutionaries of 1776 and the French ones of 1789 claimed to find the basis of their critique of the monarchies that oppressed them and their projects to replace them with new forms of society and government in the political thought of Locke and Rousseau. Influential scholars—J. N. Figgis and the Carlyles at Oxford, Friedrich Meinecke at Berlin—dedicated their own research to the development of political thought and encouraged younger scholars to follow their example.

At first, no similar consensus obtained about the method to be followed in this study. Scholars of quite different types—both traditional teachers of political theory like George Sabine and the German refugee Leo Strauss, who became a very influential teacher in the United States—agreed in seeing political theory as a Great Tradition, in which thinkers at the highest level, from Plato through Maimonides to Machiavelli and beyond, addressed one another across time and space (Strauss also believed, more controversially, that all of them concealed those of their views that would have angered the larger public). These men clearly saw past political thought as relevant to contemporary problems and debates. Others agreed, but pursued more historical lines of research. Some argued that past political thought continued to do damage in the contemporary world. For the Israeli scholar J. L. Talmon, Enlightenment theories of political and social reform mattered most because they had engendered the totalitarian programs for social reform of twentieth-century Communists and Fascists. Others, such as the Oxford scholar and public intellectual Isaiah Berlin, looked for currently ignored or forgotten figures, such as the liberal Russian political thinkers of the nineteenth century and the conservatives of what Berlin called the 'Counter-Enlightenment', and argued that their work might offer models for the solution of modern dilemmas.

Two of Meinecke's onetime students, both sent into exile in the English-speaking world, sketched elements in the 1950s and early 1960s of what became, over time, the central approach to the field. Hans Baron, who had steeped himself in the writings of Florentine humanists in the decades around 1400, argued that they had articulated a modern, secular form of republican political and social thought. More important still, he devised a theory that explained their accomplishment by reference to its context. Great changes in thought, he argued, take place in response to changes in the thinkers' political and social world. The Florentines' successful effort to resist Giangaleazzo Visconti, the ambitious duke of Milan, inspired them to find republican ideas in the writings of Cicero and other ancients and reconfigure these for their own ends. Felix Gilbert, also an expert on Florence, set out to explicate the works of the most controversial of early modern political thinkers, Machiavelli. In order to understand what was distinctive in Machiavelli's texts, Gilbert combed the Florentine political records. He used secretarial transcripts of committee meetings held in the Palazzo della Signoria to recreate the normal language of the urban elite who actually governed the city, and whose discussions were often recorded. As much in his dissent from some normal assumptions as in his acceptance of others, Machiavelli emerged—as the humanists had—not as an isolated deep thinker but as a figure in a particular, Florentine tapestry.[12]

In the 1950s and after, a new generation of Cambridge scholars made clear that approaches like these could be applied to other times and places. Peter Laslett showed that Locke's *Second Treatise of Government* had been written in response to the Exclusion Crisis rather than the Glorious Revolution of 1688, and that Locke had been seriously engaged, in his *First Treatise*, in argument with the theorist of divine right, Robert Filmer. John Pocock recreated what he described as two conflicting ways of understanding English history—that of the common lawyers, who held that the constitution had existed since time immemorial, and that of antiquaries, influenced by Renaissance humanism, who came to see the English society of the Middle Ages as a distinct feudal world, different from both what came before and what came after—and argued that this conflict had powerful consequences in the political debates of the seventeenth and eighteenth centuries.[13]

Most influential of all, Quentin Skinner showed that a richly contextual approach to political texts could yield a newly rigorous account of their meaning. By recreating the language of political argument known to a particular author, and then by teasing out the particular statement he had meant to make—his 'intention in utterance'—the historian could show what a text had meant to its authors and its immediate addressees. In many cases, this meant showing, as Laslett had, that the author of a classic work had not meant what interpreters not grounded in its local context believed he had. Even the greatest and most original works—Machiavelli's *Discourses on Livy*, Hobbes's *Leviathan*—took on their true sense only when thus set into their linguistic and historical context.[14] Over time, a distinct Cambridge School formed, each of its members pursuing distinct lines of analysis: Pocock emphasizing the distinct languages that existed in any given culture and the ways in which thinkers adopted them, while Skinner continued to emphasize the local political circumstances in which utterances took shape, and Istvan Hont, Stefan Collini, Emma Rothschild, and many others pursued the history of political, social, and economic thought into later periods, using similar methods.

Though both Skinner and Pocock drew on the earlier work of Baron, Pocock's vision of early modern republicanism differed in vital ways from Skinner's: he noted, as Skinner did not, the powerful presence of apocalyptic elements within republican thought, introduced by Savonarola and others in fifteenth-century Florence, to reappear in seventeenth-century England and the new United States. Yet these were variations within a canon. The contextual methods that Skinner and others developed inspired dozens of monographs and editions and translations of texts. The history of political thought continues to be one of the most formidably innovative areas in the history of ideas. The creators of the Cambridge School continue both to contribute their own new work to it, and to see their ideas challenged, as well as supported, by generations of younger scholars. And the method epitomized by the title of a Cambridge University Press series—*Ideas in Context*—has proved extraordinarily productive: the home for more than 150 innovative contextual studies of everything from Jesuit political theory to ideas about music in the Berlin of the 1840s.

For all its power and coherence, the Cambridge School was not wholly independent of other forms of scholarship—and its development illustrates, in its own way, the power of ideas. In the decades around 1900, the Hamburg scholar Aby Warburg created a new, interdisciplinary method for the study of the history of art and culture—one that emphasized the ways in which images, texts, and disciplines crossed linguistic, cultural, and religious borders to survive for millennia. He and his disciples, Fritz Saxl, Edgar Wind, and Erwin Panofsky, eventually created a unique library to support these studies, which was moved from Germany to England in the early 1930s and became, as it remains, a center of interdisciplinary teaching and research in London. Most members of the London Warburg Institute became famous for their interest in areas far removed from politics: the role of astrology and prophecy in pre-modern life, for example, where Warburg and others did pioneering work that has been continued, in more recent times, by students of the history of religion like Bob Scribner and Paola Zambelli and historians of natural philosophy like Lorraine Daston and Katherine Park.[15]

At its core, though, the Warburg Institute emphasized the perdurable importance of classic texts and the systems of education and scholarship built to preserve them. In the 1970s and 1980s, Skinner, Anthony Pagden, and other Cambridge scholars came into active collaboration with Charles Schmitt of the Warburg. Skinner, who originally treated the notion that older texts conditioned later ones as scornfully as Foucault, came to see that older traditions of language and argument, as well as current debates, formed part of the discursive context within which authors wrote. His book on Hobbes focused on the ways in which Hobbes had used, at central points in his political theory, the formal classical rhetoric that he had mastered as a Cambridge student and the figures of thought he had encountered in the Greek historian Thucydides, whose work he translated into English. Pagden, for his part, carried out pioneering research into the ways in which ancient texts and categories had shaped the response of early modern Europeans to the New World and the empires they created there. The Cambridge School prospered, in other words, because its borders were fluid—more fluid than its pronouncements about method suggested.[16]

The history of political thought, in other words, became a node where multiple lines of enquiry met and fused, producing a new subdiscipline. In the same period, another realm in the history of ideas, the history of science, has become a discipline in its own right, with its own departments, publications, and conferences. Like the history of political thought, that of science has deep roots. It grew from the work of eighteenth- and nineteenth-century astronomers and medical men, scientists many of whom still benefited from a classical education and still took an interest in the ancient, medieval, and early modern history of their disciplines. Like the history of political thought in its early decades, too, the history of science was pursued in multiple ways. Some of the most expert scholars in the field, such as Christian Frisch, J. Heiberg, and J. I. E. Dreyer, emphasized the canon of texts and problems. They produced critical editions of ancient and later primary sources that retain their value even now. Those who wrote histories, however, tended to cast them in an anachronistic, polemical key. Often they looked for the origins of modern science in earlier periods. Thus Andrew Dickson White argued polemically that science had had to fight, century after century, for its independence from 'theology'. A later generation would make the reverse case, insisting that science had actually grown from the scholastic theology of the Middle Ages, whose proponents had been willing to consider such outré possibilities as that the earth, rather than the cosmos, rotated.

In the first half of the twentieth century, three developments transformed the field. The first was spearheaded by scholars like the Austrian O. Neugebauer, who participated in the revolution in mathematics and physics that took place at Göttingen in the 1920s, only to leave when the Nazis seized power and make the rest of his long career in the United States. Neugebauer showed that the history of astronomy and mathematics was a story of ideas embodied in precise techniques—and made clear that only scholars willing to master those techniques, as originally practiced, could claim understanding of their development. He demonstrated that both techniques and concepts had been created over millennia, by Babylonians as well as Greeks and Muslims as well as Christians, and thus defined the history of science as an enterprise that, like the pursuits it studied, crossed cultural boundaries. And he made clear that historians of science could not confine their attention to subjects and disciplines that still formed part of modern science. The practitioners of 'miserable subjects' like astrology and alchemy had also studied the natural world and practiced ways of observing and working on it, and these two must form part of the history of science.

The second was the work of very different scholars like the sociologist Robert Merton. Already in his doctoral dissertation, Merton set out to examine how the new science of seventeenth-century Britain took shape. Working from a rich range of sources, he argued that multiple contextual circumstances, from Puritan religious beliefs to practical military requirements, played important roles in shaping the interests of scientists. Over time, Merton extended his study to the practice of science in later periods and more modern disciplines. By attending to patterns of behavior—for example, the propensity of scientists to dispute priority in the discovery of particular facts or rules, since the prestige of being the first to make a discovery was their chief form of compensation—he began to lay out the social rules that governed the system of scientific practice that formed first in the modern West and has now spread throughout the developed world. The history of science, Merton made clear, was a history of ideas embedded not only in texts and debates about them, but in institutions and machines.

In the 1950s and 1960s, finally, Herbert Butterfield, a British historian, and Thomas Kuhn, an American scientist turned historian and philosopher of science, raised the question that had provoked, but also baffled, generations of earlier scholars: how do ideas actually change? Looking first at Copernicus' heliocentric astronomy and then at multiple cases of scientific change in more recent times, Kuhn argued that powerful ideas about nature shifted not gradually, as elements of an existing theory were disproved, but with seismic rapidity—such rapidity, in fact, that to those on the other side of a change, the beliefs and methods of their predecessors became literally incomprehensible. Kuhn held that a 'paradigm' or set of rules governed practice within a science until it became unstable and needed replacement. This vision found uses across the whole range of the humanities. So did the painstaking arguments by which he tried to show that multiple factors—including wider shifts in values and beliefs—mattered as much as evidence that an existing paradigm could not account for in its downfall and replacement.[17]

Historians of science have built immense structures on these founding principles. Specialists in East Asian science, from Joseph Needham, the pioneering Cambridge scholar who organized what has become a multi-volume collaborative history of Science and Civilization in China, to Benjamin Elman and others, have recreated the forms of enquiry into nature and innovation in technology created over the millennia of Chinese history, reconstructed the principles that underlie the distinctive forms of medical therapy developed in East Asia, and revealed what happened when, in the late nineteenth-century age of imperialism, these and European ways of understanding the body and its function came into regular contact in Asian cities. Students of 'wretched subjects' like William Newman, Lawrence Principe, and Tara Nummedal have shown that it was wrong to assume, anachronistically, that alchemy had no valid technical content. In fact, early modern 'chymists' developed effective techniques for promoting the formation and growth of metallic crystals, and for assaying metals—though some of them also promised princes, quite falsely, that they could transmute base metals into gold, and more than one paid the price for the failure of the laboratory his patron had built at court. Those interested in scientific change and its modes have shed new light on the detailed, day-to-day life of scientific work and its relation to the concepts that it tests. Peter Galison and others have made clear just how often, even in very recent times, communications between scientists of different sorts have been disrupted by their inability to find a common space in which to trade information. Using terms drawn from analyses of cultures in contact, Galison has shown how groups of intellectuals, as well as merchants, from groups that disagree on basic points of method can still form 'trading zones' and use 'agents' and 'pidgin languages' to exchange ideas. Such central ideas as that of objectivity itself have been revealed as the relatively recent products of historical evolution.

At once a flourishing field of enquiry and a source of models and methods for other areas of intellectual history, the history of science has had one particularly important result: it has shown the necessity for historians of ideas to combine their enquiry into the structure of concepts with a second, equally vital enquiry into the institutions by which those concepts are adopted, preserved, and taught to younger generations, and the practices used to verify or falsify larger theories. Historians of science have shown that the apparently eternal institutions of the modern university, such as the seminar and the doctoral dissertation, have a history of their own—one bound up with ideas about the nature of science, scholarship, and research and their relation to teaching, and one that has set its stamp on modern thinkers and their ideas.[18] Like the historians of political thought, historians of political thought have also supplied models that scholars interested in very different questions—for example, the development of the humanities and of humanistic scholarship—have applied to topics far outside the history of the study of nature.

A material turn: histories of books and readers

From the start, as we have seen, historians of ideas have debated the extent to which ideas make history. How can an idea change people's feelings and behavior? Since the 1930s, new forms of scholarship have begun to offer an answer. One of these in particular, the history of books, has been particularly fertile. Two of the great events of European history—the Protestant Reformation of the sixteenth century and the French Revolution of 1789—were both provoked, their protagonists claimed, by new ideas: ideas about the relation between God and humanity on the one side, and about society and the state on the other. Each revolution was led by highly educated men who referred to authoritative texts—the Bible in the first case, the classics and modern works of radical political theory on the other. Influential French scholars proposed a way to measure the impact of the texts. Lucien Febvre examined the inventories of private libraries from the French city of Amiens, using the books that influential families had possessed as a key to the development of their thinking—and the larger 'mental climate' within which they lived. Daniel Mornet used similar information to work out in detail how widely the intellectuals of the eighteenth-century Enlightenment were read.[19]

After the Second World War, these enquiries expanded. Febvre and his disciple Henri-Jean Martin agreed that printing—which multiplied copies of any given text in a way that scribal publication never could have—radically enhanced the impact of ideas in Europe after 1450. Through both the large-scale collective enquiries that they organized, and the individual investigations that they helped to inspire, they helped to make the world of publishing a central object of historical studies. Younger scholars joined in. Roger Chartier and Peter Burke started by using statistical methods to work out which books had actually found the widest dissemination. In the course of the 1980s and 1990s, they expanded the toolbox of the book historian, drawing on anthropology and literary theory to work out the ways in which writers and readers appropriated and reconfigured texts to radically new ends. Meanwhile Donald McKenzie, Robert Darnton, David McKitterick, and others reconstructed the actual practices of early printing houses. Darnton, James Raven, and others mined archives, and traced the sometimes-twisted channels by which books that carried new messages reached readers, often in the teeth of censorship. While some of the works considered canonical in recent times attained great popularity in the later eighteenth century, it also emerged that largely forgotten texts— utopian proposals for a new social order, pornographic novels, and collections of salacious gossip about the ways of rulers and their serv- ants—actually sold best. Some of the enlightened ideas that actually reached a wide public did so in a vulgarized form, with spice of various kinds to make them more entertaining. Slanderous accounts of royal mistresses and ministers may have done more to remove the French monarchs' air of sacredness—and to promote the general viciousness that characterized political life once the Revolution took hold—than the views of Voltaire or Rousseau. Where Lovejoy called for accounts of the way high ideas were vulgarized in their passage from philoso- phy into new media, the historians of the book have charted complex scripts in which commercial interests and ideologies, censorship, and authors' intentions all have parts to play.[20]

Statistics, for all their richness, reveal only how many copies of a given book were printed or sold: a reasonable basis for an estimate of influence, but not a basis for analyzing what the text actually meant to those who read it. In 1976, the Italian cultural historian Carlo Ginz- burg showed that the rich records of the Inquisition's dealings with a dissident Friulian miller, Domenico Scandella or Menocchio, revealed the identity of the books he had owned and read. More remarkably still, by comparing Menocchio's summaries of his readings with the originals, Ginzburg reconstructed the miller's very imaginative way of reading—one that he analyzed as steeped in the materialism of an ancient peasant culture. Over the next twenty years, scholars found unexpectedly informative clues to readers' experiences in sources of many kinds, from marginal annotations to letters to publishers. More and more intellectual historians—including students of literature like William Sherman and historians of science like James Secord—now adopt the perspectives of book history and the history of reading, using information about their protagonists' education, their libraries, and their practices as scholars and writers, as well as about the recep- tion of their work by contemporary and later readers, to embed their analyses in a richer historical contexts.

In adding these new methods to their traditional ones, historians of ideas have come much closer to one set of their traditional rivals:

the historians of culture, who have been at work since the early nineteenth century, and have usually shown less interest in the direct study of ideas and their import than in the cultural institutions that propagate ideas, from the forms of education and systems of literature that exist in all organized societies to the theaters and opera houses, cabarets and cafés, that have gradually come into existence in the modern city. Historians of ideas have adopted many of the cultural historians' approaches. Such intellectual historians as Paul Grendler, Robert Black, Martin Jay, and Suzanne Marchand have recreated the educational and scholarly institutions—from the schools and universities of fifteenth- and sixteenth-century Italy to the universities, laboratories, and museums of nineteenth- and twentieth-century Germany—which formed intellectuals and within which they carried out their work. Others have turned their attention to the literary systems that existed at a given place and time, recreating the careers that writers led and the forces that acted either to further or to suppress their creative work. Richly documented studies by Robert Darnton, Ian Maclean, James Raven, and Philip Waller have drawn from publishers' records, censors' files, and literary magazines a rich account of the careers that authors made and the political, social, and ideological pressures that they faced, which did not determine, but helped to shape, every form of writing from the political pamphlet to the novel.

Crossing borders

These approaches—which do not abandon the study of ideas but ground it in the recreation of the institutions and cultural practices that mediate between creators and readers—have yielded new understandings of many stories in world history. In some ways, historians of ideas in the pre-modern world have always practiced something like the cross-cultural form of scholarship that Christopher Bayly evokes as a desideratum in his chapter for this volume. No one, for example, has done more to undermine myths of the uniqueness and creativity of ancient Greece than Neugebauer and his successors, who traced in detail how Hellenistic science grew from Near Eastern as well as Greek roots. The Warburg Institute—officially described as a center for the study of the classical tradition—has always insisted on the vital roles played by the ancient Near Eastern civilizations, by Islam and by

Judaism in the cultural traditions that the West has made its own, and on the startling ways in which particular cultural forms, from incantations to visions of strange peoples, traveled across the continents from India to England. In more recent years Warburg scholars have extended their interests to China and Tibet.

Recently, moreover, contemporary scholarly methods have begun to move as effectively across cultural boundaries as the ideas they are used to track. Innovative recent books by Benjamin Elman and Beth Berry have traced, for example, the ways in which the forms of education, scholarship, and publishing that obtained in pre-modern China and Japan did much to form the thought of intellectuals, and an important work by George Saliba has used new forms of enquiry into the nature of pre-modern science and the transmission of ideas in manuscript to enlarge our understanding of Islamic astronomy and its profound impact on the study of nature in the early modern West— and these studies have, in their turn, become models for emulation by specialists in the intellectual history of Europe and the Americas.[21] New scholarship on book history is as likely to be carried out by Chinese or Israeli scholars as by American or British ones—and yet its results are likely to be published in English and made accessible to a still wider range of readers.

Like ideas themselves, the practices of their historians have mutated over the years, multiplying and diversifying, but retaining something of their initial depth and coherence. A study that began in the world of philosophers and worked, for many years, at a high level of abstraction, the history of ideas has never abandoned its concern with formal concepts and arguments. But scholars have learned to ground this study in a rich reconstruction of contexts and to connect it with stories of images and institutions, forms of dissemination and attention. At the start of the twenty-first century, the history of ideas is a powerful sub-discipline that exemplifies the value of interdisciplinary work. Looking back to the 1930s, its practitioners can see that the Marxists and Communists of the time both exemplified, in their commitment to coherent systems of explanation and prediction, the power of ideas to move men and women—and historians.

Notes

PREFACE

1. This passage in the original reads as follows: 'Je pratique une sorte de fiction historique. D'une certaine manière, je sais très bien que ce que je dis n'est pas vrai. Un historien pourrait très bien dire de ce que j'ai ecrit: "Ce n'est pas la vérité." ... Je sais très bien que ce que j'ai fait est, d'un point de vue historique, partial, exagéré.... Et donc, mon livre et la thèse que j'y développe ont une vérité dans la réalité d'aujourd'hui.... J'espère que la vérité de mes livres est dans l'avenir', Michel Foucault, *Dits et écrits 1954–1988*, vol. ii (Paris: Gallimard, 2001), 805.
2. *Financial Times*, 10/11 Apr. 2010.
3. For an important exploration of many of these themes see Ivan Karp and Steven D. Lavins (eds.), *Exhibiting Cultures: The Poetics and Politics of Museum Display* (Washington: Smithsonian Press, 1991).
4. Münster would reuse these sentences like a building block with other correspondents, see *Briefe Sebastian Münsters, Lateinisch und Deutsch*, trans. Karl Heinz Burmeister (Frankfurt-on-Main: Insel Verlag, 1964), 156.

CHAPTER 1

I am grateful to Ulinka Rublack for her comments on this chapter. I have only generally referenced modern works which are specifically mentioned in the text or very recent works, to avoid a very long and complex apparatus. A wide range of reference material relating to this chapter can be found in e.g. John Darwin, *After Tamerlane: How Empires Rise and Fall* (London: Penguin, 2008); C. A. Bayly, *The Birth of the Modern World 1780–1914: Global Connections and Comparisons* (Malden, Mass.: Blackwell, 2004), Tony Judt, *Postwar: A History of Europe since 1945* (London: Heinemann, 2005), and in a wide range of Oxford and Cambridge histories.

1. Andre Gunder Frank, *ReOrientate: Global Economy in the Asian Age* (Berkeley and Los Angeles: University of California Press, 1998).
2. Kenneth Pomeranz, *The Great Divergence* (Princeton: Princeton University Press, 2000).
3. Sevket Pamuk, *A Monetary History of the Ottoman Empire* (Cambridge: Cambridge University Press, 2000).
4. Jürgen Habermas, *The Structural Transformation of the Public Sphere*, trans. T. Burger (Cambridge: Polity Press, 1992).
5. John Brewer, *The Sinews of Power: War and the English State 1688–1783* (London: Unwin Hyman, 1989).
6. Pamela Crossley, *A Translucent Mirror: History and Identity in Qing Imperial Ideology* (Berkeley and Los Angeles: University of California Press, 1999).

7. Eric Hobsbawm, *Nations and Nationalism since 1780* (Cambridge: Cambridge University Press, 1990); Ernest Gellner, *Nations and Nationalism* (Oxford: Oxford University Press, 1993).

8. E. P. Thompson, *The Making of the English Working Class* (London: Gollancz, 1980).

9. See, e.g. Ranajit Guha and Gayatri Spivak (eds.), *Selected Subaltern Studies* (New York: Oxford University Press, 1988).

10. David Armitage, *The Declaration of Independence* (Cambridge, Mass.: Harvard University Press, 2007).

11. Erez Manela, *The Wilsonian Moment: Self-Determination and the International Origins of Anticolonial Nationalism* (Oxford: Oxford University Press, 2007).

12. See, e.g. Susan Bayly, *Asian Voices in a Postcolonial World* (Cambridge: Cambridge University Press, 2007).

13. Niall Ferguson, *Empire: How Britain Made the Modern World* (London: Allen Lane, 2003).

14. Andrew Roberts, *History of the English-Speaking Peoples since 1900* (London: Weidenfeld and Nicholson, 2006).

15. Quentin Skinner, *The Foundations of Political Thought*, 2 vols. (Cambridge: Cambridge University Press, 1978).

16. Raymond Geuss, *History and Illusion in Politics* (Cambridge: Cambridge University Press, 2001).

17. Pierre Rosanvallon, *Counter-democracy: Politics in an Age of Distrust*, trans. Arthur Goldhammer (Cambridge: Cambridge University Press, 2008).

18. See, e.g. Tom Bottomore, *The Frankfurt School and its Critics* (London: Routledge, 2002).

19. Reinhart Koselleck, *Critique and Crisis: The Pathogenesis of Modern Society* (Oxford: Berg, 1998).

20. Sheldon Pollock, *The Language of the Gods in the World of Men: Sanskrit, Culture and Power in Pre-modern India* (Berkeley and Los Angeles: University of California Press, 2009).

21. Cemal Kafadar and Halil Inalcik (eds.), *Suleyman the Second in his Time* (Istanbul: Isis, 1993).

22. Wagle's work is forthcoming but see Narendra Wagle and A. R. Kulkarni, *Vallabha's Parasarama Caritra: An Eighteenth Century Maratha History of the Peswas* (Bombay: Popular Prakasan, 1976).

23. See the essays collected in Shruti Kapila (ed.), *An Intellectual History for India* (Delhi: Oxford University Press India, 2010).

24. See, for a historical treatment, J. Donald Hughes, *An Environmental History of the World: Humankind's Changing Role in the Community of Life* (London: Routledge, 2002).

25. Amartya Sen and Jean Dreze, *Hunger and Public Action* (Oxford: Clarendon, 1989).

26. John Iliffe, *The African AIDS Epidemic* (Cambridge: Cambridge University Press, 2005).

CHAPTER 2

1. Max Weber, *The Protestant Ethic and the Spirit of Capitalism*, trans. Talcott Parsons (New York: Charles Scribner's Sons, 1958); Margaret Jacob, *Scientific Culture and the Making of the Industrial West* (Oxford: Oxford University Press, 1997); Joel Mokyr, *The Gifts of Athena: Historical Origins of the Knowledge Economy* (Princeton: Princeton University Press, 2003); Kenneth Pomeranz, *The Great Divergence: China, Europe and the Making of the Modern World Economy* (Princeton: Princeton University Press, 2000); Robert Allen, *The British Industrial Revolution in Global Perspective* (Cambridge: Cambridge University Press, 2009).

2. Franklin F. Mendels, 'Proto-Industrialization: The First Phase of the Industrialization Process', *Journal of Economic History*, 32 (1972), 241–61; R. Bin Wong, *China Transformed: Historical Change and the Limits of European Experience* (Ithaca, NY: Cornell University Press, 1997), 32–53.

3. David Sabean, *Property, Production, and Family in Neckarhausen, 1700–1870* (Cambridge: Cambridge University Press, 1991); David Sabean, *Kinship in Neckarhausen, 1700–1870* (Cambridge: Cambridge University Press, 1997).

4. Bin Wong, *China Transformed*, 209–52; R. Bin Wong, 'Detecting the Significance of Place', in Robert Goodin and Charles Tilly (eds.), *Oxford Handbook of Contextual Political Analysis* (Oxford: Oxford University Press, 2006), 540–4.

5. Douglass C. North, *Structure and Change in Economic History* (New York: W. W. Norton, 1981).

CHAPTER 3

I am extremely grateful to Francisco Bethencourt, Caspar Hirschi, and Ludmilla Jordanova for their feedback on different stages of the manuscript, and to Simon Schaffer and Jim Secord for bibliographical advice on Leeuwenhoek and optical devices.

1. Geoffrey R. Elton, *Political History: Principles and Practise* (New York: Basic Books, 1970), 160.

2. Marc Bloch, *The Historian's Craft*, trans. Peter Putnam, preface Peter Burke (Manchester: Manchester University Press, 1992), 47.

3. Arlette Farge, *Entretiens aves Jean-Christophe Marti: Quel bruit ferons-nous?* (Paris: Les Prairies Ordinaires, 2005), 182.

4. Clara Pinto-Correia, *The Ovary of Eve: Egg and Sperm and Preformation* (Chicago: Chicago University Press, 1997), esp. 70–3; Katherine Park, *Secrets of Women: Gender, Generation, and the Origins of Human Dissection* (New York: Zone Books, 2006).

5. Georg G. Iggers, 'Modern Historiography from an Intercultural Global Perspective', in Gunilla Bugge, Sebastian Conrad, and Oliver Jan (eds.), *Transnationale Geschichte: Themen, Tendenzen und Theorien* (Göttingen: Vandenhoeck & Ruprecht, 2006), 84.

6. Anne Goldgar, *Tulipmania: Money, Honor, and Knowledge in the Dutch Golden Age* (Chicago: Chicago University Press, 2007), 279.

7. Svetlana Alpers, *The Art of Describing: Dutch Art in the Seventeenth Century* (London: Penguin Books, 1989), 18.

8. Ibid. For a more recent exploration of vision in this society see Stuart Clark, *Vanities of the Eye* (Oxford: Oxford University Press, 2007).

9. By the early seventeenth century, for instance, the inventor Cornelis Drebbel not only constructed a submarine for the Thames, but intriguingly experimented with a camera obscura in the following way: 'I take my stand in a room and…first I change the appearance of my clothing in the eyes of all who see me. I am clad in black velvet, and in a second, as fast as a man can think, I am clad in green velvet, in red velvet, changing myself into all the colours of the world. And this is not all, for then I change my clothing so that I appear to be clad in satin of all colours, then in cloth of all colours, now cloth of gold and now cloth of silver, and I present myself as a king, adorned in diamond and all sorts of precious stones, and then in a moment become a beggar, all my clothing in rags', cited in Alpers, *Art of Describing*, 13.

10. Deborah Cohen, 'Comparative History: Buyer Beware', in Deborah Cohen and Maura O'Connor (eds.), *Comparison and History: Europe in Cross-National Perspective* (New York: Routledge, 2004), 63.

11. By 1854, the poet Heinrich Heine, who lived in Germany and France, wrote that he had brought together a 'daguerreotypic history book', a 'genuine picture of the time itself in the smallest nuances' and 'daily truth'. Only this, he claimed, produced an 'authentic' historical source, see Sigfried Kracauer, *History: Last Things before the Last* (New York: Oxford University Press, 1969), 49; on Kracauer see Dagmar Barnouw, *Critical Realism: History, Photography, and the Work of Sigfried Kracauer* (Baltimore: Johns Hopkins University Press, 1984).

12. Kracauer, *Last Things*, 57.

13. Moreover, Kracauer privileged 'the camera's affinity for the indeterminate. To be sure, the photographer endows his pictures with form and meaning to the extent that he makes deliberate choices. But however selective, his prints still are bound to record nature in the raw. Like the natural objects themselves, they will therefore be surrounded by a fringe of indistinct multiple meanings', Kracauer, *Last Things*, 59.

14. Ibid. 60.

15. Carlo Ginzburg, *Clues, Myths, and the Historical Method*, trans. John and Anne C. Tedeschi (Baltimore: Johns Hopkins University Press, 1989), ch. 2. The analogy between the historian and the detective had already interested the British philosopher R. G. Collingwood: 'the hero of a detective novel is thinking exactly like a historian when, from indications of the most varied kinds, he constructs an imaginary picture of how a crime was committed, and by whom.' But the ultimate verification came through a confession, whereas for the historian there is no conclusive evidence, only the question about the authenticity of any source that might be read as presenting an answer. Collingwood returned to the analogy of the historian and detective in his final work, *The Idea of History* (1946). He contrasted Holmes's method to that of the Belgian detective figure Hercule Poirot. Holmes he disdainfully equated to 'scissors-and-paste' historians: 'they collect all the extant testimony about a certain limited group of events, and hope in vain that something will come of it.' Poirot, by contrast, poured 'scorn on the "human blood-hound" who crawls about the floor trying to collect everything, no

matter what, which might conceivably turn out to be a clue'. Collingwood agreed: 'you can't collect your evidence before you begin thinking... nothing is evidence except in relation to some definite question.' Lord Acton's dictum 'study problems, not periods' had been preached in the heyday of Holmes to bring about a more 'scientific history'; see Robin G. Collingwood, *The Idea of History* (Oxford: Clarendon Press, 1946), 281.

16. Alain Corbin, *The Life of an Unknown: The Rediscovered World of a Clogworker in Nineteenth-Century France*, trans. Arthur Goldhammer (New York: Columbia University Press, 2001).

17. Ibid., p. xiv.

18. Ibid.

19. 'To penetrate into the complex and initially rather unstructured entity that is the village, which was not only an institution but a way of life, which consisted not only of houses but of people living in competing relationships, one must clear a path through the thicket of official documents to the human beings themselves, to ask how they shaped their lives and how they perceived and changed the world around them', Claudia Ulbrich, *Shulamith and Margarete: Power, Gender, and Religion in a Rural Society in Eighteenth-Century Europe*, trans. Thomas Dunlap (Leiden: Brill Academic Publishers, 2004), 21.

20. David Cannadine (ed.), *What is History Now?* (Houndmills: Palgrave, 2002), p. xi.

21. Jon Lawrence, 'Political History', in Stefan Berger, Heiko Feldner, and Kevin Passmore (eds.), *Writing History: Theory & Practise* (London: Hodder Arnold, 2003), 183.

22. Richard J. Evans, *In Defence of History* (London: Verso, 1997), 253.

23. Quoted in Evans, *Defence*, 251.

24. Bloch, *Historian's Craft*, 22–3.

25. Ibid. 41–3; Ulrich Raulff, *Ein Historiker im 20. Jahrhundert: Marc Bloch* (Frankfurt am Main: S. Fischer Verlag, 1995), 254, quoting his work *The Feudal Society*.

26. Bloch, *Historian's Craft*, 14–16.

27. Raulff, *Ein Historiker*, 260.

28. Ibid. 17.

29. Ibid. 15.

30. Pim den Boer, *History as a Profession: The Study of History in France, 1818–1914* (Princeton: Princeton University Press, 1998), 192.

31. For an important account of such dynamics and their way of shaping the profession see Bonnie G. Smith, *The Gender of History: Men, Women, and Historical Practise* (Cambridge, Mass.: Harvard University Press, 1998).

32. Bloch, *Historian's Craft*, 57.

33. Raulff, *Ein Historiker*, 418.

34. The last among a list of five books which Bloch still intended to write in 1940 was a detective novel called 'murder in the province'. He avidly consumed English detective novels and had discussed with his team of Strasbourg colleagues a book by the literary critique Regis Messac on the influence of the detective novel on scientific thought in its increasing privileging of inductive procedures. Similarly, Bloch identified on an imaginary level with a sense of

history in which the murder has happened, and a clear problem has thus been identified around which an enquiry now needs to be skilfully organized and in which testimonies will have to be checked very carefully because of their distortions, wilful or because of failing memory, or because everyone followed the same rumour. He was fascinated by the detective novel because it was this process of encountering the intricacy of human consciousness which such an enquiry revealed—'how many men lead lives on three and four different levels, which they wish and sometimes succeed in keeping apart', Bloch asked—which often made clear answers and judgements about causes difficult, but elaborated one's ability to define complexity and comprehend different ways in which pieces can be put together and dots joined up to make for different outcomes and plots; see Raulff, *Ein Historiker*, 190–2.

35. Ludmilla Jordanova, *History in Practice* (2nd edn. London: Hodder, 2006), 5.

36. Natalie Zemon Davis, 'What is Universal about History?', in Bugge, Conrad, and Janz (eds.), *Transnationale Geschichte*, 19. For another important endorsement of 'truth' as a category in response to postmodernism see Joyce Appleby, Lynn Hunt, and Margaret Jacob (eds.), *Telling the Truth about History* (New York: W. W. Norton, 1994), for instance p. 11.

37. Cannadine (ed.), *History*, p. xi: 'As the caveat suggests, some words of caution are also called for. However fertile and vigorous the present historical scene, both within academe and outside, there are also criticisms and challenges. So much history is now being written that very few scholars can keep up with more than a tiny fraction of what is being published: all of us know more about less and less. The rise of many new sub-specialisms threatens to produce a sort of sub-disciplinary chauvinism, where some practitioners insistently assert the primacy of their approach to the past and show little sympathy with, or knowledge of, other approaches. And far too much history is written in dismal prose or impenetrable jargon which can only be understood by a few aficionados and which fails utterly to reach a broader public audience.' For Farge see *Quel bruit*, 21.

38. Jordanova, *History in Practice*, 90–2.

39. 'This skill of writing is described through adjectives such as "well" or "excellent", but not further qualified in terms of what it means to write well about particular subjects—ie love or the Holocaust', ibid., ch. 7 and p. 195.

40. Ibid. 168–70.

41. Marnie Hughes-Warrington (ed.), *Palgrave Advances in World Histories* (Houndmills: Palgrave, 2005), 3.

42. Lorraine Daston and Peter Galison, *Objectivity* (New York: Zone Books, 2007). Figs.1.1.3 provide an initial summary.

43. Ibid. 52.

44. Ibid. 359.

45. Ibid. 367.

46. Ibid. 371.

47. See, for instance, Micol Seigel, 'Beyond Compare: Comparative Method after the Transnational Turn', *Radical History Review*, 91 (2005), 62–90.

48. Jürgen Osterhammel, *Geschichtswissenschaft jenseits des Nationalstaats: Studien zu Beziehungsgeschichte und Zivilisationsvergleich* (Göttingen: Vandenhoeck & Ruprecht, 2001), 12–17; an English translation is available.

49. Farge, *Quel bruit*, 182.
50. Hayden V. White, *The Content of Form: Narrative Discourse and Historical Representation* (Baltimore: Johns Hopkins University Press, 1987).
51. Natalie Zemon Davis, *Slaves on Screen: Film and Historical Vision* (Cambridge, Mass.: Harvard University Press, 2000).
52. For results see Ulinka Rublack, *Dressing Up: Cultural Identity in Early Modern Europe* (Oxford: Oxford University Press, 2010).
53. *Symbol, Myth, and Culture: Essays and Lectures of Ernst Cassirer 1935–1945*, ed. D. P. Verene (New Haven: Yale University Press, 1979), 138.
54. A good example is Mark Markzower, *Hitler's Empire* (London: Penguin Books, 2007). I am grateful to Adam Tooze for discussing this point with me.
55. For a pioneering discussion, which also reveals many of the complications involved, see Jörn Rüsen (ed.), *Western Historical Thinking: An Intercultural Debate* (Oxford: Berghahn Books, 2002).
56. For an important engagement with understandings of archival evidence see Ann Laura Stoler's work, for example *Carnal Knowledge and Imperial Power: Race and the Intimate in Colonial Rule* (Berkeley and Los Angeles: University of California Press 2002).

CHAPTER 4

1. *Ars rhetorica*, XI, 2.
2. *Ab Urbe condita*, I, preface.
3. *Epitome of Roman History*, I, Introd.
4. *Germania*, 61 and *passim*.
5. *De oratore*, II, ix, 36.
6. *Institutes of Oratory*, 10, 1, 73.
7. *City of God*, X, 14.
8. *Speculum maius*, IV.
9. Cited by Mommsen, 'Petrarch's Conception of the "Dark Ages" ', in E. Rice, *Medieval and Renaissance Studies* (Ithaca, NY, 1959), 122.
10. *Maxims and Reflections*, ed. M. Domandi (New York, 1965), 114.
11. Dugald Stewart, *Biographical Memoirs of Adam Smith, L.L.D., of William Robertson, D.D. and of Thomas Reid, D.D. Read before the Royal Society of Edinburgh*, now collected into one volume, with some additional notes, in *Collected Works*, vol. x (Edinburgh, 1858).
12. The account of Chinese historiography comes from Peter C. Perdue, *China Marches West: The Qing Conquest of Central Eurasia* (Cambridge, Mass.: Harvard University Press, 2005), 462–518.
13. Roger Chickering, *Karl Lamprecht: A German Academic Life, 1856–1915* (Atlantic Highlands, NJ: Humanities Press, 1993); Kathryn Brush, 'Karl Lamprecht: Practitioner and Progenitor of Art History', *Central European History*, 26 (1993), 139–64.
14. John Theodore Merz, *A History of European Thought in the Nineteenth Century, Part II: Philosophical Thought* (1904–12; New York: Dover, 1965), iii. 31–2.
15. Quoted in Lewis Pyenson, 'Uses of Cultural History: Karl Lamprecht in Argentina', *Proceedings of the American Philosophical Society*, 146/3 (September 2002), 246.
16. Benedetto Croce, *An Autobiography*, trans. R. G. Collingwood (Freeport, NY: Books for Library Press, 1970; 1st pub. 1927), 50–2.

17. Henri Berr, *Hymne à la vie* (Paris: Albin Michel, 1945), 59.
18. R. G. Collingwood, *An Autobiography* (Oxford: Oxford University Press, 1951; 1st pub. 1939), 150–4.
19. Croce, *An Autobiography*, 51–2.
20. Trans. P. Putnam (New York, 1953).
21. Quoted in Ernest Samuels, *Henry Adams* (Cambridge, Mass.: Harvard University Press, 1989), 276.
22. Julie Des Jardins, *Women and the Historical Enterprise in America: Gender, Race, and the Politics of Memory, 1880–1945* (Durham, NC: University of North Carolina Press, 2003), 112 and *passim*.
23. 'The Revenge of Literature', in R. Cohen (ed.), *Studies in Historical Change* (Charlottesville, Va., 1992), 84–108.

CHAPTER 5

1. Adam Smith, *An Inquiry into the Nature and Causes of the Wealth of Nations* (original edn. 1776; online edition available at http://www.econlib.org/library/Smith/smWN.html), book 1, chapter 2, paragraph 2.
2. Unlikely but not impossible—the Melanesian *kula* trade, for instance, covered vast areas while always involving some social element.
3. 'Amber Routes', Amber Museum-gallery, http://www.ambergallery.lt/english/muziejus-gintaro_keliai.htm. For slightly older Baltic amber finds in various parts of Eastern Europe, see Marija Gimbutas, 'East Baltic Amber in the 4th and 3rd Millennium BC', *Journal of Baltic Studies*, 16/3 (Fall 1985), 234, 245; and for slightly later material in Mesopotamia, Joan Markley Todd, 'Baltic Amber in the Ancient Near East: A Preliminary Investigation', *Journal of Baltic Studies*, 16/3 (Fall 1985), 298.
4. Paul Mellars, 'The Impossible Coincidence. A Single-Species Model for the Origins of Modern Human Behavior in Europe', *Evolutionary Anthropology*, 14/1 (Jan.–Feb. 2005), 12–27. Quotations are from p. 16.
5. With a slight change of language, the same distinction could be applied to a transition from peasant to capitalist farming.
6. Karl Polanyi, *The Great Transformation* (Boston: Beacon Press, 1957), 46–7.
7. Ibid. 64.
8. See, for instance James Scott, *The Moral Economy of the Peasant* (New Haven: Yale University Press, 1976) vs. Samuel Popkin, *The Rational Peasant: The Political Economy of Rural Society in Vietnam* (Berkeley and Los Angeles: University of California Press, 1979) on Vietnam; James A. Henretta, 'Families and Farms: *Mentalité* in Pre-Industrial America', *William and Mary Quarterly*, 3rd ser. 35 (1978), 30–2 vs. Timothy Breen, 'An Empire of Goods: The Anglicization of Colonial America, 1690–1776', *Journal of British Studies*, 25 (1986), 467–99, on colonial America; E. P. Thompson, 'The Moral Economy of the English Crowd in the Eighteenth Century', *Past and Present*, 50 (1971), 76–136 vs. John Stevenson, 'The "Moral Economy" of the English Crowd: Myth and Reality', in A. J. Fletcher and J. Stevenson (eds.), *Order and Disorder in Early Modern England* (Cambridge: Cambridge University Press, 1985), 218–38 on early modern England. In each pairing, I have placed the skeptical view of moral economy last: that should not imply that these authors have necessarily had the last word.

9. e.g. Polanyi, *Great Transformation*, 58–63; Marshall Sahlins, *Stone Age Economics* (New York: Aldine de Gruyter, 1972), 191–230. There are other substantivist traditions in which initiating exchange with a stranger and establishing a social relationship with him or her is the same act, and the failure to establish such a relationship leads to hostility, rather than 'impersonal exchange' (e.g. Lévi-Strauss). In this formulation, then, commercial transactions appear extremely anomalous across any distance.

10. See Jack Goody, *The Theft of History* (Cambridge: Cambridge University Press, 2006), 26–67, for this issue as reflected in attempts to distinguish an 'archaic' from an 'ancient' or 'classical' world.

11. Fernand Braudel, *Afterthoughts on Material Civilization and Capitalism* (Baltimore: Johns Hopkins University Press, 1977), 16–20, 50–1, 62–3.

12. Ibid. 49–53.

13. Fernand Braudel, *The Wheels of Commerce* (New York: Harper and Row, 1982), 520–45. See also Charles Tilly, *Coercion, Capital, and European States, AD 990–1990* (London: Basil Blackwell, 1992).

14. Braudel, *Wheels*, 374–457; *Afterthoughts*, 53–61. For essentially Braudelian perspectives which argue that commerce in Asia was fundamentally different because no comparable symbiosis between merchants and a military-fiscal state emerged see K. N. Chaudhuri, *Trade and Civilization in the Indian Ocean: An Economic History from the Rise of Islam to 1750* (Cambridge: Cambridge University Press, 1985), 210–15, 226–8; and, based on more up-to-date research, Giovanni Arrighi, Po-keung Hui, Ho-fung Hung, and Mark Selden, 'Historical Capitalism, East and West', in Giovanni Arrighi, Takeshi Hamashita, and Mark Selden (eds.), *The Resurgence of East Asia: 500, 150 and 50 Year Perspectives* (London: Routledge, 2003), 259–333.

15. Braudel, *Wheels*, 372–3; *Afterthoughts*, 104–10. Fernand Braudel, *The Perspective of the World* (Berkeley and Los Angeles: University of California Press, 1992), 536–618.

16. Gary Gereffi and M. Korniewicz, *Commodity Chains and Global Capitalism* (Westport, Conn.: Praeger 1994). For an anticipation that the largest capitalist firms might tend to move from production back to commerce and finance, see Braudel, *Wheels*, 381.

17. Basic facts about Foxconn are available at http://en.wikipedia.org/wiki/Foxconn, accessed 2 Feb. 2009. A more scholarly account can be found in Wai Kit Choi, 'Freedom and Labor under Capitalism: From Nineteenth Century Britain to Twenty-First Century China' (Ph.D. dissertation, Department of Sociology, University of California, Irvine, 2007), 16–19, 174–9.

18. Gary Hamilton, *Commerce and Capitalism in Chinese Societies* (New York: Routledge, 2006), 146–200.

19. Jan DeVries, *The Industrious Revolution: Consumer Behavior and the Household Economy, 1650 to the Present* (Cambridge: Cambridge University Press, 2008), 122–85 discusses consumer behavior changing in response to new goods, but puts no special weight on those that came from exotic sources. (He does, however, note that the rise of 'colonial groceries' 'was no marginal phenomenon'.) Much of the debate on the importance of overseas trade has focused on the rather different question of whether its more coercive elements (especially the

slave trade) allowed for excess profits on a significant scale. Robert Findlay and Kevin O'Rourke, *Power and Plenty: Trade, War and the World Economy in the Second Millennium* (Princeton: Princeton University Press, 2007), 330–41, is a good recent statement of that debate. My own work has tried to push this discussion more in the direction of emphasizing the way in which extra-continental trade relieved ecological impasses, while remaining agnostic on its significance for capital accumulation, and arguing that the new consumer goods it provided had some significant (though unmeasurable) impact on changing work and consumption habits: see *The Great Divergence: China, Europe, and the Making of the Modern World Economy* (Princeton: Princeton University Press, 2000).

20. Werner Sombart, *Capitalism and Luxury* (Ann Arbor: University of Michigan Press, 1967), 95; Smith, *Wealth of Nations*, book 2, chapter 3, paragraph 38 and book 3, chapter 4, paragraph 15.

21. See Kenneth Pomeranz, *The Great Divergence* (Princeton: Princeton University Press, 2000), 129–32 for a brief discussion.

22. Stefan Halikowski Smith, ' "Profits Sprout Like Tropical Plants": A Fresh Look at What Went Wrong with the Eurasian Spice Trade, *c*.1550–1800', *Journal of Global History*, 3/3 (Nov. 2008), 389–418. See also Paul Freedman, *Out of the East: Spices and the Medieval Imagination* (New Haven: Yale University Press, 2008) especially pp. 76–103. Today, it is much harder for a natural source to be mysterious: things like diet pills of dubious efficacy are more likely to be rendered special by association with laboratories and/or celebrity endorsers.

23. Arthur Wright, *Buddhism in Chinese History* (Stanford, Calif.: Stanford University Press, 1959), 31–2; Ira Lapidus, *A History of Islamic Societies* (Cambridge: Cambridge University Press, 2002), 197–8.

24. Gordon Childe, *What Happened in History* (rev. edn. London: Penguin, 1954), 182.

25. Oskar Morgenstern, *On the Accuracy of Economic Observations* (Princeton: Princeton University Press, 1963), 141–63.

26. Angus Maddison, *The World Economy: A Millennial Perspective* (Paris: Organization for Economic Cooperation and Development, 2001), 362.

27. Penn World Data tables, www.bized.co.uk/dataserv/penndata/pennhome.htm.

28. Maddison, *Millennial Perspective*, 362–3.

29. Giovanni Gozzini, 'The Global System of International Migrations, 1900 and 2000: A Comparative Approach', *Journal of Global History*, 1/3 (Nov. 2006), 321–2.

30. Fernand Braudel, *The Structures of Everyday Life* (New York: Harper and Row, 1981), 427.

31. Tim Wright, *Coal Mining in China's Economy and Society, 1895–1937* (Cambridge: Cambridge University Press, 1984), 9. G. William Skinner, 'Regional Urbanization in Nineteenth Century China', in G. William Skinner (ed.), *The City in Late Imperial China* (Stanford, Calif.: Stanford University Press, 1977), 217, has a lower figure (with the cost doubling after 25 miles of transport), but one which would still be prohibitive for a great many purposes.

32. Goody, *Theft of History*, 63.

33. Note that this did not necessarily make them the best off, as they may well have worked more hours to get these goods, Moreover, since many goods and services did not pass through markets, price-based estimates of value are quite shaky.

34. Fang Xing, 'Qingdai Jiangnan nongmin de xiaofei' (The expenditures of peasants in Qing dynasty Jiangnan), *Zhongguo jingji shi yanjiu*, 11/3 (1996), 91–8; E. H. Phelps-Brown and Sheila Hopkins, *A Perspective of Wages and Prices* (London: Methuen, 1981), 14.

35. Robert Allen, 'How Prosperous Were the Romans?', www.economics.ox.ac.uk/Research/wp/pdf/paper363.pdf, 8–9, estimating (with cautions due to limited evidence) that Roman real incomes were close to those of non-British non-Dutch Europeans of the eighteenth century. Moreover, unless we think that the eighteenth-century Europeans ate much better than Romans (for which there is no evidence, and a fair amount to the contrary), their incomes (over half of which went for food) couldn't possibly be as much as double Roman incomes. And very little food traveled long distances in this period. Braudel, *Structures*, 127, estimates that long-distance grain shipments in early modern Europe were not even enough to feed 3,000,000 people.

36. Elisabeth Rosenthal, 'To Counter Problems of Food Aid, Try Spuds', *New York Times*, 25 Oct. 2008.

37. Fernand Braudel and Frank Spooner, 'Prices in Europe from 1450 to 1750', in E. E. Rich and C. H. Wilson (eds.), *The Cambridge Economic History of Europe*, vol. iv (Cambridge: Cambridge University Press, 1967), 395–404, 470–1.

38. Kevin O'Rourke and Jeffrey Williamson, 'After Columbus: Explaining the Global Trade Boom, 1500–1800', National Bureau of Economic Research, Working Paper 8186 (Mar. 2001), 9–11, 49.

39. Note that this may occur even without much actual movement of goods; as long as everybody knows that they could move easily, this may well deter local merchants throughout the zone from deviating from the 'law of one price'.

40. O'Rourke and Williamson, 'After Columbus'.

41. John Shepherd and Gary Walton, *Shipping, Maritime Trade, and the Economic Development of Colonial North America* (Cambridge: Cambridge University Press, 1972), 49–73 on productivity change, 73–7, 80–5 on security, insurance costs, and ship and crew sizes.

42. See e.g. Geoffrey Gunn, *First Globalization: The Eurasian Exchange, 1500–1800* (Lanham, Md.: Rowman and Littlefield, 2003); C. A. Bayly, *The Birth of the Modern World* (Malden, Mass.: Blackwell, 2004); Dennis Flynn and Arturo Giraldez, 'Born with a Silver Spoon: The Origin of World Trade in 1571', *Journal of World History*, 6/2 (Fall 1995), 201–21.

43. Thus a disagreement on definitions, rather than facts, underlines the debate on the history of globalization between Flynn and Giraldez and O'Rourke and Williamson. Kevin O'Rourke and Jeffrey Williamson, 'When Did Globalization Begin', NBER Working Paper 77632 (April). Available at http://www.nber.org/papers/w7632; Dennis Flynn and Arturo Giraldez. 'Path Dependence, Time Lags, and the Birth of Globalization: A Critique of O'Rourke and Williamson', *European Review of Economic History*, 8/1 (2004), 81–108; O'Rourke and Williamson, 'Once More: When Did Globalization Begin?', *European Review of Economic History*, 8/1, 109–17.

44. Carol Shiue and Wolfgang Keller, 'Markets in China and Europe on the Eve of the Industrial Revolution', *American Economic Review*, 97/4 (2007), 1189-216.

45. George Grantham, 'The Shards of Trade', unpublished paper, quoted by permission.

46. O'Rourke and Williamson, 'When Did Globalization Begin?'

47. Steven Stoll, *The Fruits of Natural Advantage: Making the Industrial Countryside in California* (Berkeley and Los Angeles: University of California Press, 1998), 52-3.

48. Niels Steensgaard, *The Asian Trade Revolution of the Seventeenth Century: The East India Companies and the Decline of the Caravan Trade* (Chicago: University of Chicago Press, 1974), 40-1.

49. Ibid. 169-71.

50. A succinct statement is Douglass North, 'The Evolution of Efficient Markets in History', http://dlc.dlib.indiana.edu/archive/00002918/01/9411005.pdf, especially 5-6. See also Douglass North and Robert Paul Thomas, *The Rise of the Western World* (Cambridge: Cambridge University Press, 1973), especially 69-70, 155-8.

51. Douglass North, *Institutions, Institutional Change, and Economic Performance* (Cambridge: Cambridge University Press,1990), 92-3, 98-100. Note, however that North sees institutional change as path dependent; thus leaders of a state with less efficient institutions may be unable to change them even if they understand the problem, and in less intensely competitive environments such institutions may survive a long time.

52. Avner Greif, 'Reputation and Coalitions in Medieval Trade: Evidence on the Maghribi Traders', *Journal of Economic History*, 49/4 (Dec. 1989), 857-82.

53. Sebouh Aslanian, 'Social Capital, "Trust" and the Role of Networks in Julfan Trade: Informal and Semi-formal Institutions at Work', *Journal of Global History*, 1/3 (2006), 383-402, esp. 390-9.

54. For instance Karen Clay, 'Trade without Law: Private-Order Institutions in Mexican California', *Journal of Law, Economics, and Organization*, 13/1 (1997), 202-31; Sebastian Prange, 'Trust in God, But Tie your Camel First: The Economic Organization of the Trans-Saharan Slave Trade between the Fourteenth and Nineteenth Centuries', *Journal of Global History*, 1/2 (2006), 219-39.

55. e.g. Philip Curtin, *Cross-Cultural Trade in World History* (Cambridge: Cambridge University Press, 1984), 320-53.

56. Lisa Bernstein, 'Opting out of the Legal System: Extra-legal Contractual Relations in the Diamond Industry', *Journal of Legal Studies*, 21/1 (1992), 115-57.

57. Avner Greif, *Institutions and the Path to the Modern Economy: Lessons from Medieval Trade* (Cambridge: Cambridge University Press, 2006), 328-38.

58. Ibid. 338-46.

59. Ibid. 347.

60. See Edmund Herzig, 'Julfan Commercial Law', cited in Sebouh Aslanian, 'From the Indian Ocean to the Mediterranean: Circulation and the Global Trade Networks of Armenian Merchants from New Julfa/Isfahan, 1605-1747' (Ph.D. dissertation, Columbia University, 2007), 256-7.

61. He Bingdi, *Zhongguo huiguan shilun* (Historical essay on Chinese native place associations) (Taibei: Taiwan xuesheng shuju, 1966); Peter Golas, 'Early Ch'ing

Guilds', in G. William Skinner (ed.), *The City in Late Imperial China* (Stanford, Calif.: Stanford University Press, 1977), 555–80.

62. Greif, 'Reputation and Coalitions', 859, 862, 876.

63. Greif, *Institutions*, 282.

64. Frederic Wakeman, 'The Canton Trade and the Opium War', in John K. Fairbank and K. C. Liu (eds.), *The Cambridge History of China*, vol. x/1 (1978), 172. By my rough calculations the USA–UK cotton trade actually surpassed the India–China opium trade over the entire course of the century, but the basic point stands nonetheless (and Wakeman is probably right for the first half of the century).

65. Sidney Mintz, *Sweetness and Power: The Place of Sugar in Modern History* (New York: Penguin, 1985), 14–18, 74–150.

66. Hans Medick, 'Plebeian Culture in the Transition to Capitalism', in Raphael Samuel and Gareth Stedman-Jones (eds.), *Culture, Ideology, and Politcs* (Cambridge: Cambridge University Press, 1982), 86, 90–5.

67. This is perhaps the weakest part of Mintz's argument, as he does not provide direct evidence of efforts to create a taste for sugar; but it seems quite plausible that other researchers will find some.

68. Mintz, *Sweetness and Power*, 52–73; on shipping costs, see Kevin O'Rourke and Jeffrey Williamson, *Globalization and History* (Cambridge, Mass.: MIT Press, 1999), 53.

69. See, e.g. Mary Douglas (ed.), *Food in the Social Order* (New York: Russell Sage Foundation, 1984); Marshall Sahlins, *Culture and Practical Reason* (Chicago: University of Chicago Press, 1976), 166–221.

70. Hans-Joachim Voth, 'Time and Work in Eighteenth-Century London', *Journal of Economic History*, 58/1 (1998), 37–40; E. P. Thompson, 'Time, Work-Discipline, and Industrial Capitalism', *Past and Present*, 38 (1967), 56–97; DeVries, *Industrious Revolution*, 87–92.

71. Braudel, *Structures*, 132–5; Phelps-Brown and Hopkins, *Perspective of Wages and Prices*, 19, 100–4; Gregory Clark, 'Yields Per Acre in English Agriculture: Evidence from Labor Inputs', *Economic History Review*, 44/3 (1991), 446; Pomeranz, *Great Divergence*, 92; DeVries, *Industrious Revolution*, 82–5; Jan DeVries and Ad Van der Woude, *The First Modern Economy: Success, Failure, and Perseverance of the Dutch Economy, 1500–1815* (Cambridge: Cambridge University Press, 1997), 629–31.

72. DeVries, *Industrious Revolution*, 123–85 summarizes a variety of evidence on this point.

73. On demography, see David Levine, *Family Formation in an Age of Nascent Capitalism* (New York: Academic Press, 1977), 58–87; Peter Kriedte, Hans Medick, and Jürgen Schlumbohm, *Industrialization before Industrialization* (Cambridge: Cambridge University Press, 1981), 77–86; on relative prices, Philip Hoffman, David Jacks, Patricia Levin, and Peter Lindert, 'Real Inequality in Europe since 1500', *Journal of Economic History*, 62/2 (June 2002), 322–55; on religion and attitudes towards work, the most famous text is Max Weber, *The Protestant Ethic and the Spirit of Capitalism* (New York: Routledge, 2001). DeVries, *Industrious Revolution*, 123–85 reviews and criticizes several of the alternatives.

74. Time spent making things for one's family (e.g. baking) rather than purchasing the goods poses very complex problems, and that of caring for family members rather than hiring help even more so; even assuming we had accurate figures on how much time went into these activities in different times and places, it is not clear that they should always be thought of as 'work' that people would prefer not to do.

75. Akira Hayami, 'Kinsei Nihon no keizai hatto to Industrious Revolution' (Modern Japanese economic development and the industrious revolution), in Akira Hayami, Osamu Saito, and Sugiyama Chuya (eds.), *Tokugawa shakai kara no tenbo: hatten, kozo, kokusai kankei* (A view from Tokugawa society: development, structure, and intenational relations) (Tokyo: Dobunkan, 1989), 19–32; DeVries, *Industrious Revolution*; Pomeranz, *Great Divergence*, 91–106.

76. Wang Yeh-chien, 'Food Supply and Grain Prices in the Yangtze Delta in the Eighteenth Century', in *The Second Conference on Modern Chinese History*, vol. ii (Taibei: Academia Sinica, 1989), 429, conservatively estimates eighteenth-century Yangzi Delta grain imports at 15–22% of total consumption; this appears to be the same as the share of Baltic grain in the consumption of the Netherlands in the mid-sixteenth century, after which that number must have declined over the next 200 years, since the amount of imports first stagnated and then declined, while population grew by about 50%. Calculated from DeVries and Van der Woude, *First Modern Economy*, 50, 198, 414. For a classic account of the importance of interregional trade in Song China, see Mark Elvin, *The Pattern of the Chinese Past* (Stanford, Calif.: Stanford University Press, 1973), 164–72.

77. On commerce, popular religion, and ideas of popular efficacy see Valerie Hansen, *Changing Gods in Medieval China, 1127–1276* (Princeton: Princeton University Press, 1990), 105–59; Stephen Teiser, 'The Growth of Purgatory', in Patricia Ebrey and Peter Gregory (eds.), *Religion and Society in T'ang and Sung China* (Honolulu: University of Hawaii Press, 1993), 128, 133–5; for offerings as reflecting 'capitalist culture', see Hill Gates, 'Money for the Gods', *Modern China*, 13/3 (July 1987), 259–77. For capitalist growth seen as the antithesis of natural processes of growth and thus demonic, see, for instance, Michael Taussig, *The Devil and Commodity Fetishism in Latin America* (Chapel Hill, NC: University of North Carolina Press, 1983).

78. Teiser, 'Growth of Purgatory'; Richard Von Glahn, *The Sinister Way: The Divine and the Demonic in Chinese Religious Culture* (Berkeley and Los Angeles: University of California Press, 2004), 135–43.

79. This period saw the break-up of large estates in the Lower Yangzi, some of which had been farmed by bondservants, giving these people freedom at the price of full exposure to the market. At approximately the same time, large numbers of these free families became dependent on producing cloth for markets in the interior to purchase grain from those areas; but adverse weather, rebellions, and other events interrupted this trade repeatedly, creating poorly understood and devastating market fluctuations. For ways in which these fluctuations affected family incomes and division of labor see Kenneth Pomeranz, 'Women's Work and the Economics of Respectability', in Bryna Goodman and

Wendy Larson (eds.), *Gender in Motion* (Lanham, Md.: Rowman and Little-field, 2005), 243–6.

80. Richard Von Glahn, 'The Enchantment of Wealth: The God Wutong in the Social History of Jiangnan', *Harvard Journal of Asiatic Studies*, 51/2 (Dec. 1991), 651–715.

81. P. Steven Sangren, *History and Magical Power in a Chinese Community* (Stanford, Calif.: Stanford University Press, 1987), 69–71. On rotating credit societies in contemporary China (noting their particular importance for small-scale entrepreneurs, especially women) see Kellee Tsai, *Back Alley Banking: Private Entrepreneurs in China* (Ithaca, NY: Cornell University Press, 2002), 71–3, 111–13; for Taiwan, see Donald DeGlopper, *Lukang: Commerce and Community in a Chinese City* (Albany, NY: State University of New York Press, 1995), 207–9.

82. Hamilton, *Commerce and Capitalism*, 225–9, 232. Interestingly the term *renqing* and the related *ganqing* are also used to explain how networks of gift exchange— often opposed to commerce in social science analysis—should work.

83. Ibid. 195–6, 235.

84. Richard Stites, 'Industrial Work as an Entrepreneurial Strategy', *Modern China*, 11/2 (Apr. 1985), 239–43.

85. Robert Shiller, Maxim Boycko, and Vladimir Korobov, 'Popular Attitudes toward Free Markets: The Soviet Union and the United States Compared', *American Economic Review*, 81/3 (June 1991), 385–400.

CHAPTER 6

I consulted with many friends and colleagues before writing this chapter and would like to thank warmly the following in particular for their advice, comments, and conservation: Sir Christopher Bayly, Nora Berend, Annabel Brett, Christine Carpenter, Richard Drayton, Andreas Fahremeir, Priyamvada Gopal, Miranda Griffin, Wolfram Kaiser, Shruti Kapila, Jon Lawrence, Nina Lübbren, Mireille Mazard, Magnus Ryan, Sarah Schneiderman, Brendan Simms, John A. Thompson, and Megan Vaughan.

1. For useful summaries of debates over definitions, see, for example, James T. Tedeschi, Thomas V. Bonoma, Barry R. Schlenker, and Svenn Lindskold, 'Power, Influence, and Behavioral Compliance', *Law & Society Review*, 4/4 (May 1970), 521–44; Michael Barnett and Raymond Duvall, 'Power in International Politics', *International Organization*, 59/1 (2005), 39–75.

2. Thomas N. Bisson, 'Introduction', in id. (ed.), *Cultures of Power: Lordship, Status and Process in Twelfth-Century Europe* (Philadelphia: University of Pennsylvania Press, 1995).

3. Colin Gordon, 'Afterword', in Michel Foucault, *Power/Knowledge: Selected Interviews and Other Writings, 1972–1977*, trans. Colin Gordon et al. (New York: Pantheon, 1980), 229–59, here 235–6.

4. Cited in David A. Baldwin, 'Power Analysis and World Politics: New Trends Versus Old Tendencies', *World Politics*, 31/2 (1979), 161–94; on the distinction between power and influence, see also David V. J. Bell, *Power, Influence and Authority* (New York: Oxford University Press, 1975).

5. Thomas N. Bisson, *The Crisis of the Twelfth Century: Power, Lordship and the Origins of European Government* (Princeton: Princeton University Press, 2009), 27.

6. On Pufendorf's view of the *translatio imperii*, see Samuel Pufendorf, *Die Ver-fassung des deutschen Reiches*, ed. Horst Denzer (Stuttgart: Philipp Reclam, 1976), 17 ff., 101, cited and discussed in U. Muhlack, *Geschichtswissenschaft im Humanismus und in der Aufklärung* (Munich: C. H. Beck, 1991), 112–13; on the unpredictable character of relations among nations, see Detlef Döring, introductions to Samuel Pufendorf's essays *Discussio quorundam scriptorum Brandeburgicorum* (1675) and *De Occasionibus Foederum inter Sueciam et Galliam et quam parum illa ex parte Galliae observata sint* (*c.*1672; *c.*1681), in Samuel von Pufendorf, *Kleine Vorträge und Schriften: Texte zu Geschichte Pädagogik, Philosophie, Kirche und Völkerrecht*, ed. Detlef Döring (Frankfurt am Main: V. Klostermann, 1995), 238, 350; Samuel Pufendorf, *Einleitung zu der Historie der vormehmsten Reiche und Staaten, so jetziger Zeit in Europa sich befinden* (Frankfurt am Main 1705, vol. i, Vorrede).

7. Frederick II, 'Memoires pour servir à l'histoire de la Maison de Brandebourg', reprinted in Johann D. E. Preuß (ed.), *Œuvres de Frédéric le Grand*, 30 vols. (Berlin: Imprimerie Royale, 1846–56), i. 272–3.

8. For synoptic overviews of the succession of powers and attempts to identify the economic, societal, and technological factors underlying it, see William H. McNeill, *The Pursuit of Power: Technology, Armed Force and Society since A.D. 1000* (Chicago: University of Chicago Press, 1982), Paul M. Kennedy, *The Rise and Fall of the Great Powers: Economic Change and Military Conflict from 1500 to 2000* (New York: Random House, 1987); F. H. Hinsley, *Power and the Pursuit of Peace: Theory and Practice in the History of Relations between States* (Cambridge: Cambridge University Press, 1963).

9. Joseph Nye, *The Paradox of American Power: Why the World's only Superpower Can't Go It Alone* (New York: Oxford University Press, 2002).

10. Arthur M. Schlesinger Jr., 'The Quagmire Papers', *New York Review of Books*, 16 Dec. 1961, 41.

11. I am indebted for these reflections to conversations with John A. Thompson of St Catharine's College, who is currently preparing a major study of US foreign policy and kindly allowed me to see his unpublished manuscript 'American Power'.

12. Max Weber, 'Politics as a Vocation', reprinted in H. H. Gerth and C. Wright (eds.), *From Max Weber: Essays in Sociology* (New York: Oxford University Press, 1958), 78.

13. Georges Duby, *La Société aux XIè et XIIè siècles dans la région mâconnaise* (Paris: Armand Colin, 1971), 131; for supporting accounts, see Guy Bois, *The Transformation of the Year One Thousand*, trans. Jean Birrell (Manchester: Manchester University Press, 1992); Jean-Pierre Poly and Éric Bournazel, *La Mutation féodale, Xe–XIIe siècles* (Paris: Presses Universitaires de France, 1980).

14. The key exposition of this view is now Bisson, *Crisis of the Twelfth Century*; for a dissenting view, see Dominique Barthélemy, *La Mutation féodale, a-t-elle eu lieu? Servage et chevalerie dans la France des Xe et XIe siècles* (Paris: Fayard, 1997).

15. Bisson, *Crisis of the Twelfth Century*, 578, 579, 580.

16. Comment by Professor Christine Carpenter, 14 Jan. 2010; I am grateful to Professor Carpenter for agreeing to discuss with me at length her thoughts on power in the setting of the medieval English state.

17. For a succinct outline of Mayer's arguments, see Theodor Mayer, 'Die Ausbildung der Grundlagen des modernen Staates im hohen Mittelalter', *Historische Zeitschrift*, 159 (1939), 457–87; on the territorialization of legal discourses, see Magnus Ryan, 'Freedom, Law and the Medieval State', in Quentin Skinner and Bo Stråth (eds.), *States and Citizens: History, Theory, Prospects* (Cambridge: Cambridge University Press, 2003), 51–62, esp. 58–9; I am grateful to Magnus Ryan for letting me see the unpublished manuscript of his Carlyle Lectures, soon to be appear in the form of a book, especially lecture 3 on 'the sense of place'.

18. Christine Carpenter, *Locality and Polity: A Study of Warwickshire Landed Society 1401–1499* (Cambridge: Cambridge University Press, 1992); for a broader formulation of the argument, see Christine Carpenter, *The Wars of the Roses: Politics and the Constitution in England, c.1437–1509* (Cambridge: Cambridge University Press, 1997).

19. John Van Engen, 'Sacred Sanctions for Lordship', in Bisson (ed.), *Cultures of Power*, 203–30, here 223–7.

20. Cited in Philippe Buc, 'Principes gentium dominantur eorum: Princely Power between Legitimacy and Illegitimacy in Twelfth-Century Exegesis', in Bisson (ed.), *Cultures of Power*, 310–28, here 310.

21. Van Engen, 'Sacred Sanctions for Lordship', 228–9.

22. Cited in Richard Tuck, 'Power and Authority in Seventeenth-Century England', *Historical Journal*, 17 (1974), 43–61, here 47.

23. David Warren Sabean, *Power in the Blood: Popular Culture and Village Discourse in Early Modern Germany* (Cambridge: Cambridge University Press, 1984), 25.

24. Nicholas Henshall, *The Myth of Absolutism: Change and Continuity in Early-Modern European Monarchy* (London: Longman, 1992), 41–2.

25. Samuel Pufendorf, *On the Law of Nature and Nations in Eight Books* (1672), book 7, chapter 4, in Craig L. Carr (ed.), *The Political Writings of Samuel Pufendorf*, trans. Michael J. Seidler (New York: Oxford University Press, 1994), 220; see also Christoph Fürbringer, *Necessitas und Libertas: Staatsbildung und Landstände im 17. Jahrhundert in Brandenburg* (Frankfurt: Peter Lang, 1985).

26. Henshall, *Myth of Absolutism*, passim.

27. See Carl Schmitt, *Gespräch über die Macht und den Zugang zum Machthaber* (Stuttgart: Klett-Cotta Verlag, 2008).

28. Vivienne Shue, *The Reach of the State: Sketches of the Chinese Body Politic* (Stanford, Calif.: Stanford University Press, 1988), 94; for a similar argument see Roy Bin Wong, *China Transformed: Historical Change and the Limits of European Experience* (Ithaca, NY: Cornell University Press, 1997), 88.

29. Madeleine Zelin, 'The Yung-Chen Reign', in Willard J. Peterson (ed.), *The Cambridge History of China*, vol. ix/1 (Cambridge: Cambridge University Press, 1988), 183–229, here 197, 223.

30. Leo K. Shin, *The Making of the Chinese State: Ethnicity and Expansion on the Ming Borderlands* (Cambridge: Cambridge University Press, 2006), 186–7.

31. James McClain, *Japan: A Modern History* (New York: W. W. Norton, 2002), 20.

32. Marius B. Jansen, *The Making of Modern Japan* (Cambridge, Mass.: Belknap Press, 2000), 47; on Tokugawa boundaries, see David L. Howell, 'Territorial

and Collective Identity in Tokugawa Japan', *Daedalus*, 127/3 (1998), 105-32, here 124.

33. McClain, *Japan*, 11-47; Jansen, *Modern Japan*, 53; Harold Bolitho, *Treasures among Men: The Fudai Daimyo in Tokugawa Japan* (New Haven: Yale University Press, 1974).

34. Conrad D. Totman, *Politics in the Tokugawa Bakufu* (Cambridge, Mass.: Harvard University Press, 1967).

35. McClain, *Japan*, 157.

36. Ibid. 153-4; Ian Neary, *The State and Politics in Modern Japan* (Oxford: Oxford University Press, 2002), 12.

37. John Gledhill, 'Legacies of Empire: Political Centralization and Class Formation in the Hispanic American World', in John Gledhill, Barbara Bender, and Mogens Trolle Larsen (eds.), *State and Society: The Emergence and Development of Social Hierarchy and Political Centralization* (London: Routledge, 1988), 302-19, here 317.

38. Donald G. McCloud, *South-East Asia: Tradition and Modernity in the Contemporary World* (Boulder, Colo.: Lynne Rienner, 1995), esp. 71-4; for a dissenting view of the role played by borders, see Mireille Mazard's forthcoming dissertation 'Political Life in the Salween Gorge' (Ph.D. thesis, Cambridge, 2010).

39. Jeffrey Herbst, *States and Power in Africa: Comparative Lessons in Authority and Control* (Princeton: Princeton University Press, 2000), 11, 12, 15, 45.

40. See John Lonsdale, 'Globalization, Ethnicity and Democracy: A View from "the Hopeless Continent" ', in A. G. Hopkins (ed.), *Globalization in World History* (London: Pimlico, 2002), 194-219, esp. 208-9.

41. Jeffrey Herbst, 'Migration, the Politics of Protest and State Consolidation in Africa', *African Affairs*, 89 (1990), 183-203, here 183.

42. Tsegaye Tegenu, *The Evolution of Ethiopian Absolutism: The Genesis and Making of the Fiscal Military State, 1696-1913* (Uppsala: Uppsala Universitet, 1996), 19, 43-55.

43. Richard Reid, *Political Power in Pre-Colonial Buganda: Economy, Society and Warfare in the Nineteenth Century* (Athens, Oh.: Ohio University Press, 2003); see also Holly Elisabeth Hanson, *Landed Obligation: The Practice of Power in Buganda* (Portsmouth, NH: Heinemann, 2003).

44. Charlotte Beradt, *Das Dritte Reich des Traumes* (Munich: Suhrkamp, 1966), 25; this and other dreams are discussed in Reinhart Koselleck, 'Terror and Dream: Methodological Remarks on the Experience of Time during the Third Reich', in Reinhart Koselleck, *Futures Past: On the Semantics of Historical Time*, trans. Keith Tribe (Cambridge, Mass.: MIT Press, 2004), 205-21.

45. George Orwell, *Nineteen Eighty-Four* (Oxford: Oxford University Press, 1990), 180.

46. Benito Mussolini, *Fascism: Doctrine and Institutions* (1935), trans. Douglas Parmée, in Adrian F. Lyttelton (ed.), *Italian Fascisms from Pareto to Gentile* (London: Cape, 1973), 37-67, here 42.

47. Luigi Sturzo, *Italien und der Faschismus* (Cologne: Gilde Verlag, 1926), cited in Wolfgang Wippermann, *Faschismustheorien: Die Entwicklung von den Anfängen bis heute* (7th edn. Darmstadt: Wissenschaftliche Buchgesellschaft, 1997), 231-4, esp. 225.

48. See the introductory essay by Max Lerner in Guy Stanton Ford, *Dictatorship in the Modern World* (Minneapolis: University of Minnesota Press, 1935, 1936), 3–20, esp. 14–16.

49. Carl J. Friedrich and Zbigniew Brzezinski, *Totalitarian Dictatorship and Autocracy* (Cambridge, Mass.: Harvard University Press, 1956).

50. R. J. B. Bosworth, '*Anno Santo 1933–4*: A Fascist Holy Year?', *European History Quarterly* (2010), forthcoming; I am grateful to Professor Bosworth for letting me see a manuscript version of this article before publication.

51. R. J. B. Bosworth, *Mussolini's Italy: Life under the Dictatorship, 1915–1945* (London: Allen Lane, 2005); see also R. J. B. Bosworth, *The Italian Dictatorship: Problems and Perspectives in the Interpretation of Mussolini and Fascism* (New York: Arnold, 1998); and R. J. B. Bosworth, 'Everyday Mussolinism: Friends, Family, Locality and Violence in Fascist Italy', *Contemporary European History*, 14 (2005), 23–43.

52. Richard J. Evans, *The Coming of the Third Reich* (London: Allen Lane, 2003).

53. Robert Gellately, *Backing Hitler: Consent and Coercion in Nazi Germany* (Oxford: Oxford University Press, 2001), 256, 257, 258; on the impact of policing, see also Robert Gellately, *The Gestapo and German Society: Enforcing Racial Policy, 1933–1945* (Oxford: Oxford University Press, 1990).

54. See for example Robert W. Thurston, *Life and Terror in Stalin's Russia, 1934–1941* (New Haven: Yale University Press, 1996); Robert W. Thurston, 'The Stakhanovite Movement: The Background to the Great Terror in the Factories, 1935–1938', in J. Arch Getty and Roberta Manning (eds.), *Stalinist Terror: New Perspectives* (Cambridge: Cambridge University Press, 1993); Robert W. Thurston, 'Reassessing the History of Soviet Workers: Opportunities to Criticize and Participate in Decision-Making, 1935–1941', in Stephen White (ed.), *New Directions in Soviet History* (London: Cambridge University Press, 1991), 160–90.

55. For a study that foregrounds these processes, see Silvia Rief, *Rustungsproduktion und Zwangsarbeit. Die Steyrer Werke und das KZ Gusen: Der Nationalsozialismus und seine Folgen* (Innsbruck: Studien Verlag, 2005).

56. John Gledhill, *Power and its Disguises: Anthropological Perspectives on Politics* (2nd edn. London: Pluto, 2000), 89–90.

57. Toyin Falola, 'Power Relations and Social Interactions among Ibadan Slaves, 1850–1900', *African Economic History*, 16 (1987), 95–114, esp. 97–9.

58. Michel Foucault, 'Two Lectures' (Lecture Two: 14 Jan. 1976), in id., *Power/Knowledge*, 78–108, here 98.

59. Cited in Bobby Baker with Larry King, *Wheeling and Dealing* (New York: Norton, 1978), 256.

60. Walter Bagehot, *The English Constitution* (2nd edn. London: Oxford University Press, 1872) viewed online at http://www.gutenberg.org/files/4351/4351–h/4351-h.htm.

61. Woodrow Wilson, *Congressional Government: A Study in American Politics* (Boston: Houghton Mifflin Company, 1885); the contrast between Bagehot and Wilson is discussed in John A. Thompson, *Woodrow Wilson* (Harlow: Longman, 2002), 25.

62. Richard J. Carwardine, *Lincoln* (Harlow: Longman, 2003), 250–7.

63. Cited in Thompson, *Woodrow Wilson*, 39.
64. Woodrow Wilson, *Constitutional Government in the United States* (based on lectures given at Columbia in 1907, 1st pub. 1908; New York: Columbia University Press, 1921), cited and discussed in Thompson, *Woodrow Wilson*, 39.
65. Cited in Thompson, *Woodrow Wilson*, 39.
66. On the 'cycle theory', see Thomas E. Cronin, 'Presidential Power Revised and Reappraised', *Western Political Quarterly*, 32/4 (Dec. 1979), 381–95, here 394; on the legislative veto, see H. G. Nicholas, *The Nature of American Politics* (Oxford: Oxford University Press, 1986), 95.
67. Arthur M. Schlesinger, *The Imperial Presidency* (Boston: Houghton Mifflin, 1973).
68. Richard M. Pious, 'Is Presidential Power "Poison"?', *Political Science Quarterly*, 89/3 (1974), 627–43.
69. See Howard J. Spitzer, 'Presidential Prerogative Power: The Case of the Bush Administration and Legislative Power', *PS: Political Science and Politics*, 24/1 (1991), 38–42.
70. Richard E. Neustadt, *Presidential Power: The Politics of Leadership from FDR to Carter* (2nd edn. New York: Wiley, 1980), 10.
71. George C. Edwards III, 'Presidential Influence in the House: Presidential Prestige as a Source of Presidential Power', *American Political Science Review*, 70/1 (1976), 101–13; George C. Edwards III, 'Presidential Electoral Performance as a Source of Electoral Power', *American Journal of Political Science*, 22/1 (1978), 152–68; Calvin Mouw and Michael MacKuen, 'The Strategic Configuration, Personal Influence, and Presidential Power in Congress', *Western Political Quarterly*, 45/3 (1992), 579–608; on the effect of opinion polls on Supreme Court adjudications, see Jeff Yates and Andrew Whitford, *Political Research Quarterly*, 51/2 (1998), 539–50.
72. See the essays in Vernon Bogdanor (ed.), *The British Constitution in the Twentieth Century* (Oxford: Oxford University Press, 2003); for a useful discussion of the issues raised by this volume, see also the review by Jon Lawrence in *Historical Journal*, 48 (2005), 1155–6. I am grateful to Jon Lawrence for sharing his understanding of these issues with me.
73. On the importance of secrecy and the challenge to it, see David Vincent, *The Culture of Secrecy: Britain, 1832–1998* (Oxford: Oxford University Press, 1998); for a less impressive discussion of the importance of executive secrecy for presidential government in the USA, see John M. Orman, *Presidential Secrecy and Deception: Beyond the Power to Persuade* (Westport, Conn.: Greenwood, 1980).
74. David S. Bell, *Presidential Power in Fifth Republic France* (Oxford: Oxford University Press, 2000), 11.
75. Christoph Schönberger, 'Gibt es im Grundgesetz ein Erbe der Monarchie? Das Amt des Bundespräsidenten zwischen Kontinuität und Diskontinuität', in Thomas Biskup and Martin Kohlrausch (eds.), *Das Erbe der Monarchie: Nachwirkungen einer deutschen Institution seit 1918* (Frankfurt am Main: Campus, 2008), 284–309.
76. See Jorma Selovuori (ed.), *Power and Bureaucracy in Finland, 1809–1998* (Helsinki: Edita, 1999); Ezra Suleiman, *Politics, Power and Bureaucracy in France: The Administrative Elite* (Princeton: Princeton University Press, 1974) and Ezra Suleiman, *Dismantling Democratic States* (Princeton: Princeton Univer-

sity Press, 2005) both make a strong case for the synergy between effective democratic government and responsive bureaucracies.

77. See Andrew Moravcsik (ed.), *Centralization or Fragmentation? Europe Facing the Challenges of Deepening, Diversity and Democracy* (New York: Council on Foreign Relations, 1998); Andrew Moravcsik, *The Choice for Europe: Social Purpose and State Power from Messina to Maastricht* (Ithaca, NY: Cornell University Press, 1999).

78. The classic exposition of this view is Ernst B. Haas, *The Uniting of Europe: Political, Social and Economical Forces* (London: Stevens and Sons, 1958).

79. See Paul Pierson and Stephan Leibfried (eds.), *European Social Policy: Between Fragmentation and Integration* (Washington: Brookings Institution, 1995); Eva Sørensen and Jacob Torfing, *Theories of Democratic Network Governance* (Basingstoke: Macmillan, 2007); for an overview that explores various methodologies, see Wolfram Kaiser, 'Networks in European Union Governance: Concepts and Contributions', *Journal of Social Policy*, 29 (2009), 131–3 and the other articles in that issue. I am grateful to Wolfram Kaiser for sharing with me his deep understanding of the historiography of the European Union.

80. Sally H. Clarke, *Consumers, the Modern Corporation and the Making of the United States Automobile Market* (Cambridge: Cambridge University Press, 2007), esp. 280–1.

81. Giles Deleuze and Félix Guattari, *A Thousand Plateaus: Capitalism and Schizophrenia*, trans. Brian Massumi (Minneapolis: University of Minnesota Press, 1987), 94, 4.

82. Francis Fukuyama, *The End of History and the Last Man* (London: Hamish Hamilton, 1992); the book elaborates arguments set out in his essay 'The End of History?', published in *The National Interest* in the summer of 1989, accessible online at http://www.wesjones.com/eoh.htm.

83. For a brief history of the Stiftung Preussischer Schlösser und Gärten, see the foundation website, esp. http://www.spsg.de/index_49_en.html.

84. On Sans Souci at Milot, Haïti, and the relationship with the Potsdam namesake, see Michel-Rolph Trouillot, *Silencing the Past: Power and the Production of History* (Boston: Beacon Press, 1995), 33–53, quotation p. xix.

85. For some compelling examples of the potentialities of this approach, see James C. Scott, *Weapons of the Weak: Everyday Forms of Peasant Resistance* (New Haven: Yale University Press, 1985); James C. Scott, *Domination and the Arts of Resistance: Hidden Transcripts* (New Haven: Yale University Press, 1990); Richard J. Evans, *Tales from the German Underworld: Crime and Punishment in the Nineteenth Century* (New Haven: Yale University Press, 1998); Natalie Zemon Davis, *Women on the Margins: Three Seventeenth-Century Lives* (Cambridge, Mass.: Harvard University Press, 1995); Natalie Zemon Davis, *The Return of Martin Guerre* (Harmondsworth: Penguin, 1983); Victoria Harris, *Selling Sex in the Third Reich: Prostitutes in German Society, 1914–1945* (Oxford: Oxford University Press, 2010).

86. Judith Butler, *The Psychic Life of Power* (Stanford, Calif.: Stanford University Press, 1997), 2.

87. Gilles Deleuze and Félix Guattari, *Kafka: Pour une littérature mineure* (Paris: Minuit, 1975).

CHAPTER 7

1. Marshall McLuhan, *Understanding Media: The Extensions of Man* (London: Routledge, 1964).
2. Asa Briggs and Peter Burke, *A Social History of the Media from Gutenberg to the Internet* (3rd edn. Cambridge: Polity, 2009), introduction.
3. Harold D. Lasswell, *Politics: Who Gets What, When, How* (New York: McGraw-Hill, 1936).
4. Albert B. Lord, *The Singer of Tales* (Cambridge, Mass.: Harvard University Press, 1960).
5. J. D. Smith, 'The Singer and the Song: A Re-assessment of Lord's "Oral Theory"', *Man*, 12 (1977), 141–53.
6. Dipesh Chakrabarty, '*Adda*: A History of Sociality', in his *Provincializing Europe* (Princeton: Princeton University Press, 2000), 180–213.
7. Eric A. Havelock, *Preface to Plato* (Oxford: Oxford University Press, 1963); Rosalind Thomas, *Literacy and Orality in Ancient Greece* (Cambridge: Cambridge University Press, 1992).
8. Ruth Finnegan, *Oral Literature in Africa* (Oxford: Clarendon Press, 1970); Karin Barber, *The Anthropology of Texts, Persons and Publics: Oral and Written Culture in Africa and beyond* (Cambridge: Cambridge University Press, 2007).
9. Frances Yates, *The Art of Memory* (London: Routledge, 1966); Mary Carruthers, *The Book of Memory: A Study of Memory in Medieval Culture* (2nd edn. Cambridge: Cambridge University Press, 2008).
10. Marcia Ascher and Robert Ascher, *Code of the Quipu: A Study in Media, Mathematics, and Culture* (Ann Arbor: University of Michigan Press, 1980).
11. Jerrold S. Cooper, 'Babylonian Beginnings: The Origin of the Cuneiform Writing System in Comparative Perspective', in Stephen Houston (ed.), *The First Writing: Script Invention as History and Process* (Cambridge: Cambridge University Press, 2004), 71–99.
12. Stephen D. Houston, 'Overture', in Houston (ed.), *The First Writing*, 3–15.
13. Harold Innis, *Empire and Communication* (Oxford: Oxford University Press, 1950).
14. Jack Goody, *The Domestication of the Savage Mind* (Cambridge: Cambridge University Press, 1977); Jack Goody, *The Interface between the Oral and the Written* (Cambridge: Cambridge University Press, 1987); Brian V. Street, *Literacy in Theory and Practice* (Cambridge: Cambridge University Press, 1984).
15. Richard Gombrich, 'When the Mahayana Began', in Tadeusz Skorupski (ed.), *The Buddhist Forum*, vol. i (London: School of Oriental and African Studies, 1990), 21–30.
16. Brian Stock, *The Implications of Literacy* (Princeton: Princeton University Press, 1983).
17. Max Weber, 'The Three Types of Legitimate Domination', in *Essays in Economic Sociology* (Princeton: Princeton University Press, 1999), 99–108.
18. Jacob Soll, *The Information Master: Jean-Baptiste Colbert's Secret State Intelligence System* (Ann Arbor: University of Michigan Press, 2009).
19. Philip A. Kuhn, *Soulstealers: The Chinese Sorcery Scare of 1768* (Cambridge, Mass.: Harvard University Press, 1990), esp. 122–4.

20. Martin Moir, 'Kaghazi Raj: Notes on the Documentary Basis of Company Rule: 1783–1858', *Indo-British Review*, 21/2 (1996), 185–93.

21. Carla Bozzolo and Ezio Ornato, *Pour une histoire du livre manuscrit au moyen âge: trois essais de codicologie quantitative* (Paris: CNRS, 1980); Michael T. Clanchy, *From Memory to Written Record: England, 1066–1307* (2nd edn. Oxford: Blackwell, 1993): Stock, *Implications of Literacy*.

22. Christine Métayer, *Au tombeau des secrets: les écrivains publics du Paris populaire, Cimetière des Saints-Innocents (XVIe–XVIIIe siècle)* (Paris: Albin Michel, 2000); Judy Kalman, *Writing on the Plaza: Mediated Literacy Practice among Scribes and Clients in Mexico City* (Cresskill, NJ: Hampton Press, 1999).

23. Brinkley Messick, *The Calligraphic State: Textual Domination and History in a Muslim Society* (Berkeley and Los Angeles: University of California Press, 1993).

24. Abdelkebir Khatibi and Mohammed Sijelmassi, *The Splendour of Islamic Calligraphy* (London: Thames and Hudson, 1976). George Makdisi, *The Rise of Humanism in Classical Islam and the Christian West* (Edinburgh: Edinburgh University Press, 1990); Houari Touati, *L'Armoire à sagesse: bibliothèques et collections en Islam* (Paris: Aubier, 2003).

25. Jonathan Berkey, *The Transmission of Knowledge in Medieval Cairo* (Princeton: Princeton University Press, 1992); Michael Chamberlain, *Knowledge and Social Practice in Medieval Damascus* (Cambridge: Cambridge University Press, 1994).

26. Elizabeth Eisenstein, *The Printing Press as an Agent of Change*, 2 vols. (Cambridge: Cambridge University Press, 1979), 3–42. Cf. Eisenstein, 'An Unacknowledged Revolution Revisited', *American Historical Review*, 107 (2002), 87–105, and Adrian Johns, 'How to Acknowledge a Revolution', ibid. 106–25.

27. Timothy H. Barrett, *The Woman Who Discovered Printing* (New Haven: Yale University Press, 2008).

28. Roger Chartier, 'Gutenberg Revisited from the East', *Late Imperial China*, 17 (1996), 1–9; Cynthia Brokaw and Kai-Wing Chow (eds.), *Print and Book Culture in Late Imperial China* (Berkeley and Los Angeles: University of California Press, 2005); Pow-Key Sohn, *Early Korean Typography* (2nd edn. Seoul: Po Chin Chai, 1982).

29. Cynthia Brokaw, 'Commercial Publishing in Late Imperial China: The Zou and Ma Family Businesses of Sibao, Fujian', *Late Imperial China*, 17 (1996), 49–92; Peter Kornicki, *The Book in Japan: A Cultural History from the Beginnings to the Nineteenth Century* (Leiden: Brill, 1998); Mary Elizabeth Berry, *Japan in Print: Information and Nation in the Early Modern Period* (Berkeley and Los Angeles: University of California Press, 2006).

30. David Landau and Peter Parshall, *The Renaissance Print 1470–1550* (New Haven: Yale University Press, 1994); Muneshige Narazaki, *The Japanese Print: Its Evolution and Essence* (Tokyo: Kodansha International, 1966).

31. Everardo Ramos, *Du marché au marchand: la gravure populaire brésilienne* (Gravelines: Musée du Dessin et de l'Estampe, 2005).

32. Francis Robinson, 'Technology and Religious Change: Islam and the Impact of Print', *Modern Asian Studies*, 27 (1993), 229–51.

33. Gerald Strauss, 'Lutheranism and Literacy', in K. von Greyerz (ed.), *Religion and Society in Early Modern Europe, 1500–1800* (London: German Historical Institute, 1984), 109–23; Robert F. Arnove and Harvey J. Graff (eds.), *National*

Literacy Campaigns: Historical and Comparative Perspectives (New York: Plenum Press, 1987).

34. Jürgen Habermas, *The Structural Transformation of the Public Sphere* (English trans. Cambridge: Polity, 1989).

35. Carlo Cipolla, *Literacy and Development in the West* (Harmondsworth: Penguin, 1969).

36. Briggs and Burke, *Social History of the Media*, 61–90. Cf. R. W. Scribner, *For the Sake of Simple Folk: Popular Propaganda for the German Reformation* (Oxford: Clarendon Press, 1994); Joad Raymond, *The Invention of the Newspaper: English Newsbooks, 1641–1649* (Oxford: Clarendon Press, 1996); Robert Darnton and Daniel Roche (eds.), *Revolution in Print: The Press in France, 1775–1800* (Berkeley and Los Angeles: University of California Press, 1989).

37. Benedict Anderson, *Imagined Communities* (3rd edn. London: Verso, 2006).

38. Robert Mandrou, *De la culture populaire aux 17e et 18e siècles: la Bibliothèque Bleue de Troyes* (Paris: Stock, 1964); Roger Chartier, *The Cultural Uses of Print in Early Modern France* (Princeton: Princeton University Press, 1987), 240–64; Julio Caro Baroja, *Ensayo sobre la literatura de cordel* (Madrid: Ediciones de la Revista del Occidente, 1969).

39. Candace Slater, *Stories on a String: The Brazilian Literature de cordel* (Berkeley and Los Angeles: University of California Press, 1982).

40. Emmanuel N. Obiechina, *An African Popular Literature: A Study of Onitsha Market Pamphlets* (Cambridge: Cambridge University Press, 1973).

41. Helen Berry, *Gender, Society and Print Culture in Late-Stuart England: The Cultural World of the Athenian Mercury* (Aldershot: Ashgate, 2003).

42. David McKitterick, *Print, Manuscript and the Search for Order, 1450–1830* (Cambridge: Cambridge University Press, 2003), 37–8.

43. Harold Love, *Scribal Publication in Seventeenth-Century England* (Oxford: Oxford University Press, 1993); François Moureau (ed.), *De bonne main: la communication manuscrite au 18e siècle* (Paris and Oxford: Universitas and Voltaire Foundation, 1993).

44. Arjun Appadurai, *Modernity at Large: Cultural Dimensions of Globalization* (Minneapolis: University of Minnesota Press, 1996).

45. Briggs and Burke, *Social History of the Media*, 121–302.

46. Daniel Lerner, *The Passing of Traditional Society: Modernizing the Middle East* (Glencoe, Ill.: Free Press, 1978), 196.

47. Ien Ang, *Watching Dallas: Soap Opera and the Melodramatic Imagination* (London: Routledge, 1985); Tamar Liebes and Elihu Katz, *The Export of Meaning: Cross-cultural Readings of Dallas* (2nd edn. Cambridge: Polity, 2004).

48. John B. Thompson, *Books in the Digital Age: The Transformation of Academic and Higher Education Publishing in Britain and the United States* (Cambridge: Polity, 2005).

49. Appadurai, *Modernity*, 21–2.

50. Dale F. Eickelman, 'Inside the Islamic Reformation', in Donna Bowen and Evelyn A. Early (eds.), *Everyday Life in the Muslim Middle East* (2nd edn. Bloomington, Ind.: Indiana University Press, 1997), 246–56.

51. Mark Poster, *What's the Matter with the Internet?* (Minneapolis: University of Minnesota Press, 2001).

CHAPTER 8

1. 'The Human Revolution: 5 Million Years Ago to 10,000BC', in Patrick K. O'Brien (ed.), *Philips Atlas of World History* (London: George Philip, 1999), 16–17.

2. Tim G. Parkin, *Old Age in the Ancient World: A Cultural and Social History* (Baltimore: Johns Hopkins University Press, 2003), 37.

3. Rivkah Harris, *Gender and Ageing in Mesopotamia* (Norman, Okla.: University of Oklahoma Press, 2000).

4. Parkin, *Old Age*, 46–51.

5. Ibid. 45.

6. Ibid. 186.

7. Shulamith Shahar, *Growing Old in the Middle Ages* (London: Routledge, 1997), 33.

8. S. R. Johansson, 'Sex and Death in Victorian England', in M. Vicinus (ed.), *Suffer and be Still* (Bloomington, Ind.: Indiana University Press, 1971), 163–81.

9. D. Herlihy, 'Life Expectancies for Women in Medieval Society', in R. T. Morwedge (ed.), *The Role of Women in the Middle Ages* (Albany, NY: State University of New York Press, 1975), 1–22.

10. Michael Anderson, 'The Social Implications of Demographic Change', in F. M. L. Thompson (ed.), *Cambridge Social History of Britain, 1750–1950*, vol. ii (Cambridge: Cambridge University Press, 1990), 27.

11. Tom Kirkwood, *Time of our Lives* (London: Phoenix, 1999), 184–95.

12. C. Haber and B. Gratton, *Old Age and the Search for Security: An American Social History* (Bloomington, Ind.: Indiana University Press, 1994). Edgar-Andre Montigny, *Foisted upon the Government? State Responsibility, Family Obligation and the Care of the Dependent Aged in Late Nineteenth Century Ontario* (Montreal: McGill-Queens University Press, 1997), 40–1.

13. *UN World Population Prospects: The 2006 Revision: 2005–2010* (Geneva: UN, 2006).

14. www.statistics.gov.uk/hub/population/deaths/life-expectancies/index.html.

15. *World Population*.

16. Amy M. Froide, *Never Married: Singlewomen in Early Modern England* (Oxford: Oxford University Press, 2005).

17. Beverley Kingston, *A History of New South Wales* (Cambridge: Cambridge University Press, 2006), 61; W. Vamplew, E. Richards, D. Jaensch, and J. Hancock, *South Australian Historical Statistics*, Monograph No. 3 (Sydney: University of New South Wales, 1986), 13–14.

18. Kingston, *History of New South Wales*, 61.

19. *Australian Social Trends* (Canberra: Australian Bureau of Statistics, 2004), www.abs.gov.au/Ausstats.

20. *Population Distribution, Aboriginal and Torres Strait Islanders*, ABS, cat. no. 4705.0, www.abs.gov.au/Ausstats.

21. www.stats.govt.nz/census.

22. *Health, US 2007*, National Center for Health Statistics, www.cdc.gov/chs (2008).

23. Office for National Statistics *Two Hundred Years of the Census*, www.statistics.gov.uk (2001).

24. Parkin, *Old Age*, 38.

25. Ibid. 139–44.
26. P. Laslett, 'Mean Household Size in England since the Sixteenth Century', in P. Laslett and R. Wall (eds.), *Household and Family in Past Time* (Cambridge: Cambridge University Press, 1972), 125–58.
27. Julian Hoppitt, 'Gregory King, 1648–1712', *Oxford Dictionary of National Biography*.
28. B. R. Mitchell, *European Historical Statistics* (abridged edn. London: Macmillan, 1978), 3–11.
29. M. Drake, 'The Census 1801–1891', in E. A. Wrigley (ed.), *Nineteenth Century Society: Essays in the Use of Quantitative Methods for the Study of Social Data* (Cambridge: Cambridge University Press, 1972), 7–46.
30. Edward Higgs, *Making Sense of the Census Revisited: Census Records for England and Wales, 1801–1901—A Handbook for Historical Researchers* (London: The National Archives and the Institute of Historical Research, 2005).
31. *200. Years of the Census* (London: Office for National Statistics, 2001), www.statistics.gov.uk.
32. B. R. Mitchell with the collaboration of Phyllis Deane, *Abstract of British Historical Statistics* (Cambridge: Cambridge University Press, 1962), 3.
33. A. Sauvy, 'Social and Economic Consequences of Ageing of Western Populations', *Population Studies*, 2/1 (June 1948), 115–24. Pat Thane, 'The Debate on the Declining Birth-Rate in Britain: The "Menace" of an Ageing Population, 1920s–1950s', *Continuity and Change*, 5/2 (1990), 283–305.
34. Thane, 'The Debate on the Declining Birth-Rate in Britain', 289.
35. R. M. Smith, 'Demography and Medicine', in W. F. Bynum and Roy Porter (eds.), *Companion Encyclopaedia of the History of Medicine*, vol. ii (London: Routledge, 1993), 1664.
36. E. G. Knox, 'Thomas McKeown, 1912–1988', *Oxford Dictionary of National Biography*.
37. S. Szreter, 'The Importance of Social Intervention in Britain's Mortality Decline', *Social History of Medicine*, 1/1 (Apr. 1988).
38. E. Gautier and L. Henry, *Population de Crulai, paroisse Normande* (Paris: INED, 1958).
39. Ibid. Smith, 'Demography', 1668–9.
40. E. A. Wrigley and R. S. Schofield, *The Population History of England, 1541–1871: A Reconstruction* (Cambridge: Cambridge University Press, 1981). E. A. Wrigley, R. S. Davies, J. E. Oeppen, and R. S. Schofield, *English Population History from Family Reconstitution, 1580–1837* (Cambridge: Cambridge University Press, 1997).
41. Laslett, 'Mean Household Size since the Sixteenth Century', in Laslett and Wall (eds.), *Household and Family in Past Time*, 125–58.
42. J. Hajnal, 'Two Kinds of Preindustrial Household Formation System', *Population and Development Review*, 8/3 (1982), 449–93.
43. Peter Czap Jr., ' "A Large Family: The Peasant's Greatest Wealth": Serf Households in Mishino, Russia, 1814–1858', in R. Wall, Jean Robin, and Peter Laslett (eds.), *Family Forms in Historic Europe* (Cambridge: Cambridge University Press, 1983), 105–50.

44. Tracy Dennison, 'Serfdom and Household Structure in Central Russia: Voshchazhnikovo, 1816–1858', *Continuity and Change*, 18/3 (2003), 419.

45. Silvia Sovic, 'European Family History: Moving beyond Stereotypes of "East" and "West"', *Cultural and Social History*, 5/2 (July 2008), 1411–64.

46. Michael Anderson, *Family Structure in Nineteenth Century Lancashire* (Cambridge: Cambridge University Press, 1971), 56.

47. Thane, *Old Age*, 119–46, 287–307, 407–35.

48. Smith, 'Demography', 1672.

49. Wrigley and Schofield, *Population History*.

50. D. V. Glass, 'Introduction', in id. and D. E. C. Eversley, *Population in History: Essays in Historical Demography* (London: Edward Arnold, 1965), 1–22. H. J. Habbakuk, *Population Growth and Economic Development since 1570* (Leicester: Leicester University Press, 1971).

51. R. D. Lee, 'Inverse Projection and Back Projection: A Critical Appraisal and Comparative Results for England, 1539 to 1851', *Population Studies*, 39 (1985), 233–48; Wrigley and Schofield, *Population History*.

52. Smith, 'Demography', 1676; J. Walter and R. Schofield, 'Famine, Disease and Crisis Mortality in Early Modern Society', in eid. (eds.), *Famine, Disease and Social Order in Early Modern Society* (Cambridge: Cambridge University Press: 1989).

53. Smith, 'Demography', 1677–8. Wrigley and Schofield, *Population History*, 384–93.

54. P. Slack, *The Impact of Plague in Tudor and Stuart England* (London: Routledge, 1985).

55. Smith, 'Demography', 1681.

56. C. Klapisch-Zuber, *Women, Family and Ritual in Renaissance Italy*, trans. L. Cochrane (Chicago: University of Chicago Press, 1985).

57. G. Levi, *Inheriting Power: The Story of an Exorcist* (Chicago: University of Chicago Press, 1988).

58. Smith, 'Demography', 1668–73; A.-S. Kälvemark, 'The Country that Kept Track of its Population: Methodological Aspects of Swedish Population Records', in J. Sundin and E. Söderland (eds.), *Time, Space and Man: Essays in Microdemography* (Stockholm: Almqvist & Wiksell, 1979), 221–38.

59. J. E. Knoedel, *Demographic Behaviour in the Past: Study of Fourteen German Village Populations in the Eighteenth and Nineteenth Centuries* (Cambridge: Cambridge University Press, 1988).

60. Sovic, 'European Family History'.

61. Smith, 'Demography', 1669–70.

62. Hajnal, 'Two Kinds'.

63. Sovic, 'European Family History'.

64. E. Garrett, A. Reid, K. Schurer, and S. Szreter, *Changing Family Size in England and Wales: Place, Class, Demography, 1891–1911* (Cambridge: Cambridge University Press, 2001).

65. R. Woods, P. Watterson, and J. Woodward, 'The Cause of Rapid Infant Mortality Decline in England and Wales, 1861–1921', Parts 1 and 2, *Population Studies*, 42 (1988), 343–66; 43 (1989), 113–32. R. Lesthaeghe, 'The Breast-Feeding Hypothesis and Regional Differentials in Infant and Child Mortality in Belgium and

the Netherlands during the Nineteenth Century', in R. M. Smith (ed.), *Regional and Spatial Demographic Patterns in the Past* (Oxford: Blackwell, 1992).

66. M. Quine, *Population Politics in Twentieth Century Europe* (London: Routledge, 1996).

67. Gunnar and Alva Myrdal, *Crisis in the Population Question* (Stockholm: Bonnier, 1934).

68. D. Kevles, *In the Name of Eugenics: Genetics and the Uses of Human Heredity* (New York: Knopf, 1985).

69. G. Bock, 'Anti-natalism, Maternity and Paternity in National Socialist Racism', in G. Bock and P. Thane (eds.), *Maternity and Gender Politics: Women and the Rise of the European Welfare States, 1880s–1950s* (London: Routledge, 1991), 233–55.

70. UN, *World Population Prospects: The 2004 Revision* (New York: UN, 2005).

71. www.statistics.gov.uk/cci/nugget.asp?ID=951.

72. Among others: David Sabean, *Kinship in Neckerhausen, 1700–1870* (Cambridge: Cambridge University Press, 1998); D. Sabean, S. Teuscher, and J. Matthieu (eds.), *Kinship in Europe: Approaches to Long-Term Development, 1300–1900* (New York: Oxford University Press, 2007); N. Tadmor, *Family and Friends in Eighteenth Century England: Household, Kinship and Patronage* (Cambridge: Cambridge University Press, 2001); M. Segalen, *Historical Anthropology of the Family*, trans. J. C. Whitehouse and S. Matthews, (Cambridge: Cambridge University Press, 1986); M. Segalen, *Fifteen Generations of Bretons: Kinship and Society in Lower Brittany* (Cambridge: Cambridge University Press, 1991).

CHAPTER 9

This chapter is dedicated to Charlotte Furth in celebration of her career-long contributions to the study of gender, medicine, and science in China. In researching this chapter I benefited from generous colleagues who suggested readings in the field of library science as well as the histories of Latin America, Africa, the Middle East, and the USA: Jenna Freedman, Nara Milanich, Lynn M. Thomas, Abosede George, Marilyn Booth, and Rosalind Rosenberg. My deep gratitude also goes to members of the Feminist Reading Group at Columbia for critiquing a draft of this chapter.

1. Jorgensen was articulating a medical theory of 'universal bisexuality' that originated in Germany in the early twentieth century and enjoyed wide circulation in Europe but fell on deaf ears in the USA. Joanne Meyerowitz, *How Sex Changed: A History of Transsexuality in the United States* (Cambridge, Mass.: Harvard University Press, 2002), quote from 98. Thomas Laqueur has mapped the transition of a 'one-sex/flesh model' to a 'two-sex/flesh model' in Europe around the seventeenth century in his *Making Sex: Body and Gender from the Greeks to Freud* (Cambridge, Mass.: Harvard University Press, 1990).

2. Simone de Beauvoir famously wrote that 'One is not born, but rather becomes, a woman.' *The Second Sex*, trans. and ed. H. M. Parshley (New York: Penguin, 1952), 301. The English translation appeared the same year Jorgensen became a media sensation; the French original *Deuxième Sex* was published in 1949. Judith Butler has credited Beauvoir for heralding the view of sex as distinct from

gender, hence opening up the possibility of gender as choice. 'Sex and Gender in Simone de Beauvoir's *Second Sex*', *Yale French Studies*, 72 (1986), 35–49.

3. John Money, 'Hermaphroditism, Gender and Precocity in Hyperadrenocorticism: Psychologic Findings', *Bulletin of the Johns Hopkins Hospital*, 96 (1955), 253–64. The definition of gender identity is from John Money and Anke A. Ehrhardt, *Man and Woman, Boy and Girl: The Differentiation and Dimorphism of Gender Identity from Conception to Maturity* (Baltimore: Johns Hopkins University Press, 1972), 4. Money's 'gender roles' recalls anthropologist Margaret Mead's 'sex roles' advanced in the 1920s. In 1964, Stoller and Greenson coined the term 'gender identity' to refer to 'one's sense of being a member of a particular sex' (Meyerowitz, *How Sex Changed*, 115).

4. http://en.wikipedia.org/wiki/Gender.

5. Money and Ehrhardt, *Man and Woman*, 18. Also in the early 1970s, feminist anthropologist Gayle Rubin coined 'the sex-gender system' to refer to 'the set of arrangements by which a society transforms biological sexuality into products of human activity, and in which these transformed sexual needs are satisfied'. In highlighting the imprint of culture, she thus questioned the assumption that heterosexuality is normative. Rubin, 'The Traffic in Women: Notes on the "Political Economy" of Sex', in Rayna Reiter (ed.), *Toward an Anthropology of Women* (New York: Monthly Review Press, 1975), 157–210.

6. Suzanne J. Kessler and Wendy McKenna, *Gender: An Ethnomethodological Approach* (New York: Wiley, 1978). Nancy Chodorow spoke of 'gender personality' and 'sex roles' of boys and girls in her 'Family Structure and Feminine Personality', in Michelle Zimbalist Rosaldo and Louise Lamphere (eds.), *Woman, Culture, and Society* (Stanford, Calif.: Stanford University Press, 1974), 48–58.

7. Besides Rosaldo and Lamphere, other pioneering anthropological works of gender include Ann Oakley, *Sex, Gender and Society* (London: Maurice Temple Smith Ltd., 1972); Shirley Ardener (ed.), *Defining Females: The Nature of Women in Society* (London: Croom Helm, 1978); Carol P. MacCormack and Marilyn Strathern (eds.), *Nature, Culture, and Gender* (Cambridge: Cambridge University Press, 1980); Sherry B. Ortner and Harriet Whitehead (eds.), *Sexual Meanings: The Cultural Construction of Gender and Sexuality* (Cambridge: Cambridge University Press, 1981).

8. Joan Kelly, 'Did Women Have a Renaissance?', in *Women, History, and Theory: The Essays of Joan Kelly* (Chicago: University of Chicago Press, 1984), 19–50, quote from 19. This essay was formulated in a course Kelly taught at Sarah Lawrence College in 1972–3. The term 'doubled vision' is from a title of one of Kelly's articles, first published in 1979 and reprinted in *Women, History, and Theory*, 51–64.

9. Fowler's *Dictionary of Modern English Usage*, 211, cited in http://en.wikipedia. org/wiki/Gender, 10 n. 6. Joan W. Scott, 'Gender: A Useful Category of Historical Analysis', *American Historical Review*, 91/5 (1986), 1053–75; reprinted in *Gender and the Politics of History* (New York: Columbia University Press, 1988), quote from 28.

10. For a genealogy of gender in the 1970s–2000s with an emphasis on European history, see Kathleen Canning, 'Gender History: Meanings, Methods, and

Metanarratives', in *Gender History in Practice: Historical Perspectives on Bodies, Class, and Citizenship* (Ithaca, NY: Cornell University Press, 2006), 3–62.

11. Linda Gordon, 'Response to Scott', *Signs*, 5/4 (1990), 852. Gordon used gender 'to describe a power system in which women are subordinated through relations that are contradictory, ambiguous, and conflictual'. Few historians of gender would dispute this usage. In her review of Scott, Laura Downs has similar misgivings about being called 'other', which to her means to be 'made to wear dark masks of negativity: that which the great white male is not'. The experience of being other, wrought of 'sorrows, misapprehension and oppression...cannot form a basis for the true knowledge of self or of history'. Laura Lee Downs, 'If "Woman" is Just an Empty Category, then Why Am I Afraid to Walk Alone at Night? Identity Politics Meets the Postmodern Subject', *Comparative Studies of Societies and History*, 35/2 (Apr. 1993), 414–37, quote from 415.

12. Kathleen Canning has summarized the debates on poststructuralism inspired by Scott in her essay 'Feminist History after the Linguistic Turn: Historicizing Discourse and Experience', in *Gender History in Practice*, 63–100.

13. Joan Hoff, 'Gender as a Postmodern Category of Paralysis', *Women's Studies International Forum*, 17/4 (1994), 443–7 quotes from 444, 445. Brazilian historians Mary Del Priore and Maria Clementina Pereira Cunha have expressed similar concerns; see Sueann Caulfield, 'The History of Gender in the Historiography of Latin America', *Hispanic American Historical Review*, 81/3–4 (2001), 454–5 n. 9. See also Claudia Koonz's disagreements with Scott about the relationship between scholarship and politics in her review, 'Post Scripts', *Women's Review of Books*, 6/4 (Jan. 1989), 19–20. For surveys of the impact of Scott's essay twenty years after its publication, see the retrospective Forum of the *American Historical Review*, 113/5 (Dec. 2008). Editors call Scott's 'one of the most important and influential articles ever published in this journal' which began publication in 1895 (p. xiv).

14. The phrase 'social category imposed on bodies' is Lisa Lindsay's, in her *Working with Gender: Wage Labor and Social Change in Southwestern Nigeria* (Portsmouth, NH: Heinemann, 2003), 11.

15. The scholarship on the histories of women, men, and gender since the 1980s has been so rich that it is impossible to mention, let alone discuss, all the important works in this chapter. Interested readers may consult the excellent review articles and introductory pamphlets in each field. For Africa, see Nancy Rose Hunt, 'Placing African Women's History and Locating Gender', *Social History*, 14/3 (1989), 359–79; Linzi Manicom, 'Ruling Relations: Rethinking State and Gender in South African History', *Journal of African History*, 33 (1992), 441–65; Nancy Rose Hunt, 'Introduction', in Nancy Rose Hunt, Tessie P. Liu, and Jean Quataert (eds.), *Gendered Colonialisms in African History* (Oxford: Oxford University Press, 1997). For East Asia, see Susan Mann, *East Asia (China, Japan, Korea)*, Women's and Gender History in Global Perspective series, ed. Bonnie Smith (Washington: American Historical Association, 1999); Gail Hershatter, 'State of the Field: Women in China's Long Twentieth Century', *Journal of Asian Studies*, 63/4 (Nov. 2004), 991–1065; Gail Hershatter and Wang Zheng, 'Chinese History: A Useful Category of Gender Analysis',

American Historical Review, 113/5 (Dec. 2008), 1404–21. For the Middle East and North Africa, see Deniz Kandiyoti, 'Contemporary Feminist Scholarship and Middle East Studies', in id. (ed.), *Gendering the Middle East: Emerging Perspectives* (Syracuse, NY: Syracuse University Press, 1996), 1–28; Marilyn Booth, 'On Gender, History,... and Fiction', in Israel Gershoni, Amy Singer, and Y. Hakan Erdem (eds.), *Middle Eastern Historiographies: Narrating the Twentieth Century* (Seattle: University of Washington Press, 2006), 211–41. For Latin America, see Marysa Navarro, 'Research on Latin American Women', *Signs*, 5/1 (1979), 111–20; Sueann Caulfield, 'The History of Gender in the Historiography of Latin America', *Hispanic American Historical Review*, 81/3–4 (2001), 449–90.

16. Booth, 'On Gender, History,... and Fiction', 220.

17. Pioneering monographs include Katherine Kish Sklar, *Catharine Beecher: A Study in American Domesticity* (New Haven: Yale University Press, 1973); Nancy F. Cott, *The Bonds of Womanhood: 'Woman's Sphere' in New England* (New Haven: Yale University Press, 1977); Bonnie G. Smith, *Ladies of the Leisure Class: The Bourgeoises of Northern France in the Nineteenth Century* (Princeton: Princeton University Press, 1981). Pioneering works on women in the Ottoman Empire and imperial China also focused on the domestic realm; see Leslie P. Pierce, *The Imperial Harem: Women and Sovereignty in the Ottoman Empire* (New York: Oxford University Press, 1993); Patricia Buckley Ebrey, *The Inner Quarters: Marriage and the Lives of Chinese Women in the Sung Period* (Berkeley and Los Angeles: University of California Press, 1993). Susan Mann has emphasized the family as the center of imperial Chinese polity in *Precious Records: Women in China's Long Eighteenth Century* (Stanford, Calif.: Stanford University Press, 1997).

18. Gerda Lerner, *The Creation of Patriarchy* (New York: Oxford University Press, 1986), 6.

19. Frederick Engels, *The Origin of the Family, Private Property and the State*, ed. Eleanor Leacock (New York: International House Publishers, 1972). The German work was first translated into English by Alex West in 1942.

20. Itsue Takamure, *Shōseikon no kenkyū* (Tokyo: Rironsha, 1966). The slogan 'In the beginning, woman was the sun' was coined by feminist activist Hiratsuka Raichō (1886–1971). See *In the Beginning, Woman Was the Sun: The Autobiography of a Japanese Feminist/Hiratsuka Raichō*, trans. Teruko Craig (New York: Columbia University Press, 2006).

21. Hiroko Sekiguchi, 'The Patriarchal Family Paradigm in Eighth-Century Japan', in Dorothy Ko, JaHyun Kim Haboush, and Joan R. Piggott (eds.), *Women and Confucian Cultures in Premodern China, Korea, and Japan* (Berkeley and Los Angeles: University of California Press, 2003), 29. See also the introduction and Piggott's chapter. For marriage and family formation in China, see Rubie S. Watson and Patricia Ebrey (eds.), *Marriage and Inequality in Chinese Society* (Berkeley and Los Angeles: University of California Press, 1991). Martina Deuchler has analyzed how the process of Confucianization engendered different results in Korea, where the native kinship structures were divergent from those in the Japanese archipelago. *The Confucian Transformation of Korea: A Study of Society and Ideology* (Cambridge, Mass.: Harvard University Press, 1992).

22. Haruko Wakita, *Women in Medieval Japan: Motherhood, Household Management and Sexuality*, trans. Alison Tokita (Tokyo: University of Tokyo Press, 2006). See also Anne Walthall, Hitomi Tonomura, and Haruko Wakita (eds.), *Women and Class in Japanese History* (Ann Arbor: Michigan University Press, 1999).

23. Alice Kessler-Harris, *In Pursuit of Equity: Women, Men, and the Quest for Economic Citizenship in 20th-Century America* (Oxford: Oxford University Press, 2001), 109. The male breadwinner ideal was entrenched in England by the beginning of the twentieth century; see Sonya O. Rose, *Limited Livelihoods: Gender and Class in Nineteenth-Century England* (Berkeley and Los Angeles: University of California Press, 1992); John Tosh, *A Man's Place: Masculinity and the Middle-Class Home in Victorian England* (New Haven: Yale University Press, 1999). For a comparison between England and France, see Susan Pedersen, *Family, Dependence, and the Origins of the Welfare State: Britain and France, 1914–1945* (Cambridge: Cambridge University Press, 1993). See also Colin Creighton's review article focusing on Britain, 'The Rise of a Male Breadwinner Family: A Reappraisal', *Comparative Studies in Society and History*, 38/2 (Apr. 1966), 310–37.

24. Elizabeth Dore and Maxine Molyneux (eds.), *Hidden Histories of Gender and the State in Latin America* (Durham, NC: University of North Carolina Press, 2000). This anthology grew out of a 1996 conference and is 'a response to Joan Scott's call to examine how politics constructs gender and gender constructs politics' (3).

25. Karin Alejandra Rosemblatt, *Gendered Compromises: Political Cultures and the State in Chile, 1920–1950* (Chapel Hill, NC: University of North Carolina Press, 2000).

26. Nara Milanich, 'Whither Family History?', *American Historical Review*, 112/2 (2007), 439–58.

27. Rosemblatt has thus called the Popular Front state 'hegemonic' (14–15). For modern states seeking to nationalize women and rationalize domesticity after the First World War, see Victoria de Grazia, *How Fascism Ruled Women: Italy, 1922–1945* (Berkeley and Los Angeles: University of California Press, 1992).

28. Lindsay, *Working with Gender*, 88.

29. Heidi Tinsman, 'Reviving Feminist Materialism: Gender and Neoliberalism in Pinochet's Chile', *Signs*, 26/1 (2000), 145–88, quotes from 147. Tinsman echoed Lila Abu-Lughod, 'The Romance of Resistance: Tracing Transformations of Power through Bedouin Women', *American Ethnologist*, 17/1 (Feb. 1990), 41–55.

30. Andrea A. Cornwall, 'To Be A Man Is More Than a Day's Work: Shifting Ideals of Masculinity in Ado-Odo, Southwestern Nigeria', in Lisa A. Lindsay and Stephan F. Miescher (eds.), *Men and Masculinities in Modern Africa* (Portsmouth, NH: Heinemann, 2003), 244. As attested by this volume, historians of Africa have produced some of the most sophisticated works on the histories of men and masculinity; by and large they have found sociologist R. W. Connell's notions of 'hegemonic masculinity' and 'subordinate masculinity' of limited applicability to colonial Africa. See R. W. Connell, *Masculinities* (2nd edn. Berkeley and Los Angeles: University of California Press, 2005).

History-minded specialists of literature have analyzed masculinities in China; see Kam Louie, *Theorising Chinese Masculinity: Society and Gender in China* (Cambridge: Cambridge University Press, 2002); Martin Huang, *Negotiating Masculinities in Late Imperial China* (Honolulu: University of Hawaii Press, 2006). For South Asia, see Mrinalini Sinha, *Colonial Masculinity: The 'Manly Englishman' and the 'Effeminate Bengali' in the Late Nineteenth Century* (New Delhi: Manchester University Press, 1997).

31. For Latin America, see Milanich, 'Whither Family History?' For China, see Patricia Buckley Ebrey and James L. Watson (eds.), *Kinship Organization in Late Imperial China, 1000–1940* (Berkeley and Los Angeles: University of California Press, 1986) and James L. Watson and Evelyn S. Rawski (eds.), *Death Ritual in Late Imperial and Modern China* (Berkeley and Los Angeles: University of California Press, 1988).

32. Lynn M. Thomas, *Politics of the Womb: Women, Reproduction, and the State in Kenya* (Berkeley and Los Angeles: University of California Press, 2003). Gendered reproduction refers to 'the intimate relationship between gender ideologies and procreative processes'. See Lynn M. Thomas, 'Gendered Reproduction: Placing Schoolgirl Pregnancies in African History', in Catherine M. Cole, Takyiwaa Manuh, and Stephen F. Miescher (eds.), *Africa after Gender?* (Bloomington, Ind.: Indiana University Press, 2007), 49. Nancy Rose Hunt first called attention to the importance of 'colonial maternities' in her *A Colonial Lexicon of Birth Ritual, Medicalization, and Mobility in the Congo* (Durham, NC: University of North Carolina Press, 1999).

33. Kathryn Burns, 'Gender and the Politics of Mestizaje: The Convent of Santa Clara in Cuzco, Peru', *Hispanic American Historical Review*, 78/1 (1998), 5–44. The convent of Santa Clara was inaugurated in 1558, followed by Santa Catalina in 1605 and Santa Teresa in 1673. For a fuller history of the convents especially in the seventeenth and eighteenth centuries, see Burns, *Colonial Habits: Convents and the Spiritual Economy of Cuzco, Peru* (Durham, NC: University of North Carolina Press, 1999). Burns chose the title of the article as a tribute to Joan Scott's book *Gender and the Politics of History*.

34. Ann L. Stoler, 'Making Empire Respectable: The Politics of Race and Sexual Morality in 20th-Century Colonial Cultures', *American Ethnologist*, 16/4 (Nov. 1989), 634–60.

35. For female genital cutting, see Thomas, *Politics of the Womb*. For sati, see Lata Mani, *Contentious Traditions: The Debate on Sati in Colonial India* (Berkeley and Los Angeles: University of California Press, 1998). For foot-binding, see Dorothy Ko, *Cinderella's Sisters: A Revisionist History of Footbinding* (Berkeley and Los Angeles: University of California Press, 2005).

36. Partha Chatterjee, 'The Nationalist Resolutions of the Women's Question', in Kumkum Sangari and Sudesh Vaid (eds.), *Recasting Women: Essays in Indian Colonial History* (New Brunswick, NJ: Rutgers University Press, 1990), 233–53; Prasenjit Duara, 'The Regime of Authenticity: Timelessness, Gender and National History in Modern China', *History and Theory*, 37/3 (Oct. 1998), 287–308; Lydia H. Liu, 'The Female Body in Nationalist Discourse: Manchuria in Xiao Hong's *Field of Life and Death*', in Angela Zito and Tani E. Barlow

(eds.), *Body, Subject and Power in China* (Chicago: Chicago University Press, 1994), 157–77.

37. *Naissance de la clinique* (Paris: Presses Universitaires de France, 1963); translated as *The Birth of the Clinic* in 1973. Volume i of *Histoire de la sexualité* (Paris: Gallimard, 1976) was translated as *History of Sexuality* in 1978.

38. Barbara Duden, *The Woman beneath the Skin: A Doctor's Patients in Eighteenth-Century Germany*, trans. Thomas Dunlap (Cambridge, Mass.: Harvard University Press, 1991), 105; German original published in 1987. The German title is 'History under the Skin' (*Geschichte unter der Haut: Ein Eisenacher Arzt und seine Patientinen um 1730*) and says nothing about 'woman'.

39. According to Duden, this involved several moves, including the placing of 'nature' opposite to 'culture' at the end of the eighteenth century, the creation of 'reproduction' as a comprehensive category encompassing the previously disparate conception, pregnancy, and childbirth in opposition to 'production' around 1850, as well as the emergence of the category of 'sexuality' with the Marquis de Sade (1740–1814). *Woman beneath the Skin*, 20–9. See also Foucault, *History of Sexuality*; Londa Schiebinger, *Nature's Body: Gender in the Making of Modern Science* (London: Pandora, 1993). The career of the category 'woman' in colonial modernity took on a vastly different trajectory. See Tani E. Barlow, 'Theorizing Woman: *Funü, Guojia, Jiating*', in Zito and Barlow (eds.), *Body, Subject and Power*, 253–90; *The Question of Women in Chinese Feminism* (Durham, NC: University of North Carolina Press, 2004).

40. Ifi Amadiume, *Male Daughters, Female Husbands: Gender and Sex in an African Society* (London: Zed, 1987), 17.

41. Oyeronke Oyewumi, *The Invention of Women: Making an African Sense of Western Gender Discourses* (Minneapolis: University of Minnesota Press, 1997), p. xi. For a review, see Lorand J. Matory, 'Gendered Agendas: The Secrets Scholars Keep about Yoruba-Atlantic Region', *Gender and History*, 15/3 (2003), 409–39. Although some critics find its historical evidence wanting, the importance of *Invention of Women* lies in its theoretical interventions. Oyewumi has inspired a conference devoted to the question of the applicability of 'gender' in studies of Africa. See Cole et al., *Africa after Gender?*

42. Afsaneh Najmabadi, 'Mapping Transformations of Sex, Gender, and Sexuality in Modern Iran', *Social Analysis*, 49/2 (Summer 2005), 54–77, quote from 55. See also *Women with Mustaches and Men without Beards: Gender and Sexual Anxieties of Iranian Modernity* (Berkeley and Los Angeles: University of California Press, 2005).

43. Judith Butler, *Gender Trouble: Feminism and the Subversion of Identity* (New York: Routledge, 1990), 7.

44. Joan H. Fujimura, 'Sex Genes: A Critical Sociomaterial Approach to the Politics and Molecular Genetics of Sex Determination', *Signs*, 32/1 (2006), 49–82, quotes from 70, 75.

45. Anne Fausto-Sterling, *Sexing the Body: Gender Politics and the Construction of Sexuality* (New York: Basic Books, 2000), 242.

CHAPTER 10

1. www.unesco.org/culture/ich/index.php. I draw heavily in this chapter on two important discussions of contemporay questions of 'culture' and 'rights: Susan Wrights, 'The Politicisation of "Culture"', *Anthropology Today*, 14/1 (1998), 7–15 and Jane K. Cowan, 'Introduction', in Jane K. Cowan, Marie–Benedicte Dembar, and Richard A. Wilson (eds.), *Culture and Rights: Anthropological Perspectives* (Cambridge: Cambridge University Press, 2001), 1–27.

2. www.unesco.org/culture/ich/index.php.

3. For a fuller analysis of the complex meanings and history of Vimbuza see Steven M. Friedson, *Dancing Prophets: Musical Experience in Tumbuka Healing* (Chicago: University of Chicago Press, 1996).

4. Details of the UNICEF campaign in Malawi can be found at http://www.unicef.org/infobycountry/malawi_40938.html.

5. Harri Englund, *Prisoners of Freedom: Human Rights and the African Poor* (Berkeley and Los Angeles: University of California Press, 2006); Thomas Hylland Eriksen, 'Between Universalism and Relativism: A Critique of the UNESCO Concept of Culture', in Cowan, Dembar, and Wilson (eds.), *Culture and Rights:* 127–49.

6. Raymond Williams, *Culture* (London: Fontana, 1981); Raymond Williams, *Keywords: A Vocabulary of Culture and Society* (London: Fontana, 1976); Terry Eagleton, *The Idea of Culture* (Oxford: Oxford University Press, 2000).

7. Eagleton, *The Idea of Culture*, 3–4.

8. J. G. von Herder, *Herder on Social and Political Culture*, ed. and trans. F. M. Barnard (Cambridge: Cambridge University Press, 1969).

9. Matthew Arnold, *Culture and Anarchy*, ed. J. Dover Wilson (Cambridge: Cambridge University Press, 1932; 1st pub. 1864).

10. Eagleton, *The Idea of Culture*, 15; Pierre Bourdieu, *The Field of Cultural Production*, ed. and introd. R. Johnson (Oxford: Oxford University Press, 1993).

11. Francis Mulhern, *Culture/Metaculture* (London: Routledge, 2000). By thanks to Stefin Collini for drawing Ruthern's wrote to my attention and for a useful discussion for Cultural studies.

12. Richard Hoggart, *The Uses of Literacy* (Harmondsworth: Penguin, 1985); Richard Hoggart, *Only Connect: On Culture and Communication* (London: Chatto and Windus, 1972); Sue Owen (ed.), *Richard Hoggart and Cultural Studies* (Basingstoke: Macmillan, 2008); Mulhern, *Culture/Metaculture*, 56–60.

13. Dai Smith, *Raymond Williams: A Warrior's Tale* (Aberteifi: Parthian, 2008); John Higgins, *Raymond Williams: Literature, Marxism and Cultural Materialism* (London: Routledge, 1996); John Eldridge and Lizzie Eldridge, *Raymond Williams: Making Connections* (London: Routledge, 1994).

14. Raymond Williams, *Culture and Society* (Harmondsworth: Penguin, 1961; 1st pub. 1958); Raymond Williams, *The Long Revolution* (Harmondsworth: Penguin, 1961); Raymond Williams, *Marxism and Literature* (Oxford: Oxford University Press, 1977); Raymond Williams, *Problems in Materialism and Culture* (London: Verso, 1980); Williams, *Culture*; Williams, *Keywords*.

15. On Hall and the Centre for Contemporary Cultural Studies: Mulhern, *Culture/Metaculture*, 98–131; David Morley and Kuan-Hsing Chen (eds.), *Stuart Hall: Critical Dialogues in Cultural Studies* (London: Routledge, 1996); Paul Gilroy, Lawrence Grossberg, and Angela McRobbie (eds.), *Without Guarantees:*

In Honour of Stuart Hall (London: Verso, 2000); Stuart Hall, 'Cultural Studies and the Centre: Some Problematics and Problems', in Stuart Hall et al. (eds.), *Culture, Media, Language: Working Papers in Cultural Studies, 1972–79* (London: Hutchinson, 1992), 15–47.

16. Stuart Hall, 'Gramsci's Relevance for the Study of Race and Ethnicity', in Morley and Chen (eds.), *Stuart Hall*, 411–40; Stuart Hall, 'New Ethnicities', in Morley and Chen (eds.), *Stuart Hall*, 262–75; Stuart Hall, 'What Is This "Black" in Black Popular Culture?', in Morley and Chen (eds.), *Stuart Hall*, 465–75; Angela McRobbie, 'Looking Back at New Times and its Critics', in Morley and Chen (eds.), *Stuart Hall*, 238–61.

17. Paul Gilroy, *'There Ain't No Black in the Union Jack': The Cultural Politics of Race and Nation* (London: Routledge, 1988). Gilroy's work is explored in more detail later.

18. Tylor quoted in Adam Kuper, *Culture: The Anthropologist's Account* (Cambridge, Mass.: Harvard University Press, 1999), 56.

19. Kuper, *Culture*, 59–60; George W. Stocking, Jr., *Race, Culture and Evolution: Essays in the History of Anthropology* (New York: University of Chicago Press, 1968), 73; Roy Wagner, *The Invention of Culture* (Chicago: University of Chicago Press, 1975).

20. Kuper, *Culture*, 61.

21. Talal Asad (ed.), *Anthropology and the Colonial Encounter* (London: Ithaca Press, 1973); George Stocking (ed.), *Colonial Situations: Essays on the Contextualisation of Ethnographic Knowledge*, History of Anthropology 7 (Madison: University of Wisconsin Press, 1991).

22. Richard Keller, *Colonial Madness: Psychiatry in French North Africa* (Chicago: University of Chicago Press, 2007).

23. Partha Chatterjee, 'The Nationalist Resolution of the Woman Question', in Kumkum Sangari and Sudesh Vaid (eds.), *Re-Casting Women* (New Delhi: Manchester University Press, 1989), 233–53.

24. Clifford Geertz, 'Deep Play: Notes on the Balinese Cockfight' (first published in 1972), reprinted in Clifford Geertz, *The Interpretation of Cultures* (New York: Basic Books, 1973); Sherry B. Ortner (ed.), *The Fate of 'Culture': Clifford Geertz and Beyond* (Berkeley and Los Angeles: University of California Press, 1999); Kuper, *Culture*, chap. 3; Anna Green, *Cultural History* (Basingstoke: Macmillan, 2008), 56–8.

25. Geertz, *The Interpretation of Cultures*, 89.

26. Ibid. 9.

27. On the cultural history of cultural history see Green, *Cultural History*; Peter Burke, *What is Cultural History* (Cambridge: Cambridge University Press, 2004).

28. E. P. Thompson, 'The Long Revolution', *New Left Review*, 9 (1961), 24–33; E. P. Thompson, *The Making of the English Working Class* (Harmondsworth: Penguin, 1976; 1st pub. 1963); E. P. Thompson, *The Poverty of Theory* (New York: Merlin Press, 1978).

29. Lynn Hunt (ed.), *The New Cultural History* (Berkeley and Los Angeles: University of California Press, 1989); Green, *Cultural History*; Roger Chartier, *Cultural History: Between Practices and Representations* (Ithaca, NY: Cornell University Press,

1988); Peter Burke, *What is Cultural History?* (Cambridge: Cambridge University Press, 2004); Victoria E. Bonnell and Lynn Hunt (eds.), *Beyond the Cultural Turn* (Berkeley and Los Angeles: University of California Press, 1999), Geoff Eley, 'Between Social History and Cultural Studies: Interdisciplinarity and the Practice of the Historian at the End of the Twentieth Century', in Joep Leerssen and Anne Rigney (eds.), *Historians and Social Values* (Amsterdam: Rodopi, 2000), 93–110.

30. Burke, *What is Cultural History?*, 3.

31. See Bonnell and Hunt (eds.), *Beyond the Cultural Turn* and Patrick Brantlinger, 'A Response to Beyond a Cultural Turn', *American Historical Review*, 107 (2002), 1500–13. These debates are also summarized in Burke, *What is Cultural History*, and Green, *Cultural History*.

32. Peter Mandler, 'The Problem with Cultural History', *Cultural and Social History*, 1 (2004), 94–118.

33. Replying to Mandler and in defence of cultural history see Carla Hesse, 'The New Empiricism', *Cultural and Social History*, 1 (2004), 201–9 and Colin Jones, 'Peter Mandler's "Problem with Cultural History" or, Is Playtime Over?', *Cultural and Social History*, 1 (2004), 209–17. On 'identity' see Rogers Brubacker and Frederick Cooper, 'Beyond "Identity"', *Theory and Society*, 29 (2000), 1–47.

34. Ranajit Guha and Gayatri Chakravorty Spivak (eds.), *Selected Subaltern Studies* (Oxford: Oxford University Press, 1988).

35. Patrick Harries, *Work, Culture and Identity: Migrant Labour in Mozambique and South Africa, c1860–1910* (Portsmouth, NH: Heinemann, 1994); Paul Landau, *The Realm of the Word: Language, Gender and Christianity in a Southern African Kingdom* (Portsmouth, NH: Heinemann, 1995); Isabel Hofmeyr, *The Portable Bunyan: A Transnational History of Pilgrim's Progress* (Princeton: Princeton University Press, 2003); Derek Peterson, *Creative Writing, Bookkeeping and the Work of Imagination in Colonial Kenya* (Portsmouth, NH: Heinemann, 2004); Nancy Rose Hunt, *A Colonial Lexicon: Of Birth Ritual, Medicalization and Mobility in the Congo* (Durham, NC: University of North Carolina Press, 2000); Rosalind Shaw, *Memories of the Slave Trade, Ritual and Historical Imagination in Sierra Leone* (Chicago: University of Chicago Press, 2002).

36. Thomas Spear, 'Neo-traditionalism and the Limits of Invention in British Colonial Africa', *Journal of African History*, 44 (2003), 3–28.

37. Susan Vogel, *Baule: African Art/Western Eyes* (New Haven: Yale University Press, 1997); Christopher B. Steiner, *African Art in Transit* (Cambridge: Cambridge University Press, 1994); Nicholas Thomas, *Possessions: Indigenous Art/Colonial Culture* (London: Thames and Hudson, 1999); Karin Barber, 'Introduction', in id. (ed.), *Readings in African Popular Culture* (London: James Currey, 1997), 1–12.

38. Megan Vaughan, 'Colonial Discourse Theory and African History, or has Postmodernism Passed us by?', *Social Dynamics*, 20 (1994), 1–23.

39. Patrick Chabal and Jean-Pascal Daloz, *Culture Troubles: Politics and the Interpretation of Meaning* (London: Hurst, 2006), 28–30.

40. John Parker and Richard Rathbone, *African History: A Very Short Introduction* (Oxford: Oxford University Press, 2007), ch. 3.

41. Jan Vansina, *Kingdoms of the Savanna* (Madison: University of Wisconsin Press, 1966); Jan Vansina, *Paths in the Rainforest* (Madison: University of

Wisconsin Press, 1990); Jan Vansina, *How Societies are Born: Governance in West Central Africa before 1600* (Charlottesville, Va.: University of Virginia Press, 2004).

42. See Vansina's own account of this, written for a non-specialist audience: Jan Vansina, 'Towards a History of Lost Corners of the World', *Economic History Review*, 35 (1982), 165–78, and his autobiographical account, *Living with Africa* (Madison: University of Wisconsin Press, 2004).

43. Nancy Rose Hunt, *A Colonial Lexicon: Of Birth Ritual, Medicalization and Mobility in the Congo* (Durham, NC: University of North Carolina Press, 1999); Lynn M. Thomas, *Politics of the Womb: Reproduction and the State in Kenya* (Berkeley and Los Angeles: University of California Press, 2003).

44. Claudio Lomnitz, *Death and the Idea of Mexico* (New York: Zone Books, 2008).

45. Kuper, *Culture*, ch. 6; Renato Rosaldo, *Culture and Truth: The Remaking of Social Analysis* (Boston: Beacon Press, 1989); James Clifford and George Marcus (eds.), *Writing Culture: The Poetics and Politics of Ethnography* (Berkeley and Los Angeles: University of California Press, 1986); James Clifford, *The Predicament of Culture: Twentieth-Century Ethnography, Literature and Art* (Cambridge, Mass.: Harvard University Press, 1989).

46. Edward Said, *Orientalism: Western Conceptions of the Orient* (London: Pantheon Books, 1978); Robert J. Young, *Postcolonialism: An Historical Introduction* (Oxford: Oxford University Press, 2001).

47. Cowan, 'Introduction', in Cowan, Dembar, and Wilson (eds.), *Culture and Rights*, 2.

48. Ibid.

49. Gilroy, *There Ain't No Black*; Gill Seidel, 'Culture, Nation and "Race" in the British and French New Right', in Ruth Levitas (ed.), *The Ideology of the New Right* (Oxford: Oxford University Press, 1985); Wright, 'The Politicization of "Culture"', *Anthropology Today*, 14/1 (1998), 7–15.

50. Seyla Benhabib, *The Claims of Culture: Equality and Diversity in the Global Era* (Princeton: Princeton University Press, 2002), 96.

51. Elizabeth A. Povinelli, *The Cunning of Recognition: Indigenous Alterities and the Making of Australian Multiculturalism* (Durham, NC: University of North Carolina Press, 2002).

52. Homi Bhabha, 'Of Mimicry and Man: The Ambivalence of Colonial Discourse', in id., *The Location of Culture* (London: Routledge, 1994), 85–92.

53. Slavoj Zizek, 'How China Got Religion', *New York Times*, 11 Oct. 2007.

54. For a critique of this approach see Stephan Palmie, *Wizards and Scientists: Explorations in Afro-Cuban Modernity and Tradition* (Durham, NC: University of North Carolina Press, 2002); Stephan Palmie (ed.), *Slave Cultures and the Cultures of Slavery* (Knoxville, Tenn.: University of Tennessee Press, 1995); Megan Vaughan, *Creating the Creole Island: Slavery in Eighteenth Century Mauritius* (Durham, NC: University of North Carolina Press, 2005).

55. Paul Gilroy, *The Black Atlantic: Modernity and Double-Consciousness* (London: Verso, 1993).

56. Roger Brubaker and Frederick Cooper, 'Beyond "Identity"', *Theory and Society*, 29 (2000), 1–47.

57. Yinka Shonibare, *Double Dutch* (Rotterdam: NAI Publishers, 2004).

CHAPTER 11

1. 'Ethnicity', in Craig Calhoun (ed.), *Dictionary of the Social Sciences* (Oxford: Oxford University Press, 2002), 148.
2. Fredrik Barth, *Ethnic Groups and Boundaries* (Boston: Little, Brown, 1969), 10.
3. Important conceptual introductions to ethnicity include Werner Sollors (ed.), *Theories of Ethnicity: A Classical Reader* (London: Macmillan, 1996); John Hutchinson and Anthony D. Smith (eds.), *Ethnicity* (Oxford: Oxford University Press, 1996).
4. Barth, *Ethnic Groups*, 15.
5. Malcolm Chapman, Maryon McDonald, and Elizabeth Tonkin, 'Introduction', in idem., *History and Ethnicity* (London: Routledge, 1989), 12, 16.
6. David Theo Goldberg, *Racist Culture: Philosophy and the Politics of Meaning* (Oxford: Blackwell, 1993), 75; Sollors, 'Foreword', in *Theories of Ethnicity*, pp. xxxii–xxxiii; Peter Wade, *Race and Ethnicity in Latin America* (London: Pluto, 1997), 15.
7. 'The Formation of a Diasporic Intellectual: An Interview with Stuart Hall by Kuan-Hsing Chen', in David Morley and Kuan-Hsing Chen (eds.), *Stuart Hall: Critical Dialogues in Cultural Studies* (London: Routledge, 1996), 484–5.
8. Barack Obama, *Dreams from my Father: A Story of Race and Inheritance* (Edinburgh: Canongate, 2007; 1st pub. New York: Times Books, 1995), pp. xvi, 82, 111; see also pp. viii–ix, 99–100, 115.
9. Mary C. Waters, *Ethnic Options: Choosing Identities in America* (Berkeley and Los Angeles: University of California Press, 1990), 18, 167.
10. Joan Wallach Scott, *Gender and the Politics of History* (New York: Columbia University Press, 1988), 42.
11. Particularly useful discussions include Verena Stolcke, 'Is Sex to Gender as Race is to Ethnicity?', in Teresa del Valle (ed.), *Gendered Anthropology* (London: Routledge, 1993), 17–37, and Nancy Leys Stepan, 'Race, Gender, Science and Citizenship', *Gender and History*, 10/1 (1998), 25–52; more generally, see Floya Anthias and Nira Yuval-Davis (in association with Harriet Cain), *Racialized Boundaries: Race, Nation, Gender, Colour and Class and the Anti-Racist Struggle* (London: Routledge, 1992).
12. Benjamin Isaac, *The Invention of Racism in Classical Antiquity* (Princeton: Princeton University Press, 2004); Miriam Eliav-Feldon, Benjamin Isaac, and Joseph Ziegler (eds.), *Origins of Racism in the West* (Cambridge: Cambridge University Press, 2009).
13. Guy Halsall, *Barbarian Migrations and the Roman West, 376–568* (Cambridge: Cambridge University Press, 2007), esp. chs. 2 and 14.
14. R. R. Davies, 'The Peoples of Britain and Ireland 1100–1400: 1. Identities', *Transactions of the Royal Historical Society*, 6th ser. 4 (1994), 6; 'Race and Ethnicity in the Middle Ages', special issue, *Journal of Medieval and Early Modern Studies*, 31/1 (Winter 2001).
15. Halsall, *Barbarian Migrations*, introduction; Patrick J. Geary, *The Myth of Nations: The Medieval Origins of Europe* (Princeton: Princeton University Press, 2002).

16. Robert Bartlett, *The Making of Europe: Conquest, Colonization and Cultural Change, 950–1350* (London: Penguin, 1994), 197.
17. Davies, 'Peoples of Britain and Ireland', 16–18.
18. David Nirenberg, 'Race and the Middle Ages: The Case of Spain and its Jews', in Margaret R. Greer, Walter D. Mignolo, and Maureen Quilligan (eds.), *Rereading the Black Legend: The Discourses of Religious and Racial Difference in the Renaissance Empires* (Chicago: University of Chicago Press, 2007), 75; see also other essays in this excellent collection, particularly the editors' 'Introduction', 1–24, and Mignolo's 'Afterword', 312–24.
19. María Elena Martínez, *Genealogical Fictions: Limpieza de Sangre, Religion, and Gender in Colonial Mexico* (Stanford, Calif.: Stanford University Press, 2008); Verena Stolcke, 'Invaded Women: Gender, Race, and Class in the Formation of Colonial Society', trans. Walden Browne, in Margo Hendricks and Patricia Parker (eds.), *Women, 'Race', and Writing in the Early Modern Period* (London: Routledge, 1994), 272–86.
20. Benjamin Braude, 'The Sons of Noah and the Construction of Ethnic and Geographical Identities in the Medieval and Early Modern Periods', *William and Mary Quarterly*, 3rd ser. 54/1 (1997), 103–42; James H. Sweet, 'The Iberian Roots of American Racist Thought', *William and Mary Quarterly*, 3rd ser. 54/1 (1997), 143–66; Colin Kidd, *British Identities before Nationalism: Ethnicity and Nationhood in the Atlantic World* (Cambridge: Cambridge University Press, 1999), 34.
21. John Lonsdale, 'The Moral Economy of Mau Mau: The Problem', in Bruce Berman and John Lonsdale, *Unhappy Valley: Conflict in Kenya and Africa*, book 2: *Violence and Ethnicity* (London: James Currey, 1992), 274. Lonsdale's nuanced analysis of 'moral ethnicity' cannot receive adequate attention here, but see his essay 'The Moral Economy of Mau Mau: Wealth, Poverty, and Civic Virtue in Kikuyu Political Thought', ibid. 315–504.
22. Terence Ranger, 'The Invention of Tradition in Colonial Africa', in Eric Hobsbawm and Terence Ranger (eds.), *The Invention of Tradition* (Cambridge: Cambridge University Press, 1983), 211–62; John Iliffe, *A Modern History of Tanganyika* (Cambridge: Cambridge University Press, 1979), 328–41; Leroy Vail (ed.), *The Creation of Tribalism in Southern Africa* (London: James Currey, 1989).
23. Iliffe, *Modern History*, 324.
24. Gyanendra Pandey, *The Construction of Communalism in Colonial North India* (Delhi: Oxford University Press, 1990), 13. On caste and racial categories, see especially Nicholas B. Dirks, *Castes of Mind: Colonialism and the Making of Modern India* (Princeton: Princeton University Press, 2001), and the essays in Peter Robb (ed.), *The Concept of Race in South Asia* (Delhi: Oxford University Press, 1997), particularly Susan Bayly's 'Caste and "Race" in the Colonial Ethnography of India', 165–218.
25. Heather Streets, *Martial Races: The Military, Race and Masculinity in British Imperial Culture, 1857–1914* (Manchester: Manchester University Press, 2004); Mrinalini Sinha, *Colonial Masculinity: The 'Manly Englishman' and the 'Effeminate Bengali' in the Late Nineteenth Century* (Manchester: Manchester University Press, 1995).

26. Sander L. Gilman, *Difference and Pathology: Stereotypes of Sexuality, Race, and Madness* (Ithaca, NY: Cornell University Press, 1985), 18, 241.

27. Robert J. C. Young, *Colonial Desire: Hybridity in Theory, Culture and Race* (London: Routledge, 1994); Ann Laura Stoler, *Carnal Knowledge and Imperial Power: Race and the Intimate in Colonial Rule* (Berkeley and Los Angeles: University of California Press, 2002); Elizabeth Buettner, *Empire Families: Britons and Late Imperial India* (Oxford: Oxford University Press, 2004).

28. Catherine Hall and Sonya O. Rose (eds.), *At Home with the Empire: Metropolitan Culture and the Imperial World* (Cambridge: Cambridge University Press, 2006); Frederick Cooper and Ann Laura Stoler (eds.), *Tensions of Empire: Colonial Cultures in a Bourgeois World* (Berkeley and Los Angeles: University of California Press, 1997).

29. Nancy Stepan, *The Idea of Race in Science: Great Britain, 1800–1960* (London: Macmillan, 1982), esp. ch. 5; Daniel J. Kevles, *In the Name of Eugenics: Genetics and the Uses of Human Heredity* (Cambridge, Mass.: Harvard University Press, 1985).

30. Matthew Frye Jacobson, *Whiteness of a Different Color: European Immigrants and the Alchemy of Race* (Cambridge, Mass.: Harvard University Press, 1998); more generally, see Ronald H. Baylor (ed.), *Race and Ethnicity in America: A Concise History* (New York: Columbia University Press, 2003). Race and ethnicity in Latin America and the Caribbean unfortunately cannot be treated here, but can be instructively compared and contrasted with historical circumstances in the United States. For an introduction, see Wade, *Race and Ethnicity*; Richard Graham (ed.), *The Idea of Race in Latin America, 1870–1940* (Austin, Tex.: University of Texas Press, 1990); Verena Martinez-Alier, *Marriage, Class and Colour in Nineteenth-Century Cuba: A Study of Racial Attitudes and Sexual Values in a Slave Society* (Cambridge: Cambridge University Press, 1974); Viranjini Munasinghe, 'Culture Creators and Culture Bearers: The Interface between Race and Ethnicity in Trinidad', *Transforming Anthropology*, 6/1–2 (1997), 72–86.

31. David R. Roediger, *Working towards Whiteness: How America's Immigrants Became White* (New York: Basic Books, 2005).

32. F. James Davis, *Who Is Black? One Nation's Definition* (University Park, Pa.: Pennsylvania University Press, 1991); Peggy Pascoe, 'Miscegenation Law, Court Cases, and Ideologies of "Race" in Twentieth-Century America', *Journal of American History*, 83/1 (1996), 44–69; Sharon M. Lee, 'Racial Classifications in the US Census: 1890–1990', *Ethnic and Racial Studies*, 16/1 (1993), 75–94.

33. Toni Morrison, *Playing in the Dark: Whiteness and the Literary Imagination* (New York: Vintage, 1993), 72.

34. Elazar Barkan, *The Retreat of Scientific Racism: Changing Concepts of Race in Britain and the United States between the Wars* (Cambridge: Cambridge University Press, 1992), esp. ch. 6. A decisive text in recasting European populations as ethnically rather than racially distinct was Julian S. Huxley and A. C. Haddon's *We Europeans: A Survey of 'Racial' Problems* (London: Jonathan Cape, 1935).

35. Rogers Brubaker, *Citizenship and Nationhood in France and Germany* (Cambridge, Mass.: Harvard University Press, 1992).

36. Saul Friedländer, *Nazi Germany and the Jews*, i: *The Years of Persecution, 1933–1939* (New York: HarperCollins, 1997), 82.

37. Norman M. Naimark, *Fires of Hatred: Ethnic Cleansing in Twentieth-Century Europe* (Cambridge, Mass.: Harvard University Press, 2001), esp. ch. 2; Michael Burleigh and Wolfgang Wippermann, *The Racial State: Germany 1933–1945* (Cambridge: Cambridge University Press, 1991).

38. Aimé Césaire, *Discourse on Colonialism*, trans. Joan Pinkham (New York: Monthly Review Press, 2000), 36.

39. Michael Mann, *The Dark Side of Democracy: Explaining Ethnic Cleansing* (Cambridge: Cambridge University Press, 2005), 353; Naimark, *Fires of Hatred*, ch. 4; Brubaker, *Citizenship and Nationhood*, 168.

40. Yasmin Khan, *The Great Partition: The Making of India and Pakistan* (New Haven: Yale University Press, 2007); Mushirul Hasan (ed.), *Inventing Boundaries: Gender, Politics, and the Partition of India* (New Delhi: Oxford University Press, 2000).

41. On these themes, see especially Vail (ed.), *Creation of Tribalism*; Peter Uvin, 'Prejudice, Crisis, and Genocide in Rwanda', *African Studies Review*, 40/2 (Sept. 1997), 91–115.

42. Naimark, *Fires of Hatred*, 195.

43. Brubaker, *Citizenship and Nationhood*.

44. Paul Gilroy, 'There Ain't No Black in the Union Jack': *The Cultural Politics of Race and Nation* (Chicago: University of Chicago Press, 1991), 61.

45. Stuart Hall, 'New Ethnicities', in James Donald and Ali Rattansi, 'Race', *Culture and Difference* (London: Sage, 1992), 252–9.

CHAPTER 12

1. Stephen B. Brush, 'Potato Taxonomies in Andean Agriculture', in David Brokensha, D. M. Warren, and Oswald Werner (eds.), *Indigenous Knowledge Systems* (Washington: University Press of America, 1980), 37–47. See also Roberto J. González, *Zapotec Science: Farming and Food in the Northern Sierra of Oaxaca* (Austin, Tex.: University of Texas Press, 2001).

2. For example, Helen Watson-Verran and David Turnbull, 'Science and Other Indigenous Knowledge Systems', in Sheila Jasanoff, Gerald E. Markle, James C. Peterson, and Trevor Pinch (eds.), *Handbook of Science and Technology Studies* (London: Sage, 1995).

3. Jack A. Goldstone, 'The Problem of the "Early Modern" World', *Journal of the Economic and Social History of the Orient*, 41/3 (1998), 249–83.

4. The precise meaning of 'objectivity' has varied over the centuries. See Lorraine Daston and Peter Galison, *Objectivity* (New York: Zone Books, 2007).

5. A founding introduction to the place of the community in making science can be found in Thomas Kuhn, *The Structure of Scientific Revolutions* (Chicago: University of Chicago Press, 1962), and the recent understanding of the social nature of science is treated by Jan Golinski, *Making Natural Knowledge: Constructivism and the History of Science* (Chicago: University of Chicago Press, reprint 2005).

6. Tim Ingold, *The Perception of the Environment: Essays in Livelihood, Dwelling and Skill* (London: Routledge, 2000).

7. Richard W. Bulliet, *Hunters, Herders, and Hamburgers: The Past and Future of Human–Animal Relationships* (New York: Columbia University Press, 2005).

8. Robert K. Merton first pointed out this phenomenon in the 1940s: 'Singletons and Multiples in Science', in *The Sociology of Science: Theoretical and Empirical Investigations* (Chicago: University of Chicago Press, 1973), 343–70. In recent years, there have been both scholarly and popular accounts of the collective nature of invention and innovation. For example, see Arnold Pacey, *The Maze of Ingenuity* (2nd edn. Cambridge, Mass.: Harvard University Press, 1992); John Waller, *Fabulous Science: Fact and Fiction in the History of Scientific Discovery* (Oxford: Oxford University Press, 2002); Clifford D. Conner, *A People's History of Science: Miners, Midwives, and 'Low Mechanicks'* (New York: Nation Books, 2005); Keith Sawyer, *Group Genius: The Creative Power of Collaboration* (New York: Basic Books, 2007); and John H. Lienhard, *How Invention Begins: Echoes of Old Voices in the Rise of New Machines* (Oxford: Oxford University Press, 2008).

9. Joyce E. Chaplin, 'Knowing the Ocean: Benjamin Franklin and the Circulation of Atlantic Knowledge', in James Delbourgo and Nicholas Dew (eds.), *Science and Empire in the Atlantic World* (New York: Routledge, 2008), 73–96.

10. Watson-Verran and Turnbull, 'Science and Other Indigenous Knowledge Systems'.

11. Francesca Bray, 'Science, Technique, Technology: Passages between Matter and Knowledge in Imperial Chinese Agriculture', *British Journal for the History of Science*, 41 (2008), 319–44.

12. Ibid. 320–1. Thomas P. Hughes was influential in introducing the view of technology as a 'system', especially in *Networks of Power: Electrification in Western Society, 1880–1930* (Baltimore: Johns Hopkins University Press, 1983). On the definition of technology, see also David Edgerton, 'From Innovation to Use: Ten Eclectic Theses on the Historiography of Technology', *History and Technology*, 16/2 (1999), 111–36.

13. Ingold, *The Perception of the Environment*.

14. Joseph Needham and Lu Gwei-Djen (eds.), *Science and Civilization in China*, /vi:/ *Medicine* ed. Nathan Sivin (Cambridge: Cambridge University Press, 2000), institutionalization of medicine: 38–42; medical doctrines: 42–5. See also Geoffrey Lloyd and Nathan Sivin, *The Way and the Word: Science and Medicine in Early China and Greece* (New Haven: Yale University Press, 2002). Lloyd and Sivin see great differences in basic concepts used to articulate ideas about nature in ancient Greece and China, saying that the Greek focused on 'nature and the elements, the Chinese on *ch'i*, yin-yang, the five phases, and the Way' (6). A medical canon was first set down in Chinese in about the second century BC, *The Inner Canon of the Yellow Emperor*.

15. See Nancy G. Siraisi, *Medieval and Early Renaissance Medicine: An Introduction to Knowledge and Practice* (Chicago: Chicago University Press, 1990), 104–6.

16. Shigehisa Kuriyama, *The Expressiveness of the Body and the Divergence of Greek and Chinese Medicine* (New York: Zone Books, 2002).

17. Lloyd and Sivin, *The Way and the Word*, 10.

18. Christopher Minkowski, 'Astronomers and their Reasons: Working Paper on Jyotiḥśāstra', *Journal of Indian Philosophy*, 30/5 (2002), 495–514, at 497.

19. Anthony Grafton, *Cardano's Cosmos: The Worlds and Works of a Renaissance Astrologer* (Cambridge, Mass.: Harvard University Press, 1999), 10.

20. Ingold, *The Perception of the Environment*, 55.

21. Lloyd and Sivin, *The Way and the Word*, 233–4. See also Joseph Needham, *Science and Civilization in China*, v: *Chemistry and Chemical Technology*, part 2: *Spagyrical Discovery and Invention: Magisteries of Gold and Immortality* (Cambridge: Cambridge University Press, 1974). A practical text, the *Bao-pu zi* of Ko Hung, is dated *c.*300 AD (Christopher Gladwell, 'Ancient and Medieval Chinese Protochemistry: The Earliest Examples of Applied Inorganic Chemistry', *Journal of Chemical Education*, 66/8 (1989), 631–33, at 631).

22. See Nathan Sivin, *Chinese Alchemy: Preliminary Studies* (Cambridge, Mass.: Harvard University Press, 1968).

23. See William Newman, 'Technology and Alchemical Debate in the Late Middle Ages', *Isis*, 80 (1989), 423–45; William Newman, 'Art, Nature, and Experiment in Alchemy', in Edith Scylla and Michael McVaugh (eds.), *Texts and Contexts in Ancient and Medieval Science* (Leiden: Brill, 1997), 304–17; William Newman, *The 'Summa perfectionis' of Pseudo-Geber* (Leiden: Brill, 1991); and William Newman, *Promethean Ambitions* (Chicago: University of Chicago Press, 2004).

24. As Geoffrey Lloyd and Nathan Sivin, in *The Way and the Word*, express it: 'the cosmopolitan blend of Syriac, Persian, ancient Middle Eastern, Indian, East Asian, and Greco-Roman traditions that formed in the Muslim world. This blend entered Europe beginning about A.D. 1000', p. xiii.

25. Antonio Barrera-Osorio, *Experiencing Nature: The Spanish American Empire and the Early Scientific Revolution* (Austin, Tex.: University of Texas Press, 2006) and Londa Schiebinger and Claudia Swan (eds.), *Colonial Botany: Science, Commerce, and Politics in the Early Modern World* (Philadelphia: University of Pennsylvania Press, 2005), Maria Portuondo, *Spanish Cosmography and the New World* (Chicago: Chicago University Press, 2009).

26. David Arnold, *Science, Technology and Medicine in Colonial India* (Cambridge: Cambridge University Press, 2000), 31.

27. Quoted in Lloyd and Sivin, *The Way and the Word*, 16.

28. Additionally, no knowledge of an object was complete without knowledge of the 'four causes': material (the matter out of which an object was shaped), formal (its form or forming essence), efficient (how it came into being), and final (why it came into being, or its use and function).

29. Serafina Cuomo, *Technology and Culture in Greek and Roman Antiquity* (Cambridge: Cambridge University Press, 2007).

30. See Harold J. Cook, 'The Cutting Edge of a Revolution? Medicine and Natural History near the Shores of the North Sea', in J. V. Field and Frank A. J. L. James (eds.), *Renaissance and Revolution: Humanists, Scholars, Craftsmen and Natural Philosophers in Early Modern Europe* (Cambridge: Cambridge University Press, 1993).

31. Ian Hacking, *The Emergence of Probability* (Cambridge: Cambridge University Press, 1975), and Theodore M. Porter, *The Rise of Statistical Thinking, 1820–1900* (Princeton: Princeton University Press, 1986).

32. Harold Cook, *Matters of Exchange: Commerce, Medicine, and Science in the Dutch Golden Age* (New Haven: Yale University Press, 2007).

33. See Pamela H. Smith, 'Laboratories', ch. 13 in Lorraine Daston and Katharine Park (eds.), *The Cambridge History of Science*, iii: *Early Modern Europe* (Cambridge: Cambridge University Press, 2006), 290–305.

34. Simon Schaffer and Steven Shapin, *Leviathan and the Air Pump* (Princeton: Princeton University Press, 1985).

35. See, for example, Henrika Kucklick, *The Savage within: The Social History of British Anthropology 1885–1945* (Cambridge: Cambridge University Press, 1991); Roy MacLeod (ed.), *Nature and Empire: Science and the Colonial Enterprise*, Osiris 15 (Chicago: Chicago University Press, 2001); and Benedikt Stuchtey (ed.), *Science across the European Empires, 1800–1950* (Oxford: Oxford University Press, 2005).

36. Kapil Raj, 'Colonial Encounters and the Forging of New Knowledge and National Identities: Great Britain and India, 1760–1850', in MacLeod (ed.), *Nature and Empire*, 119–34, at 127–31.

37. Ibid. 133.

38. Arnold, *Science, Technology and Medicine in Colonial India*, 31–3.

39. Diana Jeater, 'Imagining Africans: Scholarship, Fantasy, and Science in Colonial Administration, 1920s Southern Rhodesia', *International Journal of African Historical Studies*, 38/1 (2005), 1–26 at 23.

CHAPTER 13

1. A longer but now somewhat dated deliberation on these and related themes is J. R. McNeill, 'Observations on the Nature and Culture of Environmental History', *History and Theory*, 42 (2003), 5–43.

2. A further extension of this principle is the 'Big History' of David Christian and Fred Spier. See Christian, *Maps of Time* (Berkeley and Los Angeles: University of California Press, 2004); Spier, *Big History* (Amsterdam: Rodopi, 1996).

3. Arne Naess: Norwegian academic philosopher born in 1912 and credited with establishing a school of thought known as Deep Ecology, according to which humans are merely one among many species and ethically obliged to pursue egalitarianism within the biosphere.

4. As did the influential amateur George Perkins Marsh, American lawyer, diplomat, and polymath whose *Man and Nature* (1864) is a foundational text for many (mainly US) environmental historians. On Marsh see the special issue of *Environment and History*, 10/2 (2004) devoted to him. Richard Grove's *Green Imperialism* (Cambridge: Cambridge University Press, 1995) discusses French and British authors who exhibited awareness of environmental change in the seventeenth and eighteenth centuries.

5. *La Méditerranée* (Paris: Presses Universitaires de France, 1949).

6. Translated as *The Mediterranean and the Mediterranean World in the Era of Philip II*, 2 vols. (New York: HarperCollins, 1972). Opinions differ on the role of the French *annalistes* historians as pioneers of environmental history. See most recently Caroline Ford and Tamara Whited, 'Introduction', *French Historical Studies*, 32 (2009), 343–52, but also Geneviève Massard-Guilbaud, 'De la "part du milieu" à l'histoire de l'environnment', *Le Mouvement social*, 200

(2002–3), 64–72. The disagreements come down to what definition one prefers for the term 'environmental history'.

7. I use this term to refer to scholars of US history. It does not mean 'Americans', although in fact the great majority of Americanists are Americans; and it is more restricted than the Spanish cognate that refers to scholars of the Americas generally.

8. New Haven: Yale University Press, 1967.

9. Westport, Conn.: Greenwood Press, 1972.

10. New York: Oxford University Press, 1978.

11. New York: Hill and Wang, 1984.

12. Cronon's *Nature's Metropolis* (New York: Norton, 1991) cemented his standing among US environmental historians. Richard White, *The Roots of Dependency: Subsistence, Environment, and Social Change among the Choctaws, Pawnees, and Navajos* (Lincoln, Nebr.: University of Nebraska Press, 1983); *The Middle Ground: Indians, Empires, and Republics in the Great Lakes Region* (New York: Cambridge University Press, 1991); *The Organic Machine* (New York: Hill and Wang, 1995). Carolyn Merchant, *The Death of Nature: Women, Ecology and the Scientific Revolution* (San Francisco: HarperSanFrancisco, 1980); *Ecological Revolutions: Nature, Gender and Science in New England* (Chapel Hill, NC: University of North Carolina Press, 1989). Martin Melosi, *Garbage in the Cities* (College Station, Tex.: University of Texas Press, 1981); *The Sanitary City* (Baltimore: Johns Hopkins University Press, 2000). Joel Tarr, *The Search for the Ultimate Sink: Urban Pollution in Historical Perspective* (Akron, Oh.: University of Akron Press, 1996).

13. In *Rivers of Empire* (New York: Pantheon Books, 1985) Worster drew on Karl Wittfogel's (now much discredited) ideas about irrigation management in Chinese history.

14. Christoph Sonnlechner, 'Landschaft und Tradition: Aspekte einer Unweltgeschichte des Mittelalters', in C. Egger and H. Weigl (eds.), *Text—Schrift—Codex: Quellenkundliche Arbeiten aus dem Institut für Österreische Geschichtsforschung* (Vienna: Oldenbourg, 2000), 123–223; Brett Walker, *The Conquest of Ainu Land*s (Berkeley and Los Angeles: University of California Press, 2001).

15. In contrast, the institutionalization of environmental history came later elsewhere. For example, the European Society for Environmental History began regular meetings in 2001. SOLCHA, the Society for Latin American and Caribbean Environmental History, began operations in 2003. A Canadian network of environmental historians (NiCHE) took shape in 2006–7. An umbrella organization for environmental history around the world formed in 2006–8 and oversaw the first world congress of environmental history in 2009. The journal *Environment and History*, which published chiefly British, European, and imperial environmental history, started up in 1995. A Dutch and Flemish journal *Tijdschrift voor Ecologische Geschiedenis* (Journal for environmental history), became a regular annual in 1999. In 2004 the Croatian journal *Ekonomska i ekohistorija* was launched. An Italian-based but internationally focused journal, *Global Environment*, began publication in 2008. In every respect, the Americans enjoyed a firmer institutional footing sooner than environmental historians elsewhere. Numerically, Americanists still loom large in

the early twenty-first century, and at a guess accounted for roughly half of the environmental historians around the world as of 2009.

16. Munich: C. H. Beck Verlag, 2000.

17. The only others I know of were Rolf-Peter Sieferle, *The Subterranean Forest* (Cambridge: Cambridge University Press, 2001); and Thorkild Kjaergaard, *The Danish Revolution, 1500–1800* (New York: Cambridge University Press, 1994). Radkau, *Nature and Power: A Global History of the Environment* (New York: Cambridge University Press, 2008).

18. This blanket generalization is only that, and does not capture the minority of Americanists who read languages other than English and the larger minority who follow environmental history work written in English from around the world. A case in point is Karl Jacoby, whose *Crimes against Nature: Squatters, Poachers, Thieves and the Hidden History of American Conservation* (Berkeley and Los Angeles: University of California Press, 2001) owed something to Indian, Africanist, and British studies that presented conservation as an elite imposition upon unwilling peasantries.

19. One unhappy reader was Simon Schama, *Landscape and Memory* (New York: HarperCollins, 1995), 13.

20. Useful comment on these trends among Americanists is found in Peter Coates, 'Emerging from the Wilderness (or, from Redwoods to Bananas): Recent Environmental History in the United States and the Rest of the Americas', *Environment and History*, 10 (2004), 407–38. Some environmental change may qualify unambiguously as bad for people, such as the thinning of the stratospheric ozone layer, but it is probably good for some species of microbe.

21. From *The Sand County Almanac* (New York: Ballantine Books, 1949), one of the canonical texts of the American environmental movement.

22. James Fairhead and Melissa Leach, *Misreading the African Landscape* (Cambridge: Cambridge University Press, 1996). See also Diana Davis, *Resurrecting the Granary of Rome: Environmental History and French Colonial Expansion in North Africa* (Athens, Oh.: Ohio University Press, 2007).

23. New York: Cambridge University Press, 1986.

24. New York: W. W. Norton, 1997.

25. See, e.g. Patricia McAnany and Norman Yoffee (eds.), *Questioning Collapse* (New York: Cambridge University Press, 2009), which contains a dozen critiques of Diamond's *Collapse* (New York: Allen Lane, 2005), and *Guns, Germs and Steel*.

26. For historiographical orientation see: Ellen Arnold, 'An Introduction to Medieval Environmental History', *History Compass*, 6/3 (2008), 898–916; Wolfgang Siemann (ed.), *Umweltgeschichte: Themen und Perpektiven* (Munich: Beck, 2003); Massard-Guilbaud, 'De la "part du milieu" à l'histoire de l'environnement', 64–72; Sverker Sörlin and Paul Warde, 'The Problem of the Problem in Environmental History: A Re-reading of the Field', *Environmental History*, 12 (2007), 107–30; Jane Carruthers, 'Tracking in Game Trails: Looking Afresh at the Politics of Environmental History in South Africa', *Environmental History*, 11 (2006), 804–29; William Beinart, 'African History and Environmental History', *African Affairs*, 99 (2000), 269–302; Libby Robin and Tom Griffiths, 'Environmental History in Australasia', *Environment and History*, 10 (2004), 439–74; Libby Robin and

Mike Smith, 'Australian Environmental History: Ten Years On', *Environment and History*, 14 (2008), 135–43; Jane Carruthers, 'Africa: Histories, Ecologies, and Societies', *Environment and History*, 10 (2004), 379–406. Bao Maohong, 'Environmental History in China', *Environment and History*, 10 (2004), 475–99; Verena Winiwarter et al., 'Environmental History in Europe, from 1994 to 2004: Enthusiasm and Consolidation', *Environment and History*, 10 (2004), 501–30; V. Winiwarter and Martin Knoll, *Umweltgeschichte* (Vienna: Böhlau Verlag, 2005), ch. 3; N. Freytag, 'Deutsche Umweltgeschichte: Umweltgeschichte in Deutschland: Ertrage und Perspektiven', *Historische Zeitschrift*, 283 (2006), 383–407; Coates, 'Emerging from the Wilderness (or, from Redwoods to Bananas)'; Stéphane Castonguay, 'Faire du Québec un objet de l'histoire environnementale', *Globe*, 9 (2006), 17–49; Wilko Graf von Hardenberg, 'Oltre la storia ambientale: Interdisciplinarietà, metodologia, prospettive', *Passato e presente*, 24 (2006), 149–61; Andy Bruno, 'Russian Environmental History: Directions and Potentials', *Kritika: Explorations in Russian and Eurasian History*, 8 (2007), 635–50; Stefania Gallini, 'Invitación a la historia ambiental', *Revista Tareas*, 120 (2005), 5–28; Guillermo Castro Herrera, 'De civilización y naturaleza: notas para el debate sobre la historia ambiental latinoamericana', *Polis: revista de la Universidad Bolivariana*, 4/10 (2005). This last is an open access online and apparently unpaginated journal, available at: http://redalyc.uaemex.mx/redalyc/src/inicio/ArtPdfRed.jsp?iCve=30541022.

27. Early work included J. Donald Hughes, *Ecology in Ancient Civilizations* (Albuquerque, N. Mex.: University of New Mexico Press, 1975); Russell Meiggs, *Trees and Timber in the Ancient World* (Oxford: Oxford University Press, 1982); Robert Sallares, *Ecology of the Ancient Greek World* (Ithaca, NY: Cornell University Press, 1991), which is mainly about grain in Attica. More recently, Marcus Nenninger, *Die Römer und der Wald* (Stuttgart: Franz Steiner, 2001); Charles Redman, *Human Impact on Ancient Environments* (Tucson, Ariz.: University of Arizona Press, 2001).

28. A pioneering effort was Geoffrey Bolton, *Spoils and Spoilers: Australians Make their Environment, 1788–1980* (Sydney: HarperCollins, 1981), firmly in the declensionist tradition. More recently, Libby Robin, *Defending the Little Desert: The Rise of Ecological Consciousness in Australia* (Melbourne: Melbourne University Press, 1998). On New Zealand, Tom Brooking and Eric Pawson (eds.), *Environmental Histories of New Zealand* (New York: Oxford University Press, 2002). An overview is Donald Garden, *Australia, New Zealand, and the Pacific: An Environmental History* (Santa Barbara, Calif.: ABC-CLIO, 2005). Perhaps the most controversial and influential effort was the work of the mammalogist Tim Flannery, *The Future Eaters* (Chatswood: Grove Press, 1994).

29. Jeyamalar Kathirithamby-Wells, *Nature and Nation: Forests and Development in Peninsular Malaya* (Copenhagen: Nordic Institute of Asian Studies, 2005). Greg Bankoff and Peter Boomgaard (eds.), *A History of Natural Resources in Asia* (Basingstoke: Macmillan, 2007); Greg Bankoff, *Cultures of Disaster: Society and Natural Hazards in the Philippines* (London: Routledge, 2002); Peter Boomgaard (ed.), *A World of Water: Rain, Rivers, and Seas in Southeast Asian Histories* (Leiden: Brill, 2007); *Frontiers of Fear: Tigers and People in the Malay World, 1600–1950* (New Haven: Yale University Press, 2001); *Southeast*

Asia: An Environmental History (Santa Barbara, Calif.: ABC-CLIOCA, 2006). Harriet Ritvo (on Britain) and Mahesh Rangarajan (on India) have also produced animal-focused environmental history.

30. Influential overviews include Mark Elvin, *The Retreat of the Elephants: An Environmental History of China* (New Haven: Yale University Press, 2004); Elvin and Ts'ui-jung Liu (eds.), *The Sediments of Time* (New York: Cambridge University Press, 1998); Conrad Totman, *The Green Archipelago: Forestry in Preindustrial Japan* (Berkeley and Los Angeles: University of California Press, 1989); *Pre-industrial Korea and Japan in Environmental Perspective* (Leiden: Brill, 2004). Among many admirable monographs, see Robert Marks, *Tigers, Rice, Silk and Silt: Environment and Economy in Late Imperial South China* (New York: Cambridge University Press, 1997). For the work of Chinese scholars, see Bao Maohong, 'Environmental History in China', *Environment and History*, 10 (2004), 475–99.

31. Bao Maohong, 'Environmental History in China'; Bao also wrote *Forest and Development: Deforestation in the Philippines (1946–1995)* (Beijing: China's Environmental Science Press, 2008). T. Mizoguchi (ed.), *The Environmental Histories of Europe and Japan* (Kobe: Nagoya University Press, 2008) gives some sense of the beginnings of environmental history within Japan.

32. But see the studies of biological conservation by Douglas Weiner, *Models of Nature: Ecology, Conservation and Cultural Revolution in Soviet Russia* (Bloomington, Ind.: Indiana University Press, 1988); *A Little Corner of Freedom: Russian Nature Protection from Stalin to Gorbachev* (Berkeley and Los Angeles: University of California Press, 1999); and the work of David Moon, e.g. 'The Debate over Climate Change in the Steppe Region of Nineteenth-Century Russia', *Russian Review*, 69 (2010), 251–75. On the Arab world there is a collection of papers in *Cairo Papers in Social Science*, 26/1 (2005) and, on what are now Iraq and Iran, Peter Christensen, *The Decline of Iranshahr: Irrigation and Environments in the History of the Middle East, 500 B.C. to A.D. 1500* (Copenhagen: Museum Tusculanum Press, 1993); on the Maghrib, Diana Davis, *Resurrecting the Granary of Rome: Environmental History of French Colonial Expansion in North Africa* (Athens, Oh.: Ohio University Press, 2007). Forthcoming work by Sam White and Alan Mikhail will shortly make a strong impact on the environmental history of the Ottoman Empire and Middle East.

33. Berlin: Springer Verlag, 1990.

34. Emmanuel Le Roy Ladurie, *L'Histoire du climat depuis l'an mil* (Paris: Flammarion, 1967); Le Roy Ladurie, *Histoire humaine et comparée du climat*, 3 vols. (Paris: Flammarion, 2004–9); Christian Pfister, *Wetternachhersage: 500 Jahre Klimavariationen und Naturkatastrophen (1496–1995)* (Bern: Haupt-Verlag, 1999); Wolfgang Behringer, Hartmut Lehmann, and Christian Pfister (eds.), *Kulturelle Konsequenzen der 'Kleinen Eiszeit'* (Göttingen: Vandenhoeck & Ruprecht, 2005); Neville Brown, *History and Climate Change: A Eurocentric Perspective* (London: Routledge, 2001). On southern European agraroenvironmental history, Manuel González de Molina and Gloria Guzmán Casado, *Tras los pasos de la insustentabilidad: agricultura y medio ambiente en perspectiva histórica (siglos XVIII–XX)* (Barcelona: Icaria, 2006); Piero Bevilacqua, *La terra è finita: breve storia dell'ambiente* (Rome: Laterza, 2006) and

his 'Le rivoluzioni dell'acqua: irrigazione e trasformazioni dell'agricoltura tra Sette e Novecento', in id. (ed.), *Storia dell'agricoltura italiana in età contemporanea* (Venice: Marsilio, 1989), 255–318. For southern European work in general, Marco Armiero (ed.), *Views from the South: Environmental Stories from the Mediterranean World* (Rome: Istituto de Studi sulle Società del Mediterraneo, 2006).

35. A recent lament is Sverker Sörlin and Paul Warde, 'The Problem of the Problem in Environmental History', *Environmental History*, 12 (2007), 116. The bibliography on the ESEH website serves as an introduction to the now vast literature in European environmental history.

36. Robert Harms, *Games against Nature: An Eco-history of the Nunu of Equatorial Africa* (New York: Cambridge University Press, 1987); Tamara Giles-Vernick, *Cutting the Vines of the Past: Environmental Histories of the Central African Rain Forest* (Charlottesville, Va.: University of Virginia Press, 2002). For explorations of the use of historical linguistics, oral data, and much else, see Kairn Kliemann, *The Pygmies Were our Compass: Bantu and Batwa in the History of West Central Africa, Early Times to c.1900 C.E.* (Portsmouth, NH: Heinemann, 2002). On the promise and challenges of African environmental history, Catherine Coquéry-Vidrovitch, 'Écologie et histoire en Afrique noire', *Histoire, économie et société*, 3 (1997), 483–504. The outpouring of South African work is largely due to the efforts of William Beinart, Jane Carruthers, and their students.

37. Cambridge: Cambridge University Press, 1995.

38. Thanks in part to the series published by ABC-CLIO and edited by Mark Stoll, several volumes of which are cited here.

39. Notable works by geographers and sociologists in this vein include Neil Roberts, *The Holocene: An Environmental History* (Oxford: Oxford University Press, 1989); I. G. Simmons, *Environmental History: A Concise Introduction* (Oxford: Oxford University Press, 1993); Antoinette Mannion, *Global Environmental Change: A Natural and Cultural History* (Harlow: Longman, 1991); Bert de Vries and Johan Goudsblom, *Mappae Mundi: Humans and their Habitats in Long-Term Socio-ecological Perspective* (Amsterdam: Rodopi, 2002). The Foreign Office refugee was Clive Ponting, who wrote a provocative if unreliable survey, entitled *A Green History of the World* (London: Penguin, 1991).

40. G. J. Leigh, *The World's Greatest Fix: A History of Nitrogen and Agriculture* (Oxford: Oxford University Press, 2004); David Montgomery, *Dirt: The Erosion of Civilizations* (Berkeley and Los Angeles: University of California Press, 2007). On soils there is the collection edited by J. R. McNeill and Verena Winiwarter, *Soils and Societies* (Isle of Harris: White Horse Press, 2006) which is the work of historians, geographers, geomorphologists, pedologists, among others. Other interesting work of this stripe by non-historians includes Vaclav Smil, *Energy in World History* (Boulder, Colo.: Lynne Rienner, 1994); and Antoinette Mannion, *Carbon and its Domestication* (Dordrecht: Springer Verlag, 2006).

41. Pyne, *World Fire: The Culture of Fire on Earth* (Seattle: University of Washington Press, 1995); Guha, *Environmentalism: A Global History* (New York: Longman, 2000).

42. J. D. Hughes, *An Environmental History of the World* (London: Routledge, 2001); Sverker Sörlin and Anders Öckermann, *Jorden en ö: En global miljöhistoria* (Stockholm: Bonnier, 1998); J. R. McNeill, *Something New under the Sun: An Environmental History of the Twentieth-Century World* (New York: W. W. Norton, 2000); John F. Richards, *The Unending Frontier: An Environmental History of the Early Modern World* (Berkeley and Los Angeles: University of California Press, 2003). An environmental analysis of a world historical problem was Kenneth Pomeranz, *The Great Divergence: China, Europe and the Making of the Modern World Economy* (Princeton: Princeton University Press, 2000). Ian G. Simmons, *Global Environmental History* (Chicago: Chicago University Press, 2008) is the latest of Simmons's several global-scale environmental histories. Also of note are Anthony Penna's compact survey *The Human Footprint: A Global Environmental History* (New York: Wiley, 2009) and Edmund Burke III and Kenneth Pomeranz (eds.), *The Environment and World History* (Berkeley and Los Angeles: University of California Press, 2009), which makes contributions concerning colonialism especially.

43. Helpful anthologies include Richard Grove, Vinita Damodaran, and Satpal Sangwan (eds.), *Nature and the Orient: The Environmental History of South and Southeast Asia* (Delhi: Oxford University Press, 1998); David Arnold and Ramachandra Guha (eds.), *Nature, Culture, and Imperialism: Essays on the Environmental History of South Asia* (New Delhi: Oxford University Press, 1995); Arun Agarwal and K. Sivaramakrishnan (eds.), *Social Nature, Resources, Representations and Rule in India* (Delhi: Oxford University Press, 2000); Gunnel Cederlof and and Kalyanakrishnan Sivaramakrishnan (eds.), *Ecological Nationalisms* (Delhi: Permanent Black, 2006). A useful reader is Mahesh Rangarajan (ed.), *Environmental Issues in India* (Delhi: Pearson Longman, 2007). Note also the pioneering synthesis of Ramachandra Guha and Madhav Gadgil, *This Fissured Land: An Ecological History of India* (Berkeley and Los Angeles: University of California Press, 1992), the recent survey of Christopher Hill, *South Asia: An Environmental History* (Santa Barbara, Calif.: ABC-CLIOCA, 2008); and the ambitious volume of Sumit Guha, *Environment and Ethnicity in India, 1200–1991* (Cambridge: Cambridge University Press, 1999). For orientation, see Rohan D'Souza, 'Nature, Conservation and the Writing of Environmental History', *Conservation and Society*, 1/2 (2003), 317–32.

44. Environmental history seems to have made no impact on syntheses of Mughal history, e.g. Harbans Mukhia, *The Mughals of India* (Oxford: Blackwell, 2004). Even John F. Richards, a noted environmental historian, ignored environmental history in his volume in the new Cambridge History of India, entitled *The Mughal Empire* (Cambridge: Cambridge University Press, 1993). Richards was a pioneer in Indian land use history, often collaborating with ecologists, e.g. E. P. Flint and John F. Richards, 'Historical Analysis of Changes in Land Use and Carbon Stock of Vegetation in South and Southeast Asia', *Canadian Journal of Forest Research*, 21 (1991), 91–110.

45. Mahesh Rangarajan, *India's Wildlife History: An Introduction* (Delhi: Permanent Black, 2001).

46. James Scott, *Seeing Like a State: How Certain Schemes to Improve the Human Condition Have Failed* (New Haven: Yale University Press, 1998).

47. Probably the most influential was Ramachandra Guha, *The Unquiet Woods: Ecological Change and Peasant Resistance in the Western Himalaya* (Delhi: Oxford University Press, 1989).

48. The bibliography maintained by Lise Sedrez and colleagues included about 1,200 entries as of 2008: http://www.csulb.edu/projects/laeh/.

49. Vitale, *Hacia una historia del ambiente en América Latina: de las culturas aborigines a la crisis ecológica actual* (Caracas: Nueva Sociedad, 1983); Dean, *Brazil and the Struggle for Rubber: An Environmental History* (New York: Cambridge University Press, 1987).

50. Berkeley and Los Angeles: University of California Press, 1995.

51. Reinaldo Funes Monzote, *De bosque a sabana: azúcar, deforestación y medio ambiente en Cuba, 1492-1926* (Mexico City: Siglo XXI Ediciones, 2004). Historical geographer David Watts's *The West Indies: Patterns of Development, Culture, and Environmental Change since 1492* (Cambridge: Cambridge University Press, 1987) handles these and other themes mainly for the British Caribbean. A recent entry in Caribbean environmental history is J. R. McNeill, *Mosquito Empires: Ecology and War in the Greater Caribbean, 1620-1914* (New York: Cambridge University Press, 2010).

52. By biologist Elio Brailovsky and economist Dina Foguelman (Buenos Aires: Debolsillo, 1991). See also Juan Carlos Garavaglia, *Les Hommes de la pampa: une histoire agraire de la campagne de Buenos Aires (1700-1830)* (Paris: Éditions de l'EHESS, 2000), a work that should interest historians of the North American frontier.

53. A start on copper was made by Mauricio Folchi Donoso, 'La insustenibilidad de la industria del cobre en Chile: los hornos y los bosques durante el siglo xix', *Revista Mapocho*, 49 (2001), 149-75. An overview is Elizabeth Dore, 'Environment and Society: Long-Term Trends in Latin American Mining', *Environment and History*, 6 (2000), 1-29.

54. Pádua, *Um sopro de destruição: pensamento politico e critica ambiental no brasil escravista (1786-1888)* (Rio de Janeiro: Jorge Zahar, 2002); McCook, *States of Nature: Science, Agriculture and Environment in the Spanish Caribbean, 1760-1940* (Austin, Tex.: University of Texas Press, 2002).

55. José Drummond, *Devastação e preservação ambiental no Rio de Janeiro* (Niterói: Editora da Universidade Federal Fluminense, 1997); Sterling Evans, *The Green Republic: A Conservation History of Costa Rica* (Austin, Tex.: University of Texas Press, 1999); Shawn Miller, *Fruitless Trees: Portuguese Conservation and Brazil's Colonial Timber* (Stanford, Calif.: Stanford University Press, 2000).

56. Ezcurra, *De las chinampa a la megalopolis: el medio ambiente en la cuenca de Mexico* (Mexico City: Siglo XXI Ediciones, 1990); Paulo Henrique Martinez (ed.), *História ambiental paulista: temas, fontes, métodos* (São Paulo: Editora Senac, 2007); Janes Jorge, *Tietê, o rio que a cidade perdeu* (São Paulo: Alameda, 2006). Etelvina Maria de Castro Trindade, *Cidade, homem, natureza: uma história das políticas ambientais de Curitiba* (Curitiba: Unilivre, 1997); Cláudio Luiz Menezes, *Desenvolvimento urbano e meio ambiente: a experiencia*

de Curitiba (Curitiba: Unilivre, 1996). See also Drummond, *Devastação e preservação ambiental no Rio de Janeiro.*

57. Jair Preciado Beltrán, Cecilia Almanza Castañeda, and Roberto O. L. Pulido, *Historia ambiental de Bogotá, siglo XX* (Bogotá: Fondo de Publicaciones Universidad Distrital, 2005).

58. New York: Cambridge University Press, 2007. Guillermo Castro, *Para una historia ambiental de América Latina* (Havana: Hafner, 2004); Elio Brailovsky, *Historia ecológica de Iberoamérica: de los Mayas al Quijote* (Buenos Aires: Debolsillo, 2006); a Brazil overview, if largely historiographical, is Paulo Henrique Martinez, *História ambiental no Brasil: pesquisa e ensino* (São Paulo: Editora Senac, 2006). For Colombia, one of the countries best researched by environmental historians, Germán A Palacio, *Fiebre de tierra caliente: una historia ambiental de Colombia, 1850-1930* (Bogotá: Fondo de Publicaciones Universidad Distrital, 2006).

59. Endfield, *Climate and Society in Colonial Mexico* (New York: Blackwell, 2008); Myrna Santiago, *The Ecology of Oil: Environment, Labor, and the Mexican Revolution, 1900-1938* (New York: Cambridge University Press, 2006).

60. But see Funes Monzote, *De bosque a sabana* and the other works cited in n. 51.

61. S. Krech, J. R. McNeill, and Carolyn Merchant (eds.), *Encyclopedia of World Environmental History*, 3 vols. (Great Barrington, Mass.: Berkshire, 2004).

62. A few examples exist, e.g. Philip Curtin, Grace Brush, and George Fisher (eds.), *Discovering the Chesapeake: The History of An Ecosystem* (Baltimore: Johns Hopkins University Press, 2001). At Göttingen University the world's largest environmental history graduate program is premised on interdisciplinary approaches. Bao Maohong, 'Environmental History in China', reports that interdisciplinary collaboration is the norm in China. The methods and charms of studying strontium/calcium ratios are outlined in Shomarka Keita, 'A Brief Introduction to a Geochemical Method Used in Assessing Migration in Biological Anthropology', in Jan Lucassen, Leo Lucassen, and Patrick Manning (eds.), *Migration History in World History* (Leiden: Brill, 2010), 59-74.

63. e.g. Óscar Carpintero, *El metabolismo de la economía española: recursos naturales y huella ecológica (1955-2000)* (Madrid: CIP-Ecosocial, 2005). Social metabolism work involves trying to estimate the quantities of materials and energy that flowed through a city, a country, or some other unit of analysis. The work depends upon good raw data which makes it less appropriate for, say, pre-colonial Africa than for modern Europe.

CHAPTER 14

I wish to thank Jonathan Berkey, Peter Marshall, Meir Shahar, and Teresa Shawcross for suggestions on readings in the areas of scholarship they expertly inhabit.

1. Peter Burke, *The French Historical Revolution: The Annales School, 1929-89* (Cambridge: Polity, 1990).

2. Émile Durkheim. *The Elementary Forms of Religious Life: A Study in Religious Sociology*, trans. Joseph Ward Swain (London: George Allen & Unwin, 1915).

3. Pierre Chaunu, *La Mort à Paris, XVIe, XVIIe et XVIIIe siècles* (Paris: Fayard, 1978); Jacques Chiffoleau, *La Comptabilité de l'au-delà: les hommes, la mort et la religion dans la région d'Avignon à la fin du Moyen Âge, vers 1320–vers 1480* (Rome: École Française de Rome, 1980).

4. *The Holy Greyhound: Guinefort, Healer of Children since the Thirteenth Century,* trans. Martin Thom (Cambridge: Cambridge University Press, 1982).

5. Clifford Geertz, 'Religion as a Cultural System', in Michael Banton (ed.), *Anthropological Approaches to the Study of Religion* (London: Tavistock, 1966), 1–46; reprinted in Clifford Geertz, *The Interpretation of Cultures* (New York: Basic Books, 1973), 87–125.

6. Giles Constable, 'From Church History to Religious Culture: The Study of Medieval Religious Life and Spirituality', in Miri Rubin (ed.), *European Religious Cultures: Essays Offered to Christopher Brooke on the Occasion of his Eightieth Birthday* (London: University of London Institute of Historical Research, 2008), 3–16.

7. R. C. Boxer, *Mary and Misogyny: Women in Iberian Expansion Overseas, 1415–1815: Some Facts, Fancies, and Personalities* (London: Duckworth, 1975).

8. Rosalind Brown-Grant, *Christine de Pizan and the Moral Defence of Women: Reading beyond Gender* (Cambridge: Cambridge University Press, 1999).

9. An influential essay which discussed the category of gender opens Joan Wallach Scott, *Gender and the Politics of History* (New York: Columbia University Press, 1988; rev. edn. 1999).

10. Jean-Claude Schmitt, ' "Quand la lune nourrissait le temps avec du lait: le temps du cosmos et des images chez Hildegarde de Bingen (1098–1179)" ', in Giovanni Careri, François Lissarrague, Jean-Claude Schmitt, and Carlo Severi (eds.), *Traditions et temporalités des images* (Paris: Éditions de l'École des Hautes Études en Sciences Sociales, 2009), 73–87, figures 33–6.

11. Hildegard of Bingen, *Symphonia: A Critical Edition of the Symphonia Armonie Celestium Revelationum,* trans. Barbara Newman (2nd edn. Ithaca, NY: Cornell University Press, 1998.

12. Anne L Clark, *Elisabeth of Schönau: A Twelfth-Century Visionary* (Philadelphia: University of Pennsylvania Press, 1992). This is also true of the Muslim tradition. See the early collection of lives of Sufi women, by As-Sulamī, *Early Sufi Women: Dhikr an-Niswa al-Muta 'abbidat as-Sufiyyat Abu 'Abd al-Rahman al-Sulamī,* trans. Rkia Elaroui Cornell (Louisville, Ky.: Fons Vitae, 1999).

13. Aviad Kleinberg, *Prophets in their Own Country: Living Saints and the Making of Sainthood in the Later Middle Ages* (Chicago: University of Chicago Press, 1992); Fiona Griffiths, ' "Men's Duty to Provide for Women's Needs": Abelard, Heloise, and their Negotiation of the *Cura monialium*', *Journal of Medieval History*, 30 (2004), 1–24.

14. Amy Hollywood, *The Soul as Virgin Wife: Mechthild of Magdeburg, Marguerite Porete, and Meister Eckhart* (Notre Dame, Ind.: University of Notre Dame Press, 1995).

15. Sean Field, 'The Master and Marguerite: Godfrey of Fontaines' Praise of *The Mirror of Simple Souls*', *Journal of Medieval History*, 35 (2009), 136–49; Hollywood, *The Soul as Virgin Wife.*

16. Ivan G. Marcus, *Rituals of Childhood: Jewish Acculturation in Medieval Europe* (New Haven: Yale University Press, 1996).

17. Susanna Elm, *'Virgins of God': The Making of Asceticism in Late Antiquity* (Oxford: Clarendon Press, 1994); Kate Cooper, *The Virgin and the Bride: Idealized Womanhood in Late Antiquity* (Cambridge, Mass.: Harvard University Press, 1996).

18. In the eastern Mediterranean traditions of female priesthood may have contributed to the incorporation of women in domestic and public worship, Joan Bretton Connelly, *Portrait of a Priestess: Women and Ritual in Ancient Greece* (Princeton: Princeton University Press, 2007).

19. Meir Shahar, *The Shaolin Monastery: History, Religion and the Chinese Martial Arts* (Honolulu: University of Hawaii Press, 2008).

20. New York: Columbia University Press, 1988.

21. Caroline Walker Bynum, *Holy Feast and Holy Fast: The Religious Significance of Food to Medieval Women* (Berkeley and Los Angeles: University of California Press, 1987). Trends developed by women could become mainstream tropes as discussed in Ann Douglas, *The Feminization of American Culture* (New York: Knopf, 1977).

22. Shulamith Shahar, *Women in a Medieval Heretical Sect: Agnes and Huguette the Waldensians* (Woodbridge: Boydell and Brewer, 2001). On the subjectivity of people persecuted for religious beliefs see John Arnold, *Inquisition and Power: Catharism and the Confessing Subject in Medieval Languedoc* (Philadelphia: University of Pennsylvania Press, 2001).

23. Shannon McSheffrey, *Gender and Heresy: Women and Men in Lollard Communities, 1420–1530* (Philadelphia: University of Pennsylvania Press, 1995).

24. Peter Marshall, *The Catholic Priesthood and the English Reformation* (Oxford: Clarendon Press, 1994); Michael Mckernan, *Padre: Australian Chaplains in Gallipoli and France* (London: Allen and Unwin, 1986); Jonathan D. Spence, *The Memory Palace of Matteo Ricci* (London: Faber, 1985); Liam Matthew Brockey, *Journey to the East: The Jesuit Mission to China, 1579–1724* (Cambridge, Mass.: Belknap Press of Harvard University Press, 2007).

25. For interesting reflections on the role and power of images see David Freedberg, *The Power of Images: Studies in the History and Theory of Response* (Chicago: University of Chicago Press, 1989), and David Morgan, *Visual Piety: A History and Theory of Popular Religious Images* (Berkeley and Los Angeles: University of California Press, 1998).

26. On Islamic prayer see Constance Padwick, *Muslim Devotions: A Study of Prayer-Manuals in Common Use* (Oxford: One World, 1996).

27. On images: R. W. Scribner *For the Sake of Simple Folk: Popular Propaganda for the German Reformation* (Cambridge: Cambridge University Press, 1981); Miri Rubin, *Mother of God: A History of the Virgin Mary* (London: Alan Lane, 2009).

28. On the patronage of art and the making of images see K. J. P. Lowe, *Chronicles and Convent Culture in Renaissance and Counter-Reformation Italy* (Cambridge: Cambridge University Press, 2003); and Jeffrey F. Hamburger,

Nuns as Artists: The Visual Culture of a Medieval Convent, California Studies in the History of Art 37 (Berkeley and Los Angeles: University of California Press, 1997); on more modern periods see Colleen McDannell, *Material Christianity: Religion and Popular Culture in America* (New Haven: Yale University Press, 1995) and David Morgan, *Visual Piety: A History and Theory of Popular Religious Images* (Berkeley and Los Angeles: University of California Press, 1998).

29. Matthew Milner, *The Senses and the English Reformation* (Farnham: Ashgate, forthcoming).

30. Christopher Boyd Brown, *Singing the Gospel: Lutheran Hymns and the Success of the Reformation* (Cambridge, Mass.: Harvard University Press, 2005).

31. On the chants of religious confraternities see Eyolf Ostrem and Nils Holger Petersen, *Medieval Ritual and Early Modern Music: The Devotional Practice of Lauda Singing in Late-Renaissance Italy*, Ritus et Artes (Turnhout: Brepols, 2008); on music, conquest, and mission in the Philippines see D. R. M. Irving, *Colonial Counterpoint: Music in Early Modern Manila* (New York: Oxford University Press, 2010); on music and civic ritual see Iain Fenlon, *Ceremonial City: History, Memory, and Myth in Renaissance Venice* (New Haven: Yale University Press, 2007).

32. Helen Hills, *Invisible City: The Architecture of Devotion in Seventeenth-Century Neapolitan Convents* (Oxford: Oxford University Press, 2004).

33. In Ethel Sara Wolper, *Cities and Saints: Sufism and the Transformation of Urban Space in Medieval Anatolia* (University Park, Pa.: Pennsylvania State University Press, 2003), historical questions and architectural expertise blend to uncover a rich and complex social-religious world. See for ancient Near Eastern religions G. J. Whightman, *Sacred Spaces: Religious Architecture in the Ancient World* (Leuven: Peeters, 2007).

34. Paul Wheatley, *The Places Where Men Pray Together: Cities in Islamic Lands, Seventh through the Tenth Centuries* (Chicago: University of Chicago Press, 2001).

35. David E. Sklare, *Samuel ben Hofni Gaon and his Cultural World: Texts and Studies* (Leiden: Brill, 1996), 100–1. On Baghdad see Dmitri Gutas, *Greek Thought, Arabic Culture: The Graeco-Arabic Translation Movement in Baghdad and Early 'Abbāsid Society (2nd–4th/8th–10th Centuries)* (London: Routledge, 1998).

36. See, for example, the performance of a cathedral's life within the city, Stephen Murray, *A Gothic Sermon: Making a Contract with the Mother of God, Saint Mary of Amiens* (Berkeley and Los Angeles: University of California Press, 2004).

37. Christopher Page, *Discarding Images: Reflections on Music and Culture in Medieval France* (Oxford: Oxford University Press, 1993), 43–59; Olivier Cullin, *Laborintus: essais sur la musique au Moyen Âge* (Paris: Fayard, 2004), 91–110.

38. Walter Simons, *Cities of Ladies: Beguine Communities in the Medieval Low Countries, 1200–1565* (Philadelphia: University of Pennsylvania Press, 2001).

39. Scott G. Bruce, *Silence and Sign Language in Medieval Monasticism: The Cluniac Tradition, c.900–1200* (Cambridge: Cambridge University Press, 2007).

On sound and silence in nunneries see Anne Bagnall Yardley, *Performing Piety: Musical Culture in Medieval Nunneries* (Basingstoke: Palgrave, 2006).

40. Peter Marshall, *Beliefs and the Dead in Reformation England* (Oxford: Oxford University Press, 2002); Jane Idleman Smith and Yvonne Yazbeck Haddad, *The Islamic Understanding of Death and Resurrection* (Oxford: Oxford University Press, 2002); Leor Halevi, *Muhammad's Grave: Death Rituals and the Making of Islamic Society* (New York: Columbia University Press, 2007); David Kraemer, *The Meanings of Death in Rabbinic Judaism* (London: Routledge, 2000).

41. Commemoration of the dead and attitudes to death are closely bound in the historical literature; see, for example, Dieter Geuenich and Otto Gerhard Oexle, *Memoria in der Gesellschaft des Mittelalters* (Göttingen: Vandenhoeck and Ruprecht, 1994). The study of commemoration rituals can lead the historian of religion to consider questions usually addressed by political historians, as in John R. Neff, *Honoring the Civil War Dead: Commemoration and the Problem of Reconciliation* (Lawrence, Kan.: University of Kansas Press, 2005).

42. Ulinka Rublack, 'Grapho–Relics: Lutheranism and the Materialization of the Word', in Alexandra Walsham (ed.), *Relics and Remains* (Oxford: Oxford University Press, 2010), 144–66. For an example of an integrated approach to the culture of nunneries that combines spiritual and material practices see K. J. P. Lowe, *Nuns' Chronicles and Convent Culture in Renaissance and Counter-Reformation Italy* (Cambridge: Cambridge University Press, 2003). See also Colleen McDannell, *Material Christianity: Religion and Popular Culture in America* (New Haven: Yale University Press, 1995).

43. D. A. Brading, *Mexican Phoenix: Our Lady of Guadalupe: Image and Tradition across Five Centuries* (Cambridge: Cambridge University Press, 2001). On the power of ruins see Alexandra Walsham, forthcoming.

44. Carol Damian, *The Virgin of the Andes: Art and Ritual in Colonial Cuzco* (Miami Beach, Fla.: Grassfield Press, 1995).

45. Daniel Boyarin, *Dying for God: Martyrdom and the Making of Christianity and Judaism* (Stanford, Calif.: Stanford University Press, 1999); Israel Jacob Yuval, *Two Nations in your Womb: Perceptions of Jews and Christians in Late Antiquity and the Middle Ages*, trans. Barbara Harshav and Jonathan Chipman (Berkeley and Los Angeles: University of California Press, 2008).

46. Ora Limor, 'Pelagia's Tomb on the Mount of Olives: Sin, Repentance, Salvation', *Cathedra*, 118 (2006), 13–40 [in Hebrew]; parts in English, Ora Limor, 'Sharing Sacred Space: Holy Places in Jerusalem between Christianity, Judaism and Islam', in Iris Shagrir and Ronnie Ellenblum (eds.), *In Laudem Hierosolymitani: Studies in Crusades and Medieval Culture in Honour of Benjamin Z. Kedar* (Farnham: Ashgate, 2007), 219–31. See also Josef W. Meri, *The Cult of Saints among Muslims and Jews in Medieval Syria* (Oxford: Oxford University Press, 2002).

47. Benjamin Z. Kedar, 'Convergences of Oriental Christian, Muslim, and Frankish Worshippers: The Case of Saydnaya', in Yitzhak Hen (ed.), *De Sion exibit lex et verbum de Hierusalem: Essays in Medieval Law, Liturgy, and Literature in Honour of Amnon Linder* (Turnhout: Brepols, 2001), 59–69.

48. Bridget Heal, *The Cult of the Virgin Mary in Early Modern Germany: Protestant and Catholic Piety, 1500-1648* (Cambridge: Cambridge University Press, 2007); Benjamin J. Kaplan, *Divided by Faith: Religious Conflict and the Practice*

of Toleration in Early Modern Europe (Cambridge, Mass.: Belknap Press of Harvard University Press, 2007).

49. Spiros Vryonis, *The Decline of Medieval Hellenism in Asia Minor and the Process of Islamization from the Eleventh through the Fifteenth Century* (Berkeley and Los Angeles: University of California Press, 1971); Finbarr B. Flood, *Objects of Translation: Material Culture and Medieval 'Hindu–Muslim' Encounter* (Princeton: Princeton University Press, 2009).

50. Serge Gruzinski and Jean-Michel Sallmann (eds.), *Visions indiennes, visions baroques: les métissages de l'inconscient* (Paris: Presses Universitaires de France, 1992); Serge Gruzinski, *The Mestizo Mind: The Intellectual Dynamics of Colonization and Globalization*, trans. Deke Dusinberre (London: Routledge, 2002).

51. On the management of conversion see Seth D. Kunin, *Juggling Identities: Identity and Authenticity among the Crypto-Jews* (New York: Columbia University Press, 2009).

52. Jean-Claude Schmitt, *La Conversion d'Hermann le Juif: autobiographie, histoire et fiction* (Paris: Seuil, 2003).

53. David Nirenberg, 'Mass Conversion and Genealogical Mentalities: Jews and Christians in Fifteenth-Century Spain', *Past and Present*, 174 (2002), 3–41. On interaction between divergent confessional groups see Kaplan, *Divided by Faith*.

54. Francisco Bethencourt, *The Inquisition: A Global History* (Cambridge: Cambridge University Press, 2009).

55. Amy Singer, *Constructing Ottoman Beneficence: An Imperial Soup Kitchen in Jerusalem* (Albany, NY: State University of New York Press, 2002).

56. See the importance of cities in the 'Abbasid Empire, Amira K. Bennison, *The Great Caliphs: The Golden Age of the 'Abbasid Empire* (London: I. B. Tauris, 2009).

CHAPTER 15

1. 1387a20. *The Complete Works of Aristotle*, ed. Jonathan Barnes (Princeton: Princeton University Press, 1984), 2195.

2. Nonetheless, one should note that passive emotions or sentiments that are culturally constructed or navigated as well as the measures of navigation themselves should be the subjects of historical investigations.

3. The Manyōshū comprises some 4,500 poems and was compiled in or after AD 759.

4. *Kokin Wakashū*, Kanajo, by Ki no Tsurayuki, an editor of the anthology. In *Kokin Wakashū: The First Imperial Anthology of Japanese Poetry*, trans. Helen Craig McCullough (Stanford, Calif.: Stanford University Press, 1985), 3.

5. 'Worrying about Emotions in History', *American Historical Review*, 107/3 (June 2002), 821–45. She is in particular a sharp critic of the work of Elias and a group of American historians, such as Peter and Carlos Stearns. Also see Barbara H. Rosenwein (ed.), *Anger's Past: The Social Uses of an Emotion in the Middle Ages* (Ithaca, NY: Cornell University Press, 1998).

6. Nobert Elias, *The Civilizing Process: Sociogenetic and Psychogenetic Investigations*, trans. E. Jephcott (Malden, Mass.: Blackwell Publishing, 2000; 1st pub. 1994).

7. Eiko Ikegami, *Bonds of Civility: Aesthetic Publics and the Political Origin of Japanese Culture* (Cambridge: Cambridge University Press, 2005).

8. *Honor and Shame* (Chicago: University of Chicago Press, 1966), 39.

9. William M. Reddy, *The Navigation of Feeling: A Framework for the History of Emotions* (Cambridge: Cambridge University Press, 2001).

10. Martha C. Nussbaum, *Upheavals of Thought: The Intelligence of Emotions* (Cambridge: Cambridge University Press, 2003), 19.

11. In his *Outline of a Theory of Practice* (Cambridge: Cambridge University Press, 1977).

12. *The Fire and the Sun: Why Plato Banished the Artists* (Oxford: Oxford University Press, 1977), 1.

13. *The Secret History of Emotion: From Aristotle's Rhetoric to Modern Brain Science* (Chicago: University of Chicago Press, 2006).

14. 'Love and Knowledge: Emotion in Feminist Epistemology', in Alison M. Jaggar and Susan R. Bordo (eds.), *Gender/Body/Knowledge: Feminist Reconstructions of Being and Knowing* (New Brunswick, NJ: Rutgers University Press, 1989), 1.

15. John D. Lawson (ed.), *American State Trials* (St Louis: F. H. Thomas, 1928), xii. 731–2.

16. *Jealousy: The Evolution of an Emotion in American History* (New York: New York University Press, 1989). Peter N. Stearns and his collaborators have produced a number of works that concern the history of 'emotionology' in American history. For example, Peter N. Stearns, *American Cool: Constructing a Twentieth-Century Emotional Style* (New York: New York University Press, 1994); Peter N. Stearns with Carol Z. Stearns, 'Emotionology: Clarifying the History of Emotions and Emotional Standards', *American Historical Review*, 90 (Oct. 1985).

17. James's overly physiological understanding of emotions has been criticized by more recent psychological and neuroscientific works that take the role of cognition more seriously for understanding emotions. Contemporary brain sciences make it clear that it is not only emotions per se but the mental activities of consciousness in general that have a physiological basis. Nonetheless, although consciousness is nothing more than an expression of physical and neurological reactions, once any expressions of cognitive and emotional consciousness emerge, they would not be understood only on the basis of human anatomy and physiology.

18. Alice M. Isen and Gregory Andrade Diamond, 'Affect and Automaticity', in J. S. Uleman and John A. Bargh (eds.), *Unpublished Thought: Limits of Awareness, Intention and Control* (New York: Guildford Press, 1989), 124–52. See Reddy, *The Navigation of Feeling*, 3–33.

19. For example, we sometimes simply assume that the development of increasing self-restraint and 'internalized' and 'individualistic' mechanisms of emotional control are universal signs of modern eras. In that sense, Max Weber's thesis on Protestant ethics and the spirit of capitalism still presents the most powerful image of modern methods of emotional control, namely the combination of internalization, rationalization, and individualization of controlling emotion. Weber defined the spirit of capitalism as the ethos and habits nurtured by the Protestant ethic, which paradoxically favored the rational pursuit of economic gain. Although Weber's thesis was challenged by many scholars, theoretically and historically it still presents a powerful image of the rise of modern emotional culture.

20. Boston: Houghton Mifflin Company, 1989; originally published in 1946, 1. Due to wartime exigencies, Benedict never visited Japan, and did not speak the language.

21. Clifford Geertz, 'Us/Not-Us: Benedict's Travels', in *Works and Lives: The Anthropologist as Author* (Stanford, Calif.: Stanford University Press, 1988), 120.

22. Eiko Ikegami, *The Taming of the Samurai: Honorific Individualism and the Making of Modern Japan* (Cambridge, Mass.: Harvard University Press, 1995). For recent examples of historical studies of honor culture, see John Iliffe's work: in *Honour in African History* (Cambridge: Cambridge University Press, 2005), he examined African history from the fourteenth century to the contemporary world. Iliffe claimed the idea of honor is essential to understand the past and present of African behavior. Also see Pablo Piccato, *The Tyranny of Opinion: Honor in the Construction of the Mexican Public Sphere* (Durham, NC: Duke University Press, 2010).

23. Shōin was then imprisoned at the detention facility of the Chōshū domain, his home province. Obviously, the detention center was managed loosely so that Shōin was allowed to give moral lectures to fellow inmates there.

24. E. Ikegami, 'Shame and the Samurai Institutions, Trust worthless and Antonomy ', *Social Research*, Winter (2003).

25. *Shame and Necessity* (Berkeley and Los Angeles: University of California Press, 1993).

26. Berkeley and Los Angeles: University of California Press, 1986.

27. 'Art as a Cultural System', in *Local Knowledge* (New York: Basic Book, 1983).

28. *Perks of Yemen I Summon: Poetry as Cultural Practice in a North Yemen Tribe* (Berkeley and Los Angeles: University of California Press, 1990).

29. Other feminist scholars such as Unni Wikan who studied women's practices of shame and honor in Cairo and Oman claim the need to understand female senses of honor and shame from their own vantage points rather than considering them from male-centered vantage points. Also see Unni Wikan, 'Shame and Honour: A Contestable Pair', *Man*, 19/4 (Dec. 1984), 635–52.

30. *Popular Culture in Early Modern Europe* (New York: Harper and Row, 1978), 103–4.

31. Sōgi *Yodo no watari* cited by Ogata, Tsutomu, *Za no bungaku*, p. 34, trans. Eiko Ikegami.

32. *Bonds of Civility*.

33. 'Culture in Action: Symbols and Strategies', *American Sociological Review*, 51 (Apr. 1986), 175–208.

34. M. Berezin, 'Emotion and Political Identity: Mobilizing Affection for the Polity', in J. Goodwin, J. M. Jasper, and F. Polletta (eds.), *Passionate Politics: Emotion and Social Movements* (Chicago: University of Chicago Press, 2001).

35. Princeton: Princeton University Press, 1977.

36. *Discipline and Punish: The Birth of the Prison* (New York: Random House, 1975).

37. See, for example, Ann Laura Stoler, *Race and the Education of Desire: Foucault's History of Sexuality and the Colonial Order of Things* (Durham, NC: Duke University Press, 1995).

38. 'Honor or Order: The State and Samurai Self-Determinism', 'The Vendetta of the Forty-Seven Samurai', in *The Taming of the Samurai*.

CHAPTER 16

1. Donald Kelley, *The Descent of Ideas: The History of Intellectual History* (Aldershot: Ashgate, 2002).
2. See e.g. Joseph Levenson, *Confucian China and its Modern Fate: A Trilogy* (Berkeley and Los Angeles: University of California Press, 1968); Frederick W. Mote, *Intellectual Foundations of China* (New York: Knopf, 1971); Benjamin I. Schwartz, *The World of Thought in Ancient China* (Cambridge, Mass.: Belknap Press of Harvard University Press, 1985).
3. S. K. Heninger, Jr., *Touches of Sweet Harmony: Pythagorean Cosmology and Renaissance Poetics* (San Marino, Calif.: Huntington Library, 1974); Christiane Joost-Gaugier, *Pythagoras and Renaissance Europe: Finding Heaven* (Cambridge: Cambridge University Press, 2009).
4. On Shakespeare's learning see the classic study by T. W. Baldwin, *William Shakspere's Small Latine & Lesse Greeke*, 2 vols. (Urbana, Ill.: University of Illinois Press, 1944).
5. See Feisal G. Mohamed, *In the Anteroom of Divinity: The Reformation of the Angels from Colet to Milton* (Toronto: University of Toronto Press, 2008).
6. Thomas S. Kuhn, *The Copernican Revolution: Planetary Astronomy in the Development of Western Thought* (Cambridge, Mass.: Harvard University Press, 1966); Michael Hoskin, *The History of Astronomy: A Very Short Introduction* (Oxford: Oxford University Press, 2003).
7. Alexandre Koyré, *From the Closed World to the Infinite Universe* (Baltimore: Johns Hopkins University Press, 1957); Mordechai Feingold, 'Giordano Bruno in England, Revisited', *Huntington Library Quarterly*, 67/3 (2004), 329–46.
8. Kelley, *Descent of Ideas*.
9. Daniel Wilson, *Arthur O. Lovejoy and the Quest for Intelligibility* (Chapel Hill, NC: University of North Carolina Press, 1980); Anthony Grafton, 'The History of Ideas: Precept and Practice, 1950–2000 and Beyond', *Journal of the History of Ideas*, 67/1 (Jan. 2006), 1–32.
10. See Edward H. Schafer, *The Vermilion Bird: T'ang Images of the South* (Berkeley and Los Angeles: University of California Press, 1967); John Elliott, *The Old World and the New, 1492–1650* (Cambridge: Cambridge University Press, 1970).
11. Robert Green (ed.), *Protestantism, Capitalism, and Social Science: The Weber Thesis Controversy* (Lexington, Mass.: Heath, 1973).
12. Hans Baron, *The Crisis of the Early Italian Renaissance* (Princeton: Princeton University Press, 1955; new edn. 1966); Felix Gilbert, *Machiavelli and Guicciardini* (Princeton: Princeton University Press, 1965).
13. J. G. A. Pocock, *The Ancient Constitution and the Feudal Law: A Study of English Historical Thought in the Seventeenth Century* (Cambridge: Cambridge University Press, 1957).
14. Quentin Skinner, 'Meaning and Understanding in the History of Ideas', *History & Theory*, 8/1 (1969), 3–53—a programmatic article. For the later development of Skinner's work see e.g. his comprehensive *The Foundations of Modern Political Thought*, 2 vols. (Cambridge: Cambridge University Press, 1978).
15. See Carlo Ginzburg, 'From Aby Warburg to E. H. Gombrich: A Problem of Method', in *Clues, Myths and the Historical Paradigm*, trans. John Tedeschi and Anne Tedeschi (Baltimore: Johns Hopkins University Press, 1989).

16. Quentin Skinner, *Reason and Rhetoric in the Philosophy of Hobbes* (Cambridge: Cambridge University Press, 1996); Anthony Pagden, *The Fall of Natural Man: The American Indian and the Origins of Comparative Ethnology* (Cambridge: Cambridge University Press, 1982).

17. See Helge Kragh, *An Introduction to the Historiography of Science* (Cambridge: Cambridge University Press, 1987).

18. See William Clark, *Academic Charisma and the Origins of the Research University* (Chicago: University of Chicago Press, 2006).

19. See Elizabeth L. Eisenstein, *The Printing Revolution in Early Modern Europe* (2nd edn. Cambridge: Cambridge University Press, 2005).

20. See Robert Darnton, *The Forbidden Best-Sellers of Pre-revolutionary France* (New York: Norton, 1995); Robert Darnton, *The Devil in the Holy Water or the Art of Slander from Louis XIV to Napoleon* (Philadelphia: University of Pennsylvania Press, 2010).

21. Benjamin A. Elman, *On their Own Terms: Science in China, 1550–1900* (Cambridge, Mass.: Harvard University Press, 2005); Mary Elizabeth Berry, *Japan in Print: Information and Nation in the Early Modern Period* (Berkeley and Los Angeles: University of California Press, 2006); George Saliba, *Islamic Science and the Making of the European Renaissance* (Cambridge, Mass.: MIT Press, 2007).

Index